Essential Articles for the Study of William Blake, 1970-1984

The Essential Articles Series

Volumes Available

ESSENTIAL ARTICLES FOR THE STUDY OF
JOHN DRYDEN
Edited by H. T. Swedenberg, Jr.

ESSENTIAL ARTICLES FOR THE STUDY OF
FRANCIS BACON
Edited by Brian Vickers

ESSENTIAL ARTICLES FOR THE STUDY OF
EDMUND SPENSER
Edited by A. C. Hamilton

ESSENTIAL ARTICLES FOR THE STUDY OF
THOMAS MORE
Edited by Richard S. Sylvester and Germain Marc'hadour

ESSENTIAL ARTICLES FOR THE STUDY OF
GEORGE HERBERT'S POETRY
Edited by John R. Roberts

ESSENTIAL ARTICLES FOR THE STUDY OF
JONATHAN SWIFT'S POETRY
Edited by David M. Vieth

ESSENTIAL ARTICLES FOR THE STUDY OF
SIR PHILIP SIDNEY
Edited by Arthur F. Kinney

ESSENTIAL ARTICLES FOR THE STUDY OF
WILLIAM BLAKE, 1970-1984
Edited by Nelson Hilton

Also Available

POPE: RECENT ESSAYS BY SEVERAL HANDS
Edited by Maynard Mack and James Anderson Winn

Essential Articles for the Study of
William Blake, 1970-1984

Edited by
NELSON HILTON

Archon Books
1986

First published 1986 as an Archon Book,
an imprint of The Shoe String Press, Inc.
Hamden, Connecticut 06514

Printed in The United States of America

The paper in this book meets the guidelines for performance and durability of the Committee on Production Guidelines for Book Longevity of the Council on Library Resources.

Library of Congress Cataloging-in-Publication Data
Main entry under title:

Essential articles for the study of William Blake, 1970-1984.

(The Essential articles series)
Bibliography: p.
1. Blake, William, 1757-1827—Criticism and interpretation—Addresses, essays, lectures. I. Hilton, Nelson. II. Series.
PR4147.E78 1986 821′.7 86-1166
ISBN 0-208-02091-8 (alk. paper)

Contents

Foreword vii

Preface ix

HAZARD ADAMS
Blake and the Philosophy of Literary Symbolism 1

STUART CURRAN
Blake and the Gnostic Hyle: A Double Negative 15

FLORENCE SANDLER
The Iconoclastic Enterprise: Blake's Critique of "Milton's Religion" 33

MICHAEL RIFFATERRE
The Self-sufficient Text 57

SUSAN FOX
The Female as Metaphor in William Blake's Poetry 75

ROBERT F. GLECKNER
Most Holy Forms of Thought: Some Observations on Blake and Language 91

V. A. DE LUCA
Proper Names in the Structural Design of Blake's Myth-Making 119

DONALD AULT
Incommensurability and Interconnection in Blake's Anti-Newtonian Text 141

MORRIS EAVES
Blake and the Artistic Machine: An Essay in Decorum and Technology 175

ALICIA OSTRIKER
Desire Gratified and Ungratified: William Blake and Sexuality 211

RONALD CLAYTON TAYLOR
Semantic Structures and the Temporal Modes of Blake's Prophetic Verse 237

STEVEN SHAVIRO
"Striving with Systems": Blake and the Politics of Difference 271

SANTA CRUZ BLAKE STUDY GROUP
What Type of Blake? 301

Foreword

The resources available for the study of literature are so vast as to be almost overwhelming, particularly in the case of major authors. Few libraries have copies of all the important articles a serious student might wish to read, and fewer still can keep them easily accessible. The aim of the Essential Articles series is to bring together from learned journals and scholarly studies those essays on a standard writer or area of English literature which are genuinely essential—which will continue to appear on syllabus and reading list.

Preface

With over one thousand articles and notes about Blake appearing between 1970 and 1984, it would be blasphemous to argue that the thirteen essays collected here compass all the essential ones. To presume "essentiality" would entail assuming a knowledge of universal attributes, an enterprise which could only be marked with fear and trembling by anyone sympathetic to *Jerusalem*'s argument that "Those who dare appropriate to themselves Universal Attributes / Are the Blasphemous Selfhoods & must be broken asunder" (98.32-33).

At the outset, the editor and publisher decided not to consider articles which had already appeared in hardcover, "library" format. This one fell swoop eliminated important essays in David V. Erdman and John Grant's *Blake's Visionary Forms Dramatic* (1970), Stuart Curran and Anthony Wittreich, Jr.'s *Blake's Sublime Allegory* (1973), Morton D. Paley and Michael Phillips' *William Blake: Essays in Honour of Sir Geoffrey Keynes* (1973), Robert N. Essick's *The Visionary Hand: Essays for the Study of William Blake's Art and Aesthetics* (1973), and Phillips' *Interpreting Blake* (1978)—as well as essays appearing in hardcover annuals. Another essential decision was to emphasize articles dealing with Blake's verbal thought and practice at large. Where individual works do come to the fore in this collection (Riffaterre, Shaviro), they do so as examples of ways of reading rather than as "explications." Finally, imagining a book that might have interest and integrity as a whole, the editor resisted the possibility of assembling the ultimate doorstop in favor of something less prepossessing in volume. For all these sins of omission and commission the names of the editor and publisher appear as essential qualifiers to the title on the book's spine.

As the articles selected will suggest, the present collection has a slant toward the "textual," a note sounded from the very beginning. In this orientation the volume can at least claim to reflect the essential trajectory of literary-critical thought for the years it covers. The book thus attempts to gather together some now maturing orphans whose existence and collective testimony can help to explain why and how Blake comes to offer such a powerful example to the critical movement gathering way between 1970 and 1984. Looking back on those past "fourteen suns," one may perhaps sympathize with the astonishment of the shadowy daughter of Urthona in discovering the revolutionary force she has nourished unbeknownst for such a period: "This is eternal death: and this the torment long foretold" (*America* 2:17).

For indispensable assistance in preparing this collection I am grateful first of all to DeAnna Palmer and Connie Perry, who typed and retyped the master disk in room 255, Park Hall, University of Georgia. To all the authors and to the editors and publishers of the respective essays I am grateful for permission to reprint; particular thanks are due to Hazard Adams and, especially, Florence Sandler, for revision of their contributions.

HAZARD ADAMS

Blake and the Philosophy of Literary Symbolism

A critical tradition of some length and dignity has treated Blake as a symbolist, first with the proviso that he had to invent his own symbols, later with the argument that his symbols were archetypal, whether of Jungian or fundamentally literary shape.[1] Along with this appellation, Yeats's phrase describing Blake as a "too literal realist of the imagination" has tended to stick.[2] But Yeats's phrase has such variable meaning that unless carefully applied it obfuscates or misleads. Though he may be regarded at some very high level of abstraction as belonging to the same tradition as Baudelaire, Blake is not a symbolist at all in the obvious sense implied by the famous sonnet "Correspondances," and his techniques have little in common with Mallarmé's or with those of any of the poets discussed by Arthur Symons in one of the first studies of the symbolists.[3] Yet Blake may be treated as a more complete symbolist than those who have gone under the "symboliste" banner, if one means by symbolist a poet who regards literature as a "symbolic form" of experience, in the sense that has become common since Cassirer.[4] The view of Blake's work as more complete in its implications for critical theory than that of any poet generally regarded as symbolist has not been asserted, though implied in Northrop Frye's pioneer-

This essay, originally published in *New Literary History* 5 (1973), appeared in a longer version dealing with *Jerusalem* in *Blake Studies* 7. The shorter version was considerably revised and amended to constitute a chapter of the author's *Philosophy of the Literary Symbolic* (1983). Some of these revisions appear here. Reprinted with permission.

ing *Fearful Symmetry* and exploited in Frye's own subsequent theoretical work.[5] If Blake had exercised only this influence on Frye he would belong to a history of theories of symbolism, but his importance in this respect is far greater and his influence far more pervasive. He has had a germinal influence on the theories of numerous modern writers and made the most complete utterance of a philosophy of the literary symbolic in his time. I shall see Blake as providing a transition from purely neoclassical English views of language to those developing in the later nineteenth and earlier twentieth centuries.

In *The Marriage of Heaven and Hell,* Blake offers a fictive history, quite similar in argument to an important passage from Vico, of how poetic vision became reduced to systems of moral code.[6] The passage, comprising Plate 11 of the work, has usually been treated as offering an explanation of the cyclical decline into Urizenic abstraction of an original visionary perception. It could also be regarded as a Blakean myth of "dissociation of sensibility," if one were to follow along lines suggested by Frank Kermode.[7] Here I intend to treat it as part of the expression of a whole view of language informing the so-called prophetic books and anticipating twentieth-century ideas of "symbolic form" and constitutive poetic language.

The passage is as follows:

> The ancient Poets animated all sensible objects with Gods or Geniuses, calling them by the names and adorning them with the properties of woods, rivers, mountains, lakes, cities, nations, and whatever their enlarged and numerous senses could perceive.
>
> And particularly they studied the genius of each city and country, placing it under its mental deity.
>
> Till a system was formed, which some took advantage of, and enslaved the vulgar by attempting to realize or abstract the mental deities from their objects: thus began Priesthood.
>
> Choosing forms of worship from poetic tales. And at length they pronounced that the Gods had ordered such things.
>
> Thus men forgot that all deities reside in the human breast.

The last sentence offers a picture of the prelapsarian condition, for dissociation and Fall are identical in Blake: Human consciousness was, or properly is, to use Blake's characteristic terms, the "circumference" of experience or reality rather than its "center." One human breast properly contains the gods, who always should be, according to Blake, the servants of Man. The senses existed originally in an "enlarged" state and contained the world. This gathering in of experience was not contradicted by the first poets when they named and composed. Indeed, their activity, which we take to have been the creation of language, was the means by which "vision," as we now understand it, was established. Given Blake's emphasis on creativity, the statement about this at the beginning of the passage is put rather curiously, however; for it seems uttered from a point of view toward language opposed to that of the poets, while at the same time the total passage laments the passing away of the point of view of those poets. Were the "sensible objects" existent previous to their animation by the poets? Only, I think, as potential possibilities of vision. Blake did not intend us to imagine men, at that critical moment of the invention of language, originally confronting real inanimate sensible objects. Rather, he intended the poets by the constitutive power of language—namely metaphor—to have *created* those objects in the way a circumferential power gives life to objects—by anthropomorphizing them. It is in words that the "calling" and the "adorning" mentioned in the passage from *The Marriage* must continually take place. The enlargement of the senses and their increased number are sustained by these acts of "calling" and "adorning." The additional senses, lost in the fallen state, can be described collectively as constitutive power, or what I shall call "myth," as against a notion of passive reception of subsequently named sense data, or what I shall call "antimyth."

As the poets built language, regarded as fundamentally metaphoric, the world became realizable in words: "Till a system was formed, which some took advantage of." That brought the dissociation, for, as Blake says, "some took advantage" of what the "system" formed from myth provided. To take advantage of something is to externalize it (to make it an "it,") or in Blake's terms, to retreat to what he calls the "selfish center" from an imaginative circumference that holds everything together. This thrusts everything outside and turns the outside into inanimate or "sensible" objects, abstracted from their "mental deities," which are relegated at this point to subjective illusions and arbitrary signs by the dominating epistemology of subject/object. The object is *before* the word, the world *before* language, both temporally and epistemologically. Object negates subject. To put it another way, the poetic verbal universe is destroyed by a competing idea of language that claims for language only the power to point outward toward *things* beyond which lies nothing; or only the power to point outward toward *things* which stand "Platonically" or "religiously" for an order of ideas or mysterious beings disembodied behind the veil of those things. With language no longer containing reality in mythic form but only *pointing toward* an alien reality, a mediating or interpreting force is required, namely what Blake calls a "priesthood," to rationalize the mysteries of this "allegoric" separateness.

Now what we have here are two fundamentally opposed views of language. In that of the poets, metaphor is absolutely fundamental, not merely a collection of tropes or devices added on to an assertion that points outward from itself. Trope as device is all that is left of the synthetic and mythmaking powers of language after it has been redefined by priestly practice.

The difference is that between what Blake calls "allegory addressed to the intellectual powers," but usually "vision," and allegory which is available to the "corporeal understanding."[8] Both are forms of language, the former that of the poets, the latter that of the priesthood, the former mythical, the latter antimythical. But it is important to notice that the priesthood came after the poets and chose "forms of worship from poetic tales." The original mode of language was poetic and the whole process of externalizing language was built outward from that original mode. It is as if poetry and myth preceded religion, if one thinks of religion as a system of beliefs to which are attached codes of behavior. Inasmuch as Blake's archetypal priest Urizen is also his archetypal scientist, it would appear that for Blake poetic myth precedes science in the same way. But the main implication is that we are talking about language. To what extent is the world that Blake talks about a linguistic world or secularly "symbolic form"?

Before proceeding to that question I return to a previous one answered arbitrarily and only provisionally for the sake of launching the inquiry: Were the sensible objects Blake mentions in the passage existent previous to their animation by the poets? Or is Blake for the sake of rhetoric simply acceding to our deeply ingrained antimythical habits of externalization, or *pointing to*, in order to get *his* argument going? This is like asking what the original Edenic condition was in Blake's mythology. But that mythology does not allow us to locate Eden by pointing outward and back to it, locating it at the beginning of a stretch of external time. For one thing, the mythology is mythical, and we should not choose forms of externality from poetic tales. If we stick as closely as possible to Blake's terms, we can nearly avoid externalizing, which is the best we can do. There are in Blake some mental deities that may serve us instead. There is, for example, the story of the shapeless horrific body of Urizen that Los must in some way constitute; there is the sleeping body of the world-giant Albion, whose unorganized dreaming state is, as an alien history, the substance that must be transformed into a living vision. Both of these figures seem to imply the possibility of a living, human, unified world, adornable with the "properties of woods, rivers, mountains, lakes, cities, nations"—in other words, subject to, indeed requiring, the process of poetic naming. These horrific sleepers in Blake are the potentiality of imaginative creation. As potentiality they are not in time and history; neither are they matter that is there for the poets to confront as such. They are sheer possibilities of the imagination. Existence can be said to have its beginning in their mythical apprehension.

Another part of *The Marriage of Heaven and Hell* throws some light on this and suggests how language acts as a creative force and dynamic container of reality. In one of his "Memorable Fancies" (Plate 15) Blake describes a printing house in Hell where "lions of flaming fire" melt metals into living fluid, passing the fluid to "unnamed forms" who cast the metals into the expanse, there to be received by men in the shape of books arranged in libraries. This, according to Blake, is how knowledge is transmitted from generation to generation. The body of earth—the mass of potential reality—is turned to flux and then, in naming, it is formed linguistically. As a result, history becomes not simply an outward objective linear arrangement of events to which words refer but is embodied as the presentness of words. The past comes into the present—belongs to it—because the only place that we can find it is in its construction in words, present to our reading. This may clear up the apparent oddity of Blake's method of drawing the "visionary" heads of historical personages, for he declared that they were actually present to him as he drew them. Without resort to theories of ghosts or madness, one can argue that Blake believed he was bringing these people to presentness in his paintings—by painting them as he *sees* them (*in* his mind and *through* his eyes) according to their presentness in the words of history books.

The Marriage suggests an idea of culture as embodied in words and, perhaps, an idea of history as more real when located *in* or *as* a verbal structure than externalized, distanced, and objectified as a past. Indeed, the latter is quite impossible without making a verbal structure indulging the fiction of pastness, which in turn becomes itself a presence. Blake's idea of verbal presence, the only real existence of the past, he no doubt took from his reading of the Bible. Blake interprets Jesus' second coming as His continual presence in the presence of the Book itself. Blake has nothing good to say about the historical or so-called past Jesus, who is the supreme form of Antichrist. He is "outward ceremony," meaningless ritualized behavior that mindlessly copies or points out and backward to an historically lost and forgotten or only vaguely remembered event.[9] The opposite of this would be a shaped imaginative form, living in the immediate present, like the Bible and what it contains.

But of course it would have to be shaped. When it is shaped we do it the honor of referring to its events in the present tense. We can say that Jesus *comes.* To treat the matter otherwise is to externalize the events from the words and tacitly admit that the words don't contain and shape but only point to—in this case point *back to*—a lost past. So we may argue that when we talk of a verbal universe made by the ancient poets there is no point in referring to a *before* external to it that they transformed into a presence. Blake, facing what he will later call the "stubborn structure of the language," was acceding to our manner of speaking. However, the passage from *Jerusalem* in which he uses the phrase "stubborn structure" shows that we can apply our concept of potentiality to language itself, which the poet faces and must shape, and in the sense that the poet works in history, must reshape constantly, since it tends to harden and die into "allegory." The phrase I have mentioned appears in Plate 36 [40] as a parenthetical statement by the author himself and suggests what Los's supreme task is:

> (I call them by their English names: English the rough
> basement.
> Los built the stubborn structure of the language, acting
> against
> Albion's melancholy, who must else have been a dumb
> despair.)

By "them" Blake refers to the cities of England, who have become in the poem part of an elaborate parallel-identity with the tribes of Israel. Blake has already told us in *Milton* that he will not let his sword sleep in his hand until he has built Jerusalem in England, and his poem *Jerusalem* is a plan for that building—the establishment of linguistic or metaphorical identity in visionary time and space between holy Jerusalem and resurrected London. At this point in the poem he calls his cities by their English names; he shapes the biblical vision into the English tongue. Language is the mythic mode of constituting reality, and the mythic mode is fundamental to the antimythical, which grows from it. It stands like Los at the base of culture. Los is described here as the archetype of the ancient poets. It is he who actually makes and remakes language as a receptacle for culture. This act constantly provides the sleeping giant Albion the power of speech, of awakening, of shaping his nightmare world of flux and disorder into a reality. No longer will he be surrounded like a dumb beast by a buzzing confusion, which he has allowed to grow by his inarticulateness, his poverty of tropes, his delusion that his language only *points to* things, his succumbing to the powers of the cultural "antimyth" of subject and object.

This linguistic structure or creation of the ancient poet Los is "stubborn," and the word is harsh enough to make us query it. Freed as we now should be from the need to address ourselves to the problems of beginnings, we can see that in the myth, where to query beginnings is pointless, Los's activity is really continuous, ever-present, or eternal in the moment. The stubbornness of the structure is twofold. Language has the capacity to resist the stasis reason desires and stubbornly frustrates those who—like Urizen, Satan, and the "priesthood"—would choose to abstract a single form of worship from it (try to reduce it to a system pointing outward only to that one form—the clock world of deism or the ideal world of Platonism). This is its metaphoric, Los-like structure. On the other hand, language resists stasis only as a result of the struggle that Los has with its dangerous susceptibility to externalization and hardening. Its stubbornness, then, can point either way.

What Blake calls Golgonooza is, in one of its aspects and perhaps in its primary aspect, the city of verbal form, the "stubborn structure" itself. As it is built by Los, so does it also fall by dint of those who abstract forms of worship from it, continually exhausting its possibilities in externalization and use. As a result, Los has to be at work continually.

> Here on the banks of the Thames, Los builded Golgonooza,
> Outside of the Gates of the Human Heart, beneath Beulah
> In the midst of the rocks of the Altars of Albion. In fears
> He builded it, in rage and in fury. It is the Spiritual Fourfold
> London, continually building and continually decaying desolate!
>
> (*Jerusalem,* 53)

The work is always accomplished in the midst of the ruins that are continually made of it. In my own "allegoric" or priestly reading of the passage above, the rocks are matter or Lockean substance that is made from language by forms of verbal externalization. The altars are the forms of worship abstracted from mythical thinking. The process is eternal—timeless because internalized and thus lifted from linear, measurable time, endless when seen in time because of the constant need to refurbish the mythico-linguistic structure as it is plundered by those who use it to their purposes. It is, as Blake tells us, a "terrible eternal labor."

The labor is the eternal re-creation of the act that Blake attributes in *The Marriage* originally to the "ancient poets." Since *The Marriage* is present to us, however, it is more appropriate to say that the act is not a *re-creation of* but is *identical to* the act of the poets. Seen cyclically, Los's work as the builder of language is a "striving with systems to deliver individuals from those systems" (*Jerusalem,* 11). As the system that was formed from language (a mythology) is taken advantage of and corrupted into externality, or, in other Blakean terms, becomes the spectre of its original self, Los's eternal act of building the "stubborn structure of the language" can be seen as a struggle with a spectral or "allegorical" system grown like a "polypus" from his original system (original not in the historical sense but in the sense that his system represents the fundamental nature of language—its metaphorical nature). Thus, Los is engaged in a struggle with his spectre—language converted to a sort of antimyth. Confronted by the deterioration or purposive plundering of his system into an opposing system, he

> . . . stands in London building Golgonooza,
> Compelling his Spectre to labors mighty; trembling in fear,
> The Spectre weeps, but Los, unmoved by tears or threats, remains.
> "I must create a System or be enslaved by another Man's,
> I will not Reason and Compare; my business is to Create."
>
> (*Jerusalem,* 10)

Like those in *The Marriage* who work with molten metal to make books, Los, who is a blacksmith, uses ladles of ore, shaping potentiality into the spiritual sword.

I have argued against the idea that the "ancient poets" confronted an originally spectral situation. Los, when viewed in history, however, seems to be in a more embattled position. Thus, in spite of my argument from one point of view—the mythic—that the action of Los is not re-creation in time but original creation, I must from another point of view—that of externality, and, ironically enough, of critical interpretation—admit that Los, as the creative spirit of time, the container and maker of significant time, does have to rebuild a stubborn structure that is always turning by deterioration into its spectral negation and threatening to surround him in the form of determining history. The spectral negative stubbornness of language is for Los and for Blake the tendency of language toward generalization, abstraction, and dead trope:

> . . . it is the Reasoning Power,
> An Abstract objecting power that Negates everything.
> This is the Spectre of Man. . . .
>
> (*Jerusalem,* 10)

One of Los's duties is to try to turn a negative relationship into a true contrariety—to mythologize rather than to accede wholly to the subject-object relationship. What we have regarded as cyclical and yet without external temporal beginning we ought to consider provisionally as a dialectical contrariety between opposed linguistic tendencies. One is the purely prolific tendency of the free mythmaking imagination and the other the devouring tendency of the externalizing, purposive object-making and thus also subject-making, "allegoric," "antimythical" rationality. In *The Marriage* Blake speaks of prolific and devourer as follows:

> . . . one portion of being is the Prolific, the other the Devouring; to the devourer it seems as if the producer was in his chains, but it is not so: he only takes portions of existence and fancies that the whole.
>
> (Plate 16)

The devourer attempts to ingest the mythmaking power of language. But, in the process, that power can only turn into its opposite, because the devourer is a machine for externalizing. For the devourer to take something inside is really for him to externalize it at once in the form of the antimyth of subject and object. The devourer can never be at the circumference of his thought, but only at the center, no matter how much he devours, for devouring is using and to use is to externalize. Ultimately, however, the devourer is at the circumference of a myth of his own, but actually an antimythical fiction that insists on placing himself at the center of experience and surrounding him with infinite space and time. If he does not appreciate the irony of this situation and bring in the contrary, he is in trouble. Thus the curious difficulties Urizen has in finding a place to stand in *The Four Zoas* and his inability to attain to a circumference. He does not grasp that his antimyth is a created fictive form. He makes it surround him and determine him as a fixed "reality."

I pause now in the argument to expand a point made in passing. In measurable or externalized time, Los would seem to be condemned to a Sisyphus-like existence, building language as myth only to see it deteriorate, and then building it again. This surely sounds as if it were Hell, and it would be Hell if Los really lived in the externalized time that is the antimyth to his myth. Instead, he lives in prolific work, where every moment is imaginative creation. To put it more accurately, time and the unfallen counterpart of Hell are in him—the area of human energy out of which come Blake's famous proverbs. It is not too much to say that this energy is artistic shaping in a language, whether of words or lines or musical forms, that this unfallen Hell at the bottom of the world (the strong legs and feet of unfallen man) is an unremitting source of the symbolic. The work done here—in the mines and at the forge—is not easy, for it is accomplished against the pressure of antimyth that, from the mythic point of view, *obfuscates* particular reality with generality and abstract nothingness:

> Some Sons of Los surround the Passions with porches of
> iron and silver
> Creating form and beauty around the dark regions of
> sorrow,
> Giving to airy nothing a name and a habitation
> Delightful, with bounds to the Infinite putting off the
> Indefinite
> Into most holy forms of Thought; such is the power of
> inspiration.
> They labor incessant with many tears and afflictions,
> Creating the beautiful House for the piteous sufferer.
> (*Milton,* 28)

The porches are the forms taken by the metals of the "Memorable Fancy" we have already examined, mythico-linguistic shapings from crude potentiality. The "regions of sorrow," or fallen Hell—unshaped because symbolically uncontained and therefore rampant spectral anxieties—are made part of, enter into, a larger containing form. The House of Albion is a house of cultural myth that assigns value and meaning to his acts:

> Others cabinets richly fabricate of gold and ivory
> For doubts and fears unformed and wretched and
> melancholy.

The passage I have quoted from *Milton* ends with a description of the artist:

> Antamon takes them [the spectres] into his beautiful
> flexible hands
> As the Sower takes the seed, or as the Artist his clay
> Of fine wax, to mould artful a model for golden
> ornaments.

Blake is very hard on antimyth, for in his view his own age had come to be so dominated by it that people tended to think only in its terms, which are the terms of Bacon, Newton, and Locke. Its domination had tended to render myth trivial or material for psychoanalysis by accusing it of subjectivity while reserving objectivity for itself. When antimyth negates myth in this way Blake is prone to call it simply error, the completion of the Fall in opacity and contraction—Newton's trumpet blast.[10] Everything is reduced to Lockean material substance or the nothingness of the abstract. The antimyth comes to be regarded as the source of the single vision of truth and reality, but Blake always insists that this vision is a human construction like myth; indeed, it is built like an antitype or fallen analogy upon (or, to be consistent, underneath) the very same mythic structures that it relegates to subjectivity—poetry and the other arts.

Now both myth and antimyth are, as I apply the terms to Blake, modes of imaginative construction that result in what may be called fictions. The way of myth is synthesis and art, the way of antimyth analysis and science. The antimyth creates the mythology of the subject-object split and proceeds to divide everything by analysis into smaller and smaller units, thus draining substance of life, freedom, and will. Blake opposes the dominance of antimyth in his time by giving myth the fictive historical primacy we noted in *The Marriage of Heaven and Hell.* He also gives it a formal primacy by considering it to be the fundamental mode of imaginative construction. Myth puts together, and antimyth takes apart or devours. Because both are *modes* of activity and not themselves copies of anything, the question of which has truth or correspondence to reality is not a possible question. Indeed, the question is merely a reflection of a category, to borrow Kant's term, of the antimythic code, and is meaningful only within its terms.

Blake's insistence on the historical and formal primacy of myth suggests that without myth antimyth starves. In this sense, myth potentially contains antimyth (as the seed does the plant): antimyth can never contain myth, though it is engaged in a constant effort to devour it. Its own tendency to externalize everything prevents its self-completion and its victory.

Art, the creator of the fiction of myth and the prolific to the antimyth's devourer, the seed of thought, becomes for Blake the contrary of everything that operates by generalization toward abstract law—not just science but religion and, to some extent, history, when history rises up the scale of abstraction to form a deterministic outlook. But art, as the fundamental activity of making languages, is also the source upon which all of these modes feed, distorting the source and requiring its rebirth in the process.

Blake's view suggests that we create symbolic worlds, and that these are for all practical purposes the only worlds we have. What we have made them makes us what we are. We can only make a world with a language, indeed *in* a language. There is nothing imaginable independent of a medium to imagine *in*. Our languages constantly die into use and must be reborn. Further, each language has its own limits and requires its opposite. Blake's vision of language was that myth precedes science and reason, that the latter feeds on the former. But he also believed that in his time the devourer's language had so dominated reality in the form of "Single Vision & Newton's sleep" that civilization itself was in danger unless the contrary mythic language of poetry and art rose to the challenge of spiritual warfare. Fully antimythical language—always only an ideal of symbolic logic—is the contrary that must be reshaped back into its opposite, but only in order that the devourer may consume its contrary in prolific use. This is the "fitness and order" Blake sought; the vision of it leads to his remark: "What is the Life of Man but Art and Science?"

Notes

1. The one purely Jungian study, W.P. Witcutt's *Blake: A Psychological Study* (London, 1946), is quite unreliable. Other critics have here and there used Jungian insights. The archetypal, non-Jungian approach was originated by Northrop Frye in *Fearful Symmetry* (Princeton, 1947).

2. "William Blake and His Illustrations to the *Divine Comedy*" (1897), *Essays and Introductions* (London, 1961), p. 119.

3. Symons' *The Symbolist Movement in Literature* (London, 1899), dedicated to Yeats, studies Nerval, de L'Isle Adam, Rimbaud, Verlaine, Laforgue, Mallarmé, Huysmans, and Maeterlinck.

4. Ernst Cassirer, *Die Philosophie der symbolischen Formen* (Berlin, 1923–29); *An Essay on Man* (New Haven, 1944).

5. See especially Frye's remarks about Blake's influence on him in *The Critical Path* (Bloomington, 1971), pp. 13–14.

6. See Giambattista Vico, *The New Science* [1744], rev. tr. (Ithaca, 1968), pp. 116–20.

7. *Romantic Image* (New York, 1957), pp. 138–61.

8. Letter to Thomas Butts, 6 July 1803.

9. *The Laocoön* (c. 1820).

10. *Europe* 13, 4–5.

STUART CURRAN

Blake and the Gnostic Hyle: A Double Negative

It is, I think, appropriate to begin any discussion of Blake's relationship with literary and cultural traditions by paying tribute to Kathleen Raine's handsome and learned compilation of source materials.[1] There is no need to dwell on its deficiencies. The reviews have been unanimous in wishing for greater discrimination of Blake's central sources and of the precise attitude he took toward them. But Miss Raine has provided us with valuable foundation to which we owe respect. Construction of a sound and stable edifice of scholarship upon it will depend largely on our ability to avoid pitfalls to which past historical criticism of Blake has seemed peculiarly susceptible. True children of Albion that we are, we have codified much Error that must be annihilated. As a contribution to that undertaking, I would like to enumerate what appear to me the three major fallacies that beset our view of Blake's relationship with tradition, then proceed to take a limited—and somewhat esoteric—tradition of Christian theology and illustrate to what use, or abuse, Blake put it.

If I may offer, to begin with, a parable—a perhaps unmemorable fancy: twentieth-century Milton scholars have often thrown up their hands in combined disbelief and shock at the heretical attitude of some Romantic poets toward *Paradise Lost*. I

This essay first appeared in *Blake Studies* 4 (1972): 117–133. Reprinted with permission.

daresay those same poets would return the compliment. For their heresy consists in severely questioning the Christian conception of the universe that underlies Milton's epics: in other words, in not being content merely to praise the literary and intellectual genius of *Paradise Lost,* but to read it as revelatory of an inclusive ethical system. Undoubtedly, Milton justifies God's ways to man in terms of this system, but to Blake or Shelley it is nonetheless a miscreated universe that the heirs of Adam have been willed. The pathways of Eden, like those of heaven, are paved with God's good intentions: reality, as Milton himself suggested, is hellish. And, though most modern critics are truer to the particulars of *Paradise Lost* than some Romantics were, it is probably because their eyes are on the poem, not on Paradise. But to a poet afflicted with millenarian yearning, integrity of scholarship and absolute fidelity to source are scarcely of primary interest. They are products of the Daughters of Memory. If the Voice of the Bard is to lead us toward the future, it must be faithless to the past.

I pursue this fancy because it is still not generally recognized that poets are not scholars. They may be, and often are, learned; but their primary obligation is to mold that learning into a new vision. Blake would never have written *Milton,* nor Shelley *Prometheus Unbound,* nor Byron *Cain,* nor Keats *Hyperion,* if *Paradise Lost* had been definitive. All of these works are ultimately theodicies—justifications of the ways of God to man—and each attempts a new, more modern, more humane, or more inclusive vision than Milton's.[2] In each case *Paradise Lost* is the significant literary context, but in each case it is bent to another's purposes. The point is not to be true to Milton, but to oneself and one's age.

What is apparent of literary sources applies as well to patterns of intellectual and cultural history. When a poet invokes a tradition, it can be because the dynamics of that tradition form an exact complement to his themes. An orthodox Christian poet like George Herbert will thus use the liturgy of the Anglican church. But few great poets are so orthodox, and certainly Blake was not. He is as likely to subvert tradition as he is to call upon it for intellectual support in framing his mythology. The Neoplatonism that Kathleen Raine finds so prevalent in Blake's writing is more correctly Christian Gnosticism, a tradition Blake draws upon constantly and with commanding knowledge.[3] But he is no Gnostic. Blake would be as quickly branded a heretic by this heretical sect as by the mainstream of Christian orthodoxy.

To be conscious, then, of the traditions Blake invokes is insufficient unless we are equally sensitive to how he reworks them. But this latter task is, in turn, impossible unless we also discriminate what resources Blake had at his disposal. They are clearly not those of a modern research library. The first major student of Blake to attempt to link him to Gnostic traditions, Milton Percival, assumes that Blake was exactly as learned as he: this, despite the fact that Percival could avail himself of numerous English translations of the primitive Church fathers whom Blake would have been constrained to study mostly from Latin and Greek tomes dating from the Renaissance.[4] Much of our knowledge of Gnosticism results from extremely technical scholarship—both historical and textual—performed within the past hundred years.[5]

Ironically, to bring to Blake's writings the edifice of truth built by twentieth-century scholarship is to falsify his relationship with Gnostic traditions. The knowledge of Blake's time derived from highly biased anathemas against the Gnostics delivered by men fighting an ideological war against a spreading heresy. They are filled with propaganda, distortions, outright lies, which the eighteenth century had only begun to sift for truth. The emphasis of eighteenth-century Biblical commentators, mythologists, and philosophers, which time has placed in a diminished perspective, shed considerable illumination on common strains of Blake's thought and imagery.

Finally, if we are to adopt the careful historical methodology that Blake's genius deserves, we must end, once and for all, the most pernicious vestige of the era when mad Blake prompted irrational criticism—what I would call the flying inductive leap. Yeats and Ellis are the most famous, but neither the least nor last, to rewrite Blake by unsubstantiated assertion. The practice continues today with equal force and equal damage to truth. A perfect instance is the interpretation of Hyle, second of the twelve sons of Albion, who with his brother Hand extends the reign of evil in *Jerusalem.* There seems to have been no concerted attempt to allegorize Hyle until a minor Blake critic, Herbert Ives Jenkins, to whom we owe the discovery of many details of Blake's life at Felpham, suggested that Hyle signified William Hayley, Blake's patron during the Felpham period.[6] His suggestions were elevated into insistence by S. Foster Damon, who glossed Hyle as "the Bad Artist" and launched his career through dozens of later commentaries where all his similarities with Hayley were expounded upon, amplified—and invented.[7] Frye, Erdman, and Bloom are no exceptions. And the most recent complete edition of Blake's poems informs all the budding intellects of the British Isles that " 'Hyle' derives from 'Hayley', the self-satisfied intellectual."[8]

And yet, in *Jerusalem* Hyle is far more dangerous than that representative of fallen humanity, Scofield, whose name indubitably derives from the soldier who brought Blake to the bar on a charge of Sedition. Scofield and his friend Kox, as well as the Judges who acquitted Blake, but whom he nonetheless had reason to distrust, are all claimed as Sons of Albion, because they represent the fallen State, which bases its security upon law, order, and guns. But Hyle, more ferocious than any of these, a super-militarist who is identified as Gog, the enemy of God's kingdom, at the climax of the third chapter of *Jerusalem,* and who is subsequently turned into a winding worm of reductive Generation by Gwendolen, seems scarcely representative of the man who defended Blake and stood by him throughout that trial. Hayley is one of English literature's most vilified men, thanks largely to zealous Blakeans who have seldom matched Blake's balanced perspective.[9] That Hayley was officious and as a friend more conscious of Blake's corporeal than spiritual needs suggests a failing somewhat short of wickedness: Hayley was, indeed, a benefactor. When his efforts to secure Blake's financial independence seemed to demand forsaking his vision, Blake parted company, penned some nastily incisive epigrams, yet continued on amicable terms. Blake correctly understood his genius to be radical. But, in modern parlance, Hayley is merely a sympathetic liberal, compelled by mistaken notions of philanthropy. He is not a Fascist menace. He is not, but Hyle is.

Who, then, is Hyle? It has long been noted that ὕλη (hyle) is the Greek word for matter, but unlike the expatiations on Hayley's inadequacies of character, this observation has never been pursued. Had it been, scholars would long ago have discovered that Blake is scarcely the first writer to personify matter, that, indeed, Hyle himself is a figure with a long and notorious history of personification, most of it elaborated within the watershed of Christian Gnosticism. For both the Gnostics and Blake, Hyle is the devil: the Satanic Spectre of Natural Religion.

Blake's familiarity with this tradition should not appear to us as one of his indulgences in the esoteric, like his Cabbalistic and Rosicrucian symbolism. If it does, it is an index of our historical and cultural myopia. Having accommodated ourselves to Hyle's kingdom, a technocracy that moves mountains with atomic explosions rather than faith, we are barely capable of questioning materialist premises. But the attack on such principles by Christian radicals continued throughout the eighteenth and early nineteenth centuries, and Blake had easy access to the records of Hyle's fantastic exploits, at least through contemporary accounts of the Gnostic's holy, intellectual war with orthodox Christianity. He might easily have encountered lengthy expositions of Gnostic thought in Pierre Bayle's *Dictionary,* Isaac de Beausobre's *Historie Critique de Manichée et Manicheisme,* Nathaniel Lardner's *History of Heretics* and *Credibility of the Gospel History,* Johann Lorenz von Mosheim's *Ecclesiastical History,* Gibbon's *Decline and Fall of the Roman Empire,* any number of works of the Unitarian theologian Joseph Priestley, and perhaps even Bishop Berkeley's three dialogues between Hylas and Philenous. Far from being minor or esoteric, all these works except Beausobre's had multiple editions and are continually cited for reference by eighteenth-century historians of the church or of philosophy.[10] If a writer like Blake is capable of elevating an uncommon personification like Orcus—Latin for hell—into his symbol of energy, it is virtually impossible for him to allude to Hyle without invoking a tradition from which the character is inseparable. "Part of space," according to Lardner's account of the Manicheans, is "occupied by Hyle, the evil principle, matter"; in the opinion of Faustus, "Hyle . . . [is], in common discourse, the devil."[11] Another Manichean proselyte named

Agapius refers to Hyle "sometimes [as] nature, sometimes matter, sometimes Satan, and the devil, and the prince and god of this world."[12] The mythologists view Hyle not only as a common term for the Devil,[13] but as equivalent among ancient religions to the Egyptian Typhon and the Persian Ahrimanes.[14]

According to the Manicheans, who saw Hyle as an evil principle coexistent with God, matter was originally the prison of dark demons churning in an internecine chaos, which grew in size until it touched the edge of God's kingdom of light. There those demons, amorous of the light they lacked, attempted to merge with it and through their efforts created this world. This is a tradition well-documented by the eighteenth century, one that is central to the mythopoeic conceptions of Shelley and Byron.[15] But Blake refuses to countenance the Manicheans' first principle, that evil is eternal; and, since the Manicheans affixed this perverse outgrowth of Zoroastrianism to an original Gnostic conception,[16] Blake understandably turns to the uncontaminated source.

"The great boast of the Gnostics," says Dr. Priestley, "was their profound and intricate doctrine concerning the derivation of various intelligences from the supreme mind, which they thought to be done by emanation or *efflux*."[17] Priestley echoes Nathaniel Lardner, whose exposition I quote:

> Basilides . . . taught that from the self-existent Father was born Nus or Understanding; of Nus Logos; of Logos Phronesis, Prudence or Providence; of Phronesis Sophia and Dunamis, Wisdom and Power, of Dunamis and Sophia, Powers, Principalities, and Angels, whom they call the superior angels, by whom the first heaven was made; from these proceeded other angels and other heavens . . . Farther they say that the angels which uphold the lower heaven, seen by us, made all things in this world, and then divided the earth among themselves. And the chief of these, they say, is he who is thought to be the God of the Jews.[18]

Likely though it is that Blake's theory of emanation derives from common Gnostic traditions, it is obvious from this passage that Blake altered the inherited conceptual framework. Blake does not allegorize, but mythologizes: the degenerative theory of history we encounter in *The Four Zoas* is a radical revision of the Gnostic emanation from the divine pleroma, Blake's realm of the Eternals. In the account of the pleroma ascribed to Valentinus, we even find four principal, sexually neutral eons—Horus, Christ, the Holy Ghost, and Jesus—who seem responsible for the organization of this habitation of the Deity.[19] Thus, though Hyle as a character is a comparative late-comer to Blake's pantheon, Gnostic conceptions color Blake's original attempts to create an inclusive mythology. In order to understand how distinctive is his debt, we need only turn to his contemporary Thomas Taylor, who in 1795 published four hymns probably derived from Plotinus.[20] In obscure and often limping verse Taylor repeatedly depicts the fall of the soul from its original bliss. After describing the primeval unity in "To Neptune," Taylor portrays its rupture:

> But when the madd'ning impulse of desire,
> Produc'd by Hyle's fluctuating life,
> With silent evolution guileful spread,
> And caus'd oblivion of supernal goods;
> In evil hour, unconscious of my change,
> And fraught with seeds of bitter woe, to earth
> I rush'd impetuous.
>
> (p. 133)

There follows an account of the fall through the seven planetary spheres, as the soul is progressively enclosed by the equivalent of Blake's Mundane Shell.

> I fell; by love of outward form ensnar'd,
> And guileful nature's fascinating charms:
> Till plung'd in infancy and night profound,
> And in this earthly cumbrous shell inclos'd,
> The soul's dark prison and Tartarian tomb,
> I lost all knowledge of my former state,
> And ancient union with thy central fount.
>
> (p. 134)

An even more illuminating version of the archetypal fall occurs in Taylor's hymn, "To Venus," where the soul descends into the organization of the human body, similar to Blake's rendering in *The First Book of Urizen,* engraved in 1794, the year before Taylor's Hymns were published. And it is particularly close to the immersion of Los in materiality, which dominates the second chapter of Blake's *Book of Los,* engraved the same year, 1795.

> Unhappily from thee, I then retir'd,
> And downward verg'd, as earthly love increas'd.
> Till with insanity my soul was fill'd,
> And into Hyle's stormy darkness hurl'd.
> For then her former dignity impair'd,
> My soul unable longer to extend
> Intelligibly with the mighty world,
> Her essence with all-various powers replete,
> Through dark oblivion of thy beauteous form,
> And wonder rais'd by Nature's guileful arts,
> Lethargic tended towards solid forms,
> Full of impetuous matter's base alloy.
> Hence in her passage thro' th'etherial orbs,
> Whate'er replete with light and warmth she found,
> And well-adapted body to connect,
> This with avidity she madly seiz'd;
> Herself involving in coercive bonds,
> Form'd from these circles, and their moving lines,
> And spreading round her like a filmy net.
> . . . .
> Then wide extending, as she gradual fell,
> Each orb's entangling surfaces and lines,
> And partly downwards thro' her spirit drawn,
> And partly struggling for supernal forms,
> Her spheric figure lost in lengthening rays,
> She sunk, transmuted to a human shape.
> In baneful hour thus fall'n and obscur'd,
> And in dark Hyle's loud-resounding sea
> Deep merg'd her vestment of etherial mould,
> For one membraneous and terrene she chang'd.
> The lines too, which before with fiery light,
> And colour'd with a fiery redness shone,
> She chang'd into the grosser form of nerves.
> And last, from these interior realms assum'd
> A spirit pond'rous, humid, and obscure.

Thus with a nat'ral body cover'd o'er.
From certain surfaces membraneous form'd,
With spirit, nerves, and filmy lines combin'd,
Th' external body's harmony and root,
Thro' which its parts are nourished and sustain'd,
My clouded and lethargic soul at length
Thy perfect beauty and alluring light
Forgot, the source of energy divine.

(pp. 122–124)

That Blake was familiar with Thomas Taylor's *Four Hymns* is probably beyond proof, but the similarity of these two conceptions of the fall is stronger testimony to a working relationship than is usually advanced in the tendentious and unconvincing arguments linking the two.[21]

The farther one probes into the Gnostic theory of emanation, the more probably it seems that Blake drew from it for the particulars of his mythology. The emanation responsible for sustaining human souls, for instance, is a feminine figure denominated the First Woman, and the Mother of the Living. Perhaps derived initially from the Virgin Mother, her powers extend far beyond those exercised by Mary in the original church: she is "the principle of immortal life, and the Source . . . the Dispenser of the Spirits who share Life and Rationality."[22] In other words, she is the type of Jerusalem, who in the last line of that poem is identified as the Emanation of all Human Forms, the spiritual reality toward which all life strives.[23]

The doctrine of emanations led the Gnostics to differentiate sharply between the Supreme God and the Demiurge, or Creator of the world. As Priestley renders Irenaeus, the Gnostics "all blasphemed in supposing the Maker of all things to be an evil being."[24] Moreover, pledging an extreme allegiance to the new dispensation, the Gnostics were not loath to identify this evil Demiurge. Tertullian quotes Basilides as claiming " 'that the Creator, who is the God of the Jews, as *the most turbulent* of the angels of his order, incited sedition and frequent wars, and spilt great floods of human blood.' According to St. Epiphanius, 'he was the proudest, most ambitious, most splendid, most arrogant, and most wicked of all the Angels.' "[25] Priestley delineated the logic for this attack on the Old Testament: "considering *matter* to be the source of all evil, and the world to have been the work of a malevolent being, they thought that this same evil being, or one of a similar disposition, had been the author of the law of Moses."[26] Jehovah, the furthest emanation from the supreme Godhead and the only divinity totally committed to a material universe, is easily assimilated with the arch-enemy of God, Satan. Cerinthus implied just such a comparison in teaching his followers,

> that the Creator of this world, whom he considered also as the sovereign and law-giver of the Jewish people, was a *being* endowed with the greatest virtues, and derived his birth from the *Supreme God*; that this *being* fell, by degrees, from his native virtue, and his primitive dignity; that the *Supreme God,* in consequence of this, determined to destroy his empire, and sent upon earth, for this purpose, one of the ever-happy and glorious *aeons,* whose name was Christ . . .

Cerinthus goes on to point the obvious conclusion of this struggle, that Christ "opposed himself with vigour to the *God of the Jews,* and was, by his instigation, seized and crucified by the Hebrew chiefs."[27]

If the Demiurge is ultimately opposed to the supreme God in his predilection for a universe of matter, that creation is likewise beyond the pale of divinity. The Gnostics believed "that malevolent *genii* presided in nature, and that from them proceeded all diseases and calamities, wars and desolations."[28] This, then, is the empire to which men are subjected. Blake recapitulates the Gnostic conflation in his attack on eighteenth-century rationalism: the God of Nature is identical with the God of Moral Law in a confluence that is ultimately inhuman, ultimately Satanic. As in every sense this God of Law and Nature opposes Christ, the divine emissary, he defines himself as the Anti-Christ, the universal enemy of man's salvation. As Blake demonstrates again and again—from the *Marriage of Heaven and Hell* and *Songs of Experience* to *Jerusalem*—the God worshipped in this world is Satan. Furthermore, in resurrecting this Gnostic judgment, Blake would have found congenial the Gnostics' reputation, verified in the New Testament, for political subversion. The founder of Christian priestcraft, Peter, attacks the Gnostics as "them that . . . despise government. Presumptuous *are they,* self-willed, they are not afraid to speak evil of dignities"; "they promise . . . liberty."[29] The Gnostics seem also to have defended energetic and intelligent evil against rigid pieties: several commentators portray Christ in his harrowing of hell redeeming figures like "Cain and the people of Sodom . . . but Abel, and Enoch, and Noah, and the patriarchs, and the prophets, were not delivered, because they would not come to him."[30] Blake casts his opposing forces in similar terms in *Jerusalem,* between the few free spirits yet responsive to Christ's invitation to embrace the spiritual liberty of Jerusalem, and the proponents of virtue as a substitute for intellect, those who have accepted the material Polypus of Generation and, hoisting the banner of rigid moral law, lead their flock into the spiritual wilderness of Ulro. It is thus that Blake saw Wordsworth, and his denunciation was such that it even ruffled the placid conventionality of Henry Crabb Robinson:

> The eloquent descriptions of Nature in Wordsworth's poems were conclusive proof of Atheism, for whoever believes in Nature said B: disbelieves in God—For Nature is the work of the Devil[.] On my obtaining from him the declaration that the Bible was the work of God, I referred to the commencement of Genesis—In the beginning God created the Heaven & the Earth[.]—But I gained nothing by this for I was triumphantly told that this God was not Jehovah, but the Elohim, and the doctrine of the Gnostics repeated with sufficient consistency to silence one so unlearned as myself[.][31]

Surprising as it is that Blake's considerable debt to Gnosticism has been so widely disregarded, it is even more curious that scholars enamored of Gnostic and Neoplatonic elements in Blake have not realized that Blake casts a plague on both houses.[32] If Blake employs Gnostic doctrine to assault the Deism of his time—in effect to launch a point by point reversal of orthodox doctrine—he just as surely upholds a vision of the true Christ in opposition to Gnostic conclusions. He achieves—and it would seem deliberate—an almost classic case of infiltration and subversion. Priestley attacks Gnosticism from the relatively safe distance of fifteen centuries; but Blake, who openly recreates a

Gnostic mythos, is by far the more dangerous enemy, exploding Gnostic pretensions to the final truth from within a superficially Gnostic framework. For, if the vitality of Eastern religious traditions motivated the Gnostics to attack the worldly focus of the church, to a thinker like Blake they must have seemed lacking in the vision, not to say the courage, of their own convictions. Their commitment to spiritual reality—at least as represented by the commentaries Blake might have known—merely affirms the negative perfection of denial. For all their lengthy struggles to be recognized as God's true church, their prescription for elevating human nature is a dreary regimen of reclusion, asceticism, mortification, dogmatic rigidity, and suicidal hatred of the Self. As the underside of Christianity, Gnosticism merely attacks the Christian's willingness to compromise with Hebraic traditions; otherwise, it shares with the church it opposes its worst premises. To Blake both orthodox and heretical Christianity lose the reality of God's minute particulars in murderous abstraction. The Gnostics even refused to acknowledge the humanity of Christ: an emanation of an abstract deity, he was never contaminated by what Blake terms 'the Human Form Divine.'

Where traditional Christianity straddles the division between matter and spirit, the Gnostics cast their doctrinaire allegiance with spirit. Blake would have agreed with Priestley's assault on this as "the real source of the greatest corruptions of true religion in all ages."[33] At the beginning of *The Marriage of Heaven and Hell* Blake carefully cites the duality between flesh and spirit as the principle Error of "All Bibles or sacred codes."[34] But, as Priestley argues against the Gnostic duality in order to defend his own Socinian—that is, Unitarian—heresy, his conclusion is anathema to Blake. Priestley's *Disquisitions Relating to Matter and Spirit* attempts to fuse the duality in a way perfectly illustrative of why Blake saw Deism as the final degeneration of man.[35] To Priestley, most of whose voluminous writings support one fundamental principle, there is no such thing as independent spirit, no such thing as free will. A dogmatic and absolute Necessitarian, Priestley defines spirit as a function of matter (a theological position that, in general cultural terms, has prevailed in the modern world). If Blake opposes the false duality of the

Gnostics, his poetry is even more strenuously opposed to Priestley's materialism: indeed, his own resolution of the duality is exactly the opposite of Priestley's. The passage in *The Marriage of Heaven and Hell* continues by propounding a truth whose simplicity underlies the complexities of Blake's life-work: "Man has no Body distinct from his Soul for that calld Body is a portion of Soul discerned by the five Senses, the chief inlets of Soul in this age" (*MHH* 4). The good angels of *The Marriage* are horrified by Blake's illustration of this concept—as well they should be, for they are all Gnostics who see Blake in the service of the devil.

But the ironic truth that Blake expounds throughout his work is that the Gnostics are themselves unconsciously in league with the true devil, the materialist principle worshipped by Priestley and the other Deists. The Gnostics conceived the fall of man to have originated from the sexual commerce of Adam and Eve.[36] Desire to the Gnostics is an emotion that seals our fallen nature. In contrast, it is "the moment of desire!" (*VDA* 7:3) Oothoon craves that Blake sees as man's unconscious endeavor to transcend the bonds of materialism. Not only is *Visions of the Daughters of Albion* a concerted attack against Gnostic principles, but it portrays in Oothoon a theme common to the subsequent poetry: the awakening comprehension that Urizen, a Gnostic deity commanding hatred of the flesh, is the "Father of Jealousy" (7:12), of possessiveness, of inhuman abstraction, and—finally—of Nature. Urizen's demand for a solid without fluctuation is impossible for spiritual fulfillment: he is reduced at last to the Indefinite Void of Hyle. Gnostic asceticism renders sexuality entirely a function of the material: thus in a perverse misunderstanding Vala, the presiding genius over Nature and Natural Religion, is rendered a Holy Virgin and Jerusalem a Magdalen. But, as the Divine Vision explains in comforting Jerusalem, Mary was herself an adulteress (*Jerusalem* 61:62); Christ is born of what Oothoon would call "happy copulation" (*VDA* 7:1), of the spirit's delight in breaking down the sensual barriers erected by those who hate all life, including their own.

If a religion is founded on the proposition that 'everything that dies is holy,' it has done what the Gnostics accused the Jews of perpetrating. It has resigned the management of man's spirit to Satan. In Blake's view the Gnostics reacted against the God of

Law by transforming him into a God of Moral Virtue and Denial, finally identical with the first. As there are no exceptions to law, nor any to the Gnostics' hatred of the flesh, there are also none to the machinery of Priestley's heaven, and none to Nature's total dominion over man. Law, asceticism, deism, and nature, however various their manifestations, found their dominion upon that denial of energetic impulse which is death. The Gnostics and Necessitarians, who seem so opposed in principle, in practice worship the same deity—Hyle, the winding worm who would reduce everything in the universe to the commonalty of clay. Blake's idealist stance recognizes that nothing is so spiritual but that the timid and unimaginative can perceive it within the framework of matter. But the corollary of that truth for Blake is another: there is nothing that seems material that cannot be humanized—spiritualized—when we see through, not with the eye. If it is a failure of vision that allows man to deny the spirit and give allegiance to the laws of matter, the demon Hyle, it is the divine vision incarnate in every man—Christ, the Human Imagination—that can humanize the material and thereby end the reign of the evil principle.

Notes

1. *Blake and Tradition,* 2 vols. (Princeton: Princeton Univ. Press, 1968).

2. Obviously the term theodicy must be stretched to represent all these works. For Shelley, Byron, and Keats, indeed, the justification is humanistic rather than theistic: of man rather than of God.

3. To distinguish properly between Neoplatonism and Gnosticism would require a small book. Simply speaking, the Platonic tradition portrays a benevolent demiurge attempting to instill the pure essence into intractable matter, but failing of perfect success. The Gnostics, in contrast, see matter and all who serve it as intrinsically evil. Blake's view of Nature as a universe of death accords with Gnostic, not Neoplatonic, doctrine. Ironically, however, when man identifies Nature as human form, he becomes that Demiurge, instilling matter with the pure essence—which is finally to say what is self-evidently the case, that Blake's tradition is that of native eighteenth-century idealism. Neither Platonist nor Gnostic, Blake is a Berkeleyan.

4. Milton O. Percival, *William Blake's Circle of Destiny* (New York: Columbia Univ. Press, 1938). To question Percival's methodology is not to gainsay the intelligence or achievement of his study.

5. *The Gospel of Truth* by Valentinus, a major Gnostic document, was

discovered in 1945–46 in Egypt among scrolls containing forty-four Gnostic works written in Coptic.

6. "The Trial of William Blake for High Treason," *Nineteenth Century,* 67 (1910), 849–61; reprinted in Herbert Jenkins, *William Blake: Studies of His Life and Personality,* ed. C. E. Lawrence (London, 1925), pp. 77–78.

7. *William Blake: His Philosophy and Symbols* (Boston and New York: Houghton Mifflin, 1924), pp. 187, 190, 191.

8. *The Poems of William Blake,* ed. W. H. Stevenson (London: Longman, 1971), p. 780. Each appearance of 'Hyle' is similarly annotated.

9. This penchant for defining abstruse problems in Blake's poetry from our meagre knowledge of the biography has been aptly characterized by James Rieger as "the loosest chatter about the dead" (in "The Hem of Their Garments: The Bard's Song in *Milton,*" *Blake's Sublime Allegory: Essays on The Four Zoas, Milton, and Jerusalem,* ed. Stuart Curran and Joseph Anthony Wittreich, Jr. [Madison: University of Wisconsin, 1972]). Professor Wittreich has undertaken a defense of Hayley's formative influence on Blake's late poetics in "Domes of Mental Pleasure: Blake's Epics and Hayley's Epic Theory," *Studies in Philology,* 69 (1971), 101–29. The other 'heavies' of Blake biography, long accorded a vilification akin to Hayley's, are James Leigh, and Robert Hunt, publishers of the liberal *Examiner,* which attacked Blake's 'enthusiastic' art in 1808–09. The Brothers Hunt, without differentiation, have been condensed into Hand, the most evil of the Sons of Albion, on the strength of the printer's hand symbol, used as an editorial signature by Leigh Hunt. This designation is now universal, despite the fact that Hand appears in plate 19 of *Milton* (a late addition, say the commentators on the strength of this identification), and despite Cumberland's remark that Blake had completed sixty plates of a new prophecy (clearly *Jerusalem*) in 1807, which would make the introduction of a new character two years later at best most questionable. The circular arguments used to support Hand's identification with the Brothers Hunt are methodologically unconscionable, suggesting that Blake critics have taken a license for unravelling obscurities long ago revoked for critics of Spenser and Shakespeare. Leigh Hunt, who demonstrated his remarkable taste in championing Hazlitt, Keats, Shelley, and Browning when comparatively unknown, should be forgiven his one lapse of artistic judgment, even by those who find all visions pale in comparison with Blake's. As for Hand, he is self-evidently "The Accuser who is The God of This World," to whom Blake inscribed the epilogue of *For The Sexes: The Gates of Paradise.* His many symbolic manifestations have been delineated with an expert balance by E. J. Rose, "Blake's Hand: Symbol and Design in *Jerusalem,*" *Texas Studies in Literature and Language,* 6 (1964), 47–58.

10. After having done much of my research, I was gratified to find confirmation for Priestley's influence on Blake in Morton Paley's *Energy and the Imagination: A Study of the Development of Blake's Thought* (London: Oxford Univ. Press, 1970). Paley sees Priestley's writings as possible sources for a number of Blake's preoccupations, including those that are Gnostic in origin (pp. 8–10, 66–67). Though I hope that my findings strengthen the value of this assertion, at one point we are in fundamental disagreement, as I think Priestley and Blake would have been, whatever the evidence for their acquaintance: see below, n. 35. It is of incidental interest to note that, except for Mosheim's standard history, the investigation of early heresies by eighteenth-century scholars seems to have been the province of free-thinkers (Bayle, Beausobre) or of Dissenting ministers intent on proving their own orthodoxy, like Lardner and Priestley.

11. *The Credibility of the Gospel History* in *The Works of Nathaniel Lardner*

(London, 1788), III, 457, 458. The section of this work on "Mani, and his followers" is nearly two hundred pages in length (*Works*, III, 374–554).

12. *Credibility of the Gospel History*, in Works, III, 461.

13. Isaac de Beausobre, *Histoire Critique de Manichée et Manicheisme* (Amsterdam: J. Frederic Bernard, 1734), I, 489.

14. Beausobre, II, 250.

15. Shelley explicitly introduces a Manichean framework into the first canto of *The Revolt of Islam*, and it is likewise basic to the structure of *Prometheus Unbound* and *The Cenci*. Byron often alludes to Manichean (or Zoroastrian) machinery, as in the Hall of Arimanes in *Manfred*. Cain exhibits a profound knowledge of Manichean arguments: Byron's Lucifer is ironically a pure Gnostic.

16. "All the Gnostics were persuaded, that *evil* had some other cause than the Supreme Being, but, perhaps, none of them before Manes held that it arose from a principle absolutely independent of him. Bardesanes maintained that evil was not made by God. Marcion, Cerdon and Manes, all held that the devil and demons were unbegotten. Valentinus held that matter was self-existent, and the cause of evil." Joseph Priestley, *An History of Early Opinions Concerning Jesus Christ . . . Proving that the Christian Church was at First Unitarion* (1786), in *The Theological and Miscellaneous Works of Joseph Priestley*, ed. John T. Rutt (London: G. Smallfield, 1817–32), VI, 80–81. This work is hereafter cited as *Early Opinions*. Priestley also treats the distinction between Manichean and Gnostic thought in *A General History of the Christian Church* (1790, 1803), in *Works*, VIII, 262–63.

17. *Early Opinions*, in *Works*, VI, 81.

18. *The History of the Heretics in the First Two Centuries after Christ . . . with Large Additions by John Hogg* (1780), in *Works*, IX, 272–73.

19. John Laurence Mosheim, *An Ecclesiastical History, Ancient and Modern*, tr. Archibald Maclaine (London: Cadell and Davies, 1811), I, 229.

20. *The Fable of Cupid and Psyche, translated from the Latin of Apuleius: to which are added a poetical paraphrase on the speech of Diotima, in the Banquet of Plato; four hymns, &c. &c.* (London, 1795).

21. To this evidence should be added early lines from the hymn, "To Love," remarkably similar to Blake in diction (pp. 126–27):

> Four circling eyes adorn thy four-fold face,
> And cause thy *perfect*, and unbounded sight:
> Two golden wings emitting mental fire,
> Impell thee rapid, through the mighty world.

22. Beausobre, I, 312–13, quotes Epiphanius: "Cette *Mere des Vivans est l'Esprit*, qui est le Principe du mouvement & de la vie . . . Je crois donc, que la *Mere de la Vie*, la *Mere Lumineuse*, la *Mere des Vivans, & l'Espirit*, qui est la Premiére Femme, que tout cela n'est autre chose qu'une Emanation Divine, qui est le Principe de la Vie immortelle, & la Source, ou du moins la Dispensatrice des Ames, qui ont en partage la Vie & la Raison." This is likely a variation of the conception introduced by the original Gnostic, Simon Magus, who believed that he and his mistress Helena were divine aeons, "and that he came by the command of God upon earth, to abolish the empire of those who had formed this material world, and to deliver Helena from their power and dominion" (Mosheim, I, 143).

23. An essential distinction, however, separates Blake's from the Gnostic conception of Emanations. Blake's emanations testify to a human, if tragically fragmented, reality. The Gnostics concern themselves with heaven.

24. *Early Opinions,* in *Works,* VI, 134.

25. Beausobre, II, 15.

26. *Early Opinions,* in *Works,* VII, 176–77.

27. Mosheim, *Ecclesiastical History,* I, 145. Basilides held the same doctrine concerning the Demiurge: "These angelic beings, advanced to the government of the world which they had created, fell by degrees, from their original purity, and manifested soon the fatal marks of their depravity and corruption. They not only endeavoured to efface in the minds of men the knowledge of the Supreme Being, that they might be worshipped in his stead, but also began to war against one another, with an ambitious view to enlarge, every one, the bounds of his respective dominion. The most arrogant and turbulent of all these angelic spirits, was that which presided over the Jewish nation. Hence the Supreme God, beholding with compassion the miserable state of rational beings, who groaned under the contest of these jarring powers, sent from heaven his Son Nus, or Christ, the chief of the *aeons,* that, joined in a substantial union with the man Jesus, he might restore the knowledge of the Supreme God, and destroy the empire of those angelic natures which presided over the world, and particularly that of the arrogant leader of the Jewish people. The god of the Jews, alarmed at this, sent forth his ministers to seize the man Jesus, and put him to death" (Mosheim, *Ecclesiastical History,* I, 225–26). Beausobre quotes Manes to the effect that it was "the Devil, who raised the Jews against Christ and moved them to crucify him" (I, 228); he discusses Satan as author of the Old Testament and Mosaic Law in I, 272–73.

28. Mosheim, *Ecclesiastical History,* I, 136. Beausobre devotes several pages to an analysis of Nature as an evil principle among the Gnostics: II, 416–18.

29. 2 Peter 2:10, 19. Priestley attributes Peter's words as applicable to the Gnostics in *Early Opinions* (*Works,* VI, 112) and also cites Jude 8: they "despise dominion, and speak evil of dignities." Furthermore, he claims that Paul's remarks in 1 Tim, 6:1–4 suggest that the Gnostics had incited slaves to revolt from their masters (*Works,* VI, 112–13). The Gnostics were also taken to task for the anarchistic lack of discipline in their churches: there were no bishops in evidence, and the members took turns in leading the congregation (*Works,* VI, 113–14).

30. Lardner, citing a similar statement by Irenaeus, quotes Theodoret (*History of the Heretics,* in *Works,* IX, 377). Unfortunate as it might be to reduce Blake's delightful spontaneity to an ancient source, Lardner's account of the Adamians or Adamites provides an illuminating parallel for Thomas Butts' anecodote of discovering Blake and Catherine nude, reading Book IV of *Paradise Lost* in the garden. "Their churches are stoves, made warm for the reception of company by a fire underneath. When they come to the door they pull off their clothes, both men and women, and enter naked into the place of meeting. Their presidents and teachers do the same, and they sit together promiscuously. And so they perform their readings, and other parts of worship naked . . . they reckon their church an emblem of paradise, and themselves imitators of Adam and Eve" (Lardner, quoting Epiphanius, in *Works,* IX, 336–38).

31. G. E. Bentley, Jr., *Blake Records* (London: Oxford Univ. Press, 1969), p. 545.

32. The sole exception is Thomas Altizer in *The New Apocalypse: The Radical Christian Vision of William Blake* (East Lansing: Michigan State Univ. Press, 1967). Quoting Robinson's remembrance of Blake's remarks on Wordsworth and passages from *Vision of the Last Judgment,* Altizer observes, "Critic after critic has

seen fit to interpret [Blake's] vision in Gnostic terms, whether implicitly or explicitly," and, though he acknowledges the influence, he flatly states that Blake's ideas are "antithetically related to the dualistic and world-negating spirit of Gnosticism. No one with any historical knowledge of ancient Gnosticism could imagine for a moment that Blake's vision is Gnostic; we need only remember the deep hostility to art that is characteristic of true Gnosticism . . ." (86–87). One wishes that Altizer, so gifted in representing nuances of theology, had chosen to explore Blake's relationship with Gnosticism further.

33. *Disquisitions Relating to Matter and Spirit* (1777, 1782), in *Works,* III, 219.

34. All citations from Blake's writings refer to *The Poetry and Prose of William Blake,* ed. David V. Erdman, rev. ed. (Garden City, N. Y.: Doubleday, 1970).

35. I simply cannot accept Paley's sketchy argument that Priestley, in denying the dichotomy of soul and body in his *Disquisitions,* is anticipating Blake's position; nor can I countenance his claim that "we should not be misled by Priestley's professed materialism and Blake's hostility to materialist philosophies" into finding opposition (*Energy and the Imagination,* p. 9). It is difficult to conceive of any contemporary of Blake, as the poet would see it, more bent on codifying error than Priestley. Priestley's main tenet, which he attempted with such fortitude to prove that of the primitive church, is the prime heresy to Blake: denying the divinity of Christ. The *Disquisitions Relating to Matter and Spirit* (as well as its sequel, *The History of the Philosophical Doctrine . . .* [of] *the Nature of Matter; with its Influence on Christianity*) defines soul as an element of body, whereas Blake perceives exactly the opposite. And Priestley's argument is dangerously tendentious: he wishes religious knowledge, like physics, to be based on the methodical rules enunciated by Newton at the opening of the third book of his *Principia* (*Disquisitions,* in *Works,* III, 221). In other words, if one accepts the initial premise, one must accordingly acknowledge that spirit follows the absolute, causal laws of matter and thus deny spiritual liberty. "Jerusalem," it should be remembered, "is called Liberty among the Children of Albion," (*J* 54:5) and Blake's epic is directed squarely against the position Priestley maintains. The extremity of Priestley's defense of Necessity can be seen in *The Doctrine of Philosophical Necessity Illustrated: Being an Appendix to the Disquisitions Relating to Matter and Spirit* (1777, 1782; *Works,* III, 447–540). There, if Blake bothered to pursue the enemy in his own camp, he would have found ironic amusement in this free thinker's declaration of philosophical debt to Jonathan Edwards, a perfect union of Tirzah and Rahab. Blake might, incidentally, have been familiar with Priestley's *Letters to the Members of the New Jerusalem Church, Formed by Baron Swedenborg* (1791; *Works,* XXI, 43–86), which with an ingratiating tone discredits Swedenborg as a true prophet of God because he cannot create miracles and insinuates that his visions are only products of an enthusiastic imagination. Such a view would have been sufficient to drive Blake back to Swedenborg's defense.

36. See Priestley, *Nature of Matter; with its Influence on Christianity,* in *Works,* III, 444; also Lardner, *Credibility of the Gospel History,* in *Works,* III, 471–72; and Beausobre, II, 463.

FLORENCE SANDLER

The Iconoclastic Enterprise: Blake's Critique of "Milton's Religion"

Every man of sense, every good man, ought to hold the Christian sect in horror. The great name of theist, which is not sufficiently revered, is the only name one ought to take. The only gospel one ought to read is the great book of Nature, written by the hand of God and sealed with his seal.

—*Voltaire*

Waging Mental War for Jesus on the battlefield that was Europe at the end of the eighteenth century, Blake often found it his best recourse to thrust the weapons of triumphant Deism back on the Deists themselves. If, from Shaftesbury to Voltaire, the Deists had accused religious visionaries of being the first bigots and inquisitors, then Blake would show that, on the contrary, inquisition, oppression, and the attempt to impose uniformity were the necessary consequences of accepting as absolute the abstractions and generalizations of empirical Reason. If the *philosophes* accounted for the awesome God of traditional religion as a projection by man out of his own fear and a symptom of his lamentable lack of confidence in his own reason, then Blake would show that empirical Reason itself was a projection of man's self-limitation to his five senses and a consequence of

---

This essay first appeared in *Blake Studies* 5 (Fall 1972): 13–57; pages 16–47 of the original have been considerably edited and rewritten for this occasion by the author. Reprinted with permission.

his terrified refusal to enjoy the rigorous life of the Imagination. If the *philosophes* analyzed the history of religion as the growth of superstition and the progress of sacerdotal imposition, then Blake would expose the superstition inherent in the "Mathematical Holiness" of empirical Reason, and the derivation of Hume's Natural Religion from Druidism and the mystery cults. Shaftesbury and Trenchard had diagnosed religious enthusiasm as a disease of the mind, and Holbach had written off religion as *la contagion sacrée*; Blake, in a counter offensive, would depict empirical Reason and Materialism as the Pestilence, Newton and Locke being among its chief carriers.

Yet, while Blake defies the men of Enlightenment, it is clear that he shares much of their critique of Christianity. No *philosophe* exposes more devastatingly than Blake the process of the projection of fear that makes the God of Thunder, Old Nobodaddy; none could be more keen than he to hunt down in Christianity the psychopathology that supports priestly mystery and the historical alliance between priest and monarch. In his own day he is doing the work of Christian iconoclasm that the Reformers had left unfinished, separating the Idol from the True God, or, in Paul's words, the Religion of the Flesh ([*sarx*]) from that of the Spirit ([*pneuma*]). Luther and Calvin had indeed protested against the authoritarianism and superstition that constituted the "idolatry" of the Roman Church, but John Milton in his generation had seen the idolatries hidden even within Calvinism; Blake, for his part, must surely expose the idolatries latent in the whole cultural heritage, the legacy of Newton and Locke, but also of Milton, Luther, Calvin, and Paul. Even the affinity between Blake and the men of the Enlightenment is to be seen in the perspective of the Reformation; for Bayle, Shaftesbury, and Hume were in their own way continuing the critique that the Reformers had undertaken, simply extending their study from the superstition of paganism and Catholicism to *all* religion, which, in so far as it professed a metaphysic, was by very definition superstition. But to exchange Mystery for "Rational Demonstration in the Saviour" was, from Blake's point of view, to exchange the Whore for Satan and still to deny the Spirit. The Reformation had always had its Rationalist wing, partly in alliance, partly at odds, with the Spiritualists; the pattern is continued when, at the end of the eighteenth century, the Deists, who are the heirs of Socinius, are confronted by Blake, the antinomian prophet, who accuses them of having erected Reason into another idol.

One recognizes the concern to expose or "unveil" the idol as a basic feature of apocalyptic. Indeed, the word "apocalypse" means exactly the "revelation" or "unveiling" of something previously hidden. The Apocalypse of St. John, the model for so many Reformation writings and a favorite text for commentary, is structured around the successive "unveilings" and apotheoses of the components of the Anti-Christ (the Beasts, the Dragon, the Whore who is the False City) and then those of the Christ and his Bride, the True City, Jerusalem. It is noteworthy that the Apocalypse recapitulates, in order to transvaluate, the events of Israel's history—the Exodus attended by the plagues upon the Egyptians, the building of the City and the Temple, and (since this is a Christian apocalypse) the Crucifixion and Resurrection. Throughout this history the Body of the Anti-Christ (i.e., the Body of Sin and Death) has been hardening into definition, but so has the Body of Life, represented by the saints upon whom the Dragon makes war. Now that the Body of the Anti-Christ, the False Ruler, is fully manifest, Time is fulfilled and the Eschaton has arrived; the Anti-Christ can be cast out, and the Body of Christ, in his triumphant Second Coming, will be realized not only in the saints but in the whole cosmos.

It is part of their Reformation heritage, perhaps, that the men of the Enlightenment develop a style that may be described as "secular apocalyptic." They are frequently engaged in iconoclastic "unveiling"— *L'Antiquité dévoilée* is the title of one of Boulanger's books; *Le Christianisme dévoilée* is the title of Holbach's—and the unveiling is often a prelude to the proclamation of the triumphant Reign of Reason. From Blake's point of view, they have simply mistaken the Anti-Christ for Christ, and the Satanic Body of Death for the Body of Life. Blake himself, as Northrop Frye and Harold Bloom have pointed out, is writing apocalyptic. Indeed, he indicates as much when he chooses for two of his epics the names "Jerusalem" and "Vala"

(Vala meaning here "the Veiled One," and perhaps concealing a pun on Vale and Valour). He has under purview not merely Israel's history, but the whole history of mankind, to which, however, Israel's history provides the vital clue. Living under what is alleged to be the Reign of Reason, Blake can see clearly enough the petrifaction through history of that particular Body of Death that he calls Urizen, and its feminine part that he calls Rahab. That is, he discerns in the religion of Israel and in religion generally that Legalism and Natural Religion constantly infiltrate and undermine the Divine Imagination, the Poetic Genius, which sees that Everything that Lives is Holy. His own work of poetry is both iconoclastic and prophetic, exposing Satan and Rahab, the Dragon and the Whore, wherever they lurk within the human mind (most likely in the very forms of Holiness), and to open the eye of Vision to recognize Jesus, the Divine Imagination.

In Blake's short apocalypse, *Milton,* the task is more particularly to purge and clarify the religious vision of John Milton, master spirit, Christian, poet-prophet and republican. In Blake's corpus, *Milton* stands as prelude to *Jerusalem,* and its protagonist is the Elijah whose Second Coming is the sign of the Eschaton, the Awakening of Albion, and the "Great Harvest and Vintage of the Nations." Only Milton could play this role for Albion. And yet even Milton, in his life and poetry, had fallen victim to some degree to Satan and Rahab and been implicated in cruelty. Because Milton is, as it were, Blake's other self and because Blake loves him only just this side idolatry, the iconoclastic enterprise must begin with Milton himself; and Milton's self-purging is Blake's own.[1]

Blake announces at the outset that part of the subject his Muses must address is the corruption of love and prophecy that consists in the cult of sacrifice, sanctioned by the official doctrines of Jesus' atonement on the Cross:

> Tell also of the Flase Tongue! vegetated
> Beneath your land of shadows: of its sacrifices, and
> Its offerings; even till Jesus, the image of the Invisible God
> Became its prey: a curse, an offering, and an atonement,
> For Death Eternal . . .
>
> (2:10–14)[2]

As in the Preface "To the Jews" in *Jerusalem,* he exposes "the laws of sacrifice for sin" as the cruelty of the "elect" against the "reprobate," whether of the elect class invoking the penal law against social outcasts and malefactors, or the elect nation waging war against its enemies. The Holy War that the Hebrews waged against the Canaanites, massacring the enemy as a "devotion" to their war-god Jehovah,[3] is perpetuated in the ideological warfare of the modern world, with its "sacrifice" of countless thousands on the battlefields. The same nexus of sacrifice Blake discerns in more subtle forms in the annihilation of the other in the intimate relationships of husband and wife, parent and child.

Thus the poem's action proceeds against a background of sacrifice and ritual slaughter which takes place in London daily, "Between South Molton Street & Stratford Place: Calvarys foot" (4:21), on army parade grounds, in the prisons and on the scaffold—all built on Tyburn Rock and the sacrificial Oak Groves of the Druids. At one point in London's recent history the act had been performed publicly and in full cognizance upon a king, when Milton and Cromwell, being of the "elect," had cast themselves with conviction into the role of regicide, offering up what Milton called a "most gratefull and well-pleasing Sacrifice" unto the Lord.[4]

> Charles calls on Milton for Atonement. Cromwell is ready.
> (5:39)

The regicide pamphleteer is also, by no coincidence, the poet who expounds in *Paradise Lost* the traditional doctrine of Jesus' death on the cross as being the "satisfaction" of the "penalty" or even the "punishment" exacted by the Father as due for Adam's "transgression" and the "sins/ Of all mankind" (*P.L.* XII 393–419). Only the Spectre or Satan demands Human Sacrifices, Blake protests, while the "Sacrifices of Eternity," in accordance with the authentic voice of prophecy in the psalm, are "a Broken Spirit/ And a Contrite Heart" (*The Ghost of Abel,* p. 269). Abel himself, and the saints below the altar in the Apocalypse, surely call not for vengeance but for the Forgiveness of Sins. Only contrition and forgiveness, born of love, can respond to Jesus' laying down his own life in love.

Thus Milton, the Christian Hero of Blake's poem, hears with contrition the testimony that implicates him in the cruelties and wars of history: "Miltons Religion is the cause: there is no end to destruction" (22:39), while the witnesses must hear the prophetic voice of Los counselling them to patience lest, raging against the Satanic, they become Satanic in turn and repeat the errors of history:

> Calvin and Luther in fury premature
> Sow'd War and stern division between Papists & Protestants
> Let it not be so now! O go not forth in Martydoms & Wars.
> (23:47–49)

But Milton himself has already undertaken the act of Christian heroism which is redemption, a self-annihilation and an entering into "Eternal Death" (14:14) to confront his own Spectre and redeem his Emanation.

It is without irony that Blake shows his protagonist first waiting among the elect to attend the Marriage-supper of the Lamb, but unhappy in Eternity while his reprobate Emanation is "scatter'd thro' the deep/ In torment" (2:19–20)—no Marriage for Milton, but only Divorce! The young Milton had entered into marriage with the ominous announcement that, if chastity was the chief glory of woman, made in the image of man, then it was all the more the glory of man, made directly in the image of God.[5] A year later, smarting under the separation from his wife, he had become the advocate for divorce where marriage was nothing but "continual strife," and for the current validity of the Mosaic provisions for divorce which Jesus had surely not intended to abrogate! Even in marriage, Milton had conducted himself as the elect dealing with the reprobate: as the elect of Israel had cast off foreign wives to purify the race and reaffirm the covenant in the days of Ezra, so he would repudiate his wife who, being a Royalist, was no better than an idolator or "Canaanite," and was now "in the camp of the enemy, threatening her husband with death and disaster."[6] Though the breach was eventually healed when Mary Milton threw herself in submission at her husband's feet, Milton in his will virtually repudiated the daughters of the marriage as too "unkind" (ungrateful, but also foreign?) to inherit from their father. (And from their mother's property there was nothing to inherit.)

In Milton's life, then, there were the evidences of self-righteousness and revenge in the course of his long warfare with his Emanation. His poetry celebrated not only the Holy Matrimony of Adam and Eve but also the Lady's doctrine of Chastity and Virginity, and he has presented the bitter perplexity of Samson in his marriage-choices, which were treacherous, though God-inspired.

Hence, setting out to redeem his Emanation, the Milton of Blake's poem must confront in the wilderness his Urizenic self, who is the Mosaic law-giver and (in two senses) the director to his Emanation. The Six-fold Miltonic Female, comprising his three wives and three daughters,

> sat rang'd round him as the rocks of Horeb round the land
> Of Canaan: and they wrote in thunder smoke and fire
> His dictate; and his body was the Rock Sinai.
>
> (17:12–14)

But the Emanation is sure to turn upon him to dominate him on her own terms, weaving a covering out of poverty and pain, and she appears shortly as the siren goddesses, Rahab and Tirzah, enticing him over the Jordan not only to become the warring "King/ Of Canaan and reign in Hazor where the Twelve Tribes meet" (20:5–6) but to become implicated also in Tirzah's priestly and sexual mysteries of sacrifice (19). Milton's struggle in the wilderness recapitulates the struggle of the Son in *Paradise Regained:* the authentic prophet must repudiate kingship and priesthood. (Jesus Himself is Prophet for Blake, but neither Priest nor King.) The sexual temptation that Satan poses to the Son in *Paradise Regained* is, however, quickly dismissed in favour of the more formidable temptations of political and intellectual power. Here the temptation is more subtle: to see the Emanation reduced to domestic servant on the one hand and whore on the other is to find no need and no capacity for love itself.

The call of the Canaanite goddesses is not only Blake's shrewd comment on Milton's terrors over his "Canaanite" wife in the enemy camp, threatening his destruction; it is also a significant indication of his reading of the anxieties of Biblical religion. It is noteworthy that king and priest are presented as a composite, that they are sponsored by goddesses, and that they are *Canaanite* perversions of prophetic religion. To a "diabolical" reader of the Bible like Blake, it was clear that the kingly titles appropriated by David, and later attributed to Jesus as Son of David, were originally Canaanite titles. God's people Israel, after all, had begun as republicans, and it was a sign of their degradation, the prophet Samuel had declared, that they later insisted upon having a king after the manner of the nations round about. It was instructive that at the same time they came to envisage their God Jehovah as a king also, seated on his throne between the Cherubim in the Temple which was his new palace on Mount Zion. But the imperial style indicates to Blake's mind not God Himself (Who is Spirit) but only Urizen, the Usurper and Anti-God, who purports to be Law and Destiny. Such a God, Blake had declared, is "only an Allegory of Kings & nothing Else."[7]

Along with the sacral kingship, the Israelites had taken over the institution of priesthood with its rites of sacrifice and propitiation. Notoriously, in the reign of Manasseh, they had fallen back to sacrificing children in the cult of Moloch. But Blake sees even the regular cult of sacrifice in Israel as a Canaanite perversion from beginning to end, and the ceremony of Atonement, with the High Priest's penetration into the Holy Place and the designation of the scapegoat, as the epitome of a Mystery that is sexual as well as political.

Palace and Temple, standing side by side on Mount Zion, made explicit the political alliance between the sacral kings of the House of David and the Jehovite priesthood, the kings' appropriation and centralization of the political power that had formerly belonged to the Tribes themselves having its corollary in the Deuteronomic Reform which gave the priesthood in Jerusalem the exclusive monopoly on the performance of sacrificial rituals.

Less obvious is the sexual reference of the Temple. Jehovah, the God of Israel, who was unusual in having no divine consort, had entered into marriage with the Virgin Israel, having chosen her in the wilderness, given her the marriage-contract or covenant on Mount Sinai, and led her into the Land of Canaan as to her marriage-bed. The sign of Jehovah's cohabitation with Israel was the Temple itself, his tent or tabernacle, where the mythic At-one-ment, the *hieros gamos,* was recapitulated each year by the High Priest's entry through the curtains into the Secret Place.[8]

Exactly in the Holy of Holies in the Temple in Jerusalem Blake found the prototype for the Mystery, and in the holy things that reposed there (the Ark of the Covenant shaded by the Covering Cherub and containing the Tables of the Law) the marks of an idolatry sexual and legalistic, the throne of Satan/ Urizen and the Whore. The phrase "the Abomination of Desolation," used in Daniel to describe Antiochus' defilement of the Holy Place, Blake uses to characterize the very conception of the Holy Place. Not only the materials and the workmen for the Temple had come for Canaanite Tyre but presumably also the symbols of the cult. In Canaan itself the Cherub of Baal or of his king would couple with the Virgin Ashtoreth in the central mystery of the official fertility cult. The Hebrews, appalled by Canaanite orgies and temple prostitution, had substituted for Ashtoreth the Tables of the Law, and in place of Canaanite promiscuity had promulgated the Levitical Code that exemplified, to Blake's mind, the opposite perversion. The more subtle presence of the goddess showed itself here in a religion of Chastity, exclusiveness and revenge. (A priest "shall take a wife in her virginity. A widow, or one divorced, or a woman who has been defiled, or a harlot, these he shall not marry; but he shall take to wife a virgin of his own people, that he may not profane his own children" [Lev. 21:13–15]. "The adulterer and the adulteress shall surely be put to death" [Lev. 20:10].) But the true spirit of prophecy spoke otherwise: when the scribes and Pharisees had brought to Jesus the woman taken in adultry asking whether she should be stoned, Jesus had shamed the accusers and refused to condemn the woman.

The marriage between Jehovah and the Virgin Israel had not been harmonious. Listening to the dialogue woven through the oracles of the prophets and the Song of Songs, hearing now the tones of yearning, now of accusation, possessiveness and vindictiveness, Blake must have identified the voices of many "States," as they came to be presented in his poems—the voices not only of Jesus and Jerusalem, but also of Urizen, Satan, Vala, Rahab and Leutha.

> Thou hast played the harlot with many lovers;
> Yet return again to me, saith the Lord . . .
> (Jeremiah 3:1)[9]
> All thy lovers have forgotten thee;
> they seek thee not;
> for I have wounded thee with the wound of an enemy,
> with the chastisement of a cruel one,
> for the multitude of thine iniquity;
> because thy sins were increased.
> (Jer. 30:14)
> Return, thou backsliding Israel, saith the Lord;
> and I will not cause my anger to fall on you; . . .
> for I am married unto you
> (Jer. 3:12–14)

Even in Jeremiah, the prophecy of the New Covenant and the True Marriage, which is for Blake the Marriage of Jesus and Jerusalem, implies the end of the old cult symbols: "In those days, saith the Lord, they shall say no more, The ark of the covenant of the Lord: neither shall it come to mind" (Jer. 3:16). And in the Apocalypse of John, when the Lamb fully inhabits Jerusalem his bride, then, says the seer, "I saw no temple therein: for the Lord Almighty and the Lamb are the temple of it" (Rev. 21:22). Not only has the veil of the Temple been rent in twain, but the temple and the Holy of Holies have been altogether abolished; or rather, the sacral centre (with the full presence of God) is no longer confined to that one place but is extended everywhere. Much the same prophecy Blake reaches in *Jerusalem* at the end of plate 69, which is his most explicit critique of the Mystery of the Temple and the "False Holiness hid within the Center":

> For the Sanctuary of Eden. is in the Camp: in the Outline,
> In the Circumference: & every Minute Particular is Holy:
> Embraces are Cominglings: from the Head even to the Feet;
> And not a pompus High Priest entering by a Secret Place.
> (41–44)

Likewise, in *Milton,* before the consummation is reached, there must be the final apotheosis of the evil that sits, in its hermaphroditic complexity, in the Holy Place: the same "Dragon red & hidden Harlot which John in Patmos saw" (40:22), but hidden now no longer. It has been exposed and repudiated in the meeting of Bridegroom and Bride face to face: Milton, who has overcome, by self-annihilation, the Satan within himself, and Ololon, who casts off "the Virgin" (42:3–7). They follow the work of Jesus, who has rent

> the Sexual Garments, the Abomination of Desolation
> Hiding the Human Lineaments, as with an Ark and Curtains
> (41:25–8)

and their meeting is the prelude to the apotheosis of Jesus Himself, Who comes not as King, not as Priest, but as Prophet and Friend (*cf.* Rev. 19:10), prepared now and always to enter—to his own annihilation, Albion's "bosom of death" (42:21). As against the "Sexual Garments" of Natural Religion and Legalism, Jesus wears as a garment Love, Mental Warfare and Poetry:

> The Clouds of Ololon folded as a Garment dipped in
> blood
> Written within & without in woven letters: & the Writing
> Is the Divine Revelation in the Litteral expression:
> A Garment of War, I heard it namd the Woof of Six
> Thousand Years.
> (42:12–15)

Having asserted that Blake, in his critique of "Milton's Religion" and of the Christianity of his day to which Milton had contributed, shares to a considerable extent the criticisms of traditional religion proposed by the men of the Enlightenment I do not wish to leave the subject before I have offered some documentation to support that contention, and to describe more precisely the kinds of suggestions made by Deists, *philosophes* and mythographers on the origin of religious ideas and practices which Blake would have found helpful in defining the activities, within Judaism and Christianity, of Satan and the Whore.

It is instructive to compare Blake's views on Sacrifice and

Atonement with those of a *philosophe,* in this case the celebrated Nicholas-Antoine Boulanger in his *Recherches sur l'origine du despotisme oriental,* published posthumously in 1761, and republished in 1792 in the eight-volume edition of his collected works put out as an act of homage by the revolutionary radicals of France. Meanwhile the book had remained highly illegal in any language. Blake may well have read it in the translation by the patriot hero, John Wilkes, which appeared in 1764 with a title page that failed to indicate the author, the translator or the publisher, and misrepresented the place of publication.[10] Boulanger was one who took to an extreme that fear-theory of the origin of religion much favored in the first half of the century. Man, essentially rational, must have endured some overwhelming primaeval catastrophe, Boulanger thought, to explain his having become everywhere in historic times the victim of a double superstition, political and religious—a prey, that is, to both depotism and priestcraft. The catastrophe could have been nothing other than the Universal Deluge, of which evidence remained in two forms: the physical evidence of marine fossils found even in inland mountains, and the anthropological evidence of the legends of the Deluge told by so many diverse peoples. A deluge so great as to overwhelm the whole earth to the very mountaintops had bred in the minds of the few miserable survivors an image of a Being both powerful and vindictive enough to cause their destruction—a god-king who must be placated and blindly obeyed.

Assuming the Deity had visited one near-destruction on the earth, the survivors would think it likely that he was preparing a future destruction or "Last Judgment," and that he (whom to look upon was Death) would come in person to reign, or perhaps send his deputy, his Anointed One. The greater part of the human race would perish in the latter catastrophe, as in the former since the Great Judge would have found them unworthy to dwell on earth; but there would be again the few survivors, "the elect, the just, who had found grace in his eyes." This last belief Boulanger attributed to "a particular species of men who believed themselves to be nearer to the Divinity than any other mortals, . . . wherein will one day be traced the primitive origin of religious orders known among the Sabeans, Pagans and Jews, long before christianity, which, from imitating, was debased by them.[11] The sects of the "elect" had caused the nations in which they resided to become scourges to all others; "they were filled with a spirit of conquest, and instigated by a turbulent and ambitious hope of being possessed one day of the universal monarchy by right of inheritance. It was consequent to this fatal mistake that the Hebrews exterminated the Canaanites, to become masters of their country, as of a land promised by the Diety of their ancestors. Up to the same source will be traced all those pretended oracles, all those obscure promises of the gods, under whose sanction the Romans, fraught with intrepidity and confidence, continued their march . . . to the empire of the world."[12] One sees here in Boulanger's exposition the reason why it is just when he has taken off the "robe of promise, & ungirded himself from the oath of God" that Milton in Blake's poem denounces the Nations for still following "after the detestable Gods of Priam; in pomp/ Of warlike selfhood, contradicting and blaspheming" (14:13–16).

The first intermediaries between god and the people were the priests who claimed to know the god's mind, and even to have received from him (mostly to the accompaniment of thunders and lightnings) the demands and laws to which he required compliance as the condition of his favor. To honor the god, the priests set up his temple as the place where it was believed that he actually held his court; they alone had the privilege of entry to the mysterious presence of the god and the secret of the rituals. With their magic, their ecstatic prophets and their oracles, they were able also to command political power. (The rod of Aaron is to be recognized as the sceptre claimed by the Aaronite priesthood.) Samuel's famous warning to the Hebrews against appointing a tyrant to rule over them is evidence that the priesthood had opposed the original institution of kingship, jealous that the power it exercised over men's minds with its sacred arks and stones (the god's dead images) would be superseded by the power of a man who purported to be the *living* image of the god. Indeed, for ten years the priestly ark was forgotten in Israel, but thereafter the people's disillusionment with the king enabled the priesthood to recapture a measure of its former influence so that it came to form an alliance with the kingship or even at times to denounce the king to his undoing. Nevertheless, both priest and despot ruled in the name of the Theocracy (for Boulanger, the "universal chimera"), claiming divine right and divine sanctions.

Boulanger had suggested much that was to Blake's purpose. A Deluge of Tharmas is the trauma in Blake's universe also, and the cause of man's pathological fear, though Blake conceives of the Deluge as a mythical and psychological rather than an historical event, and the fossils that interest him are the fossilized cages of the human mind. Boulanger had also insisted that the notion of the monarchy of God is not an extrapolation from the human institution, but the other way round. The "universal chimera" of Theocracy (for Blake, the self-definition of Urizen) is the original perversion. From that flow idolatry (when the people treat the deity as a man, actually present), and then slavery (when they come to treat a man as the deity). But Boulanger is especially pertinent to Blake when he proceeds to treat of sacrifice. In the temples, Boulanger relates, there was a perpetual offering of animal and vegetable sacrifices to serve the god's table; and once the people had become accustomed to the idea that he rejoiced in blood, the priests could represent it to them that he was most gratified by *human* blood, so that "of all the nations in the world there exists not one that has not delighted in the affrightful parade of human victims." The succeeding paragraphs that take Boulanger to the Christian view of the Atonement show his irony at its most diabolical:

> Nothing, it is to be hoped, like this atrocious manner of thinking, can be said to be the basis of the christian religion, when preserved in its purity. What good protestant but detests the horrours practised in Portugal, and all the mystic cruelties of popery? Nay, what says an unenlightened pagan on this head? to wit, Plutarch! 'Is that a method of adoring the supreme Being? What a dishonour is reflected on the Divinity, by supposing him thirsty of human blood, greedy of slaughter, or even capable of exacting, or being pleased with such sacrifices? If the Typhons and the giants had conquered heaven, could they have established upon earth more abominable sacrifices?' What an instructive approach is here uttered by one of those men called Pagans, and which would even puzzle the most orthodox christian teachers to explain (if not warranted by the true prophets, the words of the most

> high and by sacred revelation, doubted of by none but abandoned infidels) why the blood of all mankind, being insufficient to appease the irritated Deity, nothing less than an effusion of divine blood was judged adequate.
>
> Let not any profane wretch dare to assert, that this was a refining on fanaticism, and the horrours above delineated: no, this is a mystery, if not conceivable by our weak senses, as the fathers of the church say, to be trembled at and believed by all the faithful, saying with them, *O profunditas! O altitudo! O impenetrabilitas consiliorum Dei.*[13]

In his delineation of the *sexual* mystery of religion one suspects that, again, Blake has been prodded by the writings of the *philosophes.* Whereas in the earlier part of the eighteenth century the men of the Enlightenment had reached a kind of consensus that religion was basically derived from man's projection onto a Deity of his own pathological fear which was then exploited by a priesthood, now in the latter part of the century the opinion had been gaining ground that perhaps the basis was rather man's projection of his *generative* faculties. All religion was at root a cult of fertility. So at least Charles Dupuis had proclaimed in his *Origine de tous les cultes* (1795)—a work which had come to be accepted as a kind of orthodoxy in the France of the Directorate.[14] His thesis threw into perspective phenomena of paganism in which the eighteenth century had always shown interest—the Priapic cults of Herculaneum, the worship of the sacred *lingam* among the Hindus, the uninhibited sexuality of the Tahitians, and the widespread dispersal of the myth of the *Kore* and of hermaphroditic symbolism. The reputation of primitive man was much enhanced among the *philosophes* when it became apparent that, far from being a fear-driven savage, he had in his own way espoused a Natural Religion, consonant with Reason.

From the chapter on Dupuis in Frank E. Manuel's splendid book, *The Eighteenth Century Confronts the Gods,*[15] two points emerge which are of particular interest for a student of Blake. On the one hand, Dupuis recognizes a double origin of religious symbolism. Not only the earth but also the sun and stars had been the object of primitive man's worship, for the movement of the heavenly bodies had been equally decisive in Nature's rhythms and seasons. (Dupuis himself was an astronomer.) Thus he established the partnership between the fertility goddess and the god who is the "Daystar" or "Lucifer," Ashtoreth and Baal—in Blake's terms, the goddess with her "moony ark" and the god in "Fiery Flame" with his "bright Paved-work/ Of precious stones by Cherubim surrounded" (*Milton* 39:24–25). On the other hand, Dupuis was one more systematizer who was confident that Christianity was as much subject to his generalizations as any other religion:

> Christ will be for us what Hercules, Osiris, Adonis and Bacchus were. He will share in common with them the worship which all peoples of all countries and all ages have rendered to universal nature and to its principal agents: and if he seems to assume a mortal body, like the heroes of the ancient poems, this will be only the fiction of a legend.[16]

"Directorate theophilanthropy was a kind of nature and science worship," Manuel remarks; "and Dupuis provided it with an origins-of-religion theory. The new cult could thus resume where the ancient religions had left off. Men could again become simple adorers of science and productive nature, and the fanatical superstitious ages of theological Christianity could be obliterated from the memory of mankind."[17]

I am not sure whether Blake had read Dupuis,[18] though it would be surprising if he had not at least become aware of the thesis, in view of the popularity of the book. Blake's "moony ark" comes rather from the icon (which he had probably engraved) in Bryant's *Antient Mythology,*[19] where the crescent shaped ark is seen floating upon the waters, while the Dove descends bearing an olive branch; sea, dove, and ark are all enclosed by the rainbow of the Noahide covenant. Since Blake was certainly familiar with Bryant's thesis about the origin of the fertility goddess, it would seem worthwhile at this point to recall the context for the icon of the ark. The systematizer of the *Antient Mythology* was also the defender of *The Authenticity of the Scriptures and the Truth of the Christian Religion,*[20] staunchly upholding in the face of the attack from Boulanger and others the uniqueness of the revelation to the Hebrews. (He upheld even the propriety of the Hebrews' extermination of the Canaanites who, after all, has usurped the land which God, the universal landlord, had specifically designated in the days of Abraham as the property of the

Hebrews!) It is instructive to see how Bryant provides Blake with many of his materials and evaluations, and yet fails to produce anything like Blake's radical critique of the relationship between Christianity and the pagan cults.

In the *Antient Mythology,* after Bryant has described the first stage of idolatry among the ancients as the development of Zabaism, deriving the worship of the god directly from a veneration for the sun, one expects him to derive the worship of the goddess just as directly from a veneration of the moon and the natural cycle of life and death apparent in the process of vegetation. He has spent some time pouring scorn upon the Euhemerists; yet when he comes to the second part of his thesis he advances what can only be called a Euhemerist position, asserting the veneration of an historical event and person. Perhaps it was the peculiar association of the goddess with the Baal that gave Bryant his clue to the origin of the mystery cults! Perhaps he found too many etymologies related to the name of Noah. Or perhaps it was simply that any self-respecting mythographer writing after Boulanger felt obliged to make the Deluge the turning-point in man's religious history. In any case, Bryant concludes that "the antients were in general materialists, and thought the world eternal. But the mundane system, or at least the history of the world, they supposed to commence from the Deluge" (III, 227). Hence, "all the mysteries of the Gentile world seem to have been memorials of the Deluge" (III, 174); the ark resting on the face of the waters was "certainly looked upon as the womb of nature, and the descent from it as the birth of the world" (III, 218). The cultic *mythos* of descent into Hades and rebirth upon emergence was an imitation, Bryant thinks, of the Patriarch's descent into the ark (a kind of "death") and his reemergence when the floodwaters had subsided. Thus Noah was the original of all the male consort-gods in the mystery cults: Osiris, Tammuz, Adonis. The post-diluvians even "called him Bal, and Baal; and there were others of their ancestry joined with him [i.e., Ham, Shem, Japhet and their sons], whom they styled the Baalim" (I, 2).

The goddess herself (Isis, Astarte, Ashtoreth, Aphrodite of Cypris) was the deified ark, the womb that bore the Patriarch; she was also represented as "Beroë in labour." (Blake would call her the Female Space hiding the Male.) And "Beroë was so called," Bryant remarks, "from the Ark being esteemed a bier, or tomb" (III, 223). The goddess of the Deluge was furthermore the goddess of marriage; for "marriage was supposed to commence at the restoration of the world, when the thread of man's life was renewed . . . To Iönah [Juno] on these occasions was added a Genius, named Hymen; the purport of whose name is a veil or covering. In the history of Hymen they probably referred to the same object which was styled [*chiton phanaitos*], the covering of Phanes: from whence that Deity after a state of concealment was at last disengaged. Satan was often depicted with his head under cover, which had an allegorical meaning" (III, 250–54). (*Indeed* it had an allegorical meaning, Blake would have agreed, and a deeper one than Bryant intended to suggest. For Blake also had surely pondered the *icon* of "Satan under the veil" in Roman art, Christian as well as pagan,[21] and found it to be another proof that the pagan Cosmocrator, apparently overthrown by the Christian god, had instead been secretly assimilated.)

Even outside the context of marriage, the goddess still has her veil. Bryant reproduces an icon of *"Juno Samia Selentis cum peplo sacro"* (III, facing p. 193), where the goddess extends with both arms the veil that falls from head to foot. She is distinguished also by her lunette, which, Bryant explains, "did not relate to the planet in the heavens"—a strange statement!—"but to the Patriarch and to the ark, for the lunette greatly resembled the sacred ship" (III, 146). If, as Bryant asserts, the lunette or crescent or pair of horns was the mark of the Diluvian (or "Typhonian") Deity, there was certainly for Blake a question to be raised about the status of the horned prophet Moses, who had inaugurated the Law and the Covenant. One more clue is provided by the *Antient Mythology* as to the nature of the unholy alliance between the Moral Law and Nature, Satan and Rahab: Beroë had as one of her male counterparts a certain "Baal Berith in Canaan; who was worshipped by the men of Shechem, and of no small repute. This, I should think, was no other than the Arkite God; with whose idolatry the Israelites were in general infected, soon after they settled in the land. 'Berith' was the name of the Ark, but signified properly a covenant" (III,

209–10). How greatly the Israelites—and the Christians—were infected by Beroë and Berith Jacob Bryant had scarcely realized!

As for the contribution of the cult of sacrifice and sacral kingship in Israel to a sacrificial doctrine of the Atonement, Bryant's apologia was as much of an embarrassment to Christianity as Boulanger's brilliantly poised offensive. When, in the *Antient Mythology,* he comes toward the end of his long-spun tale of the religious perversions of the ancient pagan world with its ritual murders, orgiastic dismemberments, child-sacrifices, Druidic hangings and beheadings (all of which turn his stomach and arouse his indignation), suddenly he turns upon himself with a most remarkable assertion that among all these sacrifices there was one, performed by the (Canaanite) Phoenicians, which belonged in a category by itself as a "mystical sacrifice" and "*a type of something to come*" (VI, 332). The language in which the effect of the sacrifice is described by Sanchoniathon strongly suggests, he thinks, the sacrificial language of the New Testament. Moreover,

> the mystical sacrifice of the Phenicians had these requisites, that *a prince was to offer it;* and *his only son was to be the victim . . .* We are informed . . . that this custom was instituted in consequence of an example exhibited by *Kronus,* who . . . was originally esteemed the supreme deity; as is manifest from his being called *Il* and *Ilus.* It was the same name, as the *El* of the *Hebrews;* and according to St. Jerome, was one of the ten names of God. (VI, 325, 328, 331)

The sacrifices had been instituted, "in consequence of a prophetic tradition, which, I imagine, had been preserved in the family of *Esau,* and transmitted through his posterity to the people of Canaan" (VI, 331).

It would be clear to Blake than any such prophetic tradition in the family of Esau had indeed come from El of the Elohim—and not from the Human Imagination Divine—and that the affinity between this "mystical sacrifice" and the sacrifice on Calvary was due not to the Canaanites' having anticipated the true antitypical event, but to the Hebrews' having succumbed to imitating the Canaanites.

Thus, from the clumsy apologia of Jacob Bryant as well as from the devastating attacks of the *philosophes,* such as Dupuis and Boulanger, it was all too evident in Blake's day that Judaism and Christianity throughout their history had been entangled in Canaanite ideas and practices—in "carnal religion" and idolatry, as the Protestant Reformers would have said. Hence Christianity's sacrificial theory of Atonement and its sexual law of Chastity; hence its tendencies to monarchism and sacerdotalism, its claim to special election and its habit of waging Holy Wars. Within this complex of perversions, there lurked the Veiled Ones, the Canaanite Baal and Astoreth, Satan and Rahab, the Dragon and the Whore.

But the Veiled Ones, in the course of history's long apocalypse, are exposed by the Poetic Genius, which brings to full manifestation not only the Body of Death but also the Body of Life which is Jesus, the Human Imagination Divine. The work of the Poetic Genius had been undertaken by the Hebrew prophets, by John of Patmos and John Milton; and now in these latter days it had been inherited by Blake himself. But lest the single works of apocalyptic should become themselves dead and idolatrous, they too must be purged and subjected to the Poetic Genius, as Blake now proceeded to purge the work of his great predecessor in the epic *Milton.*

Blake had undertaken his critique in the conviction that "Milton's Religion"—humanistic, enthusiastic and revolutionary—was the best that England and Christianity had produced; and yet that even Milton had been corrupted in part by the Spectre and the Emanation—by Urizen and Enitharmon, assuming their demonic forms as Satan and the Whore. Thus Milton had been betrayed into the assumption of "electness" and the prerogative of "sacrifice"; in public life he had been implicated in Cromwell's Wars and Martyrdoms; and in his personal life, chaste love had deteriorated all too soon into self-righteousness and revenge. In Blake's poem, therefore, Milton's task is one of self-purgation and reintegration, overcoming both his inclination to legalism (and his status among the "elect") and also the alienation from his Emanation that is implied in his doctrine of Virginity (a state of "electness" in love that is the opposite perversion from harlotry).

The poem is in many ways patterned on Milton's own *Paradise Regained,* with its temptations in the wilderness and its eventual apotheoses of Christ and Satan; and this poem, too, is about the regaining of Paradise. But *Milton* also constitutes a critique of Milton's poem; it begins with Milton's realization that Paradise had perhaps not been regained after all, since that is a state of At-one-ment, and Milton himself is not yet at-one with his own Emanation. He must cast off his "electness" so that he may redeem her, unveiling the Whore and the Virgin to disclose the true Bride. Only then can the "Great Harvest & Vintage of the Nations" begin (*Milton* 43:1) or, to find the equivalent situation in Milton's own poem, only then can Christ indeed "begin to save mankind" (*Paradise Regained* IV. 635).

The significance of Blake's critique of Milton's Religion is not private to Milton and Blake, but a prophecy for the Age, as was the Apocalypse of St. John. Milton comes as Elijah to announce the Eschaton at a time when his own life's work, in both its prophetic and Urizenic aspects, has reached definition in history. In the early nineteenth century, the Revolution, abortive in Milton's day, had reached its strength in America and France; but the Cromwellian excesses were also running at full tide in the wars and terrors perpetrated by Robespierre, Napoleon—and Pitt. As in the days of Nero and Diocletian, when St. John had composed his Apocalypse, so now, the "winepress of wrath" poured out blood upon the earth. To the *philosophes,* the Revolution has appeared under the aspect of an eschatological event, but they had been increasingly disillusioned as the Dawn of the Millennium turned into a Night of Purgatory. The Reign of Terror and the ascendency of Napoleon were enough to turn Wordsworth and Coleridge eventually into conservatives. Blake, however, remained, like Milton, a radical to the end of his days. He maintained his faith and integrity by subjecting the Revolution itself to the iconoclastic enterprise, unveiling in the deities that presided over his Age (Robespierre's Supreme Being and Rousseau's Nature) the Satan and The Whore of the Apocalypse; and he conducted the purgation of his own prophetic role in the purgation of Milton's. In the very Reign of Napoleon, Pitt, and the Anti-Christ, Blake the Visionary, as hopeful as any Deist and as hard-headed, proclaimed the apotheosis in history of Jesus, the Eternal Humanity Divine.

Notes

1. For Blake's view of Milton as poet-prophet, see especially Joseph Anthony Wittreich, Jr., Introduction to *The Romantics on Milton: Formal Essays and Critical Asides* (Cleveland and London: Press of Case Western Reserve Univ., 1970), and also his Introduction to William Hayley's *Life of Milton* (Gainesville, Fla.: Scholars' Facsimiles and Reprints, 1970). Wittreich points out that it was Hayley himself who first gave a sympathetic portrayal of Milton as religious and poetic enthusiast.

2. Blake's text is taken from *The Poetry and Prose of William Blake,* ed. David V. Erdman, rev. ed. (Garden City, N.Y.: Doubleday, 1970).

3. I use "Jehovah" rather than "Yahweh" as the form of the name familiar to Blake himself.

4. John Milton, *Eikonoklastes,* in *Complete Prose Works* (New Haven and London: Yale Univ. Press, 1953–82), III, 596.

5. Milton, *Apology for Smectymnuus* in *Complete Prose Works,* I, 892.

6. *Second Defence, C.P.W.,* IV, i, 625. Milton's sustained argument for the right of the elect to be rid of spouses who are foreign, idolatrous and defiled is to be found in *The Doctrine and Discipline of Divorce, C.P.W.,* II, esp. chapters VII and VIII. Hayley had presented Milton's advocacy of divorce in the cause of domestic liberty with so much sympathy that these sections of the *Life,* along with those of Milton's republicanism were excized from the first edition by his publisher, fearful of scandal. (See Wittreich's Introduction of Hayley's *Life,* fn. 1.)

7. Annotations to Thornton's *Lord's Prayer, Newly Translated, Poetry and Prose,* pp. 658–9.

8. The Biblical texts that support Blake's analysis are particularly, Jeremiah, Hosea and the Song of Songs. One might compare Blake's reconstruction of the relationship between Hebrew and Canaanite religion with that of contemporary scholars, e.g., William Foxwell Albright in *Yahweh and the Gods of Canaan: An Historical Analysis of Two Contrasting Faiths* (Garden City, N.Y.: Doubleday, 1968); John Gray, *Near Eastern Mythology* (Feltham: Hamlyn, 1969); Marvin Pope, Introduction to *The Song of Songs,* Anchor Bible Edition (Garden City, N.Y.: Doubleday, 1977). On the whole, the Canaanite texts discovered at Ugarit in the present century support and amplify "Sanchuniathon," who was the only authority available to the eighteenth century.

9. The Biblical text is taken from the King James Version.

10. [Nicholas-Antoine Boulanger] *The Origin and Progress of Despotism,* trans. [John Wilkes] (Amsterdam [*scilicet* London], 1764).

11. *The Origin and Progress of Despotism,* p. 92.

12. *The Origin and Progress of Despotism,* p. 93.

13. *The Origin and Progress of Despotism,* pp. 122–23.

14. Charles Dupuis, *Origine de tous les cultes, ou Religion universelle* (Paris, An III [1795]).

15. Frank E. Manuel, *The Eighteenth Century Confronts the Gods* (1959; rpt. New York: Atheneum, 1967), Chap. V, 3, "Charles Dupuis: The Phallus and the Sun-God," pp. 259–70.

16. *Origine de tous les cultes,* V, x-xi. Quoted by Manuel, p. 269.

17. *The Eighteenth Century Confronts the Gods,* p. 267.

18. I have been unable to find any English translation of Dupuis' book before 1872. But there was much discussion of fertility cults in radical circles in Blake's London. Richard Payne Knight published his *Discourse on the Worship of Priapus* in 1786, and Joseph Priestley wrote a chapter "Of the Licentious Rites of the Hindoo and other Ancient Religions" for the same volume in which he undertook to refute Dupuis. See his *Comparison of the Institutions of Moses with those of the Hindoos and Other Ancient Nations, with Remarks on Mr. Dupuis' Origin of all Religions.* (Northumberland: Printed for the Author by A. Kennedy, 1799). Stuart Curran tells me that Coleridge in 1796 mentions in a letter that he about to begin reading Dupuis.

19. Jacob Bryant, *A New System, or, an Analysis of Antient Mythology,* 3rd ed., 6 vols. (London: Printed for J. Walker, etc., 1807). Further quotations from this work are cited parenthetically within the text. The engraving of the "moony ark" is to be found in volume V, facing p. 286. Note that the "ark" (Heb. *thebah*) that is Noah's ship is to be distinguished from the "ark" (Heb. *aron*) in the Holy of Holies.

20. Jacob Bryant, *A Treatise upon the Authenticity of the Scriptures and the Truth of the Christian Religion,* 2nd ed. (Cambridge, Printed by J. Archdeacon, Printer to the University, For T. Cadell and P. Elmsley, London, 1793).

21. The best known examples of the *icon* in Christian art are probably those on the Sarcophagus of Junius Bassus in the Grotte Vaticane, and the Sarcophagus in the Museo Laterano in Rome. (See, André Grabar, *Early Christian Art from the Rise of Christianity to the Death of Theodosius* [New York: Odyssey, 1968], pls. 41 and 726.) In each case the pagan Cosmocrator under the veil is surmounted by Christ triumphantly enthroned. In the Junius Bassus design, Christ is also delivering the law.

MICHAEL RIFFATERRE

The Self-sufficient Text

My purpose is to analyze a poem using internal evidence only and to determine to what extent the literary text is self-sufficient. It seems to me that a proper reading entails no more than a knowledge of the language. Needless to say, this runs counter to the tradition of criticism. Even modern criticism, having gotten rid of the referential fallacy and having discovered the primacy of language, persists in finding thematology, as well as considerations of archetypes and topoi, essential. Reference to things has been replaced as a semantic analysis criterion by the notion of reference to the corpus of topoi, themes and motifs. Which is a devious way of relapsing into the referential fallacy. The assumption seems to be that their symbolism cannot be understood without understanding them first as metaphors for man.

My example will be taken from Blake's *Songs of Experience:*

THE SICK ROSE
O ROSE, thou art sick!
The invisible worm
That flies in the night,
In the howling storm,

Has found out thy bed
Of crimson joy,

This essay was first printed in *Diacritics* 3 (Fall 1973): 39–45. Reprinted with permission.

And his dark secret love
Does thy life destroy.[1]

All critics have seen the rose and its parasite as figures of humanity. There is no question that in some of his poems, Blake does in fact represent Man as a Worm or even a caterpillar. In *The Four Zoas,* for instance:

Man is a Worm; wearied with joy, he seeks the caves of sleep
Among the Flowers of Beulah, in his selfish cold repose
Forsaking Brotherhood & Universal love, in selfish clay
Folding the pure wings of his mind, seeking the places dark
Abstracted from the roots of Science.

(Night IX, 11) [133.11–15]

But when Blake does this, either he makes it quite explicit, or, if the equation of Man and insect is not stated, then systematic analogy in context insists on the equivalence of the two.[2] To say, however, that whenever a text mentions a worm, it is really talking about man just because this is true for other texts, is like saying that a word has the same meaning everywhere no matter what the context, or that a trope always emphasizes the same thought. On the one hand, the lesson of the worm may be applicable to human experience, without the worm's resembling Man even by analogy. On the other hand, while it may be true that the recurrence of an image reveals some obsession of the author, or is even a hieroglyph in his private world of repressed thoughts, this still does not tell us what use he makes of this obsession in the poem. In fact, an obsessive image is likely to be used to stress just about any thought irrelevant of its own specific meaning.

Unfortunately, most critics behave as if the images of the text were referring, consciously or not, but word for word, to psychological, Freudian or Jungian, symbolism. At any rate, the rose is woman and the worm, guess what. If the text does not fit the translation, the critic adds a generous sprinkling of ambiguity. A rather extreme example is this, from T. R. Henn's pen:

Womanhood, the rose, is sick; the spirit of joy has left her. She has been attacked or raped, unnaturally (in the howling storm) by lust, itself contrary to nature and joy. The flying worm is perhaps the

> *dragon (consider all the mythological stories connected with the rescue from the dragon). The lust principle (here the engraving comes in) is parasitical, selfish (the caterpillar). It has become what it is, unnatural and destructive, because of the briars of religious prohibitions.*
>
> *That is perhaps one layer of meaning. It may be that there are several more [. . .] there may be an invitation to ponder the paradox of death and birth, love bringing death, the sacrifice of the mother to the child.* (The Apple and the Spectroscope. *New York: Norton, 1966; pp. 40–41*)

This approach is usually combined with an effort to make the poem fit into a philosophical system, a system that is abstracted from other texts of Blake's. This procedure ends up in a mere paraphrase of the poem in language borrowed from the other texts.[3] This does not go without some verbal acrobatics: to wit, this interpretation of Blake *à la* D. H. Lawrence (by W. Mankowitz, in M. Bottrall, ed., *William Blake: Songs of Innocence and Experience.* London: Macmillan, 1970):

> *In it sexuality is revealed as the basis of life, the social concept of love, as something destructive to life. Love in its social definition is a negative creed of secretive joyless forbidding: love in Blake's experience is a vital matter of joy, open and sensuous. [. . .] The "Sick Rose" poem is the concrete expression of Blake's experience of the corruptive effects of "social" love upon creative sexuality. (p. 128)*

And then there is the genetic interpretation, that purports to restore to the poem its full meaning, by seeing it as the tip of an iceberg, as a condensed and therefore cryptic allusion to a complex mythological tradition. This is of course Kathleen Raine's thesis that Blake was influenced by Apuleius' version of the Eros and Psyche myth, along with its Christian interpretations: "The story of Cupid and Psyche turns upon precisely (the) ambiguous nature of love—or rather, the ambiguity of the world's differing conceptions of the god" (*Blake and Tradition.* Princeton: Princeton Univ. Press, 1968; Vol. I, p. 197). There are details in the poem that are evocative because they are not explained and seem therefore to suggest untold tales. Such details naturally become the points which the commentator believes are clarified only by the underlying story. Psyche, for instance, was at first convinced that her future husband was a serpent. For Raine, this explains the flying worm, since a worm is a serpent of sorts, and since the real Cupid does have wings.

Our exegete further notes that Psyche's family was so upset at the thought of a reptilian son-in-law that they conducted the marriage ceremony as a burial. Raine then hypothesizes that another mysterious detail in the poem, *the howling storm,* refers to the details of these rites: "the parents *who hid themselves in darkness,* the black torches and lamentations, convey the very atmosphere Blake conveys in three words" (Vol. I, p. 201. Also p. 402, fn. 51). Enough said. My point is not to poke easy fun at silly comments, but to look critically at the principle underlying them.

All the preceeding interpretations have one thing in common: they all aim outwards. These approaches find the meaning of the text in the relationship of its images to other texts. Either of two assumptions is at work here. One is that the image in the text is a metaphorical vehicle, the tenor of which is given in another text or texts. The other and more common one is that models for the use of the image are provided by the referred-to texts, inasmuch as they point to the relationship between the vehicle in our text and a tenor which is linked more visibly with it in another text.

My contention is that reading must be aimed inwards. I am not suggesting that external models for the text do not in fact exist, and that there is no intertextuality. What I am saying is that external models function, not as literary topoi, but as language stereotypes. If they were treated as topoi, they would function in the text as allusions to the contents of such topoi. They are used rather as codes, that is, as verbal structures that have no meaning *per se,* but serve as lexicon and even as prefabricated syntatic sequences for whatever meaning may be demanded by the context.

There is, undoubtedly, a topos of the flying worm and/or of the flying serpent, and it may be identified with the Eros of Eros and Psyche in those contexts which call for this meaning, but it need not always evoke Eros and Psyche, or even Eros alone. The topos is not used as mimesis, literal or metaphorical, but as semiosis: instead of creating the illusion that it reflects reality word by word, it means as a whole, as if it were a compound word. The text simply uses a lexicon and a collection of images, a sequence of representations that have been prearranged, ready-made, and tested for use. In terms of verbal artifact, the assembled product has the advantage of being familiar. Whereas an untested sequence might be objected to because of esthetic or ethic preconceptions, the tested sequence gives the reader a feeling of *déjà vu.* He readily translates this feeling into acceptability and efficacy of communication, despite his preconceived ideas. The verbal components of the topos retain their prestige even if the topos is no more than a storage bin for these usable prefabricated formulas. In occidental literatures, one cannot speak indifferently of the rose or of the cankerworm, as one would, for instance, of the daffodil, despite Wordsworth, or of the gnat, despite Vergil.

This special significance of words like *rose* and *worm* has little to do with their corresponding realities. It has to do with their relationship with other words in commonplace phrases, that is, with their status as lexical variants of a structural invariant. The word *worm,* for instance, owes its literary significance to its binary oppositions with other words. To cite only commonplaces attested in many texts, the opposition in French between *ver de terre* and *étoile,* the lowest and the loftiest. Or the relation between the worm and the foot that is about to crush it, as a symbol of total vulnerability or, paradoxically, of resistance despite this complete helplessness.[4] Or the relation that structures our poem, the relation of the worm to its habitat, the paradox of its being destructive by being constructive; the worm, for instance, builds its labyrinth in wooden beams, and in so doing destroys an edifice. You will note that the worm signifies not just by being destructive, but by being positive in its own way: Michelet called the worm "mineur obscur, travailleur caché de la nuit," even though it feeds on Death itself (*L'Insecte,* Paris: 1858; Bk. I, pp. 43–44).

The flower or the fruit is a variant of the worm's dwelling constructed through destruction. Thus, as a word, *worm* is meaningful only in the context of *flower,* and *flower* only in the context of *worm.* The word *flower,* is higher on a scale of functional synonyms than any name of fruit. And this, of course, is even truer of *rose,* since *rose* is to *flowers* what *lion* is to *animals. Flower* or *rose* is therefore, within this function, a hyperbole for "fragility" or "frailty." It also signals a semantic modification: the worm that eats a flower rather than a fruit does not destroy something useful, but rather destroys beauty or purity. The poetic effect, eventually the symbolism, and certainly the literariness, lies in the extreme nature of the resulting oxymoron. It also lies in the indissolubility of the tie between the two oxymoric components. So strong is this tie that the polar opposites tend to attract each other even when this opposition is not activated in a text, as when Shelley writes that "men go to their graves like flowers or creeping worms" (*Alastor,* 622). Obviously, the worms do not cause here the flowers' demise; but the habitual polarity of the opposites survives as contiguity and determines their companionship in death. This powerful kinship generates sequences: if a young girl is represented as conquered by Death, and if Death be the worm, then the girl is described as a flower, "Cette rose du fond du tombeau," in Hugo's "The Worm's Epic," or, in a generalized variant: "nous avons" (quoteth the worm), "nous aussi, notre fleur, le cadavre"—if Death be the worm, then the corpse itself is a flower.[5]

Polarity then is what makes the two words a semantic unit; conversely, their common significance cannot be derived from one without the other. The rose therefore must contain a worm. In this specific representation, the flower is not just the thing of beauty destined to future withering that it is singly. It is not a withering to be, but a withering in being, beauty as the latent destruction of itself, purity as the germ of impurity. For this oxymoron to work, there is no need to presuppose a hint at a human parallel, as Harold Bloom would have it.[6] Nor is there any need to compare one instance of it with another, to recognize allusions or thematic references, as Kathleen Raine and others do. All we need is a full actualization of the binary opposition in a given text. Which is the case with Blake's text. For the whole poem is derived from a matrix sentence which is our *rose vs. worm* oxymoron. The derivation is a dramatization, that is, it is obtained by further polarizing the polarity and translating it into a temporal sequence, the coexistence of the poles being described through dramatic progression, as a succession of events. And it is all the more striking, since the polarity is actualized as the story of a destruction. There are two possible types of destruction, according to whether the agent is larger or smaller than its victim. Blake's poem actualizes the second type, tokens of which are the Trojan horse within Troy, the cancer within a body, and, here, the worm. This type can be dramatized, by stressing the paradoxical smallness of the destructor: thus Victor Hugo's worm, as the cause and universal principle of Death, is "le nain partout béant" (*the chasm within a dwarf*), "un engloutissement du géant par l'atome" (*ibid.*, p. 207). Our text, instead, is generated by another form of intensification, that achieved by stressing the interiority relationship between the polar components.

Of these two, the positive pole, the rose, has always been a symbol for perfection and purity. It is therefore a contradiction in terms that this perfection should contain, not just a flaw, but the ultimate imperfection, the seed of its own death. This is an initial oxymoron, which underlines and undermines the first pole of the larger *rose vs. worm* opposition. This transformation, by the way, is imposed on the reader's perception, despite his favorable feelings about the rose, by the repetition of *sick*, by the emphasis of *thou art* (rather than *you are*), by the fact that *sick* is completely foreign in a rose context.[7] For the rose is usually the epitome of blossoming health—Rimbaud's "jeunes et fortes roses" ("Fleurs," in *Illuminations*). As Thomas Moore says: "Oft hath the poet's magic tongue/ The rose's fair luxuriance sung," and he, among others, reflects a significant tradition that links this luxuriance with health and healing and triumph over decay:

> The rose distils a healing balm,
> The beating pulse of pain to calm;
> Preserves the cold inurned clay,
> And mocks the vestige of decay.
>
> (*Ode of Anacreon,* LV)

The rose's context is one where the only negative qualification should be *withered,* a process of natural decay, not a pathological one. Thus we have a radical semantic transformation: the basic semantic feature of "health" or "integrity" or "exclusion of morbid symptoms" being inverted into "containing a morbid symptom." The *rose* pole is thus actualized at the expense of a component reversal in its basic semantic structure: from *healthy* to *sick.*[8]

A similar, if contrary, reversal occurs with the negative pole, the worm. A symbol for imperfection, impurity and death, it is periphrastically represented here as love, as a loving subject. Since love can be actualized as the subject contained within the object, this transformation reinforces the parasitic nature of the worm—a parasite indeed usually worms its way inside its victim.

Mutual interiorization (the rose engulfing the worm that devours it) results also from the hyperbole of beauty incarnated by the rose. Beauty is the emphatic, maximal degree of *appearance,* and appearance readily generates its converse, *reality.* But then, because of the infirmity of our imagination, that reality, to be represented, must be spatially located behind or within the envelope of appearance. If beauty is the greatest good, and the ultimate appearance, its contrary must be reality and the ultimate evil. If true, this rule of opposition must be verifiable by other hyperboles of beauty and purity in floral codes, and indeed it is: three of Shakespeare's sonnets hide the worm in *buds* rather than *roses.* The frail bud is to the flower what the infant is to the man, a hyperbole therefore of vulnerable innocence: "And loathsome canker lives in the sweetest bud."[9] The polarization is obvious.

Thus interiorization, thrice motivated, is the overdetermined component of the poem's structure, the motor of is effectiveness. A concealment variant actualizes the interiority structure. It has generated countless instances of the theme of the snake hidden under flowers. In codes other than floral, we find the snake in the pure crystal water of a virgin spring. And here the *appearance vs. reality* opposition translates Beauty's ailment into a danger to the spectator or passer-by, instead of danger to the appearance. But shifting the threat of destruction from beauty to its beholder is only a narrative suspense creating rationalization which does not modify the constant. In Hawthorne's apologue entitled *Egotism, or The Bosom Serpent,* the snake of Envy dwells indifferently in a man's heart or in the ornamental fountain of his garden.

Blake's poem is nothing more than the maximal actualization of the structure I have just described—two opposite poles related through interiority despite their opposition, plus the inversion of an essential semantic feature of each of these poles into its contrary.

The contained to container relation of the worm to the rose is actualized through two equally effective variants, one fantastic and one sexual. First, it is represented by the invisibility of the contained component: an invisibility that is twice stated, through the adjective and by *in the night.* This phrase, as well as *invisible,* has negative connotations of stealth and danger, which are taken up in the second quatrain by the "*dark* secret." Shakespeare had already implied than an important semantic feature of the worm is precisely its "hiddenness." And by coincidence, his worm is a metaphor for a secret love, whose repression causes the girl's beauty to wilt: "She never told her love,/ But let concealment like a worm i' the bud,/ Feed on her damask cheek" (*Twelfth Night,* II, iv). Thus, line three is overdetermined, being the result of two associative sequences. First, it develops the negative character of the *worm* as opposed to *rose.* It should be nocturnal since literary sterotypes link the rose with sunlight and the color of dawn. Second, *night* rationalizes the invisibility of the worm. Now, this worm is supernatural since its role as an aggressor demands that normal wormy semantic features such as "weakness" and "vulnerability" (essential features, which polarize its opposition with the star, with the brute force of the crushing foot, etc.) be metamorphosed into power—Clark Kent into Superman. It is further supernatural because of *invisible,* for the nocturnal explanation of *invisible* does not erase the fantastic implications of the adjective. And finally it is supernatural because supernatural objects function as stylistic markers of *horror* or of *terror.* A mimesis of the fantastic demands that semantic features of the object made fantastic be reversed: that which is motionless moves, that which moves is made motionless, rocks dance and the indiscreet onlooker is petrified. The worm being essentially a crawling animal will therefore fly. This is no gratuitous construct on my part: mythology and verbal stereotypes confirm that the *worm,* like the snake, is a polar opposite of the bird. It therefore makes sense that as a counterpart to the most down to earth, scaly reptiles, polarization should produce the feathered, aerial bird. Mythological relationships between animals are revealing in this respect. It is obviously not by chance that of all the possible relationships between animals, one of the most favored is that of enmity between birds and snakes: birds were deified because they were snake killers. Neither is it by chance that a structural inversion should further enhance this opposition of extremes in myth as well as in language. Myth: Pliny the Elder writes that even the highest and fastest flying birds can be felled by the lethal breath of some serpents (*Natural History,* 8.14; cf. 10.4). Language: a typical adynaton—that favorite trope of baroque poetry—has the snake devouring the bird, instead of the supposedly normal reverse. And it is not by chance that the mimesis of the fantastic abound in examples of the winged serpent or the flying worm—the realization of an extreme impossibility, a *coincidentia oppositorum.* For instance, Thomas Stanley's translation of one of Anacreon's most famous poems: Cupid "a bee that lurkt among Roses saw not, and was stung [. . .] help cries he, I die: A winged Snake hath bitten me" ("The Bee"). Or, in French, this significantly paradoxical description of the butterfly, in which abbé Delille telescopes the pupa and the full grown lepidopter: "Ce ver miraculeux qui [. . .] vole dans les airs."[10]

As for the *howling storm,* says Harold Bloom, the worm comes "by agency of the howling storm because a bright open love would not be received. Neither worm nor rose is truly at fault, for Nature has concealed the rose bed and so set the male and female generative contraries against one another" (*The Visionary Company,* p. 44; cf. his *Blake's Apocalypse,* p. 144: "by the agency of nature"). This is a clear case of referential fallacy, plus the usual humanizing and psychologizing generalities, the usual urge to see everything non-human as a symbol of the human. This negative pollinization that would exonerate the worm from responsibility and mitigate that of the rose is a rationalization that I find far-fetched. If this reading were correct, it would be accessible only through a subtle deduction. It would by no means compel the reader. The poem's efficacy would be a matter of choice, something reserved for connoisseurs.

What we have here is a much simpler verbal logic, that is, a continued lexical and grammatical expansion of *invisible* in *night* code. *Night* confirms and "verifies" *invisible,* and then *the howling storm* confirms and verifies *night,* inasmuch as it is a variant of "invisible," and also makes explicit the negative semantic features of *night,* stressing its role as negative marker. The generative process that produces the phrase uses the cliché *stormy night* as a matrix; this cliché need not be significant *per se* in the text; it simply increases the nightness of night. It singles out its semantic feature of "darkness." The sequence from *starless* to *cloudy* to *stormy* is a natural or logical one. The jump from implicit *starless* to explicit *stormy* is the verbal logic of polarization in stereotyped literary sequences: to wit, Coleridge: "the after gloom [makes] the darkness stormy" ("Zapolya" 2.2.1.148; cf. Wordsworth, "Peter Bell," line 777—"In darkness and the stormy night"). And then, of course, *storm* generates the cliché *howling storm,* as in Coleridge's "stormy midnight howling round."[11]

The second actualization of the contained to container relation of the worm to the rose is, as I said before, sexual. The sexual code is used twice, both from the male and then from the female viewpoint, and is used equally forcefully in each case. The worm must be a lover to the rose, instead of just being a bug or a blight to the flower. Why, one might ask, should the rose not just wilt away like all roses? The first reason is that the basic opposition of beauty and evil, despite their mutual inseparability, generates when pushed to its paradigmatic extreme a polarization of the worst evil, Death, and of the greatest good, Love. The second reason for the worm as paramour is found in the stereotyped metaphor describing a bee or butterfly's visit of a flower in terms of sexual intimacy: Hugo has written of the bumblebee's taking advantage of a flower. The third factor of overdetermination—and therefore of efficacy—is the fusion of these two chains of sexual associations with the worm's descriptive system. One of the great commonplaces of literature describes Death as the ultimate conqueror or victor: when his victim is female, the conquest is sexual. One thinks of Holbein's skeleton molesting a young woman. While the worm, as a metonym for death, devours men's cadavers, it rapes female corpses. This tidbit of necrophilia combines with a *carpe diem* motif that extends from the Renaissance to Romanticism; the girl who believes she can afford to reject her lover will fall prey to amorous maggots. To wit, Andrew Marvell's bitter verse to his coy mistress: "in thy marble vault [. . .] worms shall try/ That long preserved virginity/ And your quaint honor turn to dust." The text is true, or convincing, here because it is superimposed on literary clichés. But again these clichés are effective in the first place because they all refer to the negativation of one of the main semantic components of *love:* its life-giving nature.

The representation of female sexuality is also superimposed on a verbal cliché. The structural reversal it involves, however, does not occur at the semantic level as in the negativation I have just mentioned. It occurs at the morphemic level, and results in a transformation of the cliché itself. The cliché I am referring to is *bed of roses,* the legendary example of voluptuary sophistication, from the beds of ancient Sybaris to Marlowe's "Passionate Shepherd": "I will make thee beds of roses." From *bed of roses* to the *bed of a rose,* the pun is easy. Because *bed* easily collocates with *rose,* and because of its own independent associations with sex, *bed* is, in *rose* code, the aptest and most obvious metonym for *love* or *lust.* Or rather it is the most appropriate periphrastic expansion of the kernel word *rose,* if what is needed is an emphasis on the rose's lust. For it must be realized that "thy bed of crimson joy" is nothing more than a transform of *rose.* Such descriptive periphrastic transformations are one of the most potent tools of symbolism in literature, since they enable a writer to use literally anything to represent anything else. Rimbaud, in "Mémoire," takes the word *river* and the descriptive system of the word *bedroom* and, with the help of an implicit play on the word *riverbed,* produces a representation of the river in *bedroom* code. From time to time a verbal equation, such as "l'humide carreau tend ses bouillons limpides" ("the wet windowpane of the transparent, turbulent waters"), reminds the reader of idiolectic conventions whereby every bedroom word acquires a river meaning in this specific poem. Which makes the poem a continued metaphor. An *architecture* code, like Rimbaud's use of the *bedroom* system, is especially effective in describing any complex concept of a thing, and Blake uses it appropriately when representing not only living beings but the process of their creation:

And every Generated Body in is inward form
Is a garden of delight & a building of magnificence,

> Built by the Sons of Los in Bowlahoola & Allamanda:
> And the herbs & flowers & furniture & beds & chambers
> Continually woven in the Looms of Enitharmon's Daughters.
> (*Milton,* bk. I, 26.) [26.31–35]

Such a spreading of the meaning of one signifier over the entire descriptive sentence creates emphasis and triggers a semantic shift: Blake's *Generated Body* is no longer just a body, but an inner universe, whose every detail can be conveniently pegged with modifying adjectives. Thus, again in Blake's *Milton,* the matrix sentence *the rosebud opens* is expanded through the same code as in our poem: "the Rose still sleeps,/ None dare to wake her; soon she bursts her crimson curtain's bed/ And comes forth in the majesty of beauty" (*Milton,* bk. II, 31). In this example, the expansion is used only to give the flower the attributes of boudoir type luxury, in terms that have been conventional since at least the seventeenth century—for instance: "All the purple pride of Laces,/ The crimson curtains of thy bed" (Crashaw, "Hymn for the Circumcision of our Lord"). The cliché transforms her blossoming into the regal awakening of a queen or goddess. In "The Sick Rose," the substitution of *joy* for the *curtains* of the alcove first of all permits *joy* to attract *crimson,* an adjective that is therefore a metonym for *alcove, alcove* being a metaphor for sex. The word, of course, also happens to befit the description of a rose. It is also an elevated style word, and one that is emotion laden. But the point is that we return to the flower's color through the detour of an image that makes it somewhat off-color. This transformation, then, works as does the periphrasis *dark secret love* which expands the word *worm* into a statement of lovesickness and Death within Life. *Worm* and *dark secret love,* as well as *thou rose* and *thy bed of crimson joy,* are similar in meaning, dissimilar in significance. The transformation-produced significance, and this alone, is what gives the rose a sexual function in this text. Not the fact that there is a literary tradition that assigns the rose to Venus. And despite the traditions that make the rose a symbol for virginity.[12] All we need is the text—references to outside uses of its components can only blur its meaning. The text is and must be an entirely new experience with these words—here, the renewal of a cliché. The last two lines explain again *thou art sick,* summarizing the love story just told, as well as its dire consequences. The style is almost prosaic in that it evokes no fantastic vision like the first quatrain, and contains no image like lines 5–6. It sounds like a mere caption to Blake's pictorial version of his own poem. A mere caption, however, would be: *his love destroys her life.* The actual text adds to this minimal sentence emphasis on the statement (*does*), and emphasis resulting from the direct address (*thy*): two markers of emotion, two traits that make the sentence both a statement of fact and the mimesis of an utterance by a horrified onlooker. This dramatization, though, involves only the stylistic level of the text, its system of stresses.

The same is not true of *his dark secret love.* Harold Bloom, as we have seen, paraphrases it thusly "a bright open love would not be received" (*The Visionary Company,* p. 44). This sentimental story would seem a rather indifferent one—its interest would depend entirely on the vagaries of the reader's taste, moral curiosity, etc. However, its import does not lie in its apparent cognitive message, but rather in the way it is said. For this is no indifferent phrase: it is not just a string of words joined together by narrative logic and by the psychological motivation implemented by some story. To say with Bloom that *dark* is an exclusion of "bright" does not explain it, and I do not pretend that the variation on *night* and *invisible* fully accounts for its motivation. *Secret* is not moral deviation from the open love that would presumably be the norm for the republic of roses. The true link between these words is not found in the syntax, but, again, in their superimposition on two pretested phrases. The difference between this superimposition and the ones we discussed before is that this phrase is constructed as a new lexical coinage of the portmanteau word type—like *brunch,* or like Lewis Carroll's fantastic lepidopter, the *bread and butter-fly.* But here, the components of the portmanteau word have been kept separate. It is make up of two clichés: *dark secret,* and *secret love.* Now first of all, the sense familarity of the components gives the new phrase a ring of truth,—it seems to be especially apt. Second, *dark secret* confers on *secret* the heavy connotations of Gothic novels, novels which are built around precisely this cliché. In the same manner, *secret love* brings sinfulness to the fore. But this again would appeal only to a contingent interest of the reader, and would involve nothing but narrative structures. What counts here is the element common to both clichés, an element that is overdetermined as the point where two sequences interfere, and one that appears as an extreme, hyperbolic variant in each (both *dark secret* and *secret love* are melodramic). Thus *secret* is given special prominence. As such it summarizes and most strikingly embodies the central opposition of the fundamental semantic structure: Beauty has another face. Beauty as the Epitome of Appearance hides its own Negation. Or, the more you appear, the less you are. In other words, the last two lines are yet another transcodage, as well as the last variant of the poem's basic semantic given.

We are no longer speaking of felicitious phrasing or of compelling images at a stylistic level, but of that which makes this ending an instance of poetic language. The chief characteristic of a poetic text, as opposed to the purely cognitive use of language, is that while the text seems to progress from image to image, from episode to episode, it in fact keeps repeating the same information. The text progresses syntactically and lexically, and it keeps adding meanings, but each step forward is actually a repetition of one significance. Each of these steps is only a transcodage of that significance from one means of expression to another. The significance, of course, is found in the structure first given by the text, with its network of binary oppositions and their transformations. Every subsequent transcodage is a variant of this structure. The text has been saying all along that *the rose is sick.* And the text is nothing more than an expansion of this matrix sentence, which, by the way, is not my own perhaps questionable abstraction, but a datum provided by the title itself.

This is not to say that the poem is no more than an act of naming things for what they are, that it is content with pointing to a thing in experience. This view is held by a hostile critic who goes on to criticize "the rude identity of natural phenomena with abstract concepts (that) has nearly always ruined poetry," only to except cases when the natural phenomenon "is rightly chosen," as in this poem.[13] The poem is not a rehashing about a thing. The poem is a verbal derivation from a verbal group. Its object is not a rose and its parasite; its object is the phrase *the sick rose*, or rather the oxymoron formed by the phrase. Pound has said that "the natural object is always the adequate symbol" (*Literary Essays*. London: Faber and Faber, 1954; p. 5). True enough, so long as we remember that the natural object is represented through a verbal mimesis. The symbol is not in the parasitic relationship of a vegetable and an insect, but in an ungrammaticality—the contradiction between *rose*, an *exemplum* which excludes adjectives such as *sick*, and its association with that very adjective. The message lies in this contradiction, as well as in the fact that it is repeated through forms of maximum efficacy: the text is exemplary throughout because it is composed solely of oppositions, of polarized polarities in which the poles themselves are each realized through a structural inversion. In every case, the transformations could not involve semantic features that are more fundamental.

Because all of these phenomena are completely within the language, and because the text provides all the elements necessary to our identifying these verbal artifacts, we do not have to resort to traditions or symbols found outside the text. The mythology we need for the text is entirely encoded in the words of that text.

Even when I spoke of sexual images, I was referring to the language of sex, not to the sexual symbolism of the rose. The basic contradiction of the text is first developed in botanical code stemming from *rose;* and then, because of the interference of the descriptive system of *worm* and of Blake's own sexual obsessions, a love story is sketched. But it is only a code.[14] A potent one, no doubt, a high voltage one, but a code used only to convey a meaning that has nothing to do with love or sex. This meaning is the inseparability of Beauty and its Destruction, Death as the other face of Beauty. *Love* or *sex* is only a powerful manner of speaking to describe the close bond between two elements. This bond is the structural polarity.

One might object that I have repeatedly quoted from other texts and that I have alluded to traditional verbal conventions. These references beyond the text would seem to present a departure from my own principles. However, their sole purpose was to prove that a given phrase was indeed a stereotype. But the natural reader does not have to prove: he has only to perceive the stereotype to recognize it as such. True, some clichés of the English language may have been lost over the course of time, but the network of semantic oppositions is so tightly constructed, and the inversions of semantic relations so radical, that no one can escape their impact. The reader certainly can and does relate the poem to occurrences of its stereotypes and to similar structural transformations in other texts, but the poem stands alone without these echoes—they are not essential to a reading. The poem is not a collection of themes and motifs, whose meanings are found outside the text. These elements are indeed present inside the text but only as words, and as words that point to something other than themselves, that is, to a significance determined by the rules of a grammar valid only for this text, determined by the fact that these words actualize again and again a structure first realized in the title and in the first line.

Notes

1. For a convenient if dated list of the principal comments on the poem, see Hazard Adams, *William Blake: A Reading of the Shorter Poems* (Seattle: Univ. of Washington, 1963; pp. 326–27).

2. See the examples collected by Edward J. Rose, "Blake's Human Insect: Symbol, Theory, and Design," *Texas Studies in Literature and Language,* 10 (1968), 215–32. As often happens in literature, add the time dimension to a metaphor and you get a metamorphosis, e.g. the transformation of the worm into a serpent and then into an infant (*The First Book of Urizen,* plate 19, 11.19–36; Geoffrey Keynes Edition, 232); for other examples of metamorphosis, see Irene H. Chayes, "The Presence of Cupid and Psyche" in D. V. Erdman and J. E. Grant eds., *Blake's Visionary Forms Dramatic* (Princeton: Princeton Univ. Press, 1970; p. 226).

3. E.g., Robert F. Gleckner. *The Piper and the Bard.* Detroit: Wayne State Univ. Press, 1959; pp. 216, 261–62; Hazard Adams. *William Blake;* pp. 14–16, 146, 204; and particularly, S. Foster Damon. *William Blake: His Philosophy and Symbols.* London: Dawsons, 1969; pp. 280–81; Harold Bloom. *Blake's Apocalypse.* New York: Cornell Univ. Press, 1965; p. 144; and K. Raine, *Blake and Tradition.* Princeton: Princeton Univ. Press, 1968; vol. I, pp. 202–03.

4. E.g. Blake, *The Book of Thel,* plate 5, 9–10 (Keynes, 130): "That God would love a Worm I knew, and punish the evil foot / That wilful bruis'd its helpless form."

5. *Légende des Siècles,* XIII, "L'Epopée du ver" (Paris: Pléiade, 1950; p. 205). The poem is a veritable repository of worm motifs in Romantic imagery.

6. *The Visionary Company* (New York: Anchor Books, 1963; p. 44): "Nature has concealed the rose bed and so set the male and female generative contraries against one another. The poem's force is in its hinted human parallel, where concealment is more elaborate and the destructive rape-marriage a social ritual."

7. On the effect of the anapestic rhythm, see Alicia Ostriker, *Vision and Verse in William Blake* (Madison: Univ. of Wisconsin Press, 1965; p. 63).

8. To be sure, Robert Herrick's "The Funerall Rites of the Rose" begin with "The Rose was sick, and smiling died" (*Hesperides,* 686, 1), but the whole poem is a conceit wherein the withering of the rose is transposed into a sustained metaphor of a dying nun. The bed of roses is a sisterhood, its fragrance is an odor of sanctity, etc. The human vehicle leaves almost nothing of the botanical tenor, and the whole first line humanizes the flower completely: nowhere do we have a contextual contrast as in Blake.

9. *Sonnet* XXXV; cf. LXX, "For canker vice the sweetest buds doth love"; also XCV. Blake gives a discursive equivalent of this image: "the catterpiller chooses the fairest leaves to lay her eggs on" (*The Marriage of Heaven and Hell,* plate 9, 16; Keynes, 152).

10. *Les Trois Regnes,* canto VII (p. 244, col. 2). Cf. a similar jump in Brownings's *Cleon:* "Who, while a worm still, wants his wings" (333).

11. Coleridge, "Lines written at Shurton Bars," 73; cf. Wordsworth, "The Borderers," v. 1765: "It is a dismal night—how the wind howls!", and Keats, "Otho the Great," 5.2.49; "Howling in vain along the hollow night." The sequence I am discussing is natural, nay imperative, because it is derived from the very semantic components of the word *night.* Because this derivation is natural, this reading is preferable to Reuben A. Brower's. He sees the text as a paragram or hypogram (Saussure's term, not his) of Psalm 91: "Thou shalt not be afraid for the terror by night; nor for the arrow that flieth by day. Nor for the pestilence that walketh in darkness" (*The Fields of Light.* New York: Oxford Univ. Press, 1962; p. 7). But it is not inconceivable that Psalm 91 is one more factor of the phrase's overdetermination: after all, it is one reader's intertext.

12. The point is that the signifier *rose,* because of its semantic components "femininity" and "beauty" (one reinforcing the other) stands poised between harlotry and chastity. If the context does not impose the choice, the generative process is random, to wit Blake's hesitation, in a draft, between *the modest* and *the lustful rose* (Poems from the *Note-Book;* 1793, 13; Keynes 171).

13. Matthew Corrigan, "Metaphor in William Blake: A Negative View," *The Journal of Aesthetics and Art Criticism,* 28 (1969); p. 191. Brower, *loc. cit.,* and C. M. Bowra, *The Romantic Imagination* (Cambridge: Harvard Univ. Press, 1949; pp. 44–45); also see in the poem an "item of experience"; their reaction, however, is positive. These contrary reactions are possible only because reality is substituted for its verbal mimesis.

14. Confusing the code with the meaning it conveys leads to apparent contradictions: for an example of the pointless subtleties to which this condemns the critic trying to solve them, see D. G. Gilham, *Blake's Contrary States* (Cambridge: Cambridge Univ. Press, 1966; pp. 165–66).

SUSAN FOX

The Female as Metaphor in William Blake's Poetry

Studies of male authors' attitudes towards women have become so fashionable that a critic ought to hesitate to initiate one lest he or she dilute the real social and literary values of such studies by overworking a formula. In the poetry of William Blake, however, images of females are not merely cultural phenomena but artistic and philosophical principles, and they have been so little defined that they have clouded full understanding of his work. A study of Blake's use of females as metaphors should not only identify his complicated attitudes towards women but also reveal a serious self-contradiction in his vision of the universe.

In his prophetic poems Blake conceives a perfection of humanity defined in part by the complete mutuality of its interdependent genders. Yet throughout the same poems he represents one of those mutual, contrary, equal genders as inferior and dependent (or, in the case of Jerusalem, superior and dependent), or as unnaturally and disastrously dominant. Indeed, females are not only represented as weak or power-hungry, they come to represent weakness (that frailty best seen in the precariously limited "emanative" state Beulah) and power-hunger ("Female Will," the corrupting lust for dominance identified with women). Blake's philosophical principle of mutuality is thus undermined by stereotypical metaphors of femaleness

---

This essay first appeared in *Critical Inquiry* 3 (Spring 1977): 507–519. Reprinted with permission.

which I believe he adopted automatically in his early poems and then tried to redress but found himself trapped by in his late works.

In the margin of his 1789 edition of Lavater's *Aphorisms on Man* Blake wrote, "let the men do their duty & the women will be such wonders, the female life lives from the light of the male. see a mans female dependents you know the man. . . ."[1] The condescension disguised here, no doubt even to Blake, as appreciation marks an ambivalence towards women which is a significant feature of all Blake's poetry. He admired women, but not enough to imagine them autonomous human beings. He cites the failure of men as the cause of the failure of women, and yet throughout his works he more bitterly (though perhaps no more strongly) condemns the females for the lapse.

His ambivalence has been matched by a strong and confusing ambivalence among his critics as to how to take his combined respect and derogation. On the one hand they apologize for what seems like Blake's shrill antifeminism in promulgating such an idea as "Female Will" by sterilizing the conception of its sexual connotations:

> Another feature of the Ulro vision requiring comment is the "female will," the separated objective world that confronts us in the fallen perspective. The outer world of nature is a "Female Space" (M. 11:6) because, like a "harlot coy" increasing her price by pretending to be a virgin, it continually retreats from the perceiver. The perceiver is a human being, who may be a man or a woman—in other words Blake's "female will" has nothing to do with human women except when women dramatize it in their sexual rituals, as they do, for instance, in the Courtly Love convention.[2]

On the other hand they, like all responsive readers, must recognize that one of the most moving and provocative features of Blake's poetry is its profound psychological probing into sexual and familial relations, a probing embodied in such gender distinctions as spectre (always male, though it has a usually female counterpart in the "shadow"), emanation (almost exclusively female, with a revealing exception we shall deal with below), and Female Will. In other words, Blake's poetry has been represented both as a sexless abstraction of a universal human mentality divided metaphorically into sexual factions and as a profound study of human relations, including the sexual, in which metaphors of gender suggest not universal abstractions but the minute particulars of daily life.

It would appear that the reader must choose between these conflicting approaches, but to do so, it seems to me, is to lose half the greatness of Blake's poetry. One cannot apologize away Blake's occasional shrillness towards women by calling it merely metaphoric, because to do so is both to ignore the richness and aptness of his social observations and to beg the question of what a metaphor is anyway and why one chooses it. One cannot ignore the abstract quality of his sexual divisions, because to do so is to miss the vastest implications of his observations and to make those observations much more strident and condemnatory than we have evidence they were meant to be.

One encounters this critical dilemma in Blake's poetry only in terms of his representation of the relations of the sexes. In no other issue do abstraction and particularity seem so seriously to contradict each other. The abstract elements of Blake's political, aesthetic, and historical attitudes are compatible with their personal elements, but the personal dimension of his attitudes towards women is so ambiguous that it interferes with the generalization he would build out of it. We may see this ambiguity in every facet of his poetic vision, from its cosmology to its individual characterizations.

Of the four states of being in Blake's universe, the only realm in which females are both powerful and constructive is Beulah. In Eden, females, supposedly merged perfectly with their male contraries, have no independent power; when they attempt to assume such power, as Luvah's emanation Vala does in trying to usurp all of Albion's love, they destroy Edenic wholeness. In fallen reality, as we shall see, females are either passive or pernicious. In Beulah alone do female forms have power and use it for good. Yet even in Beulah the positive image of femaleness is tainted by condescension: a female state is necessarily a limited state in Blake's universe.

In the *Songs of Innocence*, generally considered a study of Proto-Beulaic existence, the positive internal powers of the realm are female. The little boy lost by his father is found by his mother, the black child who yearns hopelessly for his father-god's love is comforted by his mother, other mothers and nurses protect children from darkness and grief. The piper who sings of innocence and the shepherd who guards it are male, but they are no more its natural inhabitants than the poet who describes Beulah and the Divine Family who created it dwell within it. Male adults act as constructive powers in the *Songs of Innocence* only from outside its boundaries; God appears to the lost boy or an angel appears to the chimney sweep from realms beyond their comprehension. Otherwise male adults are either helpless (weeping fathers) or pernicious (beadles with disciplinary wands and fathers who sell their children)—just as female adults are in the fallen states.

The power of the females in the *Songs of Innocence* is entirely positive, though severely restricted in that the ultimate power in the *Songs* resides in males outside the borders of pure innocence—in piper, angel, father-god. The female power which governs the Beulaic vales in *The Book of Thel* is not only restricted, but negative in implication. The daughters of the seraphim seem to be the only permanent human inhabitants of the vales, and they apparently run things there amiably enough; but male powers from other realms drop in occasionally (Luvah waters his horses there, and God strolls through at dusk), and they clearly take precedence when they do. But however smoothly things are run by the pastoral female regents of the vales, their success is itself an indication of weakness: the vales of Har are a temporary abode from which one must proceed by active determination; that only daughters inhabit the place, that the youngest of those daughters attempts to leave and cannot, identifies females with failure. That identification is harmless to Blake's vision in this early poem, because at this point in the development of his vision women at their best are still domestic help-meets and not the cosmic "contraries" they will become.

By the time Blake was engaged in writing *Milton,* some fifteen years after he engraved *The Book of Thel,* his doctrine of contrariety had crystallized, and it had crystallized around the central metaphor of the relations of male and female. As M. H. Abrams observes, "all contraries, in Blake, operate as opposing yet complementary male-female powers which, in their energetic love-hate relationship, are necessary to all modes of progression, organization, creativity, or procreativity."[3] Contraries must be equal if their contrariety is not to resolve into a tyranny of one element over the other, and therefore Blake must rescue the female element of this central contrariety from its taint of weakness and failure. He attempts to do so in *Milton* in part by clarifying his derogatory representation of Beulah:

Into this pleasant Shadow all the weak & weary
Like Women & Children were taken away as on wings
Of dovelike softness, & shadowy habitations prepared for them
But every Man returnd & went still going forward thro'
The Bosom of the Father in Eternity on Eternity. . . .
[Plate 31, 11. 1–5]

According to this crucial passage it is not that women fail the rigors of existence in other realms, but that anyone who fails appears frail and feminine. Femaleness is thus not a synonym for failure in Blake's late poetry, but a metaphor for it. This does not, of course, excuse Blake of the prejudice of selecting this particular metaphor (though it is one he seems not so much to choose here as to be trapped in by his earlier poetry), and, as Jean H. Hagstrum has pointed out in a similar context, "Metaphors have a way of taking over in Blake. . . ."[4] Still, in his late prophecies Blake seems at least to be trying to rescue the idea of a separate but equal female principle from the bitterness and condescension his earlier uneasiness about women had imposed upon it. The rescue seems to me to begin in *Milton,* in which a great vision of the reconciliation of all contraries, especially sexual contraries, replaces Blake's earlier vision of sexual combat and submission. In *Jerusalem* he seems to refine his new conviction of female equality, though the refinement, as we shall see, leads to unsettling complications.

As Blake's cosmology developed, his representation of the femaleness of Beulah became increasingly more metaphoric. We may see the same pattern of increasing metaphorization in his representations of individual female characters. The stereotypic sexual role divisions of the *Songs of Innocence,* whatever their social and philosophical implications, are surely the automatic responses of a wary observer of human relations and not any systematic symbolic code: the women stand for women in these poems, and the men for men. The failure of the heroine of *The Book of Thel* is, as we have seen, a particularly feminine failure, but it foreshadows the genderless failure of active desire Blake will develop in later poems: in the context of his other works Thel suggests not just the frailty of women, but the "feminine" frailty of all human beings. In *Europe* (1794), engraved five years after the *Innocence* songs and *Thel,*[5] female characters represent not only the darker propensities Blake feared in women, but the technically genderless tyrannies of nature and religion as well. By *The Four Zoas,* which Blake probably worked on between 1796 and 1807,[6] both male and female figures have become, however pointedly realistic their battles and failures and ultimate reconciliations may seem, symbols of issues much broader than marital relationships: males are Zoas (or spectres) and females are emanations, and their union is not marriage but apocalypse.[7]

As the metaphoric value of female characters develops in these poems, so does their chief negative metaphoric identification, the Female Will, that lust for unnatural dominance which disrupts all proper order even as a female-dominated marriage supposedly disrupts proper order. Between *The Book of Thel* and *Milton,* the only positive females are those so devoid of will, or at least of the power to realize their will, as to be melodramatically helpless. Thel herself is instructive in this respect. She fails for lack of will, but we have more sympathy for her in her failure than we might have had had she succeeded and turned into, say, the Shadowy Female of *America* once she had found her voice, or Enitharmon in *Europe,* or Vala in *The Four Zoas.* Thel needs will, but not Female Will. After *Thel* and until *Milton,* the only effective will females can have is Female Will. Even Oothoon, the single female character in all Blake's poetry who is both active and good, fails to achieve what she desires because her (lower case) feminine will is not powerful enough to free her from the impositions of male authority. Thel needed will to succeed; Oothoon, paradoxically, needs Female Will, which would pervert the very goal it alone could achieve.[8] Women, it would seem from these early poems, are trapped in a reality which recognizes no female power but evil female power.

Blake's evident sympathy for lovely frail Thel and valorous Oothoon suggests a strong consciousness of the social forces which prevent sexual mutuality. Indeed, *Visions of the Daughters of Albion* has long been read as an affirmation of Mary Wollstonecraft's *A Vindication of the Rights of Women,* published one year before Blake engraved *Visions.*[9] Oothoon's courage and her embodiment not only of Wollstonecraft's ideas but of Blake's own have made her seem unimpeachable proof of Blake's feminism. Because in the poems which follow *Visions of the Daughers of Albion* there is no heroine both assertive and good (Ololon is a possible exception, though I shall question below the degree of her assertiveness), it has frequently been assumed that some personal incident converted Blake from belief in sexual equality to mistrust and derogation of women. Though I agree that the tone of many of his passages about women has a new stridency after *Visions,* I do not accept the idea of a sudden and bitter conversion. We have already noted that even in the *Songs of Innocence* and *The Book of Thel* Blake's attitude towards women is equivocal; I believe it is equivocal in *Visions* as well. It is certainly true that Oothoon speaks for Blake in this poem, that she is as noble in its context as ever Los is in the final poems (more noble; she does not make mistakes), that she indicates a real and deep capacity in Blake for recognizing wisdom and courage and righteousness and strength in women. But it is also true that, unlike Orc or Los or Milton or any other positive male figure in Blake's poetry, Oothoon is helplessly victimized by powers completely outside her control. On one level the poem is an outcry against this victimization, a passionate denunciation of the oppression of women. But on another level it exploits that victimization symbolically to make a second and equally central political point. Blake made the chief character of *Visions of the Daughters of Albion* female not just because he admired Mary Wollstonecraft and thought women at least potentially men's equals, and not just because he abhorred the oppression of women, but also because he needed a chief character who could be raped and tied down and suppressed without recourse—or rather, with the single recourse of giving birth to the revolutionary male force which can end the victimization. *Visions of the Daughters of Albion* has a heroine and not a hero partly because one of the points of the poem is that its central figure, "the soft soul of America," is a slave. Oothoon was chosen for her part not just because she was wise and brave, but also because she was female and thus powerless. Her gender is a trap—just the trap the symbolism of the poem demands. Blake rails against her being trapped, of course—he was never not libertarian. But it is one thing to despise oppression, and another to envision the means of the oppressed to end it. No woman in any Blake poem has both the will and the power to initiate her own salvation—not even the strongest and most independent of his women, Oothoon.

Oothoon, whatever limitations her gender imposes on her power, is a complete woman, strong, willing, and wise. She is the first and last complete woman in Blake's poetry. After *Visions of the Daughters of Albion* female characters will be either good (Ahania, Ololon, Jerusalem) or active (Enitharmon, Rahab, Vala), never both. Blake will divide the female character more schematically and reductively than he ever will the male: Tharmas, for example, the incarnation of chaotic passivity, is also the force which commands Los to keep building fallen humanity in *The Four Zoas;* he, like all other male forms, is both negative and positive, both weak and powerful. In *America* and *Europe* we see the pernicious Female Will rampant (in *Europe* the woeful Shadowy Female constantly giving birth gives us a passive contrary to the virulent Enitharmon); in the Books of *Urizen* and *Ahania* the emanations weep helplessly at the deeds of their powerful consorts. In *The Four Zoas* Ahania and Enion lament helplessly in the wilderness while Enitharmon and Vala proclaim their dominion and scheme to keep it. Rahab's power to corrupt opposes Ololon's sweet submissiveness in *Milton,* and Vala in her strident pride contrasts with the wise but abandoned Jerusalem in Blake's last prophecy.[10] This divided female image must necessarily be of more value as symbol than as characterization, since any character it permits is by definition partial.

The reason for this shift in emphasis from character (or at least from the representation of self-contained figures capable of complex significance, like Oothoon—Blake was never much interested in characterization in any novelistic sense) to symbol may have been the proliferation of Blake's mythic system, or it may have been a personal experience which altered his conception of women. It has often been argued that at Lambeth, where the Blakes lived from 1791 to 1800, Blake undertook an affair—or desired to undertake one—which so alienated his wife that she startled him into a new perception of feminine wrath and possessiveness.[11] It may be that such a revelation shocked Blake into accepting stereotypes of women he had long resisted—or that his own guilt and confusion made him spiteful. But whatever the cause of the emergence of female as metaphor in his poetry, the process reaches a crisis in *Milton,* in which for the first time the metaphoric representation of female characters contradicts the vision it is intended to support.

The central structural and thematic issue of *Milton* is the progressive contrariety of equal but opposite forces. That contrariety is represented principally in two pairs of characters, the brothers Rintrah and Palamabron and the conjugal couple Milton and Ololon. The action of the poem is the reconciliation of contraries which have been severed by the perpetuation of the original error of the fall ("envy of Living Form" [3:2]), and the vehicle of that reconciliation is the union of Milton and Ololon, which consolidates a complex of unions gathering throughout the poem. Their union is an affirmation of the necessary mutuality of contraries, and it depends on the equality of those mutual principles. "Redeemed" Palamabron is different from "Reprobate" Rintrah, but no weaker; both err, both fight to redress their errors, and both are essential to full human existence. Palamabron's harrow and Rintrah's plow are equally necessary to the harvest. Similarly, Milton and Ololon—male and female, visionary and sensuous, time and space—are equally and mutually necessary to the survival of humanity. Ololon, like Palamabron, is different from her contrary, and also, in principle, no weaker than he—but she seems weaker throughout the poem because, despite Blake's constant emphasis on her commitment and courage and on her identification with Jesus himself, she is associated in the poem with those feeble "female" creatures who cannot withstand Edenic battle and must retire to Beulah for comfort. She does not even complete Milton's brave passage from Eden to Ulro, but must make her way instead through a series of "emanative" steps beginning with Beulah; her new passage may have been meant to suggest that she is a bold pathfinder in her own right, but the failure implicit in any female state suggests even more strongly that she does not have such a bold path as Milton's to find.

Blake may have written *Milton* at least in part as a repudiation of the alienation from and antipathy towards women we have identified in the Lambeth poems after *Visions of the Daughters of Albion.* One of the principal errors his chief character Milton must redress is the historic John Milton's failure to achieve a full and progressive relationship with his wives and daughters, and the character Blake has been separated throughout the poem's action from his own emanation, with whom he is reunited only at the reunion of Milton and Ololon. But the metaphoric associations of femaleness which have gathered throughout Blake's poetry and which are not repudiated in *Milton* undermine the poem's central vision of the necessary mutuality of contraries.

Contraries are by definition equal, but the females in *Milton,* however crucial and powerful Blake intended them to be, are not convincingly equal to their male contraries. They participate in the same dehumanizing division of the good from the active which kept Blake's earlier female figures not only from full characterization but even from multidimensional symbolism. Throughout the poem females are either passive or pernicious. Females presented positively are passive: emanations cannot long endure the strife of Eden, Enitharmon is uncomplainingly cut off from full vision by Los, Ololon mourns by her river in Eden and only descends to Generation when she sees Milton there, Catherine is ill in her house. Active females are pernicious: Leutha, Tirzah, the Shadowy Female all create disaster by their actions, which are only imitations of the actions of males anyway and need the further actions of males to complete them.

There is some evidence in *Milton* that the passive female can be stronger in her passivity than the male in his active glory. Enitharmon's gentle love for Satan saves him by creating a space for him (his salvation is necessary to Albion's), and Ololon's lamentations consummate Milton's act of sacrifice and consolidate the Divine Family as Jesus. The positive functions of the females of the poem are equal in rigor and importance with those of the males. Yet still the metaphoric use Blake makes of femaleness is pejorative. In the passage quoted above about the function of Beulah he does not say that all females are weak, but he does say that all weakness is female: when you enter Beulah exhausted from Eden you are female, but when, restored and strong, you return to mental strife, you are male. Furthermore, that anathema "Female Will" is so strong in the poem that it corrupts any possible balance of male-female contraries: Leutha is responsible for the fall of Satan as Vala is for the fall of Albion (or at least for the imprisonment and torment of Luvah), the Divine Voice castigates the destructive half of his emanation, Babylon, for destroying their union, and if Milton confesses to having ignorantly misused Ololon, she confesses to having maliciously sought to vanquish him. Female Will may be only a metaphor for the destructive urge for dominance which knows no gender, and the femaleness of the emanations in Beulah may be only a metaphor for weakness; the metaphor in each case is surely the most immediately suggestive Blake could have employed. But precisely because of its suggestiveness that metaphor undermines the major thematic balance of the poem.

W. J. T. Mitchell suggests that the basic dichotomy of female figures—positive/passive and pernicious/active—is resolved in the character of Ololon, a positive/active female alternative:

> Ololon's final transformation into an ark and a dove, the bearer and messenger of life amidst the annihilating flood, occurs when she casts off her false femininity. Her seeking-out of Milton reverses the traditionally passive role of the virtuous heroine in epic and romance, but she does not escape this role by becoming a female warrior, a woman in the armor of a man. . . . On the contrary, she sees that the stereotypes ruling the behavior of both sexes are the basis for the vicious cycle which entraps the best efforts of Milton and the Sons of Los, and that these roles must be annihilated and recreated as human relationships before the cycle can be broken and transformed into the fruitful, liberating dialectic of contraries.[12]

Though I agree that Ololon comes closer to realizing this necessary alternative than any other female character in Blake's poetry except Oothoon, I do not think her quite so liberated as Mitchell does. She has initiated no action but has, however courageously, merely responded to Milton's act. She comes to her imperious master a humble, questioning bride, bearing like a good handmaiden the robes which will transform them both. She may have cast off what Mitchell—and surely Blake as well—would consider "false femininity," but what they might call the "true femininity" she retains is every bit as restrictive and almost as damaging to the poem's vision of mutuality. She suffers still the dependency of women in Blake's Lavater annotation: "let the men do their duty & the women will be such wonders. . . ." For all Blake's protests against John Milton's attitudes towards women, his own character Milton sounds suspiciously like the austere intellectual Adam who converses with angels in *Paradise Lost*, and his Ololon like an even meeker Eve.

Blake seems to be partly conscious of the damage his metaphoric use of females does to his vision in *Milton* in that he tries to correct that damage by implying that the metaphor is provisional. The division into sexes was a condition of the fall imposed by Urizen (38:1–4) and will cease to exist when the fall is consummated in resurrection. As the existence of sexual distinction is a condition of the fall, so is the urge for dominance which creates sexual hierarchy. Questions about the relationship between the sexes are thus referred to a better life in which there are no sexes.[13]

In *Jerusalem* Blake seems more conscious still of the difficulties inherent in his now firmly established metaphors of femaleness, more determined to correct the imbalance they imply. He introduces a masculine emanation (Shiloh, the emanation of France as Jerusalem is of Albion [49:47 and 55:27]), and asserts later that all emanations "stand both Male & Female at the gates of each Humanity" (88:11), emphasizing that the weakness attributed to females by emanation is shared by males. He transfers responsibility for the division of the sexes from restrictive Urizen to inspired Los (58:13–20), implying that there is constructive value in the separate existence of the female during the course of the fall. He reverses the genders of the speakers of several key speeches substantially repeated in *Jerusalem* from earlier poems, suggesting that his conception of sexual roles is at least partly flexible: Jerusalem speaks the tormented lines beginning "Why wilt thou number every little fibre of my Soul"

(22:20–24) spoken by Tharmas in *The Four Zoas* (I, 4:28–32), and Erin explains the concept of States to her sisters in *Jerusalem* (49:1 to 50:17, esp. 49:65–76) as the male angels explained it to their brother Milton in *Milton* (plate 32, esp. 22–29).

Jesus castigates the destructive nature of his emanation fiercely in *Milton* (plate 33), demanding her conversion; in a parallel but much milder speech in *Jerusalem* he explains her error and consoles her and promises to lead her to redemption (60:10–37; the words of the Divine Voice are sung here by slaves as in Milton they were sung by the Daughters of Beulah). The softening of Jesus' tone towards his emanation in *Jerusalem* is echoed in Blake's expanding in his last prophecy the redemptive faculty of the female—most evident earlier in Ololon's identification with Jesus—by presenting Jerusalem as the wholly positive force which Albion need only recognize and embrace to return to Eden. She is better than he is, more nearly Edenic, less perverted: her sons are the soul while his are the body (71:4–5), her sons number four times four, the perfect numbers of Edenic existence, while his only number four times three (74:23–24).

Throughout *Jerusalem* Blake seems to be redefining for this separate female form he has conceptualized a position which is wholly positive. The clearest statement of that position is lines 39:38–40: "Man is adjoined to Man by his Emanative portion:/ Who is Jerusalem in every individual Man: and her/ Shadow is Vala, builded by the reasoning power in Man." The positive function of the female is to permit union among males; her negative function is to destroy that union by rationalization. We may recognize these functions in *Milton,* though they are not explicitly defined there: the constructive function is evident in the intermediation of Beulah between Eden and Generation as well as in Ololon's uniting of Milton and Jesus, and the negative function is evidence in the acts of Leutha and Rahab and the Shadowy Female. *Jerusalem* distinguishes even more overtly than *Milton* the positive and negative functions of the female, giving Vala equal time with Jerusalem. Yet the more clearly the female roles are defined, the more circumscribed they are by male reality: female separateness is good when it permits communication among males, bad when it corrupts that communication, good when it passively awaits embrace, bad when it actively demands embrace. The more positive Blake's female becomes, the more passive, the more male-circumscribed she becomes. Jerusalem is better than Albion, but lesser. The active/positive female alternative suggested, however ambivalently, by Ololon is sabotaged in *Jerusalem* by Blake's requirement of a totally positive—and hence, even at this point in the development of his attitudes, totally will-less—female principle. The conflict between Blake's doctrine and the stereotypes of sexual relationship in which he expresses it remains.[14]

Again, Jerusalem's femaleness is more metaphoric than literal. She is not a woman or even womankind, but the emanative portion of all humanity regardless of gender; presumably the male emanation Shiloh is in the same position she is in. But the metaphor is a powerful one, one built on profound social discrimination, and it dominates the poem. That Blake's metaphor contradicts his doctrine of necessary equality between contraries is perhaps more a comment on the society in which he was educated and which he addressed than it is upon his faculties as thinker and poet, but it is a comment on his mind and art nonetheless. Metaphors are not divorced from concepts. When they conflict with the concepts they are meant to advance they attest to an uneasiness in their author's mind, and create an uneasiness in his or her reader's mind. That uneasiness is probably minor for readers of Blake's prophecies, who are most likely able to accommodate such discrepencies comfortably in their perception of the rich and significant schemes of these great poems. It may have been minor for Blake himself, though he tried frequently to adjust it. It is not minor in our conception of the poet Blake, who more than any other male writer of his time recognized the destructive effect of received attitudes towards women, but who was nevertheless to some extent a victim of those attitudes.

Notes

1. *The Poetry and Prose of William Blake*, ed. David V. Erdman (Garden City, N.Y., 1965), p. 585. All subsequent quotations of Blake will be from this edition.

2. Northrop Frye, "Notes for a Commentary on *Milton,*" *The Divine Vision: Studies in the Poetry and Art of William Blake,* ed. Vivian de Sola Pinto (1957; rpt. New York, 1968), pp. 115–16.

3. *Natural Supernaturalism: Tradition and Revolution in Romantic Literature* (New York, 1971), p. 260.

4. "Babylon Revisited, or the Story of Luvah and Vala," *Blake's Sublime Allegory: Essays on The Four Zoas, Milton, Jerusalem,* ed. Stuart Curran and Joseph Anthony Wittreich, Jr. (Madison, Wis., 1973), p. 113. Hagstrum's context is the "interpenetration of essences" implied in Blake's mingling of sexual and religious imagery and ideas.

5. The last plate of *Thel* may have been engraved later than the rest of the poem (Erdman, textual note to his edition, p. 713).

6. Ibid., p. 737.

7. As this statement suggests, the development of the male as metaphor obviously parallels the development of the female as metaphor. But Blake's metaphoric representations of males are so much more complex and comprehensive than his metaphoric representations of females, that to dwell on them would be to distort the focus of this study and to quadruple its length.

8. Morton D. Paley notes in *Energy and the Imagination: A Study of the Development of Blake's Thoughts* (Oxford, 1970), p. 251 n., that in *Milton* Oothoon, like Leutha, will become an embodiment of Female Will, tormenting Orc with her beauty (lines 18:39–45). I would add that she is purged of Will at the end of that poem, as she "Pants in the Vales of Lambeth weeping o'er her Human Harvest" (42:33).

9. Florence Sandler sees it also as a corresponding attack on Milton's idea of chastity ("The Iconoclastic Enterprise: Blake's Critique of 'Milton's Religion,'" *Blake Studies* 5, no. 1 [1972]: 43).

10. This division in the representation of female characters probably accounts for a marked duality in critical response to Blake's women. For two definitions of Blake's symbolic use of females as both negative and positive see Brian Wilkie, "Epic Irony in *Milton,*" *Blake's Visionary Forms Dramatic,* ed. David V. Erdman and John E. Grant (Princeton, 1970), pp. 364–67, and Thomas J. J. Altizer, *The New Apocalypse: The Radical Christian Vision of William Blake* (East Lansing, Mich., 1967), pp. 48–56, 95–102. An odd twist on the duality of Blake's vision of women is suggested in dissociated comments by Hagstrum and Sandler. Hagstrum notes the symbolic presence in Blake's poetry of what Freud would call the phallic woman, the imaginary masculinization of a threatening female; he cites, among other examples, the Rahab figure engraved on plate 14 of *America,* "her loins producing a phallic serpent" (pp. 108–9). For Hagstrum the phallic woman is a Blakean symbol of perversion. Sandler notes a major positive instance of what might be considered the same phenomenon in the description of Ololon in Eden as a "sweet River, of milk & liquid pearl" (*Milton,* 21:15), which Sandler associates with "the spermatic stream of the Hermeticists" (p. 21). Thus even in his rare use of this bizarre perspective on female nature, Blake's attitude is divided between positive and negative.

11. John Sutherland sees evidence of such an affair's altering Blake's perception of women in three manuscript poems ("Blake: A Crisis of Love and Jealousy," *PMLA* 87, no. 3 [May 1972]: 424–31). He hypothesizes, very reasonably, I think, a further change as Blake began his major prophecies: "Indeed, a case can be made for the poem *Vala* as growing out of a need to express this resentment, and then perhaps being retitled *The Four Zoas* as it was modified in terms of a more positive analysis" (p. 430).

12. "Blake's Radical Comedy: Dramatic Structure as Meaning in *Milton,*" *Blake's Sublime Allegory,* p. 305.

13. He makes that referral explicit in *Jerusalem,* when he calls Enitharmon "a vegetated mortal Wife of Los:/ His Emanation, yet his Wife till the sleep of Death is past" (14:13–14). "Wife" clearly implies status inferior in the sexual relationship to that implied by "emanation," but it is only a temporary inferiority, since wives will disappear altogether when the fall is reversed. It is no great comfort that only mortal, fallen women are inferior to their male counterparts, but Blake probably meant it as comfort.

14. Even in his careful attempts in *Jerusalem* to define the differences between males and females, attempts so gracious towards females that he seems self-consciously eager to be fair, he succumbs to embarrassing stereotypes of active profound males and passive feeling females: "The Female searches sea & land for gratifications to the/ Male Genius: who in return clothes her in gems & gold/ And feeds her with the food of Eden" (69:16–18); the masculine is sublime and the feminine is pathos (90:10–11).

ROBERT F. GLECKNER

Most Holy Forms of Thought: Some Observations on Blake and Language

In an extraordinary passage at the end of Blake's greatest achievement, *Jerusalem,* he describes more fully than anywhere else in his works the apocalypse—the reachievement of fourfold unity, the marriage of Albion (the Grand Man) and Jerusalem (his emanation), the reintegration of the four zoas, the four senses, the four faces of man, the four compass points, the four elements—all that had been sundered by the Fall. It reads in part:

> The Four Living Creatures Chariots of Humanity Divine
>   Incomprehensible
> In beautiful Paradises expand These are the Four Rivers
>   of Paradise
> And the Four Faces of Humanity fronting the Four
>   Cardinal Points
> Of Heaven going forward forward irresistible from
>   Eternity to Eternity
>
> And they conversed together in Visionary forms dramatic
>   which bright
> Redounded from their Tongues in thunderous majesty, in
>   Visions

This essay first appeared in *ELH* 41 (1974): 555–575. Reprinted with permission.

> In new Expanses, creating exemplars of Memory and of Intellect
> Creating Space, Creating Time according to the wonders Divine
> Of Human Imagination, throughout all the Three Regions immense
> Of Childhood, Manhood & Old Age; & the all tremendous unfathomable Non Ens
> Of Death was seen in regenerations terrific or complacent varying
> According to the subject of discourses & every Word & Every Character
> Was Human according to the Expansion or Contraction, the Translucence or
> Opakeness of Nervous fibres such was the variation of Time & Space
> Which vary according as the Organs of Perception vary & they walked
> To & fro in Eternity as One Man reflecting each in each & clearly seen
> And seeing: according to fitness & order. And I heard Jehovah speak
> Terrific from his Holy Place & saw the Words of the Mutual Covenant Divine
> On Chariots of gold & jewels with Living Creatures starry & flaming
> With every Colour, Lion, Tyger, Horse, Elephant, Eagle, Dove, Fly, Worm,
> And the all wondrous Serpent clothed in gems & rich array Humanize . . .[1]

These redemptions are the product of an enormously complicated sequence of events chronicled in the total poem, which itself is the product of the equally complex process of Blake's regeneration of himself, particularly in the poem *Milton,* so that he might become *the* poet, *the* prophet, the "Inspired Man." The sum total of these redemptions is the awakening of man from 6000 years of brutish, nightmarish human history, the annihilation of the total Creation (which was a colossal error born in the mind of the archetypal fool), and the regeneration of the fallen physicality of all things, gathered together once again into the imaginative-human forms from which they were all rudely and tragically abstracted.

> All Human Forms identified even Tree Metal Earth & Stone. all
> Human Forms identified, living going forth & returning wearied
> Into the Planetary lives of Years Month Days & Hours reposing
> And then Awakening into his Bosom in the Life of Immortality.
>
> (99:1–4)

In that life of life, as the opening of *The Book of Urizen* describes it,

> Earth was not: nor globes of attraction
> The will of the Immortal expanded
> Or contracted his all flexible senses.
> Death was not, but eternal life sprung.
>
> (3:36–39)

All of this is so incredibly grand—and bold—a conception that paradoxically we seem to have little difficulty following it, grasping it all, if not in its minute particulars, at least in its totality. For it is the fond wish of all men however debased our imaginations.

But one aspect of this cosmic rehabilitation has received less attention than is its due—that of language, words. Concomitant with the Blakean Fall into disintegration, fragmentation, and dislocation, is the fall of the Word into words, the degeneration of "Visionary forms dramatic" into language, the compromising of the free, translucent, imaginative interconversation of the Eternals into a time-bound, space-bound syntax that passively mirrors the shattered mind and the excruciatingly finite limits of fallen sense perception. This is, of course, Urizen's world, the world of eternity bereft of its fundamental humanness, and peopled by what Blake calls "human shadows" which are produced by man himself "begetting his likeness,/ On his own divided image" (*Bk. of Urizen* 19:15–16). "Cruel enormities" is what Urizen, his residual humanity stunned at the fallen condition of his eternal creations, himself calls them:

And his world teemd vast enormities
Frightning; faithless; fawning
Portions of life; similitudes
Of a foot, or a hand, or a head
Or a heart, or an eye, they swam mischevous
Dread terrors! delighting in blood.

(23:2–7)

Thus on the one hand Blake sees the process of the Fall as all but endless, a dizzying and sickening inner strife which produces finally not merely "portions of life" or portions of men, but even worse, only *similitudes* (a word borrowed, appropriately enough, from Locke) of a foot or a hand or a heart or an eye. On the other hand, this horrible process is exacerbated by shrinkage as well:

. . . their eyes
Grew small like the eyes of a man
And in reptile forms shrinking together
Of seven feet stature they remaind

Six days they. shrunk up from existence
And on the seventh day they rested
And they bless'd the seventh day, in sick hope:
And forgot their eternal life.

(*Bk. of Urizen* 25:35–42)

What is perhaps least obvious about this Fall is that the physical creation of space and time, of the solar system and earth, and of mankind all are preceded by the utterance of the first words,[2] now separated from the imaginative significations of Eternity's "visionary forms dramatic." In *The Book of Urizen,* Urizen is first seen as "a shadow of horror," as yet unrealized and unrealizable:

Dark revolving in silent activity:
Unseen in tormenting passions;
And activity unknown and horrible;

A self-contemplating shadow,
In enormous labours occupied.

(3:18–22)

Out of this portentous silence,[3] the auditory equivalent of voidness, emerge two sounds: a trumpet, heralding Blake's remarkable parody of the apocalypse, and the utterance of "Words articulate," bursting in thunders that rolled on the tops of Urizen's mountains—words which emanate, as Urizen himself says,

From the depths of dark solitude. From
The eternal abode in my holiness,
Hidden set apart in my stern counsels
Reserv'd for the days of futurity.

(4:6–9)

And those words he immediately freezes into solid form and sets down for the edification (and enslavement) of all futurity:

Here alone I in books formd of metals
Have written the secrets of wisdom
The secrets of dark contemplation
. . . .
Lo! I unfold my darkness: and on
This rock, place with strong hand the Book
Of eternal brass, written in my solitude.

Laws of peace, of love, of unity:
Of pity, compassion, forgiveness.
Let each chuse one habitation:
His ancient infinite mansion:
One command, one joy, one desire,
One curse, one weight, one measure,
One King, one God, one Law.

(4:24–40)

And one *Word,* we might add, the ultimate perversion of the Word, which in Urizen's world, despite his laws, becomes the gibberish of the tower of Babel or mere similitudes of the Word—that is, nouns, verbs, adjectives which arrogate to themselves the divine wisdom, truth, and reality of Eternity's cosmic syntax.

Therein lies the central problem of the poet—for without words is no prophecy, and without prophecy is no apocalypse. How then is the poet to regenerate or redeem the Word via the use of the fallen elements that "signal their complicity with that which makes the [Word] unrealizable,"[4] and that therefore require regeneration and redemption themselves? How can language be unBabelized and still remain comprehensible to or apprehensible by fallen man—the reader? Given the necessity of speaking words in time, or writing words in linear space, how can the poet annihilate the very temporal and spatial confines which make verbalization possible in the first place? With Urizen's original utterance of "words articulate" in mind, and his writing them down in his book of metals, how can the poet be Urizenic and at the same time prophetic, that is, Blake's Los?

In two earlier papers I attempted the beginnings of an answer to these questions. In the first I suggested that the Romantic poets twisted and strained language in such fashion that it finally militated against its own existence, aspiring toward that totality of unverbalizable communication, that act of pure intellection which we call (with a certain helplessness) silence. For example, Shelley (who, more often than not, is the best example) writes in *The Defense of Poetry* that "Poetry is a sword of lightning, ever unsheathed, which consumes the scabbard that would contain it." And in one of the most daring of metaphors for this linguistic self-immolation, in his Preface to *The Cenci* he writes: "Imagination is as the immortal God which should assume flesh for the redemption of mortal passion." Thus, the poet creates words (poetry) which in their self-annihilative power flash upon the imagination the truths (or reality) of which they are but the imperfect and evanescent conductors. Or to put it another way, as George Steiner does in his remarkable book *Language and Silence* (New York, 1967; 1st ed. 1958): "Light, . . . instead of making syntax translucent with meaning . . . seems to spill over in unrecapturable splendor or burn the word to ash" (p. 40). For the Romantic poet, however, and—as the poet so fervently hoped—for the imaginative reader, that splendor is not only not unrecapturable; it is as inextinguishable as the burnt words are consumable.[5]

While such a formulation may be conceptually acceptable in a general way, the operative particulars clearly are not—perhaps inevitably, since to talk about wordlessness even theoretically is to compromise conceptuality with the impoverished reality of words. In a recent fine essay on Shelley's veil imagery[6] Jerome McGann provides a useful metaphorical means of discussing the dilemma. In *The Prelude,* for example, Wordsworth wrote of his soul (for which we may here read "poetry" or "language") putting "Off her veil and, self-transmuted," standing "Naked, as in the presence of her God" (IV, 150–52). While we can recognize that for hundreds of years language was thought of as the clothing of thought, it is difficult, if not impossible, to conceive of thought naked of its dress. Nevertheless Wordsworth's veil (or any number of its synonymous metaphors in other poets—masks, mists of light, curtains, clouds) has to be seen as his tacit assumption that *some* manner of articulation is necessary to make the silence of pure imaginative cognition or intellection humanly conceivable.[7] The poet thus creates the veil of language while coinstantaneously stripping off that veil—creator and destroyer both. Blake typically makes the point in its most extreme (and apocalyptic) form: "God becomes as we are, that we may be as he is" *(There Is No Natural Religion)*—which is another way of saying that The Word must be made flesh, must be articulated, so that its existence may realize itself, wordless, in our unarticulatable imaginations. But the central paradox involved here is most neatly set out by Shelley. On the one hand he writes: "Poetry lifts the veil from the hidden beauty of the world"; and poetry "strips the veil of familiarity from the world, and lays bare the naked and sleeping beauty, which is the spirit of its forms." On the other: "Poetry . . . arrests the vanishing apparitions which haunt the interlunations of life, and veiling them, *or* in language *or* in form, sends them forth among mankind"; and, more succinctly: poetry "spreads its own figured curtain, *or* withdraws life's dark veil before the scene of things" *(The Defense of Poetry).* "Whatever can be Created can be Annihilated," Blake insisted (*Milton* 32:36)—except what he called "forms," that is, their eternal realities or identities. "The Oak is cut down by the Ax, the Lamb falls by the Knife/ But their Forms Eternal Exist, For-ever . . . (*ibid.* 32:37, 38). On the other hand he writes with marvelous circularity and a touch of humor that is less rare than most of us allow him:

> . . . What seems to Be: Is: To those to whom
> It seems to Be, & is productive of the most dreadful
> Consequences to those to whom it seems to Be. . . .
> (*Jerusalem* 32:51–53)

In a second paper[8] I tried to demonstrate that in certain poems, at least, Blake's verbal and syntactical strategies become as much a symbol of the world the poetry presents (whether fallen or unfallen) as are the images, actions, plot, and characters for which the words are the vehicle. Further, the Fall (as Blake interpreted it) is not only equal to the fall of the Word into words but also to the disintegration of non-discursive unity into normal syntactical patterns. Blake's linguistic problem in this sense was to create emblems of disjunctiveness while at the same time providing us the paradigmatic conjunction or identification of All by which the disjunctiveness can become meaningful. He saw quite clearly that it was not enough simply to rely on the reader's perception of the difference between abnormal or disjunctive syntax and the normal linear flow of meaningful words—for then we would merely be measuring one aspect of the Urizenic fallen world (disintegration) against another aspect of the same world (excessive order—"one King, one God, one Law"). The challenge was to construe what Harold Bloom calls a "grammar of imagination," a language that can imaginatively assume the condition of oneness and interchangeability of grammatical forms and functions, the loss of which it not only describes but enacts.

A fine example of this is from the "Preludium" to *The Book of Urizen:*

> Of the primeval Priests assum'd power
> When Eternals spurn'd back his religion;
> And gave him a place in the north,
> Obscure, shadowy, void, solitary.

If in the fallen world the priest has appropriately a "place," imaginatively there is no place; it is "void." Further, the adjectives in the last line ambiguously modify both "place" and "him," thus linking together the mutual imaginative unreality of character and landscape while ostensibly supplying them a solid context. Similarly, the four lines together form a grammatical fragment, an illusory verbal context within which the words jostle uncertainly—in a sense to be "spurn'd back" by the imaginative reader in emulation of the Eternals. But to pursue the particulars a bit further, as the "place" is "obscure," so the priest's vision is obscuring or obscured; if the "place" is "shadowy," the priest also is unsubstantial, a delusion. Blake's call for "swift winged words," then, is for the fire to do battle with Urizen's "Words articulate" (4:4) which will be ensconced in his "Book/ Of eternal brass" (4:32–33) as

> Laws of peace, of love, of unity:
> Of pity, compassion, forgiveness.
> . . . .
> One command, one joy, one desire,
> One curse, one weight, one measure
> One King, one God, one Law.
>
> (4:34–40)

And one syntax, the fallen unwinged word of lead that unfledges all flights of fire.[9]

The first chapter of *The Book of Urizen* merely expands this technique of Urizenically asserting space as well as physical identity and coinstantaneously denying them. Urizen is "a shadow of horror," "Unknown, unprolific!/ Self-closd, all-repelling," a "form'd" void or vacuum (3:1–5). That is, he is unknowable imaginatively but he is "self-known" just as he is imaginatively sterile but self-prolific, his "enormous labours" productive of "self-begotten armies," "phantasies," "horrible forms of deformity," "cruel enormities," all ultimately but "similitudes/ Of a foot, or a hand, or a head/ Or a heart, or an eye . . . (3:22, 5:16, 10:14, 13:43, 20:50, 23:4–6). Closing himself in and repelling all so that he may self-create his identity, Urizen exemplifies paradoxically his own illusoriness by way of Blake's contrapuntal imaginative syntax which undoes the Urizenic universe at its very borning. Or to put it another way: Urizen's imaginative unreality becomes the symbol for all that he is not; and conversely, his emergence as a palpable reality is annihilated by the imaginative voidness of his realization.

While I am still persuaded by the broad outlines and general directions of these two papers, the demonstrative particulars leave a good deal to be desired partly (at least) because of the inadequacies of any critical vocabulary to talk about the adequacies or inadequacies of poetic language to vehicularize ineffability whether that be conceptualized as nothingness or everythingness. In any case I am more and more convinced that Blake (as well as, of course, the other Romantic poets) quite deliberately and consistently struggled toward a transcendant or translucent syntax, whose formulations invite us to imaginatively perceive their own self-destructiveness. For while "space undivided by existence" strikes horror into all imaginative souls (*Bk. of Urizen* 13:46–47), "What can be Created Can be Destroyed" *(Laocoön),* and such annihilation of the error constitutive of "existence" is "The whole Business of Man" *(Laocoön).* In this spirit, then, let me here hazard some further observations relative to the total context and ramifications of the problem.

Though it may seem outrageously simplistic and sweeping let me suggest at the outset that everything Blake says about Man, the Universe, society, imagination and the senses—in fact, everything that he says about anything—is translatable into a comment upon language, words, the poet's task, poetry.[10] Put that way, the subject of Blake's language assumes proportions as forbidding as the intricacies of his mythology—into which we have not yet stopped probing and are unlikely to do so in the near future. My focus, however, will be on only three aspects of the total problem:

(1) What was Blake's conception of the language of Eternity, the ur-linguistic condition so to speak?
(2) What are the linguistic implications of the fall from this condition and how does Blake present "fallen" language other than merely using it himself?
(3) How does he conceive of the redemption of language, the

> reassumption of the reality and primacy of the Word, the reintegration of Babel into not merely one language but into that language that requires no temple, no building to signify it?

Initially we must recognize that Blake with two notable exceptions (*Bk. of Urizen* 3:36–39; *Jerusalem,* plates 97–99) gives us no vision at all of Eternity (or undifferentiated Imagination). He describes it, names it (precisely as Adam names the creatures in Genesis), talks about it, but its imaginative allness eludes his pen or graver. The reasons are obvious. By its very nature Eternity is neither describable nor representable. Any image (or set of images), any words, by their very nature, would compromise its imaginative (or mental) reality. He said once, in *Milton:*

> Every Time less than a pulsation of the artery
> Is equal in its period & value to Six Thousand Years.
>
> For in this Period the Poets Work is Done: and all the Great
> Events of Time start forth & are conceived in such a Period
> Within a Moment: a Pulsation of the Artery.
>
> (28:61–29:3)

From this perspective the only poem of Eternity possible must occupy no more time than this pulsation—and presumably no more space than Eliot's still point. Given the patent absurdity of such a conception Blake had to find other means of annihilating space and time while at the same time perforce capitulating to their insidious and resistless demands. Yet we do learn *about* Eternity, as I've said, and about its language, about the consititution of the Word. In Chapter IV of *Jerusalem,* for example, Blake writes:

> When in Eternity Man converses with Man they enter
> Into each others Bosom (which are Universes of delight)
> In mutual interchange—
>
> (88:3–5)

a rather startling echo of Wordsworth's marvelous phrase in *The Prelude*, "an ennobling interchange." The Word then is not so much a linguistic unit as an event, a sharing, an act of love, a coming together.[11] Blake used the splendid word "cominglings" to describe it:

> Embraces are Cominglings: from the Head even to the Feet;
> And not a pompous High Priest entering by a Secret Place.[12]

The quotation from *Jerusalem* with which this paper began accents the point:

> & every Word & Every Character
> Was Human . . .
> & they walked
> To & fro in Eternity as One Man reflecting each in
> each & clearly seen
> And seeing . . .

Thus Eternity is in the form of a man, and the Word is a man, and all things are human-formed, each in each without separation, mergeable identities interpenetrating without end.

One of Blake's finest lyrics dramatizes this conception in terms of the poet's own four-fold vision. Standing on the shore at his retreat in Felpham he feels his eyes expanding

> Into regions of air
> Away from all Care
> Into regions of fire
> Remote from Desire
> The Light of the Morning
> Heavens Mountains adorning
> In particles bright
> The jewels of Light
> Distinct shone & clear—
> Amazd & in fear
> I each particle gazed,
> Astonish'd Amazed
> For each was a Man
> Human formd. Swift I ran
> For they beckond to me
> Remote by the Sea
> Saying. Each grain of Sand
> Every Stone on the Land

Each rock & each hill
Each fountain & rill
Each herb & each tree
Mountain hill Earth & Sea
Cloud Meteor & Star
Are Men Seen Afar

(Letter to Butts, Oct. 2, 1800)

And then miraculously, epiphanically, apocalyptically, time and space are annihilated, the doors of perception are expanded infinitely, and the mental reality of Eternity is realized:[13]

My Eyes more & more
Like a Sea without shore
Continue Expanding
The Heavens commanding
Till the Jewels of Light
Heavenly Men beaming bright
Appeard as One Man
Who Complacent began
My limbs to infold
In his beams of bright gold
Like dross purgd away
All my mire & my clay
Soft consumd in delight
In his bosom Sun bright
I remaind.

(ibid.)

Aside from the loveliness of this poem (which must surely have been lost on the patient, generous, but plodding and pedestrian Butts), it serves admirably to remind us that for Blake Eternity exists within the timelessness and infinity of the human mind. Blake's visions of Eternity—and its language—then, are visions of his own mind, the mind of the totally imaginative man. "Mental Things are alone Real," he insisted in *A Vision of the Last Judgment;* "what is Calld Corporeal Nobody Knows of its dwelling Place it is in Fallacy & its Existence an Imposture Where is the Existence Out of Mind or Thought Where is it but in the Mind of a Fool." Thus just as "Eternity Exists and All things in

Eternity Independent of Creation" *(ibid.)*, just as the Word is expressed in Eternity as "Visionary forms dramatic which bright/ Redounded from [the tongues of the Four Zoas or the Divine Humanity] in thunderous majesty, in Visions/ In new Expanses"—so Blake explodes to the man he accused of being hired to depress art, Sir Joshua Reynolds: "All Forms are Perfect in the Poets Mind. but these are not Abstracted nor Compounded from Nature but are from Imagination" (Annotations to Reynolds).

The poet's mind, then, is not merely the image of Eternity, or its analogue, but is precisely that infinite reality of which nature is the mere shadow. As such, the mind contains not only all forms—perfect—but all words and the Word, Imagination complete (which is to say infinitely expanded sense perception, or mythologically, the fourfold unity of the Four Zoas). The Fall in this regard is thus the shattering of the Human Imagination into the disparate and woefully limited senses, the turning of mental reality inside out, the descent of the Word (and all perfect forms) via the viscera and pulp of the Tongue into what Blake variously calls "fabricate[d] embodied semblances" (*Four Zoas* 90:9); "similitudes/ Of a foot, or a hand, or a head/ Or a heart, or an eye (*Bk. of Urizen* 23:4–6); "the rotten rags" and "filthy garments" of Bacon, Locke, and Newton (*Milton* 41:4, 6); the linguistic world of Urizen's iron book of laws and the Tower of Babel; the poetry of Pope, Dryden, and the endless unarticulated babblings, gnashings, groanings, screamings, and ravings of Blake's own mythological fragments of man's total being.

But the fallen state of language is less easily described, for the total Fall itself in Blake is an incredibly complex and omnivorous affair. Initially, we recall, the Fall is not into Creation directly but rather into non-entity, the world of eternal Death:

> Sund'ring, dark'ning, thund'ring!
> Rent away with a terrible crash
> Eternity roll'd wide apart
> Wide asunder rolling
> Mountainous all around
> Departing; departing; departing:
> Leaving ruinous fragments of life

Hanging frowning cliffs & all between
An ocean of voidness unfathomable.
(*Bk. of Urizen* 5:3–11)

This Dali-esque landscape Blake describes variously as "space undivided by existence," the "eternal Abyss," the "dark void," the "Non-Ens." *The Book of Los* presents one of his most succinct enactments:

Falling, falling! Los fell & fell
Sunk precipitant heavy down down
Times on times, night on night, day on day
Truth has bounds. Error none: falling, falling:
Years on years, and ages on ages
Still he fell thro' the void, still a void
Found for falling day & night without end.
For tho' day or night was not; their spaces
Were measurd by his incessant whirls
In the horrid vacuity bottomless.
(4:27–36)

Aside from the parodic eternity and infinity of the Fall before a limit is placed to it by "the Divine Hand" or "Eternal Mind," the importance of this conception lies in the formlessness of error prior to the creation. Linguistically, then, the fall of the Word and its shattering of Truth (or reality) into endlessly multiplied fragments of words constitute and define error. But even that is not quite correct—for this error has no bounds. Like Urizen the Word during the Fall is

Unknown, unprolific!
Self-closd, all repelling . . .
. . . .
Dark revolving in silent activity:
Unseen in tormenting passions;
An activity unknown and horrible;
A self-contemplating shadow,
In enormous labours occupied.
(*Bk. of Urizen* 3:2–3, 18–22)

Enormous labours, of course, to no end but a perpetuation of the fall into non-entity.

The creation of the Universe, then, of the earth, of mankind, and of language is the giving of form to what otherwise would remain an eternal abstraction (and therefore unredeemable)—the limit of contraction and the limit of opacity. Accordingly the Creation is an act of mercy,

> by mathematic power
> Giving a body to Falshood that it may be cast off for ever.
> (*Jerusalem* 12:12–13)

Somewhat differently:

> . . . whatever is visible to the Generated Man
> Is a Creation of mercy & love, from the Satanic Void.
> (*ibid.* 13:44–45)

Or again, Los and his sons (the artisans of this world) are portrayed as

> Creating form & beauty around the dark regions of sorrow,
> Giving to airy nothing a name and a habitation
> Delightful! with bounds to the Infinite putting off the Indefinite
> Into most holy forms of Thought . . .
> (*Milton* 28:2–5)

Or, finally and most elaborately, in the first chapter of *Jerusalem:*

> Lo!
> The stones are pity, and the bricks, well wrought affections:
> Enameld with love & kindness, & the tiles engraven gold
> Labour of merciful hands: the beams & rafters are forgiveness;
> The mortar & cement of the work, tears of honesty: the nails,
> And the screws & iron braces, are well wrought blandishments,

And well contrived words, firm fixing, never forgotten,
Always comforting the remembrance: the floors, humility,
The cielings, devotion; the hearths, thanksgiving:
. . . .
The curtain, woven tears & sighs, wrought into lovely
forms
For comfort.

(12:29–40)

It is in this sense, of course, that "Eternity is in love with the productions of time" *(Marriage of Heaven and Hell).*

But, while Los, the eternal artificer, can do all this to provide both the hope and the possibility of redemption and a reassumption of Eternity, the Creation is Urizenic after all:

. . . the land of woven labyrinths:
The land of snares & traps & wheels & pit-falls & dire
mills:
The Voids, the Solids, & the land of clouds & regions of
waters:
With their inhabitants: in the Twenty-seven Heavens
beneath Beulah:
Self-righteousness conglomerating against the Divine
Vision:
A Concave Earth wondrous, Chasmal, Abyssal,
Incoherent!

(*Jerusalem* 13:48–53)

Put somewhat crudely and not entirely accurately, what Los creates Urizen rules over and commands—so that the wars of Blake's mythology directly pit the poet (the human imagination) against the non-poet (the sense-dominated reason-controlled man). More to the point, that war takes place within each man. As his imagination strives to produce "most holy forms of thought" for the redemption of his total being, his reason produces space-bound, time-bound monsters which struggle for personal dominion and enslave that portion of man whose vision of Eternity remains at least a glowing ember. Reason, then, which Blake describes as "once fairer than the light till fould in Knowledges dark Prison house" ("Then She Bore Pale

Desire"), along with its cohorts, the fallen infinite and innumerable senses now shrunken to four, produces "A Pretence of Art: To Destroy Art" (Annotations to Reynolds)—its human agents being Bacon, Newton, Locke, Reynolds, Gainsborough, Rembrandt, Titian, Rubens, Pope, Dryden—and all who are not, in Blake's definition, artists. The major products of their infernal creations are two: the law and bad art (which are the same thing). Blake's metaphors for these abominations are several. Bad poets are, for example, "the destroyers of Jerusalem,"

> Who pretend to Poetry that they may destroy Imagination;
> By imitation of Natures Images drawn from Remembrance
> These are the Sexual Garments, the Abomination of
> Desolation
> Hiding the Human Lineaments as with an Ark & Curtains.
> (*Milton* 41:21, 23–26)

They are the blotters and blurrers of the minute particulars of Eternity, creating instead

> Harmonies of Concords & Discords
> Opposed to Melody, and by Lights & Shades, opposed
> to Outline
> And by Abstraction opposed to the Visions of Imagination.
> (*Jerusalem* 74:24–26)

Their counterparts—the readers, perceivers, or listeners—are equally debased:

> The Ear, a little shell in small volutions shutting out
> All melodies & comprehending only Discord and Harmony
> The Tongue a little moisture fills, a little food it cloys
> A little sound it utters & its cries are faintly heard
> Then brings forth Moral Virtue the cruel Virgin Babylon.[14]

Even more terrifying perhaps than the moral law and bad poetry, which are spun out of the entrails of Urizen and recorded in his books of iron and brass, are Blake's mechanistic metaphors for fallen language.[15] Words are described in *Milton* as being laid

in order above the mortal brain
As cogs are formed in a wheel to turn the cogs of the adverse wheel.

(27:9–10)

In *The Four Zoas* this epic machinery is seen as quite literally warring with itself—devastatingly all within man's mind:

Terrific ragd the Eternal Wheels of intellect terrific ragd
The living creatures of the wheels in the Wars of Eternal life
But perverse rolld the wheels of Urizen & Luvah back reversd
Downwards & outwards consuming in the wars of Eternal Death.

(20:12–15)

In *Jerusalem* those wheels are enmeshed neatly with the loom of Locke that cocoons the human imagination (linguistically the words which clothe the thought),[16] and fashions the nets that envelope all bodies and all minds, inducing "single vision and Newton's sleep":

I turn my eyes to the Schools & Universities of Europe
And there behold the Loom of Locke whose Woof rages dire
Wash'd by the Water-wheels of Newton. black the cloth
In heavy wreathes folds over every Nation; cruel Works
Of many Wheels I view, wheel without wheel, with cogs tyrannic
Moving by compulsion each other: not as those in Eden: which
Wheel within Wheel in freedom revolve in harmony & peace.

(15:14–20)

The total effect of these wheels and cogs upon man is predictable, but what is perhaps startling is that the wheels produce in man's brain words. In *The Four Zoas,* for example, men are

bound to sullen contemplations in the night
Restless they turn on beds of sorrow. in their inmost brain

Feeling the crushing Wheels they rise they write the bitter
words
Of Stern Philosophy & knead the bread of knowledge with
tears & groans. (138:12–5)

Los' task is to combat all this, just as the human imagination must contend with the fetters of reason, the petrified forms of the law, and the vague general forms of the debased artist. Not only is he Blake's eternal artificer; he is also appropriately Time.[17] For,

Time is the mercy of Eternity; without Times swiftness
Which is the swiftest of all things: all were eternal torment.
(*Milton* 24:72–73)

And we recall, of course, that it is in the pulsation of an artery that the poet's work is done. Although Los laments endlessly that

Reasonings like vast Serpents
Infold around [his] limbs, bruising [his] minute articulations
(*Jerusalem* 15:12–13)

it is his, the poet's, the imagination's job to create these minute articulations of error so that they may be annihilated. Thus in Chapter iii of *Jerusalem* the Eternal Great Humanity urges Los to his task,

Crying: Compell the Reasoner to Demonstrate with
unhewn Demonstrations
Let the Indefinite be explored. and let every Man be
Judged
By his own Works, Let all Indefinites be thrown into
Demonstrations
To be pounded to dust & melted in the Furnaces of
Affliction:

. . . .

The Infinite alone resides in Definite & Determinate
Identity
Establishment of Truth depends on destruction of
Falshood continually
On Circumcision: not on Virginity. . . .
(55:56–66)

Accordingly Los works unceasingly and heroically with his hammer, anvil, and fires—both to give form to error that it may be annihilated, and also to re-reveal the minute particularity of a vision of Eternity:

> & in his ladles the Ore
> He lifted, pouring it into the clay ground prepar'd
> with art;
> Striving with Systems to deliver Individuals from those
> Systems.
>
> (*Jerusalem* 11:3–5)

Perhaps not extraordinarily, then, Los creates (in addition to all else he creates in his cosmic, enormous labors)

> English, the rough basement.
> Los built the stubborn structure of the Language,
> acting against
> Albions melancholy, who must else have been a Dumb
> despair.
>
> (*Jerusalem* 36:58–60)

And with that rough basement Blake (and *all* poets) must work—building enormous structures which at once embody error in annihilable form ("giving to airy nothing a habitation and a name") and provide the possibility of organizing the minute particularity of vision in order to reconstruct Eternity. "I rest not from my great task," Blake cries in propria persona in *Jerusalem,*

> To open the Eternal Words, to open the immortal Eyes
> Of Man inwards into the Worlds of Thought: into Eternity
> Ever expanding in the Bosom of God. the Human
> Imagination.
>
> (5:17–20)

And again:

> Therefore I print; nor vain my types shall be:
> Heaven, Earth & Hell, henceforth shall live in harmony.
>
> (*ibid.* 3:9–10)

That printing will be, as *The Marriage of Heaven and Hell* reminds us, "in the infernal method, by corrosives . . . melting apparent surfaces away, and displaying the infinite which was hid."

These reformulations of familiar material bring us to the key question (my number 3 above): what can Blake do, even with all his multi-artistic genius, to redeem language—or at least to make his language susceptible of redemption and a renewal of the primacy of the Word. It is both a matter of perception (predictably) and of action (rather than a matter of merely reading). To take the latter point first, reading is not a human (i.e. imaginative) activity to Blake. It is as Urizenic as all other aspects of the fallen Imagination. For example, in *The Four Zoas*

> . . . Urizen gave life & sense by his immortal power
> . . . .
> Thus in the temple of the Sun his books of iron & brass
> And silver & gold he consecrated reading incessantly
> To myriads of perturbed spirits thro the universe
> They propagated the deadly words the Shadowy Female
>   absorbing
> The enormous Sciences of Urizen ages after ages
>   exploring
> The fell destruction.
>
> (102:14, 23–28)

Or: "Los reads the Stars of Albion! the Spectre reads the Voids/ Between the Stars" (*Jerusalem* 91:36–37). Or, as "the Shadowy Female howls in articulate howlings" of the woven garments of life,

> I will have Writings written all over [them] in Human Words
> That every Infant that is born upon the Earth shall read
> And get by rote as a hard task of a life of sixty years.
>
> (*Milton* 18:12–14)

Reading, thus, is performable only by fallen man: it is the mere scanning of objects, the tracing of "dreadful letters" (*Four Zoas* 78:2), the accumulation of data, the obverse of Adam's "naming." It is a sense experience. In *Jerusalem* Blake chides us directly:

> You accumulate Particulars, & murder by analyzing, that you
> May take the aggregate; & call the aggregate Moral Law:
> And you call that Swelld & bloated Form; a Minute Particular.

> But General Forms have their vitality in Particulars: & every Particular is a Man; a Divine Member of the Divine Jesus.
> (91:26–30)

The bloated "aggregate," of course, is the "meaning" that the reader abstracts from the particulars—and then permits to assume a reality of its own—in precisely the same way that the priests in *The Marriage of Heaven and Hell* abstract deities from their objects and then pronounce them the only realities. Words thus become part of the vast machine of the physical world, cogs in a cerebral wheel to turn the adverse wheel of the reader's mind in a kind of perpetual motion machine producing nothing—which is to say, producing mere images drawn from Nature. From these, laws are abstracted that men impose upon themselves; and gods are invented, as the source of the laws, before which men then prostitute themselves. The viciousness and self-enslavement of the reading process could not be made more graphic.

At the same time Blake clearly regarded his words as the embodiments, the formalizations, the deabstractifications of error. "There is not an Error," he wrote in *A Vision of the Last Judgment,* "but it has a Man for its Agent that is it is a Man." And again, from the same work: "Error is Created Truth is Eternal Error or Creation will be Burned Up & then & not till then Truth or Eternity will appear it is Burnt Up the Moment Men cease to behold it." We are thus thrown back upon the nature of perception: not only *how* one sees, but which direction one looks. If one sees merely the words, in order arranged, settled neatly into the time and space of the page, one sees precisely as Blake's idiot questioner who cries out irritatedly: "When the Sun rises do you not see a round Disk of fire somewhat like a Guinea"? Blake's answer is what his poems demand our answer to be: "O no no I see an Innumerable company of the Heavenly host crying Holy Holy Holy is the Lord God Almighty."[18] To see the words on the page as linguistic constructs (or even metaphors and symbols)[19] is to see one's self only. One is reminded of the quip about great poetry being as a mirror: if an ass peers into it, he can hardly expect an angel to peer out. So, for Blake, his words are intended to circumscribe and circumcise "the excrementitious/ Husk & Covering into Vacuum evaporating revealing the lineaments of Man" (*Jerusalem* 98:18–19) and the minutely discriminated particulars of vision—which are apparent to all who turn their eyes *inward* "into the Worlds of Thought: into Eternity/ Ever expanding in the Bosom of God" (*Jerusalem* 5:19–20). To "read" in such fashion is to see not words at all but human forms acting out the drama of fall, redemption, and apocalypse that takes place within one's own mental universe.

Blake's advice to us is appropriately pointed. We must arm ourselves, as he did,

> With the bows of my Mind & the Arrows of Thought
> My bowstring fierce with Ardour breathes
> My arrows glow in their golden sheaves.
>
> (Letter to Butts, Nov. 22, 1802)

So armed, we must engage with the words in mental strife, entering into their worlds (which are "universes of delight") in "Mutual interchange."[20] For

> every Word & Every Character
> [Is] Human according to the Expansion or Contraction, the Translucence or Opakeness

of our "Nervous fibres" or senses (*Jerusalem* 98:25–37).

This intellectual intercourse (clearly the external analogue of sexual intercourse) makes clear Blake's otherwise seemingly peculiar notion that the sense of touch (the Tongue) is the "Parent Sense" (*Jerusalem* 98:17). Without such engagement and comingling Blake's poetry seems much wind and splutter, intellectually fascinating but cranky, and perhaps finally irrelevant to *my* situation. But Blake did not say lightly (he repeated it seven times), through the Bard of *Milton:* "Mark well my words! they are of your eternal salvation."

His poetry, then, is not an "impossible enterprise" however shabby its "equipment,"[21] "If," he writes in *A Vision of the Last Judgment,* "the Spectator could Enter into these Images in his Imagination approaching them on the Fiery Chariot of his Contemplative Thought if he could Enter into Noahs Rainbow or into his bosom or could make a Friend & Companion of one of these Images of wonder which always intreats him to leave mortal things as he must know then would he arise from his Grave then would he meet the Lord in the Air & then he would be happy." And then he will recognize the dross of language to be the Baconian-Newtonian Lockean-Urizenic illusion that obscures, debases, and falsifies, but never hides the "Visionary Forms Dramatic" redounding *from* the plate or page as they do from all unfallen tongues and minds. Thel was told about the grave: "'Tis given thee to enter/ And to return; fear nothing." In the sense that I have been attempting to develop, Blake's linguistic text, indeed the whole of each grand plate, is our "grave." It is not much to ask us to enter, but it is everything. On page 67 of his manuscript notebook, he wrote: "23 May 1810 found the Word Golden." It's clearly worth the search.

Notes

1. Plate 98, ll. 24–44. All Blake quotations are from *The Poetry and Prose of William Blake,* ed. D. V. Erdman (New York, 1965), noted by plate and line numbers (or, from *The Four Zoas,* page and line numbers).

2. Cf. Heidegger's point that although language became actualized as "conversation" and seemingly as a consequence the gods acquired names and a world appeared, in reality "the presence of the gods and the appearance of the world are not merely a consequence of the actualisation of language, they are contemporaneous with it" (quoted in Robert W. Funk, *Language, Hermeneutics and the Word of God* [New York, 1966], p. 40).

3. Portentous in the sense that it heralds noise, non-communication, but also, in a typically Blakean paradox, this silence is reminiscent of the "silence" of eternity, its visionary forms dramatic and most holy forms of thought. Similarly Joseph Mazzeo reminds us in *Renaissance and Seventeenth-Century Studies* (New York and London, 1964) that according to Ignatius Martyr the Incarnation was a descent from silence into "speech" or *logos* and Christ was thus "his word proceeding from silence" (pp. 22–23). See also Mazzeo's interesting chapter on St. Augustine's "Rhetoric of Silence."

4. Frederic Jameson, *The Prison-House of Language* (Princeton, 1972), p. 88.

5. With the ideas in this paragraph (and elsewhere in this paper) compare Stanley E. Fish's provocative thesis in *Self-Consuming Artifacts* (Berkeley and Los Angeles, 1972). For example: "A self-consuming artifact signifies most successfully where it fails, when it points *away* from itself to something its forms cannot capture"; and: "art, like other medicines is consumed in the workings of its own best effects" (3–4). Professor Fish's argument is far too complex to be summarized here; but while I am not fully persuaded by his emphasis almost wholly on "what is happening in the reader" rather than "what is happening on the page,"

his book deserves a reading by all Blake students, especially the chapter on Herbert's poetry.

6. "Shelley's Veils: A Thousand Images of Loveliness," in *Romantic and Victorian: Studies in Memory of William H. Marshall,* ed. W. P. Elledge and R. L. Hoffman (Rutherford, N. J., 1971), pp. 198–218.

7. Cf. Frederic Jameson's point about Dante's *Paradiso* in *The Prison-House of Language*: "the content of the *Paradiso* turns out to be a series of investigations of how paradise could have content; that the events of the poem are 'nothing more' than a series of dramatizations of the pre-conditions necessary for such events to be conceivable in the first place" (p. 88).

8. "Blake's Verbal Technique," in *William Blake: Essays for S. Foster Damon,* ed. A. H. Rosenfeld (Providence, R. I., 1969), pp. 321–32. The substance of the following three paragraphs is taken from this essay.

9. Cf. Shelley's *Epipsychidion,* ll. 588–90.

10. Interestingly James Rieger recently came to the conclusion that *Milton* "exists on four levels of discourse," the utterances of each higher realm being "only partially intelligible to the inhabitants of the worlds below it. That is the central stylistic problem of the poem"—"'The Hem of Their Garments': The Bard's Song in Milton," in *Blake's Sublime Allegory,* ed. S. Curran and J. A. Wittreich (Madison, Wis., 1973), p. 277.

11. Cf. Peter Brooks' interesting essay on nineteenth-century French melodrama, "The Text of Muteness," *New Literary History* (1974), 549–64, especially his notion of mute gesture as "immediate, unarticulated language of presence: a moment of victory of expression over articulation."

12. *Jerusalem* 69:43–44. Cf. 66:56: "He who will not comingle in Love, must be adjoind by Hate"—that is by the pomposity of lexical analyses which arrive at meanings through "adjoinings." Also *Jerusalem* 88:6–7, where cominglings produce "thunders of intellect."

13. Cf. Roger Easson's argument that Blake's use of the "sublime" is related to the fact that "to sublime" in chemistry means the passing of a substance "from solid to gas without passing into the intermediate liquid state" ("Blake and His Reader in *Jerusalem,*" in *Blake's Sublime Allegory,* p. 316).

14. *Milton* 5:23–27. Blake's later version of this passage, in *Jerusalem* is:

> The Ear, a little shell, in small volutions shutting out
> True Harmonies, & comprehending great, as very small:
> The Nostrils, bent down to the earth & clos'd with senseless
> flesh.
> That odours cannot them expand, nor joy on them exult:
> The Tongue, a little moisture fills, a little food it cloys,
> A little sound it utters, & its cries are faintly heard.
>
> (49:36–41).

15. Cf. Morris Eaves' interesting explication of "The Title-Page of *The Book of Urizen*" in *William Blake: Essays in Honour of Sir Geoffrey Keynes,* ed. M. D. Paley and M. Phillips (Oxford, 1973), pp. 225–30.

16. See Rieger's discussion of this in *Blake's Sublime Allegory,* espec. pp. 278–80.

17. For a useful analysis of Los' various significations and functions see E. J. Rose's "Los, Pilgrim of Eternity" in *Blake's Sublime Allegory,* pp. 83–99. Particularly related to the point of this paper are pages 89–90 where Rose describes the artist's initial act as the same as the "visionary's effort to delineate form on indefinite space—to mercifully give time to space, to draw a line."

18. *A Vision of the Last Judgment.* It is worth noting here that Karl Barth's hermeneutic methodology (as presented in the Preface to the second edition of *Römerbrief*) "is to *live* with the text until it disappears and one is confronted with the divine word itself" (Robert W. Funk, *Language, Hermeneutics, and the Word of God,* p. 11). Cf. Merleau-Ponty's distinction between the "accomplished work" and "the work which exists in itself like a thing" (Funk, p. 234).

19. Cf. Jerzy Peterkiewicz's notion in *The Other Side of Silence* (London and New York, 1970) that metaphors are structurally "scaffoldings around invisible reality" (p. 45).

20. *Jerusalem* 88:4, 5. Cf. John M. Hill's interesting thesis about *Pearl* in "Middle English Poets and the Word," *Criticism,* 16 (1974), 153–69, especially: the dreamer "speaks of a melting mind . . . which suggests that to say truly 'of that syght' requires baffled reason and melting consciousness. Comprehension, then, would mean an entering into rather than an observation of and reference to mystical domain" (p. 166).

21. Jameson, *The Prison-House of Language,* p. 158; T. S. Eliot, *East Coker* V.

V. A. DE LUCA

Proper Names in the Structural Design of Blake's Myth-Making

Blake's principles of naming in his mythopoetic works have received little systematic attention. Commentaries, to be sure, repeatedly attempt to translate particular proper names into relevant terms of discursive significance, seeking out their etymologies in disguised puns and literary borrowings. Sometimes a comprehensive rationale is offered, usually to the effect that Blake's invented names work to disrupt associations with received mythologies.[1] Such explanations, useful as they are in certain contexts, tend to subordinate to general interpretive interests an attention to the peculiar properties of these names as linguistic data. One such property of the invented name, obvious when stated though seldom discussed, is the exotic oddity of its appearance, its phonetic and orthographic remoteness from the norms of expected naming in spoken or literary usage. The strangeness of such names does not dissipate, moreover, when they are found combined in Blake's narrative with names not of his invention, names of historical, Biblical, or legendary provenance. Such combinations serve only to complicate the mystery of the poet's name-generating principles. We do not serve Blake well when we treat the palpable strangeness of his poetic surfaces as something other than strangeness, as much criticism tends dangerously to do that seeks pragmatically

---

This essay first appeared in *Blake Studies* 8 [1978]: 5–22. Reprinted with permission.

to transmute the oddities of his verse into terms conforming to his thematic arguments.[2] The exploratory investigation of Blake's naming patterns that I propose in this paper stresses the autonomy of these patterns, their independence from (although not their irrelevance to) discursive significance. In so doing, I hope to illuminate, within the limitations of my scope, some fundamental elements of the creative principles that inform the Prophecies.

In the tripartite division of my subject that follows, I seek first, within a broad context, to identify the role of proper names in Blake and then to apply in detail some systematic models of analysis to localized patterns of naming, viewed as functional modes of that general role. This investigation involves the testing of three hypotheses. The first asserts the principle of the autonomy of his names, that is, their frequently arbitrary use and the primacy of their status as self-referential and irreducible elements in his poetry. The second develops from the first and asserts the tendency for new names, sometimes whole clusters of names, to be generated out of the phonetic material of previously invented names associated with them, with only a tangential relation to their referents. The third asserts the tendency of clusters of names recurrently linked to one another or to other clusters to form mutual relations of opposition and concord, both on the phonetic level and on more complex levels of categorization. My examples are representative rather than exhaustive, and I do not claim that the hypotheses they illustrate account for all the onomastic data we may discover in Blake's writings. I do maintain, nonetheless, that their manifestations are sufficiently prevalent and clearly defined as to indicate a major element of his mythopoetic technique.

1. *The autonomy of the mythic name.* For non-adept readers, one of Blake's most puzzling habits is his way of introducing unknown proper names before presenting the context which will make these names intelligible, and sometimes no such context ever appears. To cite an extreme instance, in Night VIII of *The Four Zoas,* Los addresses Rahab, providing her and the reader with an astonishing list of his progeny:

> And these are the Sons of Los & Enitharmon Rintrah
> Palamabron

Theotormon Bromion Antamon Ananton Ozoth Ohana
Sotha Mydon Ellayol Natho Gon Harhath Satan
(*FZ* viii, 115:1–3, E365/K350)[3]

This is not the entire list, which continues for another six lines, eliding names of Blake's invention with Biblical and historical names and then unfolding into a similar catalogue of daughters. The lines quoted, however, are sufficient to provoke some essential observations. Only the first four names refer to characters of importance in Blake's myth, some (Antamon, Sotha, and Ozoth) appear sporadically elsewhere, and the rest (aside from Satan) are apparently summoned into existence for this one occasion, never to appear again. It seems gratuitous to speculate, as some commentators have done, upon the possible symbolic reference of these nonce creations, as if characters with a specifiable significance maintained an independent if shadowy existence behind them in Blake's imagination.[4] What is more readily apparent is their arbitrary effect, since nothing in the surrounding context of Los's speech serves to identify them further, nor does the elaborate specificity of the roll call contribute to the communicative value of the context. It seems clear that Blake's preoccupation with naming so far overtakes the claims of narrative continuity that whole blocks of verse comprise nothing but names, a large proportion of them wholly mysterious. The effect is incantatory, a reconstitution of a primitive numinous power inherent in a ritualized utterance of sonorous syllables. In such instances the invented name, perceived simply as an exotic element within the stream of apprehensible verbal communication, achieves an iconic status, a status that precedes its possible function as a sign representing conceptual equivalents.[5]

As semi-sacred icons, proper names in Blake seem to work like spells, encapsulated portions of imaginative energy that derive from the permanent forms of "Los's Halls" from which "every Age renews its powers" (*J* 16:62, E159/K638). Thus when the poet speaks of

the Daughters of Albion
Names anciently remembered, but now contemn'd as fictions!
Although in every bosom they controll our Vegetative powers.
(*J* 5:37–39, E146/K624)

the ambiguity of syntax and pronoun reference permits a sense in which the names rather than the Daughters exercise control. And indeed they must, for the term "Daughters" is generic and a metaphoric poetic license, whereas the Celtic names, culled out of Geoffrey of Monmouth from still more ancient sources, are irreducible, the direct equivalents in language of particular essences. If this is in fact what Blake is suggesting here, it helps to explain not only why odd names crop up so abundantly in his writings but also why there is so much attention to listing particular names ("And these their Names & their Places within the Mundane Shell"; "And these the names of the Twenty-seven Heavens and their Churches" [*M* 37:19, 35, E136/K528]), and why behind the odd names of certain characters we find the hovering presence of other odd names ("Los was the fourth immortal starry one . . ./ . . . Urthona was his name / in Eden" [*FZ* i, 3:9–4:1 E297/K264]).

To restore ancient remembrance, Blake not only lists names explicitly but frequently subjects us to verbatim repetitions of the lists, sometimes inscribing the individual components of an associated cluster of names in a virtually invariant formulaic order. Thus when the Four Zoas appear named together, Luvah and Tharmas are always placed in contiguous positions, and Urizen and Urthona either occupy contiguous positions preceding the other pair (*M* 19:16–17; 34[38]:35–36, *J* 59:11–12) or first and last positions respectively (*J* 38[43]:2–3; 63:4; 74:4; 96:41; 97:7–11); no other variations occur. Similarly we find the inflexible order of Los's Sons, Rintrah, Palamabron, Theotormon, and Bromion (*FZ* viii, 115:1–2; *M* 24:11–12; *J* 71:51; 74:2), repeated as a spell of might, although as characters the latter two at least have had virtually nothing to do since *Visions of the Daughters of Albion.* The arbitrary orderings of such names, their repetitions, the exotic appearance of the individual names themselves, supply their own *raison d'etre.* Just as Los must build "the stubborn structure of the Language, acting against/ Albions melancholy, who must else have been a Dumb despair" (*J* 36[40]:59–60, E181/K668), Blake must conjure an exacting sense of particularized mythic presences to jolt us from our complacent attachment to easy generalizations and our slumbering forgetfulness of ancient power. We must encounter the names of that power, for good or ill, as hard, "stubborn" givens in order to recognize them or to allow them to renew our own powers.

The autonomy of mythic names and their formulaic arrangements imply that they function collectively as a principle of structure in Blake's works and not a principle of conceptual reference. They serve to separate the world of Divine Vision from that of space and time and yet to enforce their necessary confrontation. If they compose *in toto* a "stubborn structure," a multi-latticed gate repelling or inviting our entrance into the Divine Vision, according to the variation of our perceptions, each separate name may be considered as a fragmented individuation of that structure, pointing to the hypothetical existence of some nameless *Ur*-name, the name of the Divine Vision itself. At the same time any given name has the potential of giving rise to new individuations, of fathering new names to cut into the continuum of the common speech. One is reminded of the speculations of the great Swiss linguist Ferdinand de Saussure, who claimed to observe in the phonetic patterns of ordinary Latin verse concealed anagrams of the names of gods and heroes.[6] However accurate his particular discoveries, they depend upon the premise that for the ancient poet the divine name has intrinsic power, distinct from its use in a particular text, and maintains a retentive hold upon succeeding poetic forms. Since this premise seems embodied in Blake's practice, if the examples set forth above are indicative, we may expect to find similar distributions of the literal substance of his mythic names in the creation of new name-formations. In this way, the name, functioning as part of a larger structural body devoted to enforcing states of separation and relation, may contain within itself a minute mirror of that larger operation. To examine this possibility, we need to focus our attention upon some more sharply particularized bits of evidence than the argument thus far has demanded.

2. *Names begetting names within the Blakean corpus.* It is never entirely clear whether Blake coins names at the dictates of narrative and thematic exigencies, whether the form of the name summons appropriate contexts, or whether context and name-formation, even if related, are essentially independent of

one another. Most critics assume the first possibility (in some cases justifiably), but I wish to test the viability of the latter two, particularly the third. Plate 14 of *Europe* provides a useful place to start. After awakening from her eighteen-hundred-year sleep, Enitharmon summons nine of her children to her presence, in the process imposing on Blake the need to invent five names he has not used before. Leutha, Oothoon, Theotormon, and Orc have appeared previously; Ethinthus, Manathu-Vorcyon, Antamon, Sotha and Thiralatha are new. Of the nine individuals so named, only Orc acts in opposed response to Enitharmon's summons, shooting into "the vineyards of red France" (*E* 15:2, E65/K245); the other eight remain silent and presumably acquiescent to their mother's demands. What is striking about these eight is that all of their names reflect prominently, though in varying proportions and with slight shiftings, phonetic elements of Enitharmon's name, as if a primary name matched its referent in propagating descendants. De Saussure's principle of an anagrammatic distribution of the phonetic content of primary names comes to mind as we observe, for example, in seven of the eight names the central phoneme *th* of *Enitharmon,* running through the list like a genetic code. The exception, *Antamon,* corroborates the rule, for this name is closer in form to the progenitor than any of the others, showing only three small alterations, a dentalizing of the *th,* an absorption of the weak phonemes *i* and *r,* and a slide from *e* to *a* in the initial vowel; in other respects the sequence of vowels and consonants remains unchanged. Similar replications and redistributions occur throughout the remainder. Each of the first two syllables of *Ethinthus* simply repeats and condenses the initial half of *Enitharmon,* the first syllable eliminating *ni,* the second transposing *ni* and eliminating the *e.* The first portion of *Manathu-Vorcyon* alters the vowels of both the second and fourth syllables of *Enitharmon* to *a* and then collocates these syllables in transposed order, eliding into a final element that resembles the final element of *Ethinthus.* (The second portion *Vorcyon* introduces new phonemes in prominent positions but curiously embeds orthographically within itself *Orc.*) The second half of *Theotormon* virtually repeats the second half of *Enitharmon* with the *th* dentalized and the vowel shifted to *o;* the shift to *o* penetrates the first two syllables as well, but the remaining letters here reflect elements in the first half of the progenitor name. *Oothoon* resembles a radical contraction of *Enitharmon,* absorbing all the phonemes into its diphthongized *o*'s except for the medial and final consonants. *Leutha, Sotha,* and *Thiralatha* all introduce phonemes not found in the progenitor name, but it appears that they pick up subsidiary elements from the "descendant" names. The *thu* combination of *Ethinthus* and *Manathu* appears transposed in *Leutha,* which introduces an *l.* The second half of *Thiralatha* in turn reflects *Leutha* with a vowel shift, the rest of the name deriving anagrammatically from *Enitharmon. Sotha* draws upon *Oothoon, Thiralatha* and the final syllable of *Ethinthus,* with consonants inverted.

The unmistakable presence of these phonetic family resemblances leads one to the inference that the generating principle of Blake's name-formations here resides in an autonomous linguistic activity and not in appropriate associations derived from the function of the characters. Thus, for example, there is nothing in the name *Ethinthus* to associate the character with a "queen of waters" (*Europe:* 14:1), but much to associate it with the name *Enitharmon,* although that represents a mother of elements. The point seems to be that Blake's myth-making activity and his verbal invention operate upon parallel but independent lines, each activity conforming to its own internal principles of elaboration; children unfold from Enitharmon's world as their names manifest an inheritance from the progenitor name. In speaking of *Enitharmon* as a "progenitor name," I am of course aware that this invention in *Europe* follows the appearance of Leutha, Theotormon, and Oothoon in *Visions of the Daughters of Albion* by at least a year. To the principle of *ad hoc* coinage of names out of a single name, we must add a principle of a gravitation of pre-existent names toward a phonetically hospitable context. Out of the storehouse of such names Blake selects those whose phonetic appearance is such as fortuitously to make them seem further examples of the anagrammatic principle determining the form of their neighbors. (It may be significant that the remaining figure of importance in *Visions of the Daughters of Albion,* Bromion, lacking the crucial *th* or its approximation in his name, is excluded here, although Enitharmon in her repressive mood would certainly want to call on him.) The ease with which these names assimilate themselves to the phonetic ambience of Enitharmon's name tends to confirm the influence of abstract letter-play upon Blake's onomastic activity.

Other types of letter-play operate in this generation of new names from old besides the kind of anagrammatic distributions we have just examined. Thus the fecund name of Enitharmon propagates not only the names of her children but of her parents as well, as Blake's developing myth calls for such roles. In the earliest extant stratum of Night I of *The Four Zoas,* the poet abruptly introduces two new figures. One is "Tharmas Parent power. darkening in the West," who calls upon "Enion [to] come forth," demanding to know from her, "Why hast thou taken Enitharmon from my inmost soul?" (*FZ* i, 4:4,11 as recreated in textual notes E 740). As Damon and others have observed, both *Tharmas* and *Enion* result from back formations of *Eni-tharm-on.*[7] This seems the most plausible derivation of the new names, since both of them appear for the first time in close proximity with their apparent progenitor, whereas other etymological associations seem secondary at best and *ex post facto.*[8] Here again the propagation of names and the propagation of mythic narrative appear to operate on independent but parallel lines. When *Enion* "comes forth" as an independent entity, the primal unity (or "inmost soul") of *Enitharmon* and *Tharmas* is also rended, leaving the latter in separate isolation.

Another major figure first appearing in *The Four Zoas* also seems to acquire a name through a similar "twinning" process:

Then behold a wonder to the Eyes
Of the now fallen Man a double form Vala appeard. A Male
And female shuddring pale the Fallen Man recoild
From the Enormity & calld them Luvah & Vala. . . .
(vii[a], 83:13–16, E351/K326)

Although the names of Luvah and Vala have occurred in profusion before this point in the poem, this passage supplies the clearest pattern to their relation. *Luvah* and *Vala* are indeed mirror "doubles," mutually inverted syllable-pairs, kept from perfect orthographic mirroring only by the silent *h* in the first name and the shift in the initial vowel (if, indeed, Blake associated the name Luvah, who first appears in *Thel* [3:7–8] as a sun-god, with "lava" as some commentators have speculated,[9] the evidence for a "mirroring" principle in the propagation of *Vala* becomes more secure). To assert such a derivation for *Vala* is not to deny the relevance of other associations attached to the name (although the "Veil" of Vala makes its first appearance in *Jerusalem* 20:3 and seems a derivative of the name rather than the reverse, while derivations from the *Eddas* seem merely remote and speculative). Rather, it places primary focus upon a self-motivating linguistic activity that appears simultaneously improvisational and structurally patterned. Such a focus gains validity in revealing another manifestation of the technique of "twinning" or symmetrical balancing that informs Blake's myth-making generally.[10]

A different mode of propagation from a progenitor name, involving the processes of both phonetic distribution and twinning, may be called phonetic devolution. Here the component elements in the first of a series of names are altered, stage by stage, as the series progresses, until a virtual transformation is attained in the final name. A salient instance occurs in Plate 34 of *Milton,* where Ololon descends from Beulah to the Ulro and passes through "the Four States of Humanity in its Repose" (*M* 34:8):

First of Beulah a most pleasant Sleep
On Couches soft, with mild music, tended by Flowers of Beulah
Sweet Female forms, winged or floating in the air spontaneous
The Second State is Alla & the third State Al-Uro;
But the Fourth State is dreadful; it is named Or-Ulro:
(*M* 34:9–13, E133/K523–24)

Of these four names, Beulah is of course borrowed from Isaiah lxii:4 and becomes prominent in Blake's work at the time of the later stages of composition in *The Four Zoas.* Blake's own coinage, Ulro, dates from the same period, but the variant forms Al-Uro and Or-Ulro appear only on this plate of *Milton,* and Alla reappears fleetingly only in *Jerusalem* 89:58. It appears highly likely then that the three latter names are nonce formations, created to give specificity to Ololon's descent. The phonetic relationships of the names to one another comprise a descent of their own, a structure to match the mythic narrative. This structure becomes apparent if we transcribe the names of the four states in order vertically, aligning similar elements directly beneath one another. Thus:

B			eul	ah	
	Al		l	a	
	Al		Ul		ro
		Or	Ul		ro

The matrix formed by this vertical transcription allows us to perceive, first, a persistence of the phoneme *l* throughout the series, like the encoding *th* of Enitharmon's progeny in *Europe;* second, a progression from a pair of bi-syllabic to a pair of tri-syllabic names; third, a progression from orthographic asymmetry in the first name in each pair to symmetry in the second. Subsidiary patterns of descent reinforce this devolving structure. Thus *Alla* inherits the final syllable of *Beulah,* transposing its sounded letters to form the first syllable. *Al-Ulro* directly inherits the first syllable of *Alla,* blends an echo of this syllable with the more remotely inherited *ul* of *Beulah* to form the second syllable, and adds the new final element *ro. Or-Ulro* directly inherits this final element and reproduces it in reverse to form the first syllable, while preserving in its medial position the *ul* from the immediate antecedent. *Alla* thus partakes of Beulah, *Al-Ulro* of *Alla, Or-Ulro* of *Al-Ulro,* but with progressive mutations, in which the *a* sound so prominent in the upper part of the series disappears, leaving a name which partakes, as it were, only of "Ulro" substance. Just as Ololon descends through the Four States of Humanity in its Repose from a "most pleasant" to a "dreadful" state, the reader's eye also descends through a small phonetic universe of names, whose patterned stages of alteration mirror not the conceptual associations of their mythic referents but a diagrammatic abstract of their devolution.

Several implications emerge this consideration of representative clusters of name-formation. These formations suggest that Blake's creative methods conjoin a high degree of spontaneous invention with an equally high degree of ordered patterning. Names seem to spin off from other names in a centrifugal profusion that betrays little evidence of any laborious conceptualizing preceding the process. These repeated spin-offs give to the surface of Blake's prophetic poems much of its cluttered and arbitrarily-wrought appearance. At the same time, however, we observe a centripetal tendency operating which counteracts the effects of this centrifugal invention. The inventions do not issue in random isolation but in clusters bound together by patterns of mutual relation. These self-subsistent structures of relation, moreover, show a marked tendency to correlate with analogous patterns of mythic narrative, correlated in turn (as the mass of hermeneutic commentary on Blake has shown so successfully) with patterns of discursive concept. Diverse and independent patterns thus tend to gravitate toward one another as Blake shapes his material. If this is the case, we can expect that names formed in previous contexts may gravitate together in new contexts to form mutual relationships, as the need arises for mirroring structures correspondent to particular patterns of myth or concept. These considerations bring us to my third hypothesis about Blake's principles of naming.

3. *Organized patterns of internal relation among associated names.* Some of these patterns manifest themselves on the levels of phonetic arrangement and orthography, as in the instances considered above, and some, particularly those involving names borrowed from external sources, bring into play elements that relate to their derivation and their contextual associations. To cite an instance of the former patterning, we may examine a cluster of names occurring in the long description of the "World of Los" in *Milton.* Around the precincts of Golgonooza Blake groups the regenerative forms of Bowlahoola and Allamanda (*M* 24:48–50, 27:42–43, 29:25) and situates these among the unregenerate forms of "The Lake of Udan-Adan, in the Forests of Entuthon Benython" (*M* 26:25, E122/K512; cf. also 27:43, 50). If we apply the principle of binary opposition fundamental to structuralist analysis and occasionally applied by its adherents to Blake's verse, we can observe more precisely how the relationships formed by these names as linguistic data mirror the relationships of their referents.[11] The internal affinities that bind together *Golgonooza, Bowlahoola,* and *Allamanda* are clear enough (I suspect that the two latter are nonce spin-offs from

the former, previously invented in *The Four Zoas*): the three tetrasyllabic names end in *a*, the first two syllables of each rhyme assonantally with the second two (if one allows the diphthongized *o*'s in the second half of *Bowlahoola* and *Golgonooza* to pass as an eye-rhyme and assumes the medial *o* of *Golgonooza* to be pronounced as a *schwa*), *Golgonooza* and *Bowlahoola* rhyme assonantally, and *Bowlahoola* is bound to *Allamanda* by an identity of its second syllable.[12] The affinities between *Udan-Adan* and *Entuthon Benython* are these: both are compound names, with an identical number of syllables in the component halves of each name, a replication of the final syllable in each component half, and differentiation between the elements of each half preceding the final syllable. The termination upon *n* in each name further binds the two together. Both sets of names are thus characterized by repetitions in the halves of each individual name and a sharing of elements with associate names in the set. But the two sets are distinguished from one another by a differentiation of elements common to one set but not the other, and vice versa, for example, the opposition between closed syllable and open syllable terminations in the respective half-names and between single-term and compound-term names. All the names are thus bound together in relation, as are their referents, but they also form two opposing classes in confrontation. As an autonomous pattern of phonetic oppositions and concordances, the relation of the names is in no way dependent upon the relation of the regions in Los's World but may well serve as a microcosmic paradigm of this large relation, an abstract anatomy of that world's organization.

In other passages we encounter clusters of names set in a matrix which enforces more compactly a sense of their mutual internal relationships. The naming of the Zoas is a case in point:

> Four Universes round the Mundane Egg remain Chaotic
> One to the North, named Urthona: One to the South,
> named Urizen:
> One to the East, named Luvah: One to the West named
> Tharmas
>
> (*M* 19:15–17, E111/K500)

The compass points locate the Four Zoas geometrically in a conceptual space that is not space at all, for the Zoas are simultaneously universes, persons, and principles in the human psyche and culture. Given this indeterminancy of literal location, Blake's diagrammatic precision here becomes self-referential, pointing not to actual space but to a spatialization of abstract elements. The binary patterns that inform the relations of the names here become clear if we set them up in the diagrammatic scheme Blake suggests:

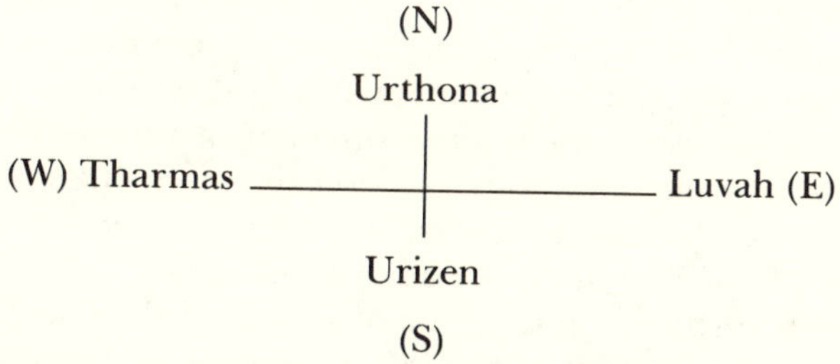

The North-South axis, *Urthona-Urizen,* distinguishes itself from the East-West, *Luvah-Tharmas,* by the following properties: the names in the first pair each have three syllables, those of the second, two; the first pair is marked by identity of the first syllable *(Ur)* and differentiation in the remaining syllables, whereas *Luvah-Tharmas* match final syllables through assonantal rhyme but vary initially; the first pair begins with vowels, the second with consonants; the first pair is vocalically rich, containing in the two names all five vowels, the second pair vocalically poor, sharing only the two back vowels *a* and *u.* To this opposition generated between the two directional axes, we must add oppositions between the poles of each axis. Thus the latter syllables of *Urthona* display the back vowels *o* and *a* and proceed to a final vowel; those of *Urizen* display the front vowels *i* and *e* and proceed to a final consonant. The opposition between *Luvah* and *Tharmas* is less marked (perhaps because we think more readily of North and South poles than of East and West), yet even here there is a contrast between the two closed syllables of *Tharmas* and the two open of *Luvah.* All of these phonetic antagonisms are balanced by a collective tendency toward phonetic inclusiveness. The accents in the four names fall, starting counterclockwise with *Urizen* upon *i, u, o,* and *a,* as many of the primary vowels as a fourhold scheme can hold (*Urizen* may incorporate a stressed phonetic *e* as well as an orthographic *i,* if a possible punning reference to "your reason" influences its pronunciation), and the succession of these vowels around the compass roughly resembles the succession of vowel positions in the mouth.

The niceties of these phonetic arrangements amount to more than some sort of subconscious verbal gamesmanship. The Zoas comprise the various faculties of Albion, the primal human community now fallen into ruins and relations of antagonism instead of mutual support. Thus the dynamic system of opposition, congruence, and complement among the phonetic parts of the names precisely mirrors the situation of the Zoas, forever pulling away from one another, yet seeking each other to reconstitute the totality of the primal man. The system of relationships made manifest in the orientations of the Zoas is of course a much later formulation than the invention of the names themselves (*Luvah* is a creation of 1789, *Urizen* and *Urthona* of 1793, *Tharmas* of approximately 1797), and it is hardly credible that Blake had it cunningly in mind from the start. It is more likely that having accumulated such names over the course of years, the poet begins to sense their potentiality to enter schematic relations with one another and hence their appropriateness to represent a quaternary scheme independently developing in his mythic conceptions. The precise polarities generated by the components of preexistent names thus correspond by more than miraculous accident to the polarities of a later conceptual mapping. Blake's gravitating sense of the relationships possible among these names eventually crystallizes and precipitates into the compact transcription of the map itself, a microcosm of Albion's divisions and his latent unity.

If small clusters of names, like those in the "Four Universes" passage, represent microcosmic anatomies of imaginative reality, individuated components of an unnamed unity, the whole poetic body of the later Prophecies, particularly *Jerusalem,* may be taken as its macrocosmic form. *Jerusalem* represents, among other things, a vast storehouse of names, derived from Blake's inventions and from external sources, often linked in collective chains. In their proliferation these names are suggestive of a shattered unity, and in their aggregate of its potential restoration. As we examine the type of names that occur in *Jerusalem,* a quaternary pattern, such as informs the names of the Zoas, emerges. Four categories of names, grouped according to the source of their derivation, dominate the poem, first, names of Blake's invention, like Los and Enitharmon, Vala and Luvah (to cite the most prominent); second, Biblical names, particularly the names of the Twelve Sons of Israel; third, names derived from ancient British tradition, particularly those of the twelve Daughters of Albion, Cambel, Gwendolyn, Conwenna, Cordella, Ignoge, Gwiniverra, Gwinefred, Gonorill, Sabrina, Estrild, Mehetabel and Ragan (*J* 5:41–44); and fourth, names that hover between nonce invention and external derivation, particularly the twelve sons of Albion, Hand, Hyle, Cogan, Kwantok, Peachey, Brereton, Slayd, Hutton, Scofield, Kox, Kotope, and Bowen (*J* 5:25, 27). The significance of this last set of names, taken as a whole, is not to be found in autobiographical allusion or the presumption of such, but in their approximation to contemporary English names in shape and pronunciation, though with orthographic distortions that render them bizarre and faintly ludicrous, like many of the inventions of Dickens. As a group these deformations of modern English names contrast markedly with the mellifluous and polysyllabic names of Albion's daughters, "Names anciently remembered" because derived from the mythography of a Britain that has new slipped into legend. A similar contrast appears between the clearly foreign (though familiar) Hebraic names and the Lambeth-minted (though exotic) names of Blake's private myth, one set coming from an ancient Bible, the other from a new "Bible of Hell: which the world shall have" (*MHH* 24).

The four sets of names thus organize themselves about two intersecting lines of polarity, according to their provenance, one a polarity of the ancient and the contemporary, the other a polarity of the sacred and the secular. Once again, an appropriation of a model of structuralist analysis may help us make sense of the pattern these polarities create. In *The Savage Mind,* Lévi-Strauss observes a fourfold pattern in the naming of animals in our culture, based on two kinds of polar distinctions. One of these pertains to the creatures' perceived similarity or dissimilarity to the name-giving culture in form or activity; the other pertains to their conceptual relation to that culture, which is seen either as *metonymic* (contiguity to the individuals of that culture) or as *metaphoric* (parallel but independent representation of the culture as a collective whole). His aim, to show that the principles of naming form "a coherent system," applies to our similar account of the profuse naming in *Jerusalem.*[13] Thus we find that the names of the Sons and Daughters of Albion both belong to a metonymic order relative to the poet's culture, the former because they are contiguous to the poet's locality in space (since their names approximate those of contemporary Englishmen), the latter because they are contiguous in time (representing the locality's ancient Celtic inheritance). The Biblical names and those of Blake's invention belong, on the other hand, to a metaphoric order. The Sons of Israel represent an independent parallel to the Sons of Albion, removed from them in both time and space but related to them though elaborate equations which stud the poem (particularly *J* 16:35–58, 71:10–49). The Blakean names belong to characters who occupy contemporary space and time (e.g., "Los stands in London building Golgonooza," *J* 10:17, E151/K629, "Luvah is France," *J* 66:15, E216/K702), but these characters are "Giant forms," not contiguous to any individuals within the poet's society but above them, below them, and in them. Putting these relationships and distinctions together, we thus discover that names of the Sons of Albion represent metonymic contemporaries, those of Blake's "Giant forms" metaphoric contemporaries, those of the Daughters of Albion metonymic ancestors, and those of the Sons of Israel metaphoric ancestors. The system of names elicited through this analysis thus provides a structure that separates and conjoins propinquity and remoteness in space and time, paradigm and corporeal existence, a mirror of the fragmentations and pulls toward unity which are *Jerusalem*'s essential theme.

It may be observed that for three of the four categories of names, there are certain pre-eminent names belonging to characters whose activity persists in the period of apocalypic reawakening: Los of the Blakean names, Albion of the names from British tradition, Jesus and Jerusalem of the Hebraic. There is no representative of the contemporary English names, an indication that these deformations of the corporeal present are states to be purged away. In the last plates of *Jerusalem* three of these pre-eminent names drop out, one by one, Los at *J* 96:32, absorbed in Jesus, Jesus at *J* 96:42, Albion at *J* 97:6, until all the diverse attributes of Humanity converge to be identified in one name, which concludes the poem: "And I heard the Name of their Emanations they are named Jerusalem" (*J* 99:5, E256/K747). Thus all the invented exotic names and the recondite borrowed ones disappear, leaving finally a traditional name central to English spiritual culture. In view of all the stress I have placed upon the arbitrary autonomy of Blake's naming principles, a final word on this situation is necessary here.

In citing at various points in this paper models of structuralist analysis as germane to my approach, I have implicitly recommended the relevance of that analysis to Blake, predicated as it is upon the assumption of autonomous pattern-making powers that lie behind the semantic and discursive surfaces of texts. That such powers operate pervasively in Blake's creativity I think is unquestionable, but it is a year of dearth indeed when criticism discovers number, weight, and measure as the deep essence of that activity, as if the poet were Urizen with his rectilinear diagrams, "unknown, abstracted/ brooding secret" (*Urizen* 3:6–7, E69/K222). A similar reservation is reflected in the frequently encountered objections to structuralism as coldly abstract and deterministic. But it is the particular genius of a poet such as Blake to make structures manifest, to energize them as aids to vision and not to enslave himself to their control. Blake should be viewed not in the context of Lévi-Strauss's tribal community, unknowingly transmitting through myth concealed ruling codes, but as one of Lévi-Strauss's composers, a creator and master of structure.[14] The dialectical structurings that abound through Blake's work (and his patterns of naming represent only one) are the frames of his gates to imaginative vision and not its virtual objects. Those objects are "exemplars of Memory and of Intellect," seen "according to the Expansion or Contraction" of our liberated senses (*J* 98:30, 36, E255/K746). And to that liberty Blake applies a familiar name, for "Jerusalem is called Liberty among the Children of Albion" (*J* 54:5, E201/K684).

Earlier in this paper, I spoke of Blake's more recondite

names, the names used to form notations of structural organization, as "semi-sacred icons," suggestive in their irreducible particularity of the Divine power in its individuated form. Although the exotic mystery of their appearance enhances their iconicity, the mystery in no way forms the basis of their sacred character, a notion that would be anathema to Blake. Their strange form, rather, is really a way of exemplifying our own estrangement from the Divine Vision, seen as remote and obscure in our fallen state. Once perceived as such, these names become tools in the dialectical workshop of our regeneration, like cogs "formd in a wheel to turn the cogs of the adverse wheel" (*M* 27:10, E123/K513). When the poet depicts unfallen states, however, as in the last plates of *Jerusalem* or in his evocations of prelapsarian unity, he strives to create a climate of familiarity:

> The fields from Islington to Marybone,
> To Primrose Hill and Saint Johns Wood:
> Were builded over with pillars of gold,
> And there Jerusalems pillars stood.
>
> (*J* 27:1–4, E170/K649)

The quaternary cluster of names here belong to no conceptual space of abstract polarities but are drawn from a unified, contemporary, near-to-home locale, pressed into merger with a name equally familiar yet from ancient and sacred sources (although not sacred in any sense connoting hierophantic lore). To give us the liberty of our ancestral home, Blake here speaks to us in the names we know. When at the end of *Jerusalem* he presses all disparates toward identification with its eponymous protagonist, we recognize in its final utterance a name to destroy the power of the mystery of names, a name to bring us home.

Notes

1. It hardly seems profitable to note comprehensively the attempts of Blake's commentators to identify allusive references in his proper names, since the attempts are so common and the identifications so varied. I cite individual instances of such identification where they are relevant to my own discussion. Probably the most extensive and scrupulous effort appears scattered through

the notes of Harold Bloom's "Commentary" in *The Poetry Prose of William Blake*, ed. David V. Erdman, 4th printing, rev. (Garden City, N.Y.: Doubleday, 1970), pp. 807–889. The part that Blake's name-inventions play in a reaction against received myth is best explained by Northrop Frye in *Fearful Symmetry: A Study of William Blake* (Princeton: Princeton Univ. Press, 1947), p. 119: "This is why we meet so many new names in Blake and find ourselves reading about Vala and Urizen instead of Venus and Zeus. . . . To Venus and Zeus we bring memories and associations rather than a concentrated response, and are thus continually impelled to search outside the poem being read for its meaning." This is a sensible observation, but Frye would have Blake himself searching outside of his own poem if only to discover what to avoid, a view which grants less autonomy to the generative principles behind his naming than I am prepared to accept. For a recent comment similar to Frye's but stressing the primacy of Blake's invented names as the "real" names of the eternal beings, see Roger Murray, "Blake and the Ideal of Simplicity," *Studies in Romanticism*, 13 (Spring 1974), 93.

2. Jerome J. McGann has expressed this cautionary view in a most pointed way: "To the degree that one regards Blake's art as an object of analysis and interpretation, to that degree any criticism fosters such a view, to that degree has Blake been misused, even . . . misread" ("The Aim of Blake's Prophecies and Uses of Blake Criticism," in *Blake's Sublime Allegory: Essays on The Four Zoas, Milton and Jerusalem*, ed. Stuart Curran and Joseph A. Wittreich [Madison: Univ. of Wisconsin Press, 1973], pp. 3–4).

3. All references are from E: *The Poetry and Prose of William Blake*, ed. David V. Erdman, 4th printing, rev. (Garden City, N.Y.: Doubleday, 1970) and K: *The Complete Writings of William Blake*, ed. Geoffrey Keynes, 3rd printing, rev. (Oxford: Oxford Univ. Press, 1971) using the following abbreviations *FZ: The Four Zoas; M: Milton; J: Jerusalem; MHH: The Marriage of Heaven and Hell; Urizen: The Book of Urizen.*

4. See, e.g. Bloom, "Commentary," E 881, and S. Foster Damon, *A Blake Dictionary: The Ideas and Symbols of William Blake* (Providence: Brown Univ. Press, 1965), p. 253.

5. See W. F. H. Nicolaisen, "Names as Verbal Icons." *Names*, 22 (September 1974), 104–110, a recent onomastic study which discusses how certain writers empower names to function as "verbal icons" or "pseudo-sacred images, in both sound and sense . . . removing them irrevocably from the realm of lexicographical definition and from the normal linguistic processes of encoding and decoding" (p. 109). Onomastic studies have, however, devoted scant attention to invented mythopoeic names. In "Ariston's Immortal Palace: Icon and Allegory in Blake's Prophecies," *Criticism*, 12 (Winter 1970), 1–19, I have argued for the presence of "iconic," anti-allegorical elements in Blake's myth-making generally. In the present context, see especially my point about the names of Golgonooza, Bowlahoola, and Allamanda in *Milton*, overtly proclaimed in certain passages as Eternal names, to which possible conceptual equivalents are mere terrestrial attachments (see pp. 10–11 and *M* 24:48–50, 27:42–43).

6. See "Les anagrammes de Ferdinand de Saussure," Textes préséntes par Jean Starobinski, *Mercure de France*, 350 (February 1964), 243–262. For a compact, general account of de Saussure's investigations see Charles Rosen, "Art Has Its Reasons," *New York Review of Books*, 16 (June 17, 1971), 35–36.

7. See *A Blake Dictionary*, p. 401.

8. Bloom suggests that the names of Tharmas and Enion derive from the sea god Thaumas and the shore goddess Eione in Hesiod's *Theogony* ("Commentary," E 866). Attractive as the suggestion seems, it makes the approximation of

the names to a split *Enitharmon* a fabulous linguistic coincidence and contradicts as well Frye's insight that Blake strives to sever from his creations associations of received myth, particularly classical (see Note 1, above). Instead of assuming that watery associations, in classical garb, determine the name and function of Blake's mythic characters, it may be best to assume that Blake "begins with Tharmas" as an arbitrary name, which attracts to itself by a process of association an ancient literary name and its attendant role. In a similar fashion, associations of Tharmas with doubt (*FZ* iv, 48:21) or later in *Milton* and *Jerusalem* with the Tongue may prompt identifications with "doubting Thomas" or the bold Thomas Paine, but the adventitious character of these associations suggests that *Tharmas* generates a hypothetical *Thomas* rather than the reverse. For the "Thomas" suggestion, see David V. Erdman, *Blake: Prophet Against Empire,* rev. ed. (Garden City, N.Y.: Doubleday, 1969), 298 ff.

9. See Erdman, *Prophet Against Empire,* p. 333.

10. Possibly the most intensive study of Blake's use of symmetrical divisions, mirroring, contrariety, and complementary opposition, observed in a single text, appears in Robert E. Simmons, "*Urizen:* The Symmetry of Fear," *Blake's Visionary Forms Dramatic,* ed. David V. Erdman and John E. Grant (Princeton: Princeton Univ. Press, 1970), pp. 146–173. Blake's fascination with "Contrary States" is of course pervasive throughout his writings and readily obvious to his readers.

11. The *locus classicus* for the structuralist principle of binary opposition, examined on the level of elementary phonetic discrimination, appears in Roman Jakobson and Morris Halle, *Fundamentals of Language* ('s-Gravenhage: Mouton, 1956), p. 38 f. For an application of the principle to Blake's verse on the syntactic level, see Jakobson's "On the Verbal Art of William Blake and Other Poet Painters," *Linguistic Inquiry,* 1 (January 1970), 3–23, and on the level of imagery, Michael Riffaterre, "The Self-sufficent Text" [reprinted in the present collection]. Speaking of "The Sick Rose," Riffaterre observes that "significance . . . is found in the structure first given by the text, with its network of binary oppositions and their transformations" (p. 44).

12. This may be the appropriate point to explain my avoidance generally in this paper of a precise technical vocabulary of phonetic description. Such a vocabulary would lack usefulness for a variety of reasons: first, because the patterns that Blake engenders depend on nothing more finely discriminated than would be readily accessible to a reader's general sense of common pronunciation and spelling; second, because there are no secure ways of determining Blake's pronunciation of his own invented names; and third, because in forming his patterns, he conflates phonetic elements with orthographic, relying on the latter to enforce sensed relationships established by the former. Thus the second vowels in *Bowlahoola* and *Golgonooza* accord to the ear, the second of the latter accords, to the eye, with the first and third of the former, and our general powers of analogy allow us to perceive similar kinds of patterning in the fourfold vocalic repetitions in Golgonooza and Allamanda (o-o-o-o-, a-a-a-a), where eye and ear suggest differentiation. None of this should be unexpected from a poet whose "every letter is studied and put into its fit place" (*J* 3, E144/K621). As Karl Kroeber has widely pointed out in discussing Blake's orthographic appeals to the eye, not only does graphic art accompany the text but "the poetry as poetry also is 'graphic' " ("Delivering Jerusalem," in *Blake's Sublime Allegory,* p. 349).

13. *The Savage Mind,* English version (Chicago: Univ. of Chicago Press, 1966), p. 208. Lévi-Strauss's argument (pp. 204–208) is too closely reasoned to reproduce here, but he emerges with a quaternary scheme in which birds are seen as "metaphorical human beings," dogs as "metonymical human beings,"

cattle as "metonymical inhuman beings," and racehorses as "metaphorical inhuman beings" (p. 207). I have freely adopted his model without necessarily endorsing these particular conclusions.

14. Thus Lévi-Strauss can say, at one point, "We are not claiming to show how men think the myths, but rather how they myths think themselves out in men and without men's knowledge" ("Overture to *le Cru et le cuit,*" trans. Joseph H. MacMahon, in Structuralism, ed., Jacques Ehrmann [Garden City, N.Y.: Doubleday, 1970], p. 46), but elsewhere in the same piece he speaks of a composer's score as cognate to the analysis of myths in revealing structure (p. 51) and of the "*creator* of music [as] a being like the gods" (p. 55, italics mine), or in Blakean terms, as one who has access to the Divine Vision. These later reflections seem to remove some of the implacable determinism suggested in his account of the transmission of structures.

DONALD AULT

Incommensurability and Interconnection in Blake's Anti-Newtonian Text

One of Blake's central purposes in constructing anti-Newtonian narrative was to create in his readers an experience of the bankruptcy of the kinds of assumptions about the interconnections in knowledge, perception, and reality which were embedded in the doctrine of *prisca sapientia*—the "ancient wisdom" which was believed by Newton and his contemporaries to have been revealed to Moses and to have been passed through the Hermetic Tablet and philosophers like Epicurus and the atomists.[1] Blake saw that this doctrine of the "one true system," which could connect such otherwise diverse modes of explanation as Biblical exegesis, alchemy, and scientific demonstration, presupposed a particular kind of single, coherent, unified world toward which all true explanation must point.[2] Blake also saw that such a "coherent" world (which Newton nevertheless believed needed to be explained) required, at the level of explanation, the rejection, suppression, and ruling out of massive aspects of human experience. Blake's methods of arming his reader against this desire to achieve such a false intergration of modes of explanation include: 1) the utilization of "incommensurable" deployment of narrative detail, to draw the reader's attention to

This essay first appeared in *Studies in Romanticism* 16 (Summer 1977): 277–303. Reprinted with permission.

conflicts which arise in the very nature of explanation; 2) the explicit attribution to the Spectre on the threshold of apocalypse (in *Jerusalem* Chapter 4) of an achieved *prisca sapientia* (in the precise context of the conflicts surrounding the doctrine in the seventeenth-century confrontation of science and alchemy); and 3) specific techniques opposed to the suppression both of the reader and of valid alternative modes of experience (a suppression which is characteristic of Newton in his Biblical and his scientific narrative). For example, Blake's technique will characteristically emphasize interconnections of characters and events (both in the "plot" and in the reader's experience), not by suppressing and rejecting "false" alternatives, but by highlighting the very "facts" of incommensurability on which the narrative insists.

It is significant that recent Newton scholarship has been intensely directed toward creating a new image of Newton, a Newton who was attempting to grapple with and integrate into a single system his work in empirical science, alchemy, the Hermetic tradition, and Biblical exegesis, but who failed (at least publicly) to achieve such an integration. For our purposes, it is also significant that Paul Feyerabend, in his "anarchist" work *Against Method,*[3] has simultaneously developed his most extended arguments (flying in the face of most entrenched concepts of scientific logic) for the existence of "incommensurable" frameworks of thought. Feyerabend attempts to show that even systems which may seem to bear structural analogies to one another really share no "facts," statements or theories. The world which implicitly lies behind Feyerabend's attack on conventional ideas of the way science "progresses," it seems to me, is a complex multiverse, not unlike Blake's, in which elements of crucial importance always escape explanation by any unified system, though they may be explained in another system, which, by the same token, allows other elements to escape. Since these two directions of recent scholarship—the attempts to find interconnections between systems of explanation which had previously been felt to be remote from one another or mutually exclusive of one another and the attempt to show that systems which seem comparable (such as classical and relativistic mechanics) are in fact incommensurable—are constructed to illuminate the history and philosophy of science, and, for our purposes, Newton in particular, it would be interesting (and significant) if insights developed for the analysis of science could shed light on techniques in Blake's poetry (a task, of course, for which they were not intended).

I

It must be made clear at the outset that the conflicting ways "facts" and "explanations" enter into Blake's radical narrative share only *some* of the characteristics of Feyerabend's incommensurable frameworks of thought. Blake's apparently "incommensurable" explanations of events are not mutually exclusive: they share the universal psychological/perceptual principle that exclusion or suppression of any central narrative element completely reorganizes the field of explanation. And frameworks which seem experientially incommensurable in Blake's narrative, though they may consciously be forgotten by the reader because of their mutual interference, are contained latently in a network of subconscious layering or sedimentation.[4] For Feyerabend, on the other hand, it seems incommensurable frameworks are mutually exclusive. For example, statements which use terms from both relativistic and classical mechanics "do not exist" (*Against Method,* p. 276). Feyerabend says of perceptual incommensurability: "These [incommensurable] families [of concepts] cannot be used simultaneously and neither logical nor perceptual relations can be established between them" (pp. 228–29). This principle requires that successive stages of perception in the individual (which are mutually incommensurable) cause previous phases to "disappear" or be "suppressed" (pp. 274, 228). Successive stages do not overlap, nor are previous stages contained in later phases: one system *replaces* another. For Feyerabend, scientific theories are related to one another in the same way. When a new theory succeeds an older one, only those elements explainable by the prior system which can be "distorted" to fit into the language of the new system are "remembered"; all others are suppressed (pp. 177–78). Feyerabend argues that the reason for the "illusion that we are dealing with the same subject matter," though in fact the theories share no common facts, is the confusion between "instrumentalistic" and "realistic" interpretation of the meaning of "facts."[5] What Feyerabend is suggesting, it seems to me, is that the assumption of a single world to be explained behind the variety of appearances gives rise to the illusion that all explanations which point toward that single world must themselves be mutually commensurable, coherent, and unified—part of a continuous unfolding process.

Feyerabend describes the "Swiss cheese" theory of language as follows: "Every cosmology (every language, every mode of perception) has sizeable lacunae which can be filled, *leaving everything else unchanged*" (*Against Method,* p. 266). This theory, it seems to me, is perfectly characteristic of Newton's approach to his own scientific enterprise, while it is precisely opposed to Blake's narrative ontology. In a revealing article, "Classical Empiricism," not directly related to the problem of incommensurability, Feyerabend, I think, bears out the accuracy of this view of Newton.[6] I would like to contrast the significance (and narrative form) of the *exclusion* (or temporary suppression) of elements or facts from a field of explanation in Newton and in Blake by contrasting Newton's "ray theory" of light (as Feyerabend has analyzed it) with some structural properties of Blake's narrative in *The Four Zoas,* Night I.

Feyerabend notes that Newton is able to *illustrate* his ray theory, but that, by means of idealizations, he regards his illustrations as an experimental basis for the truth of the theory ("Classical Empiricism," p. 160). Newton idealizes his illustrations in two ways. First, "peculiarities of each single experiment and those features of it which do not allow for an immediate description by the theory are *omitted*" (p. 162; my italics). This allows irrelevant or stray data to disappear. Second, experiments which readily express the theory are "*preferred* [my italics] to others which do not allow us to read the theory in one glance. Thus the different refrangibility of light is demonstrated in the most convincing fashion by the *experimentum crucis.*" Newton says, "If this demonstration be good, *there needs no further examination of the thing* [italics supplied by Feyerabend] . . . and seeing I am well assured of the truth and exactness of my own observations, *I shall be unwilling to be diverted by any other experiment* (p.

163; last italics mine). Lacunae in his theory—such as the absence of an explanation of diffraction by means of the initial properties attributed to light—are filled by Newton's addition of "new original properties" to light, in the manner, as Feyerabend notes, of *ad hoc* hypotheses. Certain features are suppressed in order to establish the theory, then these features are smuggled back in and distorted in the sense that they are explained by properties of light other than those originally postulated. This can happen, it seems, because the suppressed data are conceived now as somehow derivative or secondary to the phenomena which illustrate the theory. Huygen's "wave theory" of light, the contemporary challenger of Newton's theory, seized, as it were, the data Newton initially suppressed and made that data fundamental, while rectilinear propagation of light (which Newton's theory most easily accounted for as primary) could be explained with less radical addition of *ad hoc* properties to his light waves ("Classical Empiricism," pp. 166–67). Though these two theories are not in all ways incommensurable (for example, they do not mutually suspend "universal principles" of construction in the way Feyerabend feels is central to completely incommensurable systems [*Against Method,* p. 269]) the way these two theories constitute their data in terms of inverse priorities, which, in each case, gives rise initially to exclusion of some data from the field of explanation, causes radically conflicting constructions of what the data in fact *are.* Newton does not exploit the possibility that the data he omits initially may in fact constitute an alternative aspect of "reality" which, when taken into account, makes "facts" fit into the "world" in a totally different way. He wants to suppress that possibility ("no further examination of the thing") and desires to fill lacunae leaving all else unchanged. Further, Newton cannot make the focus of his demonstration the possibility that filling the lacunae might invert the whole nature of the field or that, more radically, *both* explanations may be necessary because the phenomena themselves are self-conflicting and not part of a unified world of the kind he is presupposing.

Blake's narrative, on the other hand, repeatedly derives both its plausibility and much of its characteristic power from the contrast between explanations because of the exclusion or suppression of elements from the narrative field. In *The Four*

Zoas, Night I,[7] the narration is divided into two major portions: the first two-thirds presents the sexual division of the characters Tharmas and Enion as narratively primary, from which warfare is generated (by a series of sequential surfacings of data suppressed in the initial confrontation between Tharmas and Enion)[8] in the form of an extended "Nuptial Song" at the feast of Los and Enitharmon; the final third of the Night (located in "Eternity") presents, in a story told by the Messengers of Beulah, the confrontation and warfare between Urizen and Luvah (who were subsidiary in the previous two-thirds of the Night) as narratively primary, from which sexual division between Tharmas and Enion is generated.[9] In the first portion of the Night, Los and Enitharmon engage in a conversational confrontation (which is a version of the confrontation between Tharmas and Enion with which the poem opens) in which we get somewhat conflicting versions of a story which introduces the characters Luvah, Vala, Urizen, and the Fallen Man into the narrative.[10] In the second segment of the Night, as noted before, these characters, who were most deeply embedded in the narrative of the first segment, become primary, with this important exclusion: the character Vala is completely absent from the Messengers' account. The fact that the Messengers' complete ignorance (or suppression) of Vala's interconnection with the events they are "explaining" accompanies an inversion of the narrative/ontological field is no accident. Blake specifically revised the first part of this Night—by deleting an extended conversation between Enion and the Spectre regarding Enion's slaying of Enitharmon[11]—so that at the one point at which the reader expects the two major sections of Night I to intersect or overlap (at Enitharmon's causal relation to Tharmas and to Enion), the reader is confronted with an inversion or reversal of narrative "facts."[12] The narrator's account in the first segment of the Night is incommensurate with the Messengers' narration in the second section because the elements of explanation are no longer precisely the same, though they bear the same names, recreating the conditions of the illusion that incommensurable theories explain the same neutral "facts." Blake thus creates experientially conditions of incommensurability precisely analogous to those of the inverted deployment of facts in the competing ray and wave theories discussed above. Though there is a universal principle operating in both explanations, i.e., that inclusion or exclusion of key elements of the field radically inverts narrative/ontological priority, and thus does not conform to the most systematic account Feyerabend gives of incommensurability (the requirement of mutually suspending universal principles), yet, the ray and wave theories are also incommensurable in the way perceptual levels are incommensurable: they cannot be consciously experienced simultaneously.

II

While Blake's narrative dramatizes a surface form which appropriates incommensurability by enacting in the plot alternative arrangements and priorities of "facts," his narrative simultaneously signals the possibility of the reader's construction of an interconnected network of relationships. Blake is here depending on the reader's sharing a desire to find interconnections between aspects of characters who retain the same names and events which share analogous properties despite their radically conflicting ways of entering into the narrative. The kinds of interconnections and interconstitutions of characters and events Blake is striving to have the reader construct are related, yet opposed, to the "Newtonian" drive to find interconnections between what might appear to be incommensurable frameworks of explanation. But the Newtonian version of interconnectedness can survive *only* by the suppression of accumulated "irrelevant," "stray," or "false" data, while Blake's interconnection can be constructed *only* by refusing to suppress the surface incommensurability of frameworks of perception.

The most explicit evidence of the importance Blake attached to the specific kind of interconnection of systems of knowledge which attracted Newton is perhaps located in a crucial passage in *Jersualem* Chapter 4 in which the Spectre makes one last desperate attempt to conquer Los:

> The Spectre builded stupendous Works, taking the Starry
> Heavens
> Like to a curtain & folding them according to his will

Repeating the Smaragdine Table of Hermes to draw Los
down
Into the Indefinite, refusing to believe without
demonstration
Los reads the stars of Albion! the Spectre reads the Voids
Between the stars; among the arches of Albions Tomb
Sublime
(*J.* 91:32–37, E, p. 249)

In his annotation to this passage, W. H. Stevenson remarks: "B[lake]'s knowledge of the Tablet, and of Hermes appears to have been sketchy in the extreme, for the propositions [of the Hermetic Tablet] had little or nothing in common with the science of demonstration with which B. identifies them" (p. 828). Until recently the last portion of this proposition would have been held as true by most historians of science while the first portion would have been challenged by many Blake critics anxious to prove that Blake himself was steeped in the Hermetic tradition.[13] As noted above, however, the problem of the relevance to Newton's scientific achievement of the mass of (usually unpublished) work he did in alchemy and Hermeticism (as well as Biblical exegesis) is currently the focus of the work of a number of historians of science. And it is clear that Blake had more than a "sketchy" knowledge of Hermeticism. It is no accident that in the passage quoted from *Jerusalem* Blake has the Spectre relating three central areas of Newton's research: 1) a Biblical reference to Psalms 104.2 ("the heavens like a curtain"); 2) a reference to the basic occult and alchemical text ("the Smaragdine Table of Hermes"); and 3) a reference to that for which Newton was publicly most famous ("refusing to believe without demonstration"). This last phrase, which yokes Biblical and occult imagery to science, is syntactically ambiguous in that it may attach to the Spectre's motive in luring Los ("The Spectre . . . refusing to believe without demonstration"); or it can be seen as the state in which the Spectre wishes to lure Los ("Into the Indefinite, refusing to believe . . ."); or it may actually refer to the state into which Los is temporarily lured ("refusing to believe without demonstration/ Los reads the stars . . ."); or, more likely, all three. Further, "demonstrations" itself is here ambiguous for it may be based on experimental evidence (empirical) or on pure thought (rational), or it may be a version of the "Demonstrations of Los" (*J.* 90:57, E, p. 248) on the previous plate which in part establishes the precise context for the Spectre's actions. The phrasing of the passage, in addition, works in apparent opposition to the content of the Hermetic Tablet which begins, "True without error, certain, and most true. What is below is like that which is above, and what is above is like that which is below."[14] In the passage itself, however, the Spectre seems to oppose that which is below, "down/ Into the Indefinite," to that which is above, "the Starry Heavens," except that the curtain-like heaven which the Spectre folds is itself an image of the "Indefinite." Further, the absolute skepticism of "refusing to believe without demonstration" seems to be opposed to the faith stated in the Tablet; and yet even here Blake seems to have done his homework, for the "truth" of the Table was seen by alchemists to need unravelling by "the practical work of the fire" ("Newton's Alchemical Studies," p. 172). In the Spectre's actions, then, Blake identifies the newly emerged scientific mentality with a consolidation of prophetic and occult language by having the need for "demonstration" both cause and result from the very Biblical and Hermetic consciousness which seems to oppose it. In addition, since Los "reads the stars" (astrological prediction, associated with alchemical magicians like Paracelsus[15]) while the Spectre "reads the Voids/ Between the Stars" (associated most immediately with Newton's resurrection of the "Void" as an official concept in Western thought), these two opposed actions are revealed to be inter-constitutive, much after the manner of figure and ground in perception. Thus, through dramatic interconnection Blake cuts through several dimensions of incommensurability and allows opposed systems simultaneously to constitute interlocked features of his narrative field.

As noted before, from Newton's point of view, the ground for the interconnection of these traditions is *prisca sapientia,* the lost philosophy of Moses—as P. M. Rattansi has described it: "an ancient Mosaic theology-cum-natural philosophy which had become separated after Pythagoras" ("Newton's Alchemical Studies," p. 172). Evidence that Newton believed he was filling in gaps in a lost philosophical and religious system originating with

Hebraic writers is ample in his manuscript drafts (See "Newton and the 'Pipes of Pan' ") but is also implicit in his published *Chronology of Ancient Kingdoms Ammended.* Betty Jo Teeter Dobbs writes: "Newton tended to emphasize the importance of the Hebraic transmission of God's Word, for he thought that the Brachmans of India had learned their religion, albeit in a corrupted form, from the 'Abrahamans,' or sons of Abraham, from which he thought the name 'Brachman' derived" (*Foundations,* p. 108). In this chronology Newton was arguing for a single unified proto-philosophy and religion which had been dispersed and transformed only to be reformulated by him in his system of the world. As early as *The Song of Los* (and to a lesser degree earlier in the "Religion" tracts) Blake seems to have amended Newton's amendment of ancient chronology because he has *both* Eastern and Western philosophy spring from a common source in the Sons of Los and descend through Hermes Trismegistus and Pythagoras to Newton and Locke:

Adam shudderd! Noah faded! black grew the sunny African
When Rintrah gave Abstract Philosophy to Brama in the East

. . . .

Noah shrunk, beneath the waters;
Abram fled from the steps of Chaldea;
Moses beheld upon Mount Sinai forms of dark delusion
To Tristmegistus. Palamabron gave an abstract Law:
To Pythagoras Socrates & Plato

. . . .

Till a Philosophy of Five Senses was complete
Urizen wept & gave it into the hands of Newton & Locke
(*The Song of Los* 3:10–11, 15–19; 4:16–17; E, p. 66)

Though Blake has complicated the chronological relations, it is clear that he is referring directly to *prisca sapientia,* which greatly influenced Newton and his neoplatonic contemporaries, but Blake treats these forms of ancient wisdom as "forms of dark delusion." Further, since Blake places a period after "Tristmegistus," he leaves open the syntactic possibility that "Moses beheld . . . forms of dark delusion/ *To* Tristmegistus.", making a pun on "beheld" so that it implies that Moses "held out" delusions to Hermes. Blake refers to a different aspect of this same interconnection of forms of explanation in his manuscript poem "Mock On Mock On," where he identifies "The Atoms of Democritus/ And Newtons Particles of Light" as "sands upon the Red sea shore/ Where Israels tents do shine so bright" (E, p. 469). It is unlikely that Newton would have perceived any ironic tone in these lines of Blake's; nor, perhaps, would he have disagreed with them, for privately Newton had intended to add classical annotations to the second edition of the *Principia* to show that the key propositions in the *Principia* were anciently known ("Newton's Alchemical Studies," p. 172). J. E. McGuire has indicated that Newton's belief that his system was a *prisca sapientia*

> involves more than merely placing a body of doctrine in a venerable tradition: it also involves the notion that there is one true philosophy of nature to which certain thinkers have given a partial expression. This true philosophy of nature Newton considered himself to be expounding in these "classical" scholia to the Third Book. . . . This sort of historical approach to truth in theology and natural philosophy allows for the *selection and rejection* [my emphasis] of doctrines expressed by other thinkers in terms of the criteria of the prisca employed: or, *since no thinker had been able to express the complete truth* about phenomena, the nature of *the doctrines being defended* ("Transmutation and Immutability," p. 94; my emphasis).

Thus, while *prisca sapientia* requires mutual support from all areas of knowledge, Newton is free to pick and choose those ancient hints which agree with his evolved doctrine and to exclude those observations and theories which disagree. For example, at one point Newton had included Descartes and Aristotle as expressing his own system, but "on reflection he could later reject them as being in opposition to the 'true' doctrine, which finally included, for Newton, only the philosophy of Epicurus and the atomists [including Moses who Newton believed was an atomist]" ("Force," pp. 4ff.). But, in any case, the "Tabula Smaragdina" was conceived of as the central means of transmitting the *prisca* to Newton's time, and it was intimately connected with the practical work of alchemy ("Newton's Alchemical Studies," p. 172).

In order to see more clearly what Blake has achieved in the *Jerusalem* passage cited earlier, we need to look more carefully at the aspects of alchemy and Hermeticism which were relevant to Newton. One thing that emerges from recent studies of Newton's alchemy and Hermeticism is that his ideas were constantly undergoing transformation and refinement, and that he was attempting, through efforts like his massive alchemical *Index* ("Alchemy in Newton's Career," pp. 202 ff.), to unify the differing alchemical texts he studied. And the alchemical and Hermetic elements of his thought themselves at times gave rise to interfering modes of explanation. For example, as R. S. Westfall has clearly shown, the three basic elements of the Hermetic tradition which were crucial to Newton—nature as active, organic, and psychic—survived in Newton's mature thought in many ways, not the least of which was a doctrine of a multiplicity of specific forces which would help explain the sympathies and antipathies of agents in nature ("Newton and the Hermetic Tradition," pp. 184–93 *et passim*). Whereas his earlier aetherial spirit had in mechanical (and also alchemical) fashion reduced all bodies to one common matter, rendering affinities mysterious, "in contrast, his specific forces, reflecting the radical nominalism of the Hermetic tradition and implying a multiplicity of irreducible substances, threatened constantly to shatter the unity of natural processes into a myriad of particular agents" ("Newton and the Hermetic Tradition," p. 193). On the other hand, in his alchemical studies he tended to make a sharp demarcation between "mechanical" and "vegetable" processes in nature ("Newton's Alchemical Studies," p. 176; "Alchemy in Newton's Career," pp. 219 ff.), rather than emphasizing the interpenetration of the spiritual and the physical prevalent in the Hermetic tradition ("Newton and the Hermetic Tradition," p. 184). The distinction between "mechanical" and "vegetable" processes is closely connected with the interrelated ideas of the aetherial "spirit" and the "seeds" (or "semen") of things. At one point, Newton seems to espouse a theory in which the "gros mechanicall transposition of parts" ("Alchemy in Newton's Career," p. 219) belongs to "vulgar chemistry" (a surface structure of sorts) underpinned by a more fundamental activity (a form of deep structure) which he identified as a "spirit":

> There is therefore besides ye sensible changes wrought in ye textures of ye grosser matter a more subtile secret & noble way of working in all vegetation which makes its products distinct from all others & ye immediate seat of those operations is not ye whole bulk of matter, but rather an exceedingly small portion of matter diffused through the mass wch if it were separated there would remain a dead & inactive earth.
> (quoted in "Alchemy in Newton's Career," p. 221)

Rattansi develops this idea by indicating that for Newton, "What distinguished vegetation from mechanism was the fact that it consisted of an interaction between the aether as an activating principle and the 'rudements' or seeds of things, that is 'that substance in them that is attained to the fullest degree of maturity that is in that thing' " ("Newton's Alchemical Studies," p. 176). This interaction between a universal aether and a multiplicity of seeds of substances (appearing, as we have seen, in another guise in the form of the coexistence of universal attraction with a multiplicity of specific forces) is related to the problem of psychic qualities and vegetative processes in the realm of minerals itself. In his essay on Newton's alchemy, Westfall isolates two "logically independent" themes in alchemical texts which worked together to influence Newton's way of dealing with this problem: 1) "generation by male and female as a process universal in nature, in the mineral kingdom as well as in the animal and vegetable"; and 2) "the need to purge and purify in order that the spiritual seeds of things can attain their ends" ("Alchemy in Newton's Career," p. 213). Westfall quotes a passage which Newton copied repeatedly in his alchemical notes: " 'I say our true Sperm flows from a Trinity of Substances in one Essence,' Philalethes wrote, 'of which two are extracted out of the Earth of their Nativity to the Third, and then become a pure milky Virgin-like Nature, drawn from the Menstruum of our Sordid Whore' " (pp. 213–14 and n. 80, p. 313). Though Westfall does not note the explicit Biblical tone infused into this passage, the easy translatability of the male/female propagation of metals into pseudo-Biblical imagery of the Incarnation of Jesus would have further confirmed to Newton the commensurability and simultaneous appropriateness of both the alchemical and the Biblical languages in a common system of explanation. One of Newton's own manuscripts, *The Vegetation of Metals,* repeated as its theme "the alchemical conviction that metals propagate by male and female" ("Alchemy in Newton's Career," p. 222). And in his early letter to Oldenburg, Newton attributes imagery to the aether itself which bears analogy to the male seeds of Sendivogius which are cast into the earth "as a man's seed is cast into a woman's womb" (*Foundations,* p. 157). In this early version, the aether descends to the female center of the earth which is in "perpetuall working," and the aether is ultimately cast forth again, "for nature is a perpetuall circulatory worker" (*Foundations,* p. 206).

Newton's attraction to this kind of organic, psychic, sexual, and animate language to explain the innermost workings of nature tends to be disguised in most of his public pronouncements, where we get accounts which are sexually neutral and conservative in their ontological assertions. We get public reference to "active principles" and a hypothetical "aether" in the *Opticks* and to an "electric and elastic spirit" in the *Principia,* but it is clear that Newton suppressed (or rejected) a significant aspect of his private speculations. Even a principle such as the "analogy of nature"—that there is an analogy between macroscopic and microscopic functions—was felt by Newton to "prejudice" his readers (a version of the Hermetic principle that what is above is like that which is below), as so he suppressed reference to it. In an unpublished manuscript Newton says: "This principle of nature being very remote from the conceptions of Philosophers I forebore to describe it in that Book [*Principia*] least I should be accounted an extravagant freak & so prejudice my Readers against all those things wch were ye main designe of the Book" (quoted in "Force," p. 165). Newton's refusal to invoke sexual metaphors publicly in the context of his speculations on the relations between mechanical and vegetable processes may be related to personal factors, however. Frank E. Manuel has noted Newton's intense dislike for "Emanative" theories of creation precisely because they characterize creation as sexual activity, an emission of God's substance. Newton writes: "The Gnostics after the manner of the Platonists and Cabbalists considered the thoughts or ideas or intellectual objects seated in Gods mind as real Beings or substances, and supposed them to be male and female and to generate by emission of substance, as animals generate."[16] The possibility that God generated the world "as animals generate other animals of the same species by seminal emissions" was, according to Manuel, greeted by Newton with great distaste (pp. 72–73), despite the fact that such a concept of the primacy of sexuality in the creation would be in keeping with the sexual imagery of alchemical interaction. Manuel leaves as a question "whether Newton's aversion to emissions and emanations . . . has covert origins in the intimate experience of this lone man" (p. 73). Whatever the cause, we find here a key example of Newton's explicit rejection of a theory ("Emanation") which could have given support to his speculations in other areas of research, a framework which both attracted and disturbed him. Newton's failure to achieve publicly the successful interconnection of his fields of research is directly related to his willingness to suppress incommensurable theories if they threatened to interfere with the coherent physical system he had developed experimentally and mathematically. This suppression in turn contributed to a public official philosophy associated with Newton which would seem almost totally divorced from Newton's covert researches if it were not for the work of recent scholars in this field.

We have come a long way around to help establish the framework of the drive toward interconnection of incommensurable frameworks in Newton's own career,[17] which lies behind the plausibility of the actions of the Spectre in *Jerusalem* Chapter 4. It is significant that the larger context in which the Spectre achieves his temporary *prisca sapientia* involves: 1) the sexual division of Los and of all of nature; 2) the "Demonstrations of Los," which involve transforming inorganic rocks into vegetation; and 3) Los's "secret desire" to utter an ontology of genuine interconnectedness in the body of Jesus, which the Spectre attempts to parody with his *prisca*. It should be clear that each of these features directly relates to the intersections of the different traditions we have been discussing. First, since early in Chapter 1 of *Jersualem* Los's Spectre has been connected with sexual division and jealousy (*J.* 7:9 ff.; E, p. 148). In the context of Chapter 4 he knows himself to be "the author of their [Los and Enitharmon's] divisions & shrinkings" (*J.* 88: 35; E, p. 245). Albion's Spectre, however, though he is said to tear forth from

Albion's "Loins" (E, p. 171), has been primarily associated with "Reason," "Demonstration," and the reduction of life to mineral forms.[18] Since both of these versions of the Spectre are central to this context, and since sexual division might otherwise seem irrelevant to "demonstration," it is important that the character on plate 91 is referred to as (unspecified) "the Spectre." In the plot there is a parallel set up between Los and the narrator. As soon as Los beholds and describes an androgynous "Jerusalem," he divides into male and female; immediately after the narrator beholds and describes the hermaphroditic "Covering Cherub," there is a universal sexual division enacted in the narrative itself (*J*. 85:22 ff., 86:50 ff., 89:9 ff., 90:2 ff.; E, pp. 241–47). In both cases Los seems to derive strength and something like a visionary perspective on the meaning of sexual division, so that the Spectrous powers are frustrated in their attempt to weaken Los. In a process he calls the "Demonstrations of Los" (which is simultaneously the speech he makes about sexual division and the process of vegetation he initiates), Los causes the "Little-ones," the members of Jesus and Jerusalem's body which have been condensed into rocks, to "Vegetate/ Beneath Los's Hammer, that Life may not be blotted out" (90:50–51; E, p. 248). This process of animating vegetation out of inorganic minerals reverses the process we saw in Newton in which the "vegetation of metals" is publicly suppressed and the sexual imagery complex of a spermatic seed-aether gets absorbed into a mechanical or electric context in public pronouncements. Such a transformation is explicitly enacted by the Daughters of Albion in Chapter 3:

> They cut the Fibres from the Rocks groaning in pain they Weave;
> Calling the Rocks Atomic Origins of Existence; denying Eternity
> By the Atheistical Epicurean Philosophy of Albions Tree
> Such are the Feminine & Masculine when separated from Man
> They call the Rocks Parents of Men, & adore the frowning Chaos
>
> (*J*. 67:11–15; E, p. 218)

The Daughters turn up in the context of Chapter 4 (as a narrative response to Los's "Demonstrations") as the "Maternal Humanity" whom "Deists" worship publicly while they are secretly "mocking god & Eternal Life." The Deists thus become perpetrators and victims of a process in which sexual division itself is suppressed in such a way that sexual generation is rendered a *derivative* aspect of nature, so that inorganic rocks (Epicurean Atoms) become the sexually neutralized "Parents of Men." Thus the very process by which Newton's secret speculations concerning the interconnection of all knowledge grounded in a psychic, organic, and sexual vision of nature issued in a public espousal of the kinds of explanations Blake (and Newton himself) saw as characteristic of Epicureanism is explicitly dramatized by Blake as the context in which the Spectre achieves his willed interconnection of vastly disparate modes of explanation into a single system.

Equally significant is the fact that Blake has the Spectre achieve his "stupendous Works" by distracting Los from the lived sexual division Los has just undergone at the Spectre's hands. Prior to the Spectre's achievement of *prisca sapientia* in the narrative, Los orders the Spectre to "obey my most secret desire" (91:3; E, p. 248) which, Los continues to demonstrate, is the utterance of a visionary ontology or artistic organization grounded in Jesus: "He who would see the Divinity must see him in his Children . . . he who wishes to see a Vision; a perfect Whole/ Must see it in its Minute Particulars . . . & every/ Particular is a Man; a Divine Member of the Divine Jesus" (91:18, 20–21, 29–30; E, p. 249). The Spectre, however, performs a parody of Los's secret desire by constructing a *false* unification (the *prisca*) explicitly at the expense of diverting, distorting, and ironically suppressing the sexual division Los is living through. As the Spectre, God-like, folds the heavens he seems implicitly aware of Galatians 3:28 where the consideration of the spiritual offspring of Jesus, his children (to which Los has just referred), yields a transcendence of sexual division: "there is neither male nor female: for ye are all one in Christ Jesus." The Spectre smuggles a disguised version of Los's sexual division into his *prisca* by its appearance in the "Smaragdine Table of Hermes" itself. Though we, as readers, are not given the content of the Table in the narrative, we witness the plot in which Los supposedly hears it. In the Table "one thing" which is the source of all things is described in the following way: "Its father is the sun, its mother the moon, the wind carried it in its belly, its nurse is the earth. . . . Separate the earth from the fire the subtle from the gross, gently with great art. It ascends from the earth to the heaven and again descends to earth and receives the power of things both superior and inferior" (Damon, p. 183). Rattansi reports that in Newton's manuscript commentary on the Table he interprets this activity in a rather unsexual way ("Newton's Alchemical Studies," pp. 175–76). And the fact that Blake does not give us the Table itself but narratively suppresses its content while referring to it parallels the way the sexual imagery in the Table distorts, partially obscures, and partially satisfies Los's own sexual desires. The Spectre's achievement, then, of the interconnection of the three explanatory languages (Biblical, Hermetic, scientific) is an explicit and implicit subversion of Los's secret desire to transcend sexual division by uttering the true gospel of organized interconnection in Jesus. The Spectre's version of transcending sexual division is to reverse Los's action of causing vegetation to emerge from the rocks: the Spectre wants to thwart Los's desire to integrate in Jesus by creating a false integration which is the hermaphroditic world of inorganic forms. The organization of knowledge which the Spectre and Newton strive to achieve is thus seen in *Jerusalem* Chapter 4 as a type of consolidation of the anti-Christ. Los responds to this luring false integration of knowledge by smiting the Spectre on his anvil and dividing the Spectre into a separate space, in a direct parody of the Spectre's attempt at alchemical purification (by sexual suppression) and amalgamation (by false integration). This purgation by Los of his Spectre issues in another pseudo-alchemical action, the "amalgamation" of the nations in Los's furnace (*J.* 92:1 ff.; E, p. 249)—which is, of course, both the furnace of the smith and of the alchemist. This amalgamation in Los's furnace is significantly said to involve "taking refuge in the Loins of Albion." This action brings Los back to a confrontation with his sexually divided partner, his "Emanation" Enitharmon, an action which the Spectre had hoped by means of his *prisca* to suppress.[19]

III

The illusion of interconnectedness of the sort which gave rise to *prisca sapientia* must be, as we have seen, based on massive will to suppress conflicting data. It also requires suppression of the possibility that nature may be constituted in such a way that no single explanatory system can contrue all "facts" completely and unambiguously. In this section I would like to consider how the "Newtonian text" and the "Newtonian narrator" are linguistic expressions of the "Newtonian" drive toward interconnection of incommensurables through suppression; but "Newtonian texts" are by no means restricted to Newton: his is simply an extreme form of a narrative stance which Blake's narrative systematically opposes. The Newtonian narrator stands forth most clearly in Newton's manuscript interpretations of Biblical prophecy, but it also exists in disguised form in his scientific works as well.

We have seen that Newton proceeds on the assumption of the ultimate unambiguity of nature—the phenomena which support his theories cannot be ruled out, reinterpreted, or made derivative unless overwhelming evidence be adduced. In his Fourth Rule of Reasoning in Philosophy in the *Principia* Newton forbids the interference of "any contrary hypothesis that may be imagined," once a theory has been developed on an experimental basis, "till such time as other phaenomena occur, by which they [the deduced propositions] may either be made more accurate, or liable to exceptions."[20] Newton's research program discourages, as we have seen in the context of the ray theory above, the exploration of simultaneously incommensurable theories which may *reconstruct* the "phaenomena" in a totally different way. Newton's tendency to forbid alternative constructions of phenomena becomes exaggerated in his analysis of Biblical language. With regard to his construing of the Book of Revelation he says:

> Hence if any man shall contend that my Construction of the Apocalypse is uncertain, upon pretence that it may be possible to find out other ways, he is not to be regarded unless he shall show wherein what I have done may be mended. If the ways he contends for be less natural or grounded upon weaker reasons, that very thing is demonstration enough that they are fals, and that he seeks not [after] truth but [labours

> for] the interest of a party. And if the way which I have followed be according to the nature and genius of the Prophecy there needs no further demonstration to convince it.
>
> (quoted in Manuel, Appendix A, p. 121)

It should be apparent that the Newtonian narrator is here utilizing exactly the same technique for suppressing competing theories of interpretation that he uses in his experimental arguments for the ray theory. In that context he had said, "If this demonstration be good there needs no further examination of the thing. . . . I shall be unwilling to be diverted by any other experiment." We have seen that Newton cannot unambiguously define the phenomena on which he bases his "experiments" because the experiments presuppose a selection and construction of data which will support the theory out of the sea of possible phenomena. In the context of apocalyptic language, however, his attempt to rule out alternative interpretations requires the invocation of even more blatant rhetorical strategies as the basis of "demonstration." The Newtonian text (the "I") asserts itself as the fundamental criterion by which other interpretations must be judged. Those who disagree because they can construe the apocalypse in a different way "are not to be regarded" *unless they first disprove* Newton's construing of the text. And what are the grounds for disproving the authoritative voice of the Newtonian text? Newton sets up criteria which are even less explicitly formulable than "experiment" (which we have seen is itself never really formulated): if the objector's reasons are "less natural or grounded on weaker reasons, that very thing is demonstration enough." As we shall see, Newton does try to define "natural," but it becomes clear that only the Newtonian text-voice is capable of making the final discrimination between alternative constructions because, rhetorically, the Newtonian voice could never seek the "interest of a party" but always seek "truth." It is simply the assertion of the text itself—that it has followed the "nature and genius of the Prophecy" which is "demonstration" enough.

The stance that alternative constructions of prophetic language must be ruled out is based on Newton's assertion of the unambiguity of the Biblical text: "Tis true that an Artificer may make an Engin capable of being with equal congruity set together in more ways than one, and that a sentence may be ambiguous: but this Objection can have no place in the Apocalypse, becaus God who knew how to frame it without ambiguity intended it for a rule of faith" (quoted in Manuel, Appendix A, p. 121). A characteristic of the Newtonian text is that it objects to itself and thus attempts to take that function away from the reader. Here the self-objecting text acknowledges the possibility of alternative constructions of phenomena *("with equal congruity set together in more ways than one")* but asserts its own preference for unambiguity as *God's* preference and skillfully shifts the reference of "it" in the last part of this utterance to subvert the reader's capacity to object. The Newtonian voice shifts from "God . . . knew how to frame it [the Apocalypse]" to God "intended it [the unambiguity of apocalyptic language] for a rule of faith." In this shift Newton implicitly equates the Apocalypse with unambiguous language in the experience of the reader.

When Newton attempts to define what he means by interpretation according to the nature and genius of the prophecy, he does so in terms of an explicit movement toward an analogy between techniques appropriate to the analysis of prophetic language and of nature. Rule 8 begins, "To [prefer] choose those [interpretations] constructions which *without straining reduce* contemporary visions to the greatest harmony of their parts" (quoted in Manuel, Appendix A, p. 120; my italics). That the italicized words beg as many questions as they answer sheds further light on Newton's coercive attitude toward his reader. Again, Rule 9: "To [prefer] choose those [interpretations] constructions which *without straining reduce* things to the greatest *simplicity*. . . . Truth is ever to be found in simplicity and not in the multiplicity and confusion of things. . . . He is the God of order and not of confusion" (quoted in Manuel, Appendix A, p. 120). Who but the "God of order" himself (or his inspired interpreter) can recognize the "true" simplicity and harmony to which the apparent "confusion" of the prophetic texts (and nature itself) can be "reduced" without "straining"? Who, in fact, would be able to recognize a "strained" interpretation without utilizing the "rules for methodizing the Apocalypse" or the "rules for interpreting the words and language of the scripture" which Newton presents to his reader? It is quite clear that this

Newtonian voice equates "multiplicity" with "confusion" and therefore needs to ground his direction of the reader's responses in a similar need for reduction of multiplicity to univocality. The Newtonian narrator in fact admits that his goal is to exert control over the reader's perception and judgment: "I shall lay down certain [Rules] general Rules of Interpretation, the consideration of which may prepare the judgment of the Reader and enable him to know when an interpretation is genuine and of two interpretations which is best" (quoted in Manuel, Appendix A, p. 115). Newton's "rules" thus are intended to act as a kind of grid which the reader is urged to place over Biblical language while he is reading it and over other interpretations while reading them. This grid will filter out all irrelevant associations which might enter the reader's mind, since there are quite strict semantic limits placed on meaning of Biblical language by Newton's method.

Like his "Rules of Reasoning in Philosophy," Newton's "rules" for reading Biblical language establish a coercive relationship between reader and text. In his Biblical exegesis the gap between the literal word and the meaning disappears: the Newtonian narrator asserts the semantic limits of the possible meanings of the text, making the text usurp the reader's role. As the text assumes the reader's role, the reader is forced outward and alienated from the text. Despite the assumption of reference to and verification in an external world which obeys the rules of unambiguity which his rules construct, Newton's scientific text also is centripetal in relation to itself and centrifugal in relation to the reader: it turns in on itself, and the reader is forced outward. The reader is separated from the text as the elements of the text are separated, isolated from one another.

In the opening section of Book I of the *Principia,* Newton introduces the notion of ultimate vanishing ratios. An arc is inscribed and circumscribed with a series of rectangles which are increased in number and the ratio of their areas placed on a sliding scale in which the number of rectangles increases infinitely as the sharp-edged images dissolve at infinity into the curve of the arc itself. Newton invites the reader to visualize the process by presenting a visual illustration of the first stage of the process (Fig. 1). Figure 2 represents an intermediate stage

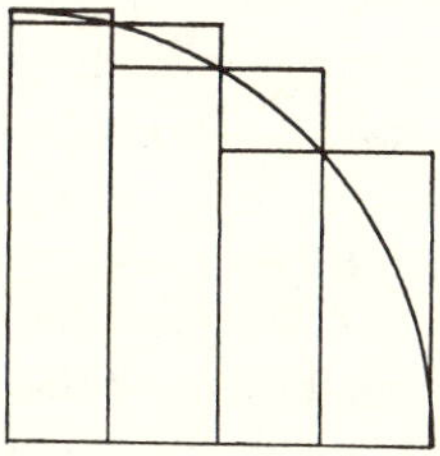

Fig. 1

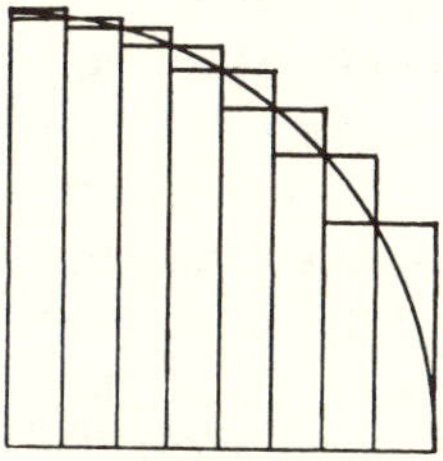

Fig. 2

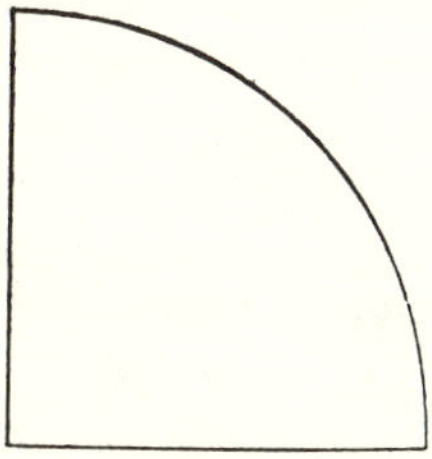

Fig. 3

(which Newton does not represent). Figure 3 represents the final stage in which the rectangles have all been absorbed into the arc. We can see that the event at the moment of the disappearance of the rectangles into the arc is the key to the process, but it cannot itself be visualized (at least not as a static image on the page). Since we are given an illustration of the first stage of the process, the illusion arises that the transformation takes place in the reader. But the transformation lies in the text and not in the reader. The final stage is unvisualizable by the kind of illustration which sets the process in motion, and so the disappearance of the rectangles resides in the assertion of the text itself. Again the Newtonian text is self-conscious of its own limitations: it raises objections for the reader, specifically in this example by a lengthy disclaimer concerning the final step of the process. The text attempts to usurp the active role of the reader by making the text object to itself.

A second example of Newton's relation to his reader in the *Principia* involves his explication of absolute space, time, and motion in his "Scholium" to "Definitions." Just as the arc toward which the rectangles proceed requires a limit to perceptual possibility, so Newton's assertion of absolute space, time, and motion requires perceptual limits of another sort. For Newton, if there were no absolutes, there could always be a new hypothetical perspective from which any motion or group of motions could appear relative—with the exception of certain kinds of accelerated motion. The man on a ship may appear at rest with respect to himself but is in motion with respect to a set of coordinates (or viewer) on shore. And this viewer, and the viewer on the boat, are in different relative motion with respect to coordinates on the sun, and so on. The conceptual limit to these relative spaces is absolute space, and to these relative motions is absolute motion. This implied absolute world has to be decoded by the text from the variety of spaces, times, and motions which constitute "common" perception. Newton's strategy is to render the multiplicity of perspectives ultimately referable to the one absolute framework which embraces all others and makes them "relative" with respect to itself. Only the text, the disembodied narrator, perceives absolute space, time, and motion as they are, simply by asserting them.

The similarity between Newton's stance in these examples and the other forms of narrative explanation we have encountered in his works should be evident. Further, the mathematical notation—in conjunction with graphic illustrations which, by convention, cannot bear an ironic or parodic relationship to the scientific text—removes the reader's participation in the process: everything has been worked out by the text. Yet the jumps between the steps of proof raise the greatest problem for a reader of Newton: the mathematical operations are performed invisibly, with the sequence of equations or steps of proof as the visible traces of the underlying continuous process of thought.

We have seen that Blake's narration opposes the assumptions of Newtonian methods of explanation and the Newtonian desire to construct a world of interconnections on the basis of suppression of alternative perspectives. Now we can see how Blake's text opposes the assumptions of the Newtonian text as well. In Night I of *The Four Zoas,* as has been shown, Blake forces the reader to come to grips with an experience of radically incommensurable explanations of the narrative nexus of events. On the other hand, Blake implants signals which appeal to the reader's desire to find interconnection beneath surface incommensurability. The basic formula which lies behind the interrelation of these two narrative processes is: incommensurability does not entail disconnection; and interconnection does not entail unity.

Whereas Newton tended to avoid utilizing doctrines or techniques which he felt would alienate his readers—"least I should be accounted an extravagant freak & prejudice my Readers against all those things w[ch] were y[e] main designe of the Book" (quoted in "Force," p. 165)—Blake directly assaults the reader and challenges him to come to terms with the unusual form of his narrative. In the following brief outline of some of Blake's techniques, I will focus on *The Four Zoas* where we have the greatest evidence of Blake's conscious revision, and therefore of clues to his intentions toward his readers.[21] All of Blake's poetic techniques in *The Four Zoas* flow out of this premise: relationships constitute the identity of characters and events.[22] Perhaps more accurately, Blake's characters are relationships between events which are named and them proceed to act as if they were independent characters with lives of their own. Characters, events, and perspectives are completely interconnected, but only by implication. Since the characters suppress (or are unaware of) their mutual interconnectedness and treat themselves as isolated entities, even the narrator is unable to make connections for the reader for the narrator takes on the aspects of the characters and events he is narrating. All interconnection which emerges must reside in the reader's taking up Blake's narrative challenge and creating the interconnectedness to which the narrator and characters are blind. Apart from perspective relationships there are no events in *The Four Zoas*. There is no substructure of specifiable events which is distorted or partially interpreted by the perspectives. The identity of characters and events, in this sense, is constituted by perspective. "Perspective," in turn, is a product of the drive toward the suppression of multiplicity into unity, a drive which we have seen is overwhelmingly strong in Newton. Thus what Blake's *Four Zoas* narrative constructs is, from the point of view of Newtonian narrative, an impossibility: a series of eccentric, mutually incommensurable universes which intersect precisely at their lacunae. Blake utilizes overlapping imagery, diction, and syntax primarily at those points where there is a conflict between perspectives. These are large and complex claims which cannot be fully documented here. But let us turn briefly to a few examples in the poem in order to see how the assumption of a single universe toward which all explanation must point—the basic assumption on which the Newtonian research program is based—is completely subverted by Blake's text.

We have already seen how Blake utilizes the technique of incommensurable frameworks of explanation in Night I by inverting the narrative/ ontological field and then overlapping these two fields at a narrative lacuna: in the first portion of the Night Enitharmon is born of Enion; in the second section Enitharmon is murdered by Enion and embalmed in her bosom as a corpse.[23] This narrative fact is not unique. From the opening of the poem Blake has been striving to dissolve a solid framework right before our eyes. It is as if we were to walk around an object to perceive various perspective aspects of it, and the more aspects we perceived the more we became convinced that the object did not exist. Blake's revisions of the opening lines of the poem reveal his evolving concern with the reader's participation in his poem, the thwarting of grammatical expectations by the spatial layout of his words and punctuation, and the transformation of his verbal narrative into a form of visual participatory theatre. In the final version of these lines Blake deletes the original reference to "Whosoever reads" and to the consequences "If with his Intellect he comprehend the terrible Sentence" of the poem. The final version frustrates all attempts at causal connection by deleting the predicate forms which allow the language to be divided into causally related phrases.

Throughout the poem Blake distinguishes between two sources of information: the constantly modulating voice of the narrator and the spoken words—or interpolated visions and memories—of characters who appear in the main narrative. Initially it seems as if there are two distinct and contrapuntal streams of information alternating with each other, the narrative action apparently happening *after* the events in remembered visions, and visions apparently referring to the primal or original "fall" of "Man." Since the characters rarely talk about or remember what has been happening within the narrative, their speech gestures act as decoys to draw attention away from the actions they are engaged in and which are disguised by their speech gestures. Virtually every such interpolated vision in the poem can be read as a fictional transformation by characters of relationships between already present characters and events. Thus, while information *seems* to be divided between two discrete sources (the narrator proper and interpolated visions in the poem) with minimal overlapping of events, these two streams of information are aspects of one another and transformations of each other. Narrative events do not occur *after* a primal "fall," nor do interpolated visions refer to a primal "fall" in the dim past. The "fall," such as it is, occurs in the narrative by the very fact of an apparent opposition between narrative and interpolated information, by the actions of speakers intending their speech gestures away from the present narrative context and fictionalizing that context in parables involving other character names. The "fall" also occurs in the reader insofar as he retains the "Newtonian" assumption of separation and denies the subliminal dialectic experience of overlapping yet incommensurable contexts.

The most powerful way in which Blake manipulates his narrative/interpolated vision relationships is to use them as "perspective analyses" of prior events. A simple perspective analysis of a prior event re-enacts the same event within the same fictional framework—as when the initial conversation in the poem between Tharmas and Enion is twice re-enacted, once in the metaphorical action of weaving and once again in the metaphor of sexual union. Blake overlaps context by repetition of syntax and diction to scramble causal order and make us see the two later actions as *versions* of the conversations. These successive analyses further *make the initial event possible* by establishing the conditions for the first event. The most complex mode of perspective analysis "embeds" subsequent events in prior plots. The structures of Nights I, III, IV, VIIa, VIIb, VIII, and IX all can be visualized as involving "brackets" of information within which sub-groups of information are embedded. An embedded plot means that previous actions are being re-enacted within a *new* fictional framework: new characters re-enact prior events, transforming the perspective, thereby revealing information suppressed within the previous fictional framework. The Los/Enitharmon plot of Night I is the first embedded structure of the poem: these characters act out in great detail the actions of the Tharmas/Enion plot.

The continual alteration of Blake's perspective techniques throughout the poem works as a check on the reader's lapse into a fixed set of expectations. Blake keeps altering the meaning of the same perspective rules in order to reveal ever more complicated interconnections between characters and events in the constitution of which the reader participates. In this context the unsettling and unsatisfactory characteristics of Night IX suggest that Blake did not want to make the events of Night IX the logical conclusion of the poem: Blake does not depict *on the page* a complete and final apocalypse which is a narrative imitation of a *future* renovation or redemption and which thereby displaces responsibility for the apocalypse away from the individual reader. Rather, the embedded structure of Night IX strongly suggests that the "Last Judgement" is an act of consciousness Blake expects the reader to be able to make in relation to the unsatisfactory "End" of Night IX. The poem's "Dream" does "End" only *after* the final action is completed.[24] Blake wants the reader to assume responsibility for his own redemption by seeing that such a redemption cannot be depicted on the page. Night IX superimposes the two halves of Night I and inverts them. In Night IX the Tharmas/Enion bracket is the innermost narrative structure, being enclosed within the Luvah/Vala segment which is in turn enclosed within the Urizen/Fallen Man plot, which is itself contained by a fusion of the Los/Enitharmon sexual plot with the imagery of war. Tharmas and Enion assume the role of children as Los and Enitharmon did in Night I, and the "Eternals" eventually interact with the main characters of the narrative at a great "Feast," unlike Night I where the Eternal and narrative perspectives were askew. The continual frustration of our desire that complete joy will characterize the reunion of males with their female counterparts points toward the opposite movement in the Night—the eventual separation of the "female form" from the Eternals themselves.[25] The sinister suggestion of the Lamb of God as a sexual rival to Albion is suppressed, as is the sexual locus of the fall. As in Night I, the Eternals are blind to their sexual potential and subtly and inadvertently establish the conditions for the primal fall.[26]

A grasp of the perspective structure of this complex poem yields the possibility of an ironic reading. That such a reading is not necessary is evident from the range of Blake scholarship which has found the conclusion of the poem unsatisfactory without trying to argue that such an experience might be intentional on Blake's part.[27] The heretical nature of the poem's suppressed "awful Sentence" is in perfect keeping with the bizarre sexual drawings which Blake sketched in the margins of the text.[28] In *The Four Zoas* Blake locates the grounds of normal perception of objects and language in a sexual vision, "the torments of Love and Jealousy," which he treats as a drive toward suppression of complexity into simplicity, by focussing or localizing attention, a suppression which inevitably frustrates itself. The more his characters attempt to hide, the more information emerges. Unlike the Newtonian narrator, he wants us to become aware of the sexual basis of our perceptual prejudices by teaching us a new way to experience relationships which are simultaneously incommensurable and interconnected. Can we blame Blake for making the effort to reorganize our perceptual faculties, for trying to wake us from what he once called "Single vision & Newtons Sleep"?

Notes

1. See P. M. Rattansi, "Newton's Alchemical Studies," in *Science, Medicine and Society in the Rennaissance. Essays to Honor Walter Pagel,* ed. Allen G. Debus (New York: Science History Publications, 1972), pp. 167–82; and J. E. McGuire and P. M. Rattansi, "Newton and the 'Pipes of Pan,' " *Notes and Records of the Royal Society of London,* 21 (1966), 108–43. (In further references these two essays will be cited by title within the text.) See also Betty Jo Teeter Dobbs, *The Foundations of Newton's Alchemy: or 'The Hunting of the Greene Lyon'* (Cambridge, London, New York, Melbourne: Cambridge U. Press, 1975), hereafter cited as *Foundations.*

2. Implied in J. E. McGuire, "Transmutation and Immutability: Newton's Doctrine of Physical Qualities," *Ambix,* 14 (1967), 94 ff., hereafter cited as "Transmutation and Immutability" in the text; and in Paul Feyerabend, *Against Method: Outline of an Anarchist Theory of Knowledge* (London: NLB; Atlantic Highlands: Humanities Press, 1975), pp. 260 ff., hereafter cited as *Against Method* in the text.

3. See note 2, above.

4. This phenomenon in Blake's narrative epistemology is analogous to Maurice Merleau-Ponty's analysis of perception in "Ourselves, and the Natural World," in *Phenomenology of Perception,* trans. from the French by Colin Smith (New York: Humanities Press, 1962), pp. 346–65; and in Merleau-Ponty, "The Child's Relations with Others," in *The Primacy of Perception: And Other Essays on Phenomenological Psychology, the Philosophy of Art, History and Politics,* ed. with an introduction by James M. Eddie (Evanston, Ill.: Northwestern U. Press, 1964), pp. 96–155.

5. *Against Method,* p. 274. "Using an 'instrumentalistic' interpretation of the themes which sees in them no more than instruments for classification of

certain 'facts' one gets the impression that there is some common subject matter. Using a 'realistic' interpretation that tries to understand the theory in its own terms such a subject matter seems to disappear although there is the definite feeling (unconscious instrumentalism) that it must exist."

6. Paul Feyerabend, "Classical Empiricism," in *The Methodological Heritage of Newton,* ed. Robert E. Butts and John W. Davis (Toronto: U. of Toronto Press, 1970), pp. 150–70, hereafter cited by title in the text.

7. All quotations by Blake are taken from William Blake, *The Poetry and Prose of William Blake,* ed. David Erdman (Garden City, N.Y.: Doubleday, 1970), hereafter cited as E. Since Blake left *The Four Zoas* in manuscript, the order of pages and the organization of various Nights is arguable. I am here assuming Erdman's ordering, which seems to me to be the most interesting and the most characteristic of Blake's techniques. But for a different (and much briefer) ordering of Night I, see *The Poems of William Blake,* ed. W. H. Stevenson (London: Longman; New York: Norton, 1970), pp. 292–306.

8. This analysis involves a rather complex methodological approach I have been developing which involves surfacing of "embedded" structures. I deal with this notion in more detail in section III of this essay.

9. The final third of Night I is extremely problematic to treat as if it were nearly in a final state, for the pages were bound out of order and Erdman rearranged them to make narrative sense. Even this rearrangement leaves problems which it would take us too far afield here to discuss. I believe Erdman's order is basically correct and am proceeding on that basis.

10. In section III of this essay I develop some of the background for this assertion. I am trying to call attention to the *way* Blake introduces characters into the narrative and the importance of the *order* in which he does so. Los and Enitharmon are contending over their relation to their parents, Tharmas and Enion, but they act out this contention by generating four other character names (which enter in an interlocked community) as verbal counters or displacements of their own actions. They primarily contend over the meaning/function of the terms "Luvah" and "Vala." As soon as their speeches end, all four characters mentioned in their vision pop into the narrative and begin to assume lives of their own.

11. See Erdman's textual notes, pp. 740–43. In the deleted section Enion admits "murdering" Tharmas' "Emanations," which, on one level of course, are a version of Enion, but, on another, of Enitharmon (for Tharmas' Emanations are said to be Enion's "children").

12. On MS p. 4 Tharmas says, "It is not Love I bear to Enitharmon It is Pity/ She hath taken refuge in my bosom" (E, p. 297); on MS p. 22 the Messengers of Beulah report that Enitharmon "fled/ And tharmas took her in pitying" (E, p. 307).

13. For Newtonian criticism, see note 1, above, and the following: R. S. Westfall, "Newton and the Hermetic Tradition" (hereafter cited by title in the text), in Debus, *Science, Medicine and Society;* Westfall, "The Role of Alchemy in Newton's Career" (hereafter cited as "Alchemy in Newton's Career" in the text), in *Reason, Experiment, and Mysticism in the Scientific Revolution,* ed. M. L. Righini Bonelli and William R. Shea (New York: Science History Publications, 1975), pp. 189–232; and J. E. McGuire, "Force, Active Principles, and Newton's Invisible Realm," *Ambix,* 15 (1968), 154–208 (hereafter cited as "Force" in the text). The Blake scholarship abounds in this area, but two studies almost completely devoted to this topic may suffice for the time being: George Mills Harper, *The*

Neoplatonism of William Blake (Chapel Hill: U. of North Carolina Press, 1961); and Kathleen Raine, *Blake and Tradition* (Princeton: Princeton U. Press, 1968).

14. I'm using the version quoted by S. Foster Damon's *A Blake Dictionary: The Ideas and Symbols of William Blake* (Providence: Brown U. Press, 1965), pp. 182–83.

15. See Henry M. Pachter, *Paracelsus: Magic into Science* (New York: Collier Books, 1951, 1961), esp. pp. 62 ff.

16. Quoted in Frank E. Manuel, *The Religion of Isaac Newton: The Fremantle Lectures 1973* (Oxford: Clarendon Press, 1974), p. 69.

17. Even though much of the material presented is based on the soundest scholarship of fine historians of science, the conclusions reached must be tentative. Westfall himself says, "What alchemy meant to Newton and the role it played in his scientific life remain . . . matters for interpretation" ("The Changing World of the Newtonian Industry," *Journal of the History of Ideas*, 37 [1976], 180). Further, when I point to the striking similarities between recent analysis of Newton's career and Blake's plot in *Jerusalem*, I am by no means insisting that Blake was privy to Newton's secret speculations (though one might wish there were proof of such). The parallels obtain because Newton's was a paradigmatic case of the kind of quest seventeenth- and eighteenth-century thinkers found themselves engaged in. It *is* of significance, however, that Newton himself was engaged in such a quest at its highest levels of research.

18. Especially *J.* 28:1 ff. (E, pp. 172–73). But this identification occurs in a number of places.

19. It is useful to note here that in her analysis of Newton's alchemy Betty Jo Teeter Dobbs invokes Jung's theory that the alchemical process is one which enacts an integration of the "persona" and the "shadow," or suppressed side of consciousness. The act of sinking into the shadow, embodied in alchemy by the process of putrefaction, death, and blackness, a "process of reducing matter to *nigredo*," required that the structure of matter itself be somewhat indefinite (in order to embody psychological projections) and therefore discourages the specific kinds of chemical analyses which emerged later (*Foundations*, pp. 32–34). The integration of the "shadow" into the "self" by means of projecting psychic function into the external medium of alchemical experiment then unleashes more deeply hidden pairs of psychic functions, which are the mysterious symbols of alchemy which persist through the centuries (*Foundations*, pp. 31–32). Two things are crucial here: first, the "integration" achieved by alchemical projection, which involves purification and separation as a prior step, is seen by Blake as a model of false interconnection (though he can transform this model for more positive uses). This false integration is a real lure for consciousness, however, and almost defeats Los in *Jerusalem* Chapter 4. Second, the indefinite concept of "matter" which Dobbs argues is central to successful projection of psychic contents onto an external medium makes alchemy incommensurable with the evolving specific mechanical and architectural models of matter which Newton was trying to develop. Newton ended up suppressing the alchemical urge for psychic wholeness (albeit from Blake's viewpoint this satisfaction of the urge for wholeness was a false one) in favor of the neutralized forms of classical mechanics.

20. Newton, *The Mathematical Principles of Natural Philosophy*, trans. Andrew Motte, 1729, with an introduction by I. Bernard Cohen (London: Dawson of Pall Mall, 1968), II, 205.

21. Any analysis of *The Four Zoas* opens a bucket of worms, as almost any

statement can be challenged. But that is what makes working with it fun. Erdman considers the possibility that Blake intended not an engraved poem but a unique illuminated manuscript in "The Binding (et cetera) of *Vala*," *The Library*, 5th ser., 19 (1964), 112–129. This might mean that Blake intended himself as the primary "reader."

22. In a book now nearing completion, tentatively titled "Perspective Ontology: Blake's Radical Narrative in *The Four Zoas*," I argue this point (and those that follow) in painstaking and elaborate detail through the whole poem. In this space I can only give a summary of some of the major ideas. This principle was suggested by and adapted from clues I first encountered in Ernst Cassirer, *Substance and Function and Einstein's Theory of Relativity* (New York: Dover Publications, 1953), and Alfred North Whitehead, *Process and Reality: An Essay in Cosmology* (New York: Harper & Row, 1929, 1957).

23. There are a variety of ways of interpreting this disjunction—including shifting the meaning of being "born" to being "murdered" and "embalmed." But in any case some inversion of explanatory coordinates is required to make the event make narrative sense.

24. Blake deleted the word "Dream" from the title but not from the phrase "End of the Dream" in Night IX. Since all the characters actually go to sleep right before the ambiguous appearance of a benign "Beulah"-like region (which is associated with "sleep") and immediately thereafter Blake gives us "End of the Dream," this "Dream" could be that from which the characters awaken, or that from which Blake expects the reader to awaken. In either case the pastoral dawn or the last few lines of the poem could be a form of the "false morning" which lies behind the actions of the whole poem, being introduced in Night I. It may be that Blake expects the reader to wake from the dream at this point, realizing that the mild vision of "Beulah" is really the delusive nightmare which generates the poem's horrors.

25. It seems shocking that at the point Tharmas and Enion reunite (at the Feast of Night IX), the "Eternal Man" splits into "Many Eternal Men" who suddenly "see/ The female form now separate" (*FZ* 133:5–6; E, p. 386).

26. This interpretation is a radical reversal of current speculation, but it does take into account the perceptual basis of the poem. In the context of the separation of the female, an Eternal speaks and tries (simplistically) to summarize the "fall," but, in the process, reveals his ignorance of the conditions of Beulah, "seeking the places dark/ Abstracted from the roots of Science then inclosd around/ In walls of Gold we cast him like a Seed into the Earth" (*FZ* 133:14–16; E, p. 386). This Eternal has a sense of the consequences of the Eternals' potential sexuality, but he perceives it quite differently from the earlier "revelling among the flowers of Beulah."

27. In rather different context, James C. Evans in "The Apocalypse as Contrary Vision: Prolegomena to an Analogical Reading of *The Four Zoas*," *TSLL*, 14 (1972), 313–28, and David Wagenknecht in *Blake's Night: William Blake and the Idea of Pastoral* (Cambridge: Belknap Press of Harvard U. Press, 1973), have suggested that the "apocalypse" is the "fall" but have not developed this idea in the way I have suggested.

28. Although Blake's illuminations are often bizarre and highly sexual, John E. Grant in a recent article ("Visions in *Vala:* A Considering of Some Pictures in the Manuscript," in *Blake's Sublime Allegory*, ed. Stuart Curran and Joseph A. Wittreich, Jr. [Madison: U. of Wisconsin Press, 1973], pp. 141–202) characterizes many of the (partially erased) drawings as pornographic (p. 191). What the infra-red camera recovers is a startling array of voyeurism—such as

two youths glaring (the male with an erased erection) at a huge gorilla-like figure astride a supine female in a position strongly suggesting fellatio, the male having "a long, hoselike phallus" (p. 189). Also scenes of defecation, anal penetration with a dildo, and a bat-winged penis-scrotum being chased by a female make evident a degree of sexual explicitness which even Blake may have been unwilling to work up into a final form (pp. 182–83). These radical gestures are visualized on pages in which the narrative is most evasive and suppressed. The central image of the verbal interchange between Urizen and Ahania is that of a "shadow," and the action depicted in Ahania's vision completely evades the female's involvement in the events which are unfolding. It is perhaps the least sexual of all the accounts of the primal fall in the poem. A close attention to verbal details of this sequence, however, from the point of view of perspective analysis and characters' verbal fictionalization and disguising of bodily gestures reveals that the sexual scenes not only make sense; they become necessary. One of the poem's central themes is the massive repression of sexuality by Urizen into the labyrinths of his mathematical universe, a universe which increasingly takes on sexual characteristics. The other characters act out the distorted sexual results of Urizen's cosmic sexual repression.

MORRIS EAVES

Blake and the Artistic Machine: An Essay in Decorum and Technology

"Mechanism" has been used in the history of ideas as a key term to describe the ideologies and cosmologies of the Enlightenment. Blake's use of the term is an episode in the history of that important metaphor. He used "machine" to describe and criticize a major line of development in the history of the arts, as when he said, "He who makes a design must know the Effect & Colouring Proper to be put to that design & will never take that of Rubens Rembrandt or Titian to turn that which is Soul & Life into a Mill or Machine."[1] His loathing of artistic machines is unmistakable and unequivocal: "vile tricks," he calls them, which "cause that every thing in art shall become a Machine" (*DC,* E, 537). "A Machine is not a Man nor a Work of Art it is destructive of Humanity & of Art" (PA, E, 564).[2]

Blake's use of "machine" as a critical metaphor has been passed over, but its background spreads out and down into his most rudimentary artistic principles, which he held firmly in defiance of the most common and rudimentary artistic principles of his century. Some of Blake's basic artistic ideas have been missed because they involve more than one art and a synthetic vision, if that is the word, of the relation between the arts and the rest of the culture. This, then, is an essay in the history of some ideas about art that involve ideas about commerce, science,

---

Reprinted by permission of the author and of the Modern Language Association of America from *PMLA* 92 (1977): 903–927.

and especially their intermediary, technology. To see what technology may have to do with the history of the arts, we must try to think of art, for the time being, as a technology. That is, instead of describing evolving artistic styles, we want to describe evolving systems of production and reproduction—systems of production being in some sense almost always systems of reproduction—in art.

The basic issue might be clarified by noticing how the limitations of a familiar machine impose limitations on the user. If the observant human pot-scrubber, whose washing by hand is almost infinitely adaptable, wishes to trade handwork for mechanized work, he will discover for himself the classic Romantic confrontation between mechanism and organism. The only way to go from one to the other is by *translating* the principles of one into the principles of the other. To save labor, the organic pot-scrubber gives up the privilege of using dishes that are too small, too large, too dirty, or too fragile. He ends up accepting a mechanical mean, which may be golden for the work it saves, but the quality of the translation is brass. For the user who hesitates to adapt, the machine has no answer except other more specialized machines or a highly complex machine that can adjust in steps (one button for especially dirty, one for especially fragile).

As the dishwasher affects the user, so the technology of reproducing works of art affects the artist. An artistic machine provides a system of translation for the sake of extension. The printing press is a particularly appropriate representative of the class, since printing is fundamentally a branch of engraving whose heredity has been obscured by its own mechanical evolution and the near death of the paternal trunk. Outlining human speech in movable type is made possible by translation, which depends upon fragmentation. One way to look at *speech* is as a translation of sensations and conceptions into auditory signs, often accompanied by gestures, for the sake of communication. *Writing* is a translation of auditory signs into visual signs for communication at a greater temporal or spatial distance, with the concomitant loss of many qualities that facilitate communication, such as pitch, volume, and gesture. *Printing* is a translation of one set of visual signs into another, made possible by the division of words into uniform letters, for the sake of repetition. The capacity for repetition inherent in print makes possible an immense extension in time and space simply by making feasible an increase in quantity.

In printing, as in dishwashing, the system of mechanical execution tends to limit the human tasks that can be performed. In the arts, the problem becomes the limits imposed by mechanical execution upon human conception. To a large extent, for instance, the writer is a slave to the press, and he adjusts accordingly. The easiest way to adjust, and the one discovered by modern humanity after long experience with the press, is for a writer to make himself over in the image of the printer by writing with a typewriter and by imitating the forms and conventions of the press. Take, for example, the novelist who wishes to make the page, rather than the chapter, the unit of narration in a novel. He probably cannot, because the typesetter, not the writer, is the master of the page. A novelist cannot consider the position of a word or sentence on the page; therefore in novels the position of words and sentences on the page is insignificant, and no reader ever thinks to consider it. The unlucky novelist with a regard for the mystical significance of number is liable to suffer if he hopes to work out his literary mathematics at any level less gross than the number and disposition of his chapters. But the graphic artist, who has usually controlled the elements in his composition, has had the option of using upper and lower as significant metaphors, and traditionally he has used them so. The rule for poets, who have traditionally made some attempt to control the appearance of their lines on the page, the poetic line being a unit ill suited to print, is that in a print culture the impression of sincerity and profundity increases in proportion to uniformity, which is a product of the mechanical principles by which the press operates.

I. Intermeasurability in Art

The history pertinent to Blake's term "machine" begins in the Renaissance, when engravers began to develop shop styles that could reproduce many kinds of pictures well and, at the same time, could be judged according to such rational economic characteristics as predictability, for instance, and consistency, efficiency, productivity, and profitability. It should be recognized that almost from the beginning the technology of picture reproduction was a constellation in the Gutenberg galaxy,[3] economically tied to the technology of word reproduction, the printing press, which set a mechanical and economic pace that the picture reproducers could never match from the Renaissance until the engraving trade went the way of the carriage trade at the beginning of this century. The printing press was always faster, always cheaper, and the translation from sounds to print that it provided was always less obvious than the translation from one visual medium to another.[4] On the other hand, their kinship means that many of the observations that can be made of word reproduction can be made of picture reproduction. Their economic and technological evolutions overlap; and, of course, whatever characteristics all technologies share, printing and engraving share. Furthermore, the evolution of the printing press as a technology was inextricably part of the economic evolution of the printing and publishing business, which we do not have space to discuss. The most important development (for our subject) was the creation of technological and economic intermediaries between the artist and the audience. The economic middleman and his systems—whether a mechanical invention in the ordinary sense, like the printing press, or a system of organizing production, sales, and distribution—were firmly in place and beginning to be noticed frequently by artists and authors in Blake's century. Of course Blake was not alone in observing that the middleman and his systems were turning words and pictures into a "portable commodity," in McLuhan's phrase.

Blake's century inherited and improved the systems of art making that had been developing since the Renaissance, and it is mainly to these systems that he is referring with his term "machines." Under the economic and technological pressures of the printing press, it did not take the artists of the Renaissance long to learn how to meet commercial need with a system of production based on a rational division of labor (the fundamental idea that, combined with motion, gives us the assembly line) and a graphic technique (a "style" in esthetic terminology) to match. "To match" means a great deal more than it may seem to, and we will be exploring that as we go.

The efficiently produced copies of Raphael's paintings that came out of Marcantonio's shop were the products of a process of systemization that affected important elements in artistic theory and practice for the next several centuries.[5] Between Marcantonio and the artists of Blake's time, Rubens is the most important artist-businessman in this line of development. He was influential in England, and what Blake calls "the Enterance of Vandyke & Rubens into this Country since which English Engraving is Lost" (PA, E, 561) is an easily documented event in the history of art.[6] In line with the commercial tradition represented in that "well known Saying" quoted by Blake, that "Englishmen Improve what others Invent" (PA, E, 565), the eighteenth century inherited and steadily improved Rubens' methods of production, which were not confined to printmaking. He refined ways of producing works of art in nearly every marketable medium and employed at least the elementary techniques, refined almost to perfection in subsequent centuries, of creating markets where none exist for a particularly profitable product.

We can see these developments with Blake's eyes if we go back to the technological and commercial ideas behind the "systems" of reproduction. For any division of labor to work, there has to be a product that is divisible. The combination of a divisible product of manufacture and a division of labor for producing it is sometimes called in intellectual histories "the rationalization of industry," which was, of course, essential in the Industrial Revolution, when manufacturing processes were "rationalized" on a very large scale. But that kind of rationalization of production had been used on a smaller scale—not revolutionizing the economy, but revolutionizing certain kinds of production—for a long time. Again, printing with movable type is a good example. The letter is the atom of printed language. If sentences cannot be divided into words and words into something like letters, movable type is an impossibility. Consider pictures in the same light, and we can see an aspect of the historical problem in the technology of picture reproduction and perhaps catch a glint of the technical solution that Blake saw as the very death of art.

If pictures could be divided into something parallel to

letters in words, then they could be easily reproduced (Illus. 1). Nothing quite so efficient happened until the inventions of photography and the halftone screen in the nineteenth century, but all the systems of art production evolved in just that direction. In painting, which we have not said much about, the example that comes immediately to mind is the system of portrait painting, practiced by Joshua Reynolds and most other painters of the time, in which labor was rationally divided so that the portraitist painted only the head and left the rest to the drapery painters, animal painters, hand painters, marine painters, and landscape painters—a legion of specialists, journeymen "finishers." Many of the most bizarre stories passed around in the painting trade during the century concern this division of labor: the one-man painting factory who adhered to a method so efficient that he could paint the twelve apostles while his wife got supper on the table; the warehouse of partly finished commissions left by Kneller at his death; the cartel of leading portraitists whose entire monopoly depended upon the services of a single drapery painter; and the famous mistakes made when a system seemed so efficient that the human operators who were plugged into it dozed for a moment and produced an admiral with two hats, or a lady in shepherdess garb who had burned to be seen posing in her finery.[7] Sometimes the scale of operation was limited to one painter in his studio; sometimes it was extended only beyond the portraitist as far as his favorite drapery man; sometimes it was as large as the workshops in which French engravers had manufactured their *estampes galantes;*[8] and yet again, by the end of the century, it could be as large as the scale on which Rudolph Ackermann in London produced his hundreds of thousands of colored prints manufactured at tables lined with French émigré laborers.[9] Though artists and critics made fun of it now and then, on the whole this division of labor—matched to a divison of techniques—was accepted as esthetically legitimate. It extended chronologically from Van Dyck and Kneller to Reynolds; hierarchically from the commonest hacks to presidents of the Royal Academy; and, although some of the manifestations and implications are different, across the arts from literature to architecture.

In engraving, the most versatile atom into which all pictures

A

B

Illustration 1. (A and B) If pictures could be divided into something parallel to letters in words, then they could be easily reproduced. Here are two systematic ways of dividing pictures for printed reproduction: (A) the face of Washington as engraved with conventional cross-hatching on the dollar bill, and (B) a familiar painting (White House Collection) reproduced by a coarse halftone screen.

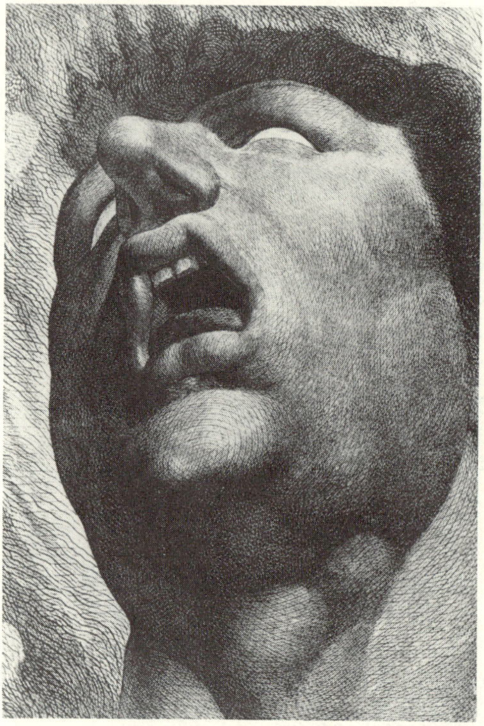

C

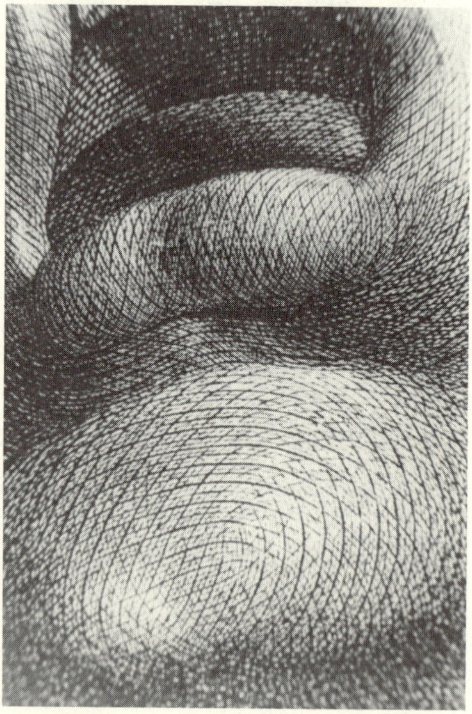

D

Illustration 2. (C & D) This print (C), probably of Satan's head, is the product of a fairly typical eighteenth-century collaboration between designer and engraver, in this case Fuseli and Blake, respectively. Blake's work on the lips and chin (D) is a fine representation of the dot-and-lozenge technique of cross-hatching, which in 1790 was as flashy and as standardized as the tap-dancing in a movie musical in 1945. (By permission of the Trustees of the British Museum.)

E *Morning Amusement*

F

Illustration 3. (E & F) The detail (F) from Blake's very early print *Morning Amusement* (E) (1782), after Watteau, is a good example of eighteenth-century "high finish" in a popular mode, stipple engraving. This sort of slickness must startle the eyes of those who learned who Blake was by looking at his original work. Here we see him just doing his job as a skilled reproductive engraver. Obviously Blake would have preferred never having to do journeywork, even of this fancy kind. But he did it consistently, and his argument is not against commercial copying but against not being able to tell the difference between the principles and techniques that produce good copies and the principles that produce good art. (By permission of the Trustees of the British Museum.)

G

Illustration 4. (G) A halftone screen reproducing only itself, to show the intermeasurable units of which it is composed, and by which it becomes so efficient a reproducer of tones. The halftone screen is the direct technological descendent of reproductive engraving techniques. Many of the screens are named after engraving techniques and media; thus "mezzotint" screens, "circular" screens, etc.

Illustration 5. (H & I) The effects of systematic techniques of reproduction can be drastic if the original artist does not design for the system of execution—and the result is the same in either case. Is the white-line etching (H) on the facing page (detail from *Death's Door,* Mrs. Charles J. Rosenbloom, Pittsburgh) what Blake showed R. H. Cromek when he came to see how Blake was getting along with the illustrations to Blair's *Grave* that Cromek had commissioned? That seems likely. If so, it is no wonder that Cromek, one of those enterprising Traders whose minds are "on the Many. or rather on the Money," hired Schiavonetti to "execute" Blake's "conceptions," with the result shown in the lower illustration (I) (detail; by permission of the Trustees of the British Museum).

Schiavonetti knew his work, and he knew how to load every rift with neoclassical values. Blake's stark background would have looked barbaric to him, so he subdued it to the point of inoffensiveness with fine, light hatching, just enough tone to set off the figure. Blake's figure radiates light like a human sun; Schiavonetti's figure is posing in front of a natural rising sun. Schiavonetti corrected the distorted face and body of Blake's figure, taking away all but a "reasonable" amount of stress in the posture. And finally, he carried over into his engraving the strong outlines of Blake's figure, but he softened them considerably with fastidious patterns of hatching and stipple. In his white-line print Blake has outlined the body of the figure with a single white line, for a peculiar effect that would have looked simply crude to Schiavonetti, who did the opposite, blending the outline with the shading of the muscles. Thus Blake called his "finishing" engraver "Assassinetti" (E, 495) for his pains.

H

I

MARIN. CVRÆVS DE LA CHAMBRE, REGI A SANCT. CONSIL. ET MEDICVS ORDINARIVS
R. Nanteuil ad viuum delineabat et sculpebat

J

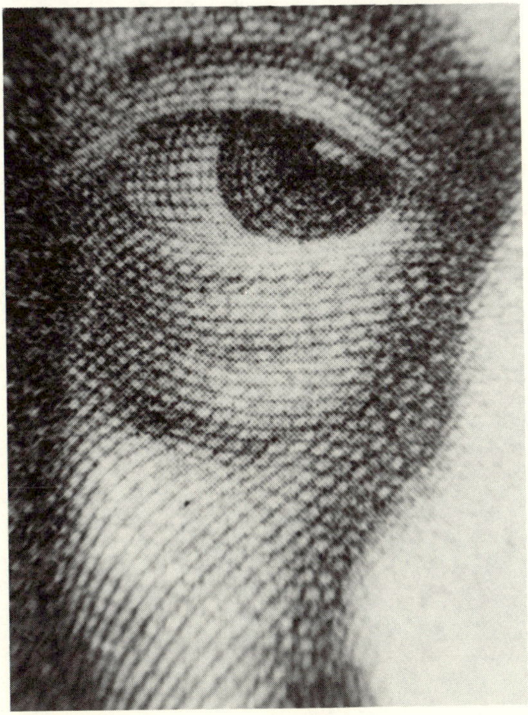

K

Illustration 6. (J, K, & L) Robert Nanteuil's seventeenth-century engraved portrait of *Marin Cureau de la Chambre* (J) from the court of Louis XIV and two details (K, L) show how the capabilities of systematic techniques of engraving were developed for the reproduction of tonal values. The viewer, of course, should admire the luxurious realism of the folds of cloth and the subtle shading of the face—as smooth as the manners of the court in the best fantasies of the courtiers. (By permission of the Trustees of the British Museum.)

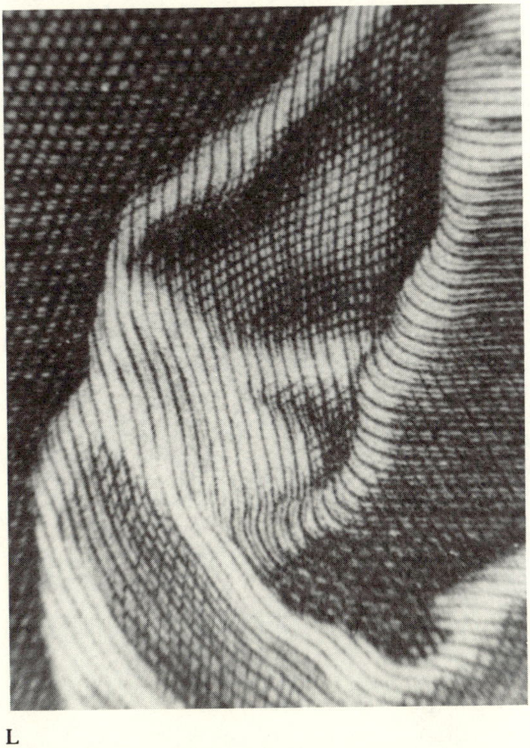

L

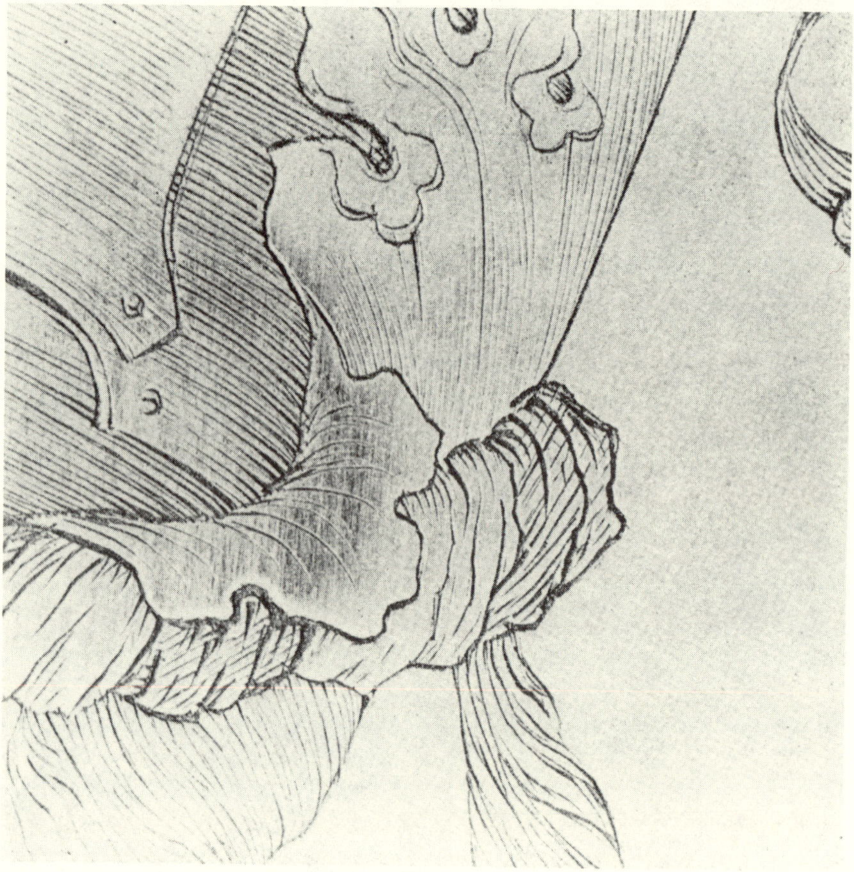

M

Illustration 7. (M) A magnified detail from a line engraving on a copper plate, to illustrate the simplest and most direct use of the medium. (Hesketh Hubbard, ed., *How to Distinguish Prints* [Woodgreen Common, Eng.: Print Society, 1926], p. 55, top illustration.)

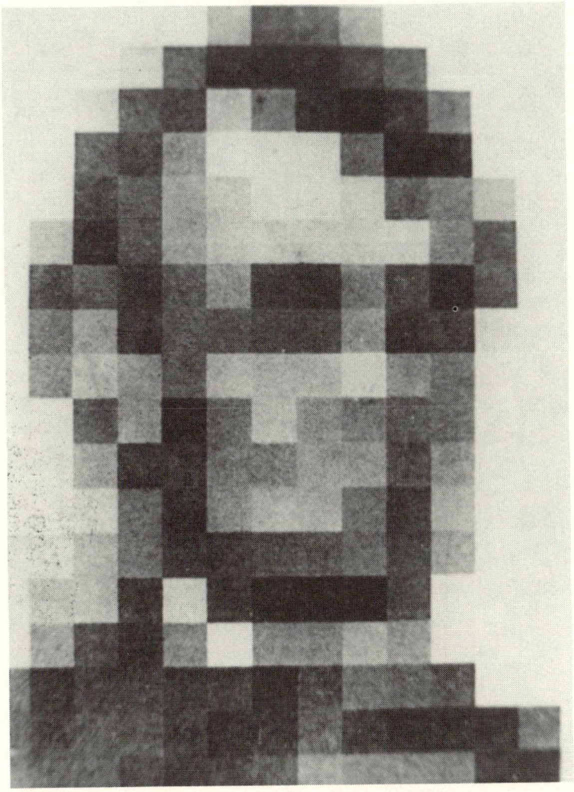

N

Illustration 8. (N) The "block portrait" reproduced here was made originally to test the human ability to recognize faces, as in police sketches, for example. The method calls for the imposition of a uniform grid over a photograph and the averaging, by computer, of all tones within each grid to a single tone. The experiment was described by Leon D. Harmon in "The Recognition of Faces," *Scientific American*, Nov. 1973, pp. 70-82. (By permission of Leon D. Harmon and Bell Laboratories.) This is a mechanical simulacrum, a model if you will, of the "Artistic Machine" as Blake, conceived of it, a system of representation imposed upon a "vision" and destroying it. The reproduction shows clearly the characteristics of such "machines," whether the modern printed halftone and the electronic televison picture or the systematic techniques of engraving in Blake's time: intermeasurability; tone (general effect, "generalization") superior to detail (line, "minute particulars"); and fragmentation ("broken lines, broken masses, and broken colours," *DC*, E, 529). "Harmony" is the effect obtained by a method of obscuring the "atoms" that compose the picture: squinting, throwing it out of focus, or looking at it from a distance. The paradox important to Blake is that, the closer one looks at such pictures, the more obscure they become.

O

P

Illustration 9. (O, P, Q, & R) Blake's engraved plate 12 of his *Illustrations of the Book of Job* (O) and a detail (P), and a detail from the watercolor drawing that Blake later made into plate 12 (Q) and a halftone reproduction of the detail from the watercolor (R). Since the *Job* engravings were both "designed" and "executed" by Blake himself—without a finishing engraver to impose a standard system of visual translation—we can compare Blake's engraving with the reproduction obtained from an Artistic Machine, in this case a halftone that simulates mechanically the effect of a systematic engraving technique. (Illustrations O and P, by permission of the Trustees of the British Museum; Q and R courtesy of the Fogg Art Museum, Harvard University, bequest of Grenville L. Winthrop.)

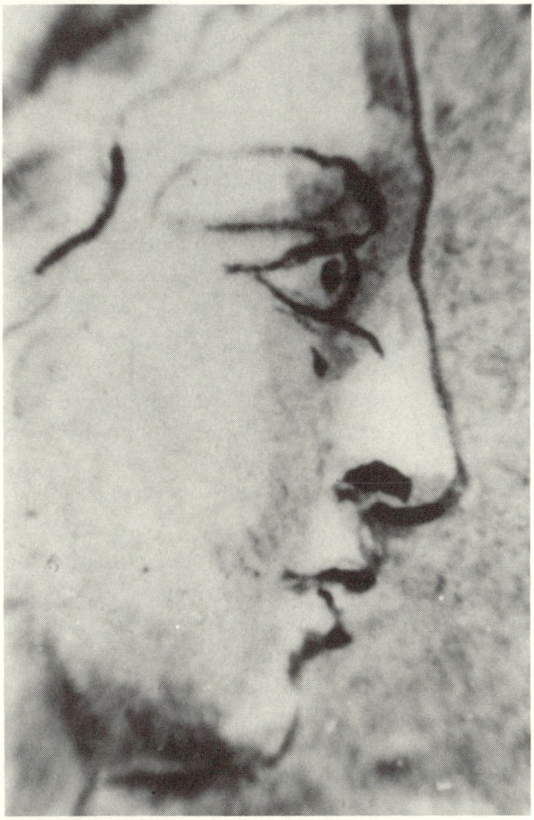

Q

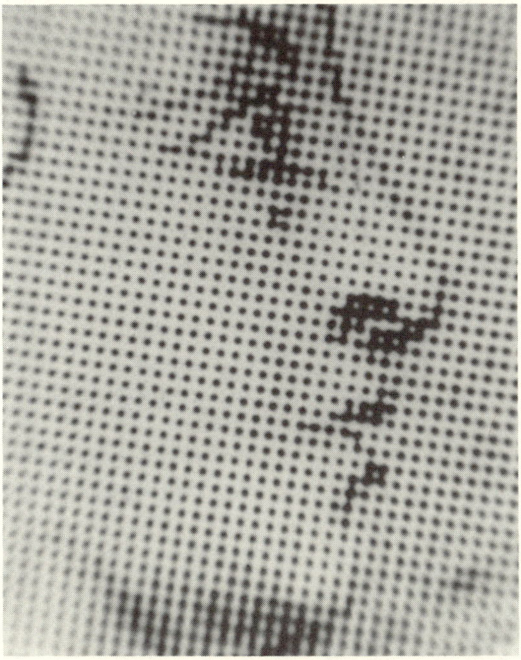

R

could be divided was the "lozenge" of cross-hatching, which was (approximately) an infinitely adjustable quadrilateral that could be combined with others of its kind into vast nets or webs of varying density to create whatever light or shadow was needed at any point in a design (Illus. 2). (For the reader with little or no knowledge of printmaking, a good example might be the face of George Washington as etched for the dollar bill by George Smillie in 1918, using techniques common two centuries earlier.) The same possibilities were latent in the dot, and eighteenth-century engravers learned to use quite homogeneous forms of stipple (Illus. 3). Mezzotint represents the discovery that to create tone without line it is easier to start from black and go to grays than to start from white. The "atom" of mezzotint, despite superficial differences in the method of production, is still the dot, as it is in stipple—but a dot in relief, created by roughening the surface of the plate.

The perfect system of reproduction would reproduce anything perfectly. Because there is no perfect system, the reproductions will always be imperfect. The technological gap between the original and the reproduction is what interests us, because we can safely guess that the difference that occurs in the gap is significant and affects the artists' originals not only now but also in the future and affects as well the audience, its understanding of the work, judgment of the work, artistic expectations, and so on. The most drastic hypothesis—the one to which Blake seems to have subscribed—would be that the system, the artistic machine, in the middle between artist and audience was capable of making everything over in its image. We have seen this tendency in the dishwasher, though it is not limited to "machines" in the sense of metal things with motors and gears but extends to the systemization of almost any procedure. We notice every day that the mechanization of one thing—tasks like washing dishes or moving down a road at a high speed comfortably—tends to force the mechanization of other things—the consumer's desires in the marketplace or the process used to manufacture the product—if the mechanical advantage gained by the systemization is great enough.

Blake noticed that systemization is most often based on a principle of intermeasurability—that is, the division of something (a product or a procedure or, most often, both) into rational units (Illus. 4), to arrive at a system of translation by which two or more things can be dealt with in the same way. Blake connected intermeasurability with contemporary science, especially the Newtonian idea of "a space composed of points, and a time composed of instants, which had an existence independent of the bodies and events that occupied them,"[10] a doctrine that corresponded to a contemporary notion in art. We could just as easily say, for instance, that eighteenth-century artists believed in a space composed of points, a time composed of instants, and so on. The separation of time and space from bodies and events in Newtonian physics corresponds to the separation of form and content in neoclassical esthetics.[11] Blake was thinking of this correspondence when he asked, "What Man of Sense will lay out his Money upon the Lifes Labours of Imbecillity & Imbecillitys Journeymen or think to Educate a Fool how to build a Universe with Farthing Balls" (PA, E, 568)[12]—farthing balls being the commercial version of a Newtonian atom, "A Thing that does not Exist" (*Letters*, 162). Note the train of Blake's thought in asserting individuality and identity against the mechanistic Newtonian atomism: "a Line is a Line in its Minutest Subdivisions: Strait or Crooked It is Itself & Not Intermeasurable with or by any Thing Else. Such is Job"—Blake means both his Job engravings and Job as a biblical character who asserts his identity against intermeasurability—"but since the French Revolution Englishmen are all Intermeasurable One by Another, Certainly a happy state of Agreement to which I for One do not Agree" (*Letters*, 162). He goes on to say that "Experimentalists must suppose" that "Up & Down" are "the same Thing" (*Letters,* 162), meaning simply that technology and eighteenth-century science had no choice but to believe in intermeasurability, without which they could not systemize.

But Blake's thought goes beyond a simple distinction between artistic method and scientific method to claim that a mechanical method at one point mechanizes everything that depends upon it: "Englishmen are all Intermeasurable." Furthermore, he connects intermeasurabilty not only with physical theories and artistic theories but also with political theories: "I know too well that a great majority of Englishmen are fond of

The Indefinite which they Measure by Newton's Doctrine of the Fluxions of an Atom, A Thing that does not Exist. These are Politicians & think that Republican Art is Inimical to their Atom" (*Letters,* 162). With this apparently crazy leap Blake is only saying that a mechanical advantage is often a commercial advantage—and that science and commerce are often partners in a foursome with technology and politics.[13] To put the matter simply, Blake wanted to live in a society based on artistic principles, and he found himself living in one based on technological principles. The result was the intrusion of commercial technology into art in the form of "artistic machines." The intrusion takes the following form. The system of reproduction is fixed and cannot change. The artist can change his original to accommodate it—match it—to the system, and the *system* thus becomes the *style* of the artist who is willing to become what the machine can behold. This is what Blake called the Limits of Opacity and Contraction, man becoming the machine he creates in order to get a mechanical advantage, which is usually a commercial advantage, certainly not often an artistic one. Historically, artists learned to draw for the systems to which they were subject. This is what sympathetic critics of Rubens mean when they refer to his sketches as "rugged";[14] another way of describing them would be "general" and "well adjusted": general enough to survive execution by an efficient system of reproduction and still have the trademark "Rubens" on them. The most efficient behavior for artists was to learn to draw for their systems of reproduction. If they failed to learn, the result in the finished product was the same anyway, the machine making over in its own image all things that pass through it. The artistic product of the machine becomes what the machine is able to behold. Blake had this experience many times, perhaps never so memorably as with Cromek and his "finishing" engraver Schiavonetti (Illus. 5).[15]

II. Technology, Decorum, and the Bounding Line

In lamenting the state of the arts in his time, Blake lamented most of the loss of drawing in art, the loss of the line: as "absurd

Nonsense about dots & Lozenges & Clean Strokes [is] made to occupy the attention to the Neglect of all real Art" (PA, E, 571); "Engraving by Losing drawing has Lost all Character & all Expression" (PA, E, 561). The loss of drawing Blake saw not as a simple esthetic choice—giving up the line in return for "painterly" values—but as a sacrifice of true art to commerce, whose requirements were dictating the principles of art. Linearity, like its negation, intermeasurability, is a metaphor of explicitness for Blake that is not only artistic (in the narrow sense). Remarks about "the hard and wirey line of rectitude and certainty in the actions and intentions" and the line as the "great and golden rule of art, as well as of life" show the interpenetration of art and life in Blake's thinking. Thus the consequences of the artistic battle between linearity and intermeasurability are immense. Art divided, life divides, and the leviathans of the culture take over: "Leave out this l[i]ne and you leave out life itself; all is chaos again, and the line of the almighty [i.e., the imagination] must be drawn out upon it before man or beast can exist" (*DC*, E, 540).

Blake's dedication to the artistic line and to its inevitable product, the minute particular, has been discussed many times, and he has been placed where he belongs in art history, on the side of two-dimensional linearists in the old esthetic battle between the linear and the painterly schools.[16] But there is an aspect of the conflict that is technological and economic as well as esthetic. The capabilities of the systems of reproduction that I have outlined were in the reproduction of tonal values (Illus. 6). No matter what classical geometry says, points do not combine to make a satisfactory line, and neither do lozenges, and yet points are as necessary to the systemization of picture reproduction as they are to the systemization of geometry. Systematic techniques need an atomistic basis. On the other hand, the easiest thing to do with a copper plate and a burin is to make a line or some other coherent mark (Illus. 7); nothing is harder to make than a tone. Until tonal media such as aquatint and mezzotint became popular in the eighteenth century, tones had in fact to be built up from systems of lines in all the standard systems of engraving. From the Renaissance through the nineteenth century engraving was thought of as a medium of translation and reproduction, following the fashions initiated in other media, oil painting for example, where the painters favored color and tone over line. Color and tone come easily to oil; line does not. As a parasitic medium of translation and reproduction, engraving worked to adapt, and its entire history can be described almost accurately as an extended search for ways of subverting, usually by disguising, what naturally happens when an engraver's tools are put to metal.

Now Blake loved the line and loved engraving, and we can see how his artistic principles and his medium match, though we cannot say which came first. He liked also to combine media where lines were easy to make—tempera with engraving as a base, for instance, or watercolor with lines of pen and ink—and he avoided the favorite "painterly" medium, oil, which he said was invented by his favorite villains, Rubens and Van Dyck (*DC,* E, 521). But the difference between Blake and many other "linearists" is that, in the historical shift from line to tone and color, he saw art being sacrificed to commerce. As everyone knows, he identified a "class of men" that he variously called false artists, counterfeiters, and Quack Doctors of the "Contemptible Counter Arts" (PA, E, 569), "whose whole art and science is fabricated for the purpose of destroying art" (*DC*, E, 529) and replacing it with "the Lifes Labour of Ignorant Journeymen Suited to the Purposes of Commerce" (PA, E, 562)—an art completely adjusted to the requirements of commerce. Out of this belief came his paranoid-sounding remarks about the attempts of "Sr Joshua & his Gang of Cunning Hired Knaves" (AR, E, 625) to destroy his career and the careers of other true artists, "to Starve me out by Calumny & the Arts of Trading Combination" (PA, E, 566).

To find out why Blake connected bad art with the methods of commerce, we need to resort to the traditional critical problem of *decorum,* the prissy term that covers the relationship between form and content in the arts. Blake's position on decorum has been largely overlooked in favor of those colorful angry remarks of his on the line, generalization, minute particulars, and the like. They are important, of course, but subsidiary to the larger and more central problem of form and content, and it is decorum that makes sense of Blake's complaint about the effects of commerce on art. Since Blake saw the technological and economic effects of systems of reproduction in terms of the relationship between form and content, we can make that our touchstone, and generate other esthetic issues from it.

The division of labor that forces the division of the object of the labor—the product—also forces the division of conception from execution, because the conception is one stage in the division of labor and execution is another. When this division is formalized, the result is the sort of thing Blake saw in the engraving trade: conception was assigned to the original artist; execution to someone else. If execution were by means of a simple and perfect system of reproduction, of course, the division would not matter. But Blake indicated the true state of affairs when he spoke of "the Lifes Labour of Ignorant Journeymen Suited to the Purposes of Commerce no doubt for Commerce Cannot endure Individual Merit its insatiable Maw must be fed by What all can do Equally well" (PA, E, 562). That is, the systems of execution used in Blake's time were systems of translation "improved" ("A Man who Pretends to Improve Fine Art does not know what Fine Art is," PA, E, 562) by centuries of trial and error, manned by journeymen who could learn the system, owned by commerce, and ready for hire to the highest bidders:

> While the Works [deleted *of Translators*] of Pope & Dryden are lookd upon as the Same Art with those of Milton & Shakespeare while the works of Strange & Woollett [eminent contemporary commercial engravers] are lookd upon as the same Art with those of Rafael & Albert Durer there can be no Art in a Nation but such as is Subservient to the interest of the Monopolizing Trader [deleted *who Manufactures Art by the Hands of Ignorant Journeymen till at length Christian Charity is held out as a Motive to encourage a Blockhead & he is Counted the Greatest Genius who can sell a Good for Nothing Commodity for a Great Price [.] Obedience to the Will of the Monopolist is calld Virtue and the really Industrious Virtuous & Independent Barry* [the artist] *is driven out to make room for a pack of Idle Sycophants with whitlors* [i.e., *whitloes* sores] *on their fingers*] Englishmen rouze yourselves from the fatal Slumber into which Booksellers & Trading Dealers have thrown you Under the artfully propagated pretence that a Translation or a Copy of any kind can be as honourable to a Nation as an Original. . . . (PA, E, 564–65)

In a system of translation, conception or the original "design" begins to be regarded as "information" or "content," which will be given its final shape, its "form," by the standard systems of translation. Like any other trade engraver, Blake found himself on either end of the process many times, but seldom on both ends, and that is the problem. To Blake's mind the artistic process is a perfect combination, an indivisible continuum, of conception and execution, content and form. The artistic sign of the presence of such a continuum is a coherent "bounding line" (*DC*, E, 540), which is "a Line in its Minutest Subdivisions: Strait or Crooked It is Itself & Not Intermeasurable with or by any Thing Else" (*Letters,* 162). An artistic machine cannot produce such a line, and the absence or presence of one is the telltale sign of true art or false.

The legitimization of the division of conception from execution, content from form, poisons true art, in Blake's opinion. But the division is a central assumption behind the most important principles in the mainstream of eighteenth-century esthetics. The systemized relationships between conception and execution become the set of matched categories we call "decorum," governed by the principle of "propriety." The most common criticism of Blake's art in his time was that he could conceive but not execute: "the Lavish praise I have recieved from all Quarters for Invention & Drawing has Generally been accompanied by this he can concieve but he cannot Execute" (PA, E, 571). Such a criticism could never have been made if a division between conception and execution had not been a naturalized, perhaps unconscious, assumption. The very important neoclassical ideas of "imitation," "high finish," "refinement," "regularity," and "correctness" are parts of an esthetic based on consensus, and they are not possible without assuming a separation between conception and execution: "Why are we to be told that Masters who Could Think had not the Judgment to Perform the Inferior Parts of Art as Reynolds artfully calls them. But that we are to Learn to Think from Great Masters & to Learn to Perform from Underlings? Learn to Design from Rafael & to Execute from Rubens?" (AR, E, 628). "Invention [i.e., conception] depends Altogether upon Execution or Organization. as that is right or wrong so is the Invention perfect or imperfect. Whoever is set to

Undermine the Execution of Art is set to Destroy Art Michael Angelos Art Depends on Michael Angelos Execution Altogether" (AR, E, 626). In the Library of the Royal Academy Blake would say to George Moser, the Keeper, "These things that you call Finishd are not Even Begun how can they then, be Finishd? The Man who does not know The Beginning, never can know the End of Art" (AR, E, 628).

Blake defended his art repeatedly on the grounds that were soon after to become a Romantic esthetic commonplace in the idea of "organic form": that conception and execution are not divisible, are one and the same thing, that each must necessarily be perfectly appropriate to the other, or the result is absolute artistic incoherence:

> I have heard many People say Give me the Ideas. It is no matter what Words you put them into & others say Give me the Design it is no matter for the Execution. These People know Enough of Artifice but Nothing of Art. Ideas cannot be Given but in their minutely Appropriate Words nor Can a Design be made without its minutely Appropriate Execution[.] The unorganized Blots & Blurs of Rubens & Titian are not Art nor can their Method ever express Ideas or Imaginations any more than Popes Metaphysical Jargon of Rhyming[.] Unappropriate Execution is the Most nauseous of all affectation & foppery He who copies does not Execute he only Imitates what is already Executed Execution is only the result of Invention[.]
>
> (PA, E, 565)

From his eighteenth-century lexicon he may choose a word Pope and Reynolds would have been comfortable with, "appropriate," to express the relationship of conception to execution, but Blake leans very far toward the radical position that conception *is* execution—the identity of form and content: "Execution is only the result of Invention." Pope, Titian, Rubens, and Rembrandt allowed "their Method" to interfere and got "unorganized Blots & Blurs" as a result. Blake is claiming to have no method and thus asking to be judged by his execution: "I know my Execution is not like Any Body Else I do not intend it should be so[.] none but Blockheads copy one another[.] My Conception & Invention are on all hands allowd to be Superior My Execution will be found so too" (PA, E, 571).

Blake's position may be most easily seen is terms of contrasting metaphors. Romantic criticism replaced neoclassical metaphors of balance, as in the matched categories of decorum, with metaphors of integrity. Thus in Romanticism the artistic version of self-division is the division between the artist and the work of art. A number of positive Romantic metaphors show the aim for an integrity of artist and work, so that the work seems to be thought of as the direct projection of the artist's imagination. "Sincerity" and the "true voice of feeling" describe this kind of integrity, and, of course, there is the pervasive organic metaphor, used almost indiscriminately to describe both the creative process and the artistic results of it. Blake uses a number of such metaphors—"appropriateness," "expression," "intention," "physiognomy"—all of which work to connect mental conception with physical and formal execution.

The technology of reproduction that I have outlined offers a subversive countermetaphor, of artistic conception radically separated from artistic execution by a nonartistic intermediary—a "machine" that interrupts the "expression" of the artist's "intention." In Blake's opinion neoclassical esthetics, as embodied for example in the scheme of decorum, whose root metaphors are hierarchy and balance rather than integrity, subverted all possibility of true art by sanctioning the interruption between conception and execution. That is the complaint Blake has in mind when he reacts to Reynolds' idea of a "composite style": "There is No Such a Thing as A Composite Style" (AR, E, 641)—in art, that is, though there can be nothing else when commerce and art combine.

The literary and artistic incoherence that Blake saw in Pope, Titian, Rubens, and Rembrandt is the result, Blake thought, of the separation of form from content by "Method," that is, systematic techniques of translation and production. If we understand the causes of "unorganized Blots & Blurs" in Blake's terms, then we can make new sense of Blake's view of some major neoclassial artistic tenets. Since we do not have the space to take up all the ideas that fit into this framework, let us take as a final instance the principle of "harmony" in the arts, which is strongly related to the fragmentation that an artistic machine causes.

Harmony is one of those neoclassical principles that drift over into Romanticism without much change, so that we find Coleridge, for example, using it as a principle around which to organize his discussion, ostensibly of the painter Allston, really of beauty and artistic unity, in the essays on *Genial Criticism* (1814). Harmony, Coleridge says in the third essay, is the unity achieved by the fine arts when they succeed in the Platonic aim of reducing the Many to One, achieving "*multeity in unity,*" which as it happens is an idea as important to science and technology as to metaphysics, theology, and esthetics.[17] Coleridge's treatment simply adjusts a neoclassical idea to some Romantic premises, but they are the premises to which Blake objected most strenuously when he read Wordsworth, where he found a lot of talk about the fitting of the mind to nature, which Blake saw, not as an original premise on which to base the writing of a new poetry, but as an ominous new step in the application of Lockean epistemology to art that had been evolving for a century at least. He came down hard on Wordsworth, and he would have been equally rough on Coleridge for being a neoclassicist under the skin with his definitions of harmony and unity, confusion of particulars and general ideas, association of universals with geometric forms, and accommodation of the imagination to the natural world.

At least in Blake's terms, Coleridge's passages on harmony and unity will not bear the interpretation one might be tempted to give them on Romantic grounds: that the One is an "organic" (as opposed to a mechanical) unity to which the Many contribute. When criticizing the "disharmony" of Wordsworth's "style" in Chapter xxii of *Biographia Literaria,* Coleridge defines the harmony he was looking for just as any neoclassical critic would have: ". . . the business of the writer, like that of a painter whose subject matter requires unusual splendor and prominence, is so to raise the lower and neutral tints, that what in a different style would be the *commanding* colors, are here used as the means of that gentle *degradation* requisite in order to produce the effect of a *whole,*" a sentence that, if Coleridge had been in one of his more imitative moods, he could have paraphrased from any number of passages in Reynolds' *Discourses.* "Degradation" is a favorite eighteenth-century word for describing artistic harmony, and Blake incorporates it, along with the geometric image of the pyramid and images of systemization (frame) and force (plank), into a serious parody in *Jerusalem* 45[31], where Los explores simultaneously the artistic and social interior of Albion with his lamp and sees

> . . . every Minute Particular of Albion degraded & murderd
> But saw not by whom; they were hidden within in the minute particulars
> Of which they had possessd themselves; and there they take up
> The articulations of a mans soul, and laughing throw it down
> Into the frame, they knock it out upon the plank, & souls are bak'd
> In bricks to build the pyramids of Heber & Terah. But Los
> Searchd in vain: closd from the minutia he walkd, difficult.
> (45[31].7–13, E, 192)

Minute particulars are lost, of course, because harmony is an overall blending of line and tone, "soft and even tints without boundaries, and of endless reflected lights, that confuse one another," in order to give the work of art "softness and evenness, by a twelvemonth's labour" (*DC,* E, 538); in short, "one Generalizing Tone" (E, 507).

In the well-known, but less well understood, remark that "Demonstration Similitude & Harmony are Objects of Reasoning Invention Identity & Melody are Objects of Intuition" (AR, E, 648), Blake's theory of knowledge is not so important to us as the company that harmony keeps: an artistic principle whose roots are not in art (intuition) but in science, technology, and commerce (reasoning). The opposition between melody and harmony used here (in the margins of a book on painting) perhaps obscures the fact that Blake was thinking of the visual and literary arts as well as music. He is careful to make the application complete in *Jerusalem:*

> I tell how Albions Sons by Harmonies of Concords & Discords

> Opposed to Melody, and by Lights & Shades, opposed to
> Outline
> And by Abstraction opposed to the Visions of Imagination
> (74.24–26, E, 227)

Blake shows how harmony might be used as a legitimate artistic term in his late annotations to Berkeley's *Siris:* "Harmony [and] Proportion are Qualities & Not Things The Harmony & Proportion of a Horse are not the same with those of a Bull Every Thing has its own Harmony & Proportion Two Inferior Qualities in it For its Reality is Its Imaginative Form" (E, 653), the political version of which, "One Law for the Lion & Ox is Oppression" (E, 43), he had etched into *The Marriage of Heaven and Hell* as early as the 1790s.

On the other hand, when among the paragraphs "On Homers Poetry" that Blake etched around 1820 he included the cryptic assertion that ". . . Unity is the cloke of folly . . ." (E, 267), he meant the kind of unity that painters, for instance, were trying to achieve with chiaroscurist techniques. In Blake's opinion, the object of artistic harmony is to disguise the true fragmentation and incoherence beneath the surface of a work of art with the *appearance* of unity, harmony being the most common synonym for unity in neoclassical discussions. Systematic techniques, such as chiaroscuro—not any emphatic use of light and shade, of course, but the systematic techniques that the word designated in Blake's time—for achieving harmony he regarded as ways of covering up the truth with an artificially imposed pattern (Illus. 8). Thus where the painters and critics of his age found in Rembrandt's work lessons in chiaroscurist harmony,[18] Blake found a bag of tricks; where the age found models of harmony and high finish, Blake found "unorganized Blots & Blurs."

The confrontation here has technological roots in a characteristic mechanical paradox: coherence and unity in the artistic machine kill all hope of coherence and unity in the artistic product. So Blake talks of "broken lines, broken masses, and broken colours" in the "Venetian and Flemish practice" (*DC,* E, 529) that he thought had ruined eighteenth-century art. The point here is that, for the artist who does not conceive in its terms, the artistic machine may as well be net or a stone wall. The machine does not change, and it *is* the execution. The array of artistic conceptions flies into pieces at the machine, and only the fragments that the machine can accept get through. These artistic scraps come out sifted into perfect order, but the order is the order of the laws of the machine, not the laws of art, of which there are none. Or, to put it another way, the order of the machine is substituted for the order of art, and the order of art is sacrificed (Illus. 9). This is why Blake can say that the "Blots & Blurs of Rubens & Titian" are "unorganized" and "not Art" (PA, E, 565) and that "All Rubens's Pictures are Painted by Journeymen & so far from being all of a Piece. are The most wretched Bungles" (AR, E, 644). All the arts, conceived in freedom, are executed under the laws of the artistic machine.

But, after all, the machines do not grind and stamp for art, and the system woven into the engravings and the printed pages that come off the press are not woven by the artist. An artistic machine is an impossibility; there are only commercial machines. For a long time there may be some confusion as to who dictates to whom—for example, the grammarian to the printer, or vice versa—but only because there are always artists and estheticians busy converting the rules of commerce into rules of art, often unconsciously, hypnotically, as in Blake's metaphor of "Newton's sleep," but also often consciously, "Picture traders Music traders & Rhime traders" with an "Eye . . . on the Many. or rather on the Money," "A Pretence of Art: To Destroy Art" (PA, E, 569; AR, E, 645, 631). If he had not known it before—though, of course, he had—Blake could have learned in reading Reynolds' *Discourses* that principles of manufacture can become esthetic principles and that in a commercial empire the approved art is at many points an allegory of commerce. "Economy" as a principle of artistic style and good business simultaneously may advertise its promiscuous relations with art and commerce more boldly than most such principles, but in a commerical empire the approved esthetic is never an obstacle to business.

Blake was a skilled reproductive engraver himself. Prints reproduced with this essay show how well he could use even the most ostentatious, complicated, and fashionable techniques of reproduction. The question of self-contradiction naturally arises. Obviously, Blake would have preferred never having to do journeywork. But he did it consistently, devoting much of his energy to reproducing the work of others, and in 1799 he wrote in a letter to Dr. Trusler that "To Engrave after another Painter is infinitely more laborious than to Engrave one's own Inventions. . . . [But] I have no objection to Engraving after another Artist. Engraving is the profession I was apprenticed to . . ." (*Letters,* 30–31). Blake's argument is not against commercial copying but against not being able to tell the difference between the principles and techniques that produce good copies and translations and the principles that produce good art. He thought that in the practice and theory of Reynolds the two were confused and that Reynolds' *Discourses* proved it. And, of course, Blake's feelings about Reynolds extended to the artistic principles for which Reynolds was the leading representative in his century.

Moreover, the proper distinction to be made between Blake and his contemporary artists is not that he had a horror of systematic cross-hatching and they did not. The evidence, at least as I read it, will not support that. Blake did not always write tolerantly, but the artistic principles he wrote about are fundamentally tolerant, or at least broad. They do not exclude webs, nets, dots, lozenges, color, tone, rhyme, heroic couplets, or any other aspect of graphic or literary technique. It was rather the transforming of these methods of convenience into artistic principles of imitation, harmony, correctness, and high finish that infuriated Blake, who always could see through the superficial levels of artistic practice into basic artistic principles. Thus Blake's broad principles exclude the ignorant insistence on any single technique. He saw this insistence for what we now say it genuinely was: fashion, represented equally by the poets' obsession with couplets and the artists' with "Chiaro Scuro" and "clean strokes" and dots and lozenges. When he said "I defy any Man to Cut Cleaner Strokes than I do or rougher when I please. . . . Drawing is Execution & nothing Else . . ." (PA, E 571), he was speaking from his basic artistic belief in appropriateness—of conception to execution, means to ends. The worship of a single technique is the worship of the Artistic Machine, which can be

Satan himself. Like his hero Los, Blake watched his culture very closely, keeping the "Divine Vision in time of trouble." And every so often in his vigilance he would issue the kind of clear morning call to artists with which *Milton* begins:

> Rouze up O Young Men of the New Age! set your foreheads against the ignorant Hirelings! For we have Hirelings in the Camp, the Court & the University: who would if they could, for ever depress Mental & prolong Corporeal War. Painters! on you I call! Sculptors! Architects! Suffer not the fash[i]onable Fools to depress your powers by the prices they pretend to give for contemptible works or the expensive advertizing boasts that they make of such works; believe Christ & his Apostles that there is a Class of Men whose whole delight is in Destroying. We do not want either Greek or Roman Models if we are but just & true to our own Imaginations, those Worlds of Eternity in which we shall live forever; in Jesus our Lord. (Preface to *Milton,* E, 94)

Here we could leave Blake and continue to wander idea by idea over the entire battleground of neoclassical and Romantic esthetics, and then, because there is no particularly good reason for stopping there, beyond artistic principles and the arts, since they are implicated in the transformation of Enlightenment culture in the fullest sense. I have tried only to sketch narrowly, with specialized attention to the ideas of one artist in one small span of time, the relationship of a few basic artistic theories and practices to nonartistic areas of the culture. I would end by offering the personal opinion, though my arguments have been confined so as not to depend very largely upon it, that artistic theories and practices can always be seen in some coherent relationship with the rest of the culture, always at some level interacting vigorously with it, and that such relationship is soon headed for the attention it deserves. This, I confess, is a bookmaker's estimate, coming just when the writings of Marshall McLuhan, Buckminster Fuller, and company have sunk almost out of sight from their height of fashion. I would even admit to betting on a long shot, if it were not for feeling that the sinking at one level has been hiding a sinking-in at a deeper level and observing just recently a new stir of interest in regenerating that sort of study boldly but soundly, with better theory and procedure but without giving up any of the intellectual energy that was spent so generously on those early studies. What I am now trying to pass off as a prediction may only be a scholar's daydream—and, for as long as anyone can remember, scholarship has shared with politics the sophisticated magic of talking marketable hallucinations into walking ghosts for a time—but I predict, anyway, a remarkable increase in our knowledge about the place of the arts in the culture.[20]

Notes

1. Blake's "Public Address" from his Notebook, quoted here from p. 564 of David V. Erdman, ed., *The Poetry and Prose of William Blake,* 4th ed., rev. (New York: Doubleday, 1970), the source of most of my quotations from Blake. For the letters, the text is Geoffrey Keynes, ed., *The Letters of William Blake* (Cambridge: Harvard Univ. Press, 1968). The abbreviations used in the essay are E for Erdman, *Letters* for Keynes, AR for Blake's annotations to Joshua Reynolds' *Discourses, DC* for *A Descriptive Catalogue of Pictures,* PA for the "Public Address."

2. There are a number of other revelant passages; see, e.g., E, 537, 570, 571, and, for that matter, almost any of the instances listed under "machine," "mechanical," etc., in *A Concordance to the Writings of William Blake,* ed. David V. Erdman (Ithaca: Cornell Univ. Press, 1967). The larger context of the metaphor in systems of geometry and mathematics cannot even be sketched here, but is at least indicated by this remark from Plato: "By beauty I do not mean, as most people would suppose, the beauty of living figures or of pictures, but, to make my point clear, I mean straight lines and circles, and shapes, plane or solid, made from them by lathe, ruler and square. These are not, like other things, beautiful relatively, but always and absolutely" (*Philebus* 51c), compared to one of the sentences that Blake engraved around his Laocoön: "The Gods of Greece & Egypt were Mathematical Diagrams See Plato's Works" (E, 271).

3. I am, of course, thinking of the train of thought and association established by Marshall McLuhan in *The Gutenburg Galaxy: The Making of Typographic Man* (Toronto: Univ. of Toronto Press, 1962), especially the uses he found for pictorial conventions in discussing the conventions of the printed page. The relationship is closer than it might seem at first, because printing is technologically a branch of engraving.

4. Of course this is not to say that artists and public were always aware of the graphic translation—certainly not always aware of the effects. But the distinction between "original" and "copy" or "translation" works one way in the graphic arts, a different way in literature. Blake observed, however, that in both arts his century had lost track of the relative values of originals and translations or copies, and, at worst, had decided in favor of copies over originals.

5. This statement weakly summarizes in one sentence the argument first advanced by William Ivins in *Prints and Visual Communication* (London: Routledge and Kegan Paul, 1953). Ivins had a great deal to say on matters closely related to the subject of this essay, not only in *Prints and Visual Communication* but also in his other works, especially *How Prints Look: Photographs with a Commentary*

(1943) and *Art and Geometry: A Study in Space Intuitions* (1946). Readers who want more information about the procedures in Rubens' shop and an extended discussion of the development of systematic printmaking techniques should see *Prints and Visual Communication* and perhaps Mayor, n. 8 below.

6. The rhetoric here and throughout the essay is what might be called, for the sake of a point, empathic. That is, in order to make Blake's ideas clear, I try to write from inside them—as though I believed them. I have been partial in selecting from a range of art-historical facts the facts that Blake thought were most important, and I have tried to see them as he saw them. I am interested in explaining why Blake hated Rubens and Rembrandt; I assume that the reader is not particularly interested to hear whether I think Blake's taste was defective.

7. The best source of such stories is William T. Whitley's *Artists and Their Friends in England 1700–1799* (1928; rpt. New York: Benjamin Blom, 1968), 2 vols. Those mentioned here are from Vol. I, pp. 23–24, 22, 53–55, 104, respectively.

8. *Estampes galantes,* in which the French upper classes celebrated their own fantasies of themselves at play in a manner not very different from English Restoration comedy, were a pre-Revolutionary fashion. They were produced for the most part in medium-sized workshops, where a fairly strict divison of labor was the rule. See A. Hyatt Mayor, *Prints and People: A Social History of Printed Pictures* (New York: Metropolitan Museum of Art, 1971), near Illus. 596–97 (n.p.).

9. Ackerman was a carriage designer turned print entrepreneur who fed the massive appetite for books illustrated with color prints at the turn of the century, using hack poets, popular illustrators, and an efficient system of production that could be operated on a scale vast for the time.

10. Bertrand Russell, *A History of Western Philosophy* (New York: Simon, 1954), p. 540.

11. Art historians will notice that I am using "neoclassical" not as they usually do, in a special narrow sense, but as literary historians do—to designate broadly a group of related esthetic principles generally held, though obviously not without significant variation and change, by most important English writers and artists, musicians and architects, from the Restoration to the end of the eighteenth century.

12. Blake always uses "journeyman" perjoratively, as a synonym for "hireling." "Journeyman" originally designated a day laborer, one who had completed an apprenticeship and qualified for daily wages. But his position as a master's employee soon gave "journeyman" the figurative connotations of "underling," slavishly doing the bidding of another. Thus for Blake's time the *OED* cites Horace Walpole: "The colouring was worse . . . than that of the most errant journeymen to the profession."

13. The mediator between science and commerce is technology, a fact that is usually clear enough, but occasionally obscured by the attitude of scientists. The history of commerce and science is evidence of their kinship. Jacob Bronowski, writing as a scientist and humanist defending the effects of science on scientists and civilization, sketched the historical relationship in *Science and Human Values,* 2nd ed. (New York: Harper, 1963), p. 21, n. 3. Science and commerce have shared their histories not because their goals are the same but because they share a material object of interest, nature, and techniques for dealing with it.

14. Mayor, near Illus. 427.

15. For the story of the disastrous wrangle between Blake and double-

dealing Cromek over the project to illustrate Blair's *Grave*—finally designed by Blake but engraved by Schiavonetti—see G. E. Bentley, Jr., "The Promotion of Blake's *Grave* Designs," *University of Toronto Quarterly,* 31 (1962), 339–53; *Blake Records* (Oxford: Clarendon, 1969), pp. 166–74; "Blake and Cromek: The Wheat and the Tares," *Modern Philology,* 71 (1974), 366–79.

16. See Nikolaus Pevsner, "Blake and the Flaming Line," Ch. v of *The Englishness of English Art* (New York: Praeger, 1956), pp. 117–46; Ch. iv of Robert Rosenblum, "The International Style of 1800: A Study in Linear Abstraction," Diss. New York Univ. Institute of Fine Arts 1956; and Rosenblum's *Transformations in Late Eighteenth-Century Art* (Princeton: Princeton Univ. Press, 1967), pp. 154–59, 189–91. The most recent assessments have been made by W. J. T. Mitchell, "Blake's Composite Art," and Jean Hagstrum, "Blake and the Sister-Arts Tradition," in *Blake's Visionary Forms Dramatic,* ed. David V. Erdman and John E. Grant (Princeton: Princeton Univ. Press, 1970), pp. 57–81, 82–91. There are books forthcoming by Mitchell and by David Bindman that may enlarge and refine what we know about Blake in relation to the linear tradition, but the basic point is unlikely to change much.

17. In *Science and Human Values,* p. 22, n. 8, for instance, Bronowski makes it the main pursuit of science and art, quoting Coleridge for the latter. The phrase "universal unity" is used by Potts, the character who speaks most of Bronowski's opinions in the dialogue "The Abacus and the Rose," p. 118. The definition of science as "the search for unity in hidden likenesses" is Bronowski's own, p. 13. Also see Potts's poem that ends "The Abacus and the Rose," p. 119.

18. The model for harmony in discussions of painting is often Rembrandt, whom we sometimes almost think of as an artistic hero, at least as a rebellious, idiosyncratic, independent thinker who would have no truck with standard artistic doctrine and practice. But Blake's century used Rembrandt chiefly for his realism and his chiaroscuro, corrected and regularized in the way that Pope corrected and regularized Donne's satires. Rembrandt was filtered, in other words, through the main principles of the century; he was not influential in shaping those principles. When the century produced works that it thought were "in the manner of Rembrandt," we hardly recognize Rembrandt in them today. They are pale, highly finished imitations. Likewise, the theoretical use of Rembrandt as a model of graphic harmony in critical discussions gives us a Rembrandt who is barely recognizable.

19. This is the view tentatively adopted by Robert N. Essick in "Blake and the Tradition of Reproductive Engraving," *Blake Studies,* 5 (Fall 1972), 59–103, an otherwise informative essay.

20. An earlier version of this paper was delivered at the conference on "Blake in the Art of His Time" at the University of California, Santa Barbara, in March 1976. Michael Fischer and Hugh Witemeyer of the Univ. of New Mexico and Marvin Morillo of Tulane Univ. made a number of valuable suggestions. An NEH Summer Stipend in 1975 and various grants made through the Research Allocations Committee of the Univ. of New Mexico supported much of the preliminary research.

ALICIA OSTRIKER

Desire Gratified and Ungratified: William Blake and Sexuality

To examine Blake on sexuality is to deal with a many-layered thing. Although we like to suppose that everything in the canon "not only belongs in a unified scheme but is in accord with a permanent structure of ideas,"[1] some of Blake's ideas clearly change during the course of his career, and some others may constitute internal inconsistencies powerfully at work in, and not resolved by, the poet and his poetry. What I will sketch here is four sets of Blakean attitudes toward sexual experience and gender relations, each of them coherent and persuasive if not ultimately "systematic;" for convenience, and in emulation of the poet's own method of personifying ideas and feelings, I will call them four Blakes. First, the Blake who celebrates sexuality and attacks repression, whom we may associate with Freud and even more with Reich. Second, a corollary Blake whom we may associate with Jung, whose idea of the emanation—the feminine element with man—parallels Jung's concept of the anima, and who depicts sexual life as a complex web of gender complementarities and interdependencies. Third, a Blake apparently inconsistent with Blake number one, who sees sexuality as a tender trap rather than a force of liberation. Fourth, and corollary to that, the Blake to whom it was necessary, as it was to his patriarchal precursor Milton, to see the female principle as subordinate to the male.

This essay first appeared in *Blake/An Illustrated Quarterly* 16 (Winter 1982–83): 156–165. Reprinted with permission.

Blake number one is perhaps the most familiar to the common reader, although professional Blakeans have paid little attention to him lately. He is the vigorous, self-confident, exuberant advocate of gratified desire, writing in his early and middle thirties (that is, between the fall of the Bastille and the execution of Louis and the declaration of war between England and France) the early *Notebook* poems, the *Songs, The Marriage of Heaven and Hell* and the *Visions of the Daughters of Albion.* A few texts will refresh the memory. Among the *Notebook* epigrams we are told that

Love to faults is always blind
Always is to joy inclind
Lawless wingd and unconfind
And breaks all chains from every mind
(E463)[2]

Abstinence sows sand all over
The ruddy limbs & flaming hair
But Desire Gratified
Plants fruits of life & beauty there
(E465)

What is it men in women do require?
The lineaments of Gratified Desire
What is it Women do in men require?
The lineaments of Gratified Desire
(E466)

It was probably these lines that converted me to Blake when I was twenty. They seemed obviously true, splendidly symmetrical, charmingly cheeky—and nothing else I had read approached them, although I thought Yeats must have picked up a brave tone or two here. Only later did I notice that the epigrams were tiny manifestoes announcing an identity of interest between sexuality and the human imagination.

During these years Blake wrote numerous minidramas illustrating how possessiveness and jealousy, prudery and hypocrisy poison the lives of lovers. He pities the chaste ("The Sunflower") and depicts the pathos of chastity relinquished too late ("The

Angel"), looks forward to a "future Age" when "Love! sweet Love!" will no longer be thought a crime, while protesting its repression by Church and State in his own time. One of his two major statements about sexual repression in *Songs of Experience* is the deceptively simple "The Garden of Love," in which the speaker discovers a Chapel built where he "used to play on the green." The Garden has a long scriptural and literary ancestry. "A garden shut up, a fountain sealed, is my sister, my bride," in the Song of Solomon. It is the site of the *Roman de la Rose.* It is where Dante meets Beatrice, it is Spenser's garden of Adonis and Milton's Paradise—"In narrow room, Nature's whole wealth." The garden is, in brief, at once the earthly paradise and the body of a woman. Probably Blake saw it so. Later he would draw the nude torso of a woman with a cathedral where her genitals should be. The briars at the poem's close half-suggest that the speaker is being crowned with something like thorns, somewhere about the anatomy, and it anticipates Blake's outraged demand, near the close of his life, in the *Everlasting Gospel:* "Was Jesus chaste? or did he/ Give any lessons of chastity?" Since the design for "The Garden of Love" depicts a priest and two children kneeling at an open grave beside a church, the forbidden love may be a parent as well as a peer, and the speaker might be of either sex: all repression is one. It is important that the tone here is neither angry nor self-righteous, but pathetic and passive—indeed, pathetically passive, for after the opening "I went," the governing verb is "saw." That the speaker only "saw . . . my joys and desires" being bound with briars and did not "feel" anything, should shock us into realizing that this speaker, at least by the poem's last line, has been effectively self-alienated. Repression has worked not merely from without, but from within.[3]

The other major statement is "London," where Blake hears the clanking of the mind-forg'd manacles (chains such as "Love . . . breaks from every mind") he will later associate with Urizen. Economic exploitation sanctioned by blackening churches and political exploitation sanctioned by bleeding palace walls are grievous, but "most" grievous is sexual exploitation, perhaps because it is a denial of humanity's greatest virtue, charity, as sweep's cry and soldier's sigh are denials of faith and hope; or perhaps because, to Blake, sexual malaise precedes and produces all other ills:

> But most thro' midnight streets I hear
> How the youthful Harlots curse
> Blasts the newborn Infants tear
> And blights with plagues the Marriage hearse
>
> (E27)

That final stanza is Blake's most condensed indictment of the gender arrangements in a society where Love is ruled by Law and consequently dies; where virtuous females are pure, modest, and programmed for frigidity, so that healthy males require whores; where whores have ample cause to curse; and where their curses have the practical effect of infecting young families with venereal disease as well as with the more metaphoric plague of unacknowledged guilt.[4] Through his hissing, spitting and explosive alliteration Blake creates an ejaculatory harlot who is (and there are analogues to her in Spenser, Shakespeare, Milton) not the garden but the snake. That a syntactic ambivalence common in Blake makes her one who is cursed by others as well as one who curses, does not diminish the point.

The point recurs polemically in *The Marriage of Heaven and Hell,* where, according to Auden, "the whole of Freud's teachings may be found."[5] Here "Prisons are built with stones of Law, brothels with bricks of Religion," "Prudence is a rich ugly old maid courted by Incapacity," and we are exhorted: "Sooner murder an infant in its cradle than nurse unacted desires" (E 36–37). Here too is the famous pre-Freudian précis of Freud's theories on suppression: "Those who restrain desire, do so because theirs is weak enough to be restrained; and the restrainer or reason usurps its place and governs the unwilling. And being restrained it by degrees becomes passive till it is only the shadow of desire" (E 34). For Freud, this process was always in some degree necessary and irreversible, as *Civilization and its Discontents* and "Analysis Terminable and Interminable" ultimately confess. But Blake—and this is what makes him more Reichian than Freudian—joyfully forsees the end of discontent and civilization too: "For the cherub with his flaming brand is hereby commanded to leave his guard at tree of life, and when he does, the whole creation will be consumed, and appear infinite, and holy where it now appears finite & corrupt. This will come to pass by an improvement of sensual enjoyment" (E 38).[6]

In all such texts Blake is not only attacking the powers of repression, particularly institutional religion, which in the name of reason and holiness attempt to subdue desire. He is also asserting that gratified desire *does* what religion *pretends* to do: gives access to vision, the discovery of the infinite. Moreover—and this is a point to which I will return—Blake in these texts does not stress the distinction between male and female, or assign conspicuously different roles to the two sexes. Youth and virgin suffer alike under chastity, man and woman have identical desires, and the "ruddy limbs and flaming hair" of which an ardent imagination makes a garden, and an abstinent imagination makes a desert, may belong interchangeably to a lover or a beloved, a male or a female.

The poem in which Blake most extensively elaborates his celebration of love and his critique of repression is *Visions of the Daughters of Albion,* printed in 1793. *Visions* is also the poem most clearly delineating male sexual aggressiveness as a component of Urizenic patriarchy, and illustrating the kinds of damage it does to both males and females. First of all, Bromion is a number of things which to Blake are one thing. He is the slaveowner who converts humans into private property and confirms his possession by impregnating the females, the racist who rationalizes racism by insisting that the subordinate race is sexually promiscuous, the rapist who honestly believes that his victim was asking for it; and, withal, he does not actually experience "sensual enjoyment." But if Bromion represents the social and psychological pathology of sexual violence, Theotormon represents its pitiable underside, sexual impotence. "Oerflowd with woe," asking unanswerable questions, weeping incessantly, Theotormon does not respond to Bromion's insult to his masculinity ("Now thou maist marry Bromion's harlot," [pl. 2.1]). Playing the hesitant Hamlet to Bromion's rough Claudius, intimidated slave to coarse slave-master, Theotormon has been victimized by an ideology that glorifes male aggressiveness, as much as by that ideology's requirement of feminine purity. Dejected and self-flagellant (design, pl. 6), he cannot look Oothoon in her intellectual and erotic eye as she maintains her spiritual virginity and offers him her love, not only because she is damaged goods but because she is taking sexual initiative instead of being "modest." Only with incredulity and grief does Oothoon realize this (pl. 6.4–20).

Most of *Visions* is Oothoon's opera. Raped, enslaved, imprisoned, rejected, the heroine's agonized rhapsody of self-offering rushes from insight to insight. Though she begins by focusing on her individual condition, her vision rapidly expands outward. She analyzes the enchainment of loveless marriage and the unhappy children it must produce, she praises the value of infant sexuality and attacks the ethos which brands joy whoredom and sublimates its sexuality in twisted religiosity. She also bewails other ramifications of the tyranny of reason over desire, such as the abuse of peasant by landlord, of worker by factory owner, of the faithful by their churches. For Oothoon life means being "open to joy and to delight where ever beauty appears," and the perception of any beauty is an erotic activity in which eye and object join "in happy copulation." Made desperate by her lover's unresponsiveness, she cries out for "Love! Love! Love! happy happy Love! free as the mountain wind!/ Can that be Love, that drinks another as a sponge drinks water?" Though remaining herself "bound" to Bromion, she nevertheless concludes with a vision of the vitality of all free things:

> Arise you little glancing wings, and sing your infant joy!
> Arise and drink your bliss, for every thing that lives is holy!
> (*VDA* 8.9–10)

Blake in *Visions* has created a heroine unequalled in English poetry before or since. Oothoon not only defines and defends her own sexuality rather than waiting for Prince Charming to interrupt her nap, and not only attacks patriarchal ideology root and branch, but outflanks everyone in her poem for intellectuality and spirituality, and is intellectual and spiritual precisely because she is erotic. Shakespeare's comic heroines, though witty and sexy, are of course not intellectuals, much less revolutionaries. The Wife of Bath strongly resembles Oothoon as a voice of "experience, though noon auctoritee" who "spekes of wo that is in marriage," celebrates sexuality as such and female sexuality in particular, and lectures to the Apollyon of Judeo-Christian misogyny from his own texts. Yet she lacks Oothoon's generosity, and has been locked by men's contempt into a perpetuation of the war of the sexes. (If, though, we amend the portrait of the Wife as she appears in the Prologue by that "imaginative portion" of her which is her Tale, we have something different. Here perhaps is the Wife as she would be—neither offensively-defensively bawdy, nor angrily polemical, but lively and charming—telling the wish-fulfilling story of a rapist enlightened and reformed, of male violence, ignorance and pride transformed by the "sovereyntee" of feminine wisdom and love.) Hawthorne's Hester Prynne comes close to being what Oothoon is, even to the point of foreseeing that "in Heaven's own time, a new truth would . . . establish the whole relation between man and woman on a surer ground of mutual happiness."[7] But Hawthorne cannot sustain or elaborate the vision he glimpses, and sends Hester back in the end to her knitting, her works of charity, and a lifelong celibacy which—unlike Oothoon's—is supposed to be voluntary.

Blake number two appears later than Blake number one, and shifts his psychological principles from an essentially socio-political to an essentially mythic base. Beginning with *The Book of Urizen,* engraved in 1794, and throughout his major prophecies, the poet relies on an idea of humanity as originally and ultimately androgynous, attributing the fall of man and what John Milton called "all our woe" not to female narcissism but to specifically male pride, male competitiveness, or male refusal to surrender the self, and depicting a fallen state in which sexual division—lapse of unity between male and female as one being—is the prototype of every division within the self, between self and other, and between humanity and God.

The mythology of these poems posits a hero who is both Great Britain and all mankind, and who lives in Eternity or Eden as one of a family of Eternals who collectively compose One Man, Christ. Albion's "Human Brain," the equivalent of Jung's collective unconscious, houses four energetic Jungian Zoas, each of whom has a feminine counterpart or emanation.

At Man's Fall, precipitated in *Urizen* by Urizen's pride, in *The Four Zoas* and *Milton* by rivalry between Urizen and Luvah, and in *Jerusalem* by Albion's selfish refusal to maintain erotic union with his saviour and his insistence on mortal virtue, Albion lapses into what Blake variously calls sleep, death and disease, and what the rest of us call human history. The Zoas simultaneously lapse into lower forms and mutual conflict instead of harmony, and are disastrously divided from their emanations. As the late Blake formulaically puts it, "The Feminine separates from the Masculine & both from Man." Bodies grow around them, inimical "To the embrace of love":

> that no more the Masculine mingles
> With the Feminine, but the Sublime is shut out from the Pathos
> In howling torment, to build stone walls of separation, compelling
> The Pathos, to weave curtains of hiding secresy from the torment.
>
> (*J* 90.10–13)

At the close of his three longest poems Blake imagines an apocalypse in which selfhood is relinquished and male and female are reunified:

> And the Bow is a Male & Female & the Quiver of the Arrows of Love
> Are the Children of this Bow: a Bow of Mercy & Loving-Kindness: laying
> Open the hidden Heart in Wars of mutual Benevolence Wars of Love
> And the Hand of Man grasps firm between the Male & Female Loves.
>
> (*J* 97.12–15)

To say that Blake's emanations resemble what Jung calls the anima is to say that they represent a man's interior "female part," the "life-giving aspect of the psyche" and the "a priori element in his moods, reactions and impulses, and whatever else is spontaneous in psychic life."[8] As a positive figure the Blakean emanation like the Jungian anima is a benevolent guide to the unconscious life. As a negative figure she is seductive and destructive. She seems also to represent a man's emotionality, sensuousness, sensitivity, receptivity—all that makes him potentially effeminate—which in a fallen state he rejects or believes to be separated from himself, and must recover if he is to gain psychic wholeness. According to Jung, of course, an individual man changes and develops during the course of his lifetime but "his" anima does not. She remains static, and his only problem is to accept her existence as a portion of himself. What is particularly fascinating about Blake, then, is that he invents not one but a set of female beings, each appropriate to the Zoa she belongs to, each with her own personality and history of transformations, not radically different from the personalities in highly symbolic fiction and drama, and able to shed light very often on characters we thought we knew as well as on larger issues of sexual complementarity.

The first figures we encounter in *The Four Zoas,* for example, are Tharmas and Enion—humanity's Sensation—in the midst of a marital quarrel. Tharmas and Enion are bucolic characters of the sort that the wheels of history run over: good but not too bright, easily confused. We may recognize their like in mythic pairs like Baucis and Philemon, Deucalion and Pyrrha, and the Wakefield Noah with his farcically shrewish wife. Fictionally, and especially when a sentimental English novelist needs a pair of innocent parent-figures, they are legion: they are Sterne's Shandies, Goldsmith's Vicar and Mrs. Wakefield, and a troop of Dickensian folk like the Micawbers and Pockets, Casby (nicknamed "The Patriarch") and Flora, and perhaps most interestingly, the Gargeries of *Great Expectations.*[9] Across the Atlantic, they stumble through the fiction of writers like W. D. Howells and John Steinbeck. What Tharmas lacks when he loses Enion is his own sense of coherence. Without her he is a frantic and suicidal "flood" of feelings. What she lacks without him is resistance to pain. In her fallen form she becomes a grieving Demeter-figure who laments the sufferings of all earthly creatures,[10] and Blake gives her some of his best lines:

> Why does the Raven cry aloud and no eye pities her?
> Why fall the Sparrow & the Robin in the foodless winter?
> (*FZ* I.17.2–3)

> It is an easy thing to triumph in the summers sun
> And in the vintage & to sing on the waggon loaded with corn
> It is an easy thing to talk of patience to the afflicted
> To speak the laws of prudence to the houseless wanderer
> . . . .
> It is an easy thing to laugh at wrathful elements
> To hear the dog howl at the wintry door, the ox in the slaughter house moan . . .
> While our olive & vine sing & laugh round our door & our children bring fruit & flowers
> Then the groan & the dolor are quite forgotten & the slave grinding at the mill
> And the captive in chains & the poor in the prison & the soldier in the field
> When the shattered bone hath laid him groaning among the happier dead.
> It is an easy thing to rejoice in the tents of prosperity
> Thus could I sing & thus rejoice, but it is not so with me.
>
> (*FZ* II.35.16–36.13)

Enion gives birth to Los and Enitharmon, the Eternal Prophet and his Muse, who from the start are as arrogant and self-absorbed as their parents are humble and selfless. Enitharmon espouses parent-abuse:

> To make us happy let them weary their immortal powers
> While we draw in their sweet delights while we return them scorn
> On scorn to feed our discontent; for if we grateful prove
> They will withhold sweet love, whose food is thorns & bitter roots.
>
> (*FZ* I.10.3–6)

Soon she turns these arts on her twin and consort, becoming a seductive and maddening tease. She is the muse who won't come across, taunting the poet with failure and giving her alliance to Reason (Neoclassicism, let us say) instead of Prophecy, while forbidding the poet to love anyone but herself. As a couple, the Los and Enitharmon who are united "in discontent and scorn" uncannily resemble the self-destructive, sullen, jealous, incestuous or quasi-incestuous couples in novels like *Wuthering Heights, Women in Love,* and *The Sound and the Fury:* novels which in the light of Blake we can read as visions of a primitive creative energy thwarted by the impossibility of creativity in a culturally collapsed world they never made. Enitharmon is also La Belle Dame Sans Merci, she is Pip's Estella, or Lady Brett, or Marlene Dietrich in *The Blue Angel;* which is to say that she is the feminine agent of male sexual humiliation, who is herself governed by *ennui.*

A third couple is Urizen and Ahania: Reason and the Faith or Idealism necessary to it. Early in *The Four Zoas,* Urizen as cosmic architect places Ahania in a zodiacal shrine and burns incense to her. Here we have Blake's version of the "pedestal," and of that neo-Platonically inspired sexual reverence which prefers ladies pure, exalted and static rather than adjacent and active. When Ahania is uncomfortable in her shrine and tries to give her spouse some advice about returning to Eternity, he seizes her by the hair, calling her "Thou little diminutive portion that darst be a counterpart," and throws her out of heaven, declaring "Am I not God? Who is equal to me?" (*FZ* III.42.21–43.9). Without Ahania, Urizen is Doubt instead of Faith, and degenerates in the course of *The Four Zoas* from Prince of Light, to tyrannic parody of Milton's God, to William Pitt opposing the Bread Bill of 1800, to the Dragon Form of Antichrist. Ahania falls from being a sky goddess who opened her mouth once too often to "the silent woman" about whom feminist critics are presently writing a good deal.[11] Until just before the end of *The Four Zoas* Ahania has nothing further to say. As "the furrowed field" she is a figure of complete submission. We should compare her possibly to those other victims of exacerbated and anxious male intellect, Hamlet's Ophelia and Faust's Gretchen.[12]

Luvah and Vala, last of the Zoas and Emanations, are in their unfallen form lover and beloved, the Eros and Psyche of Man. Fallen, Luvah is born into this world as the revolutionary babe and flaming youth who must become a sacrificed god in epoch after epoch, while Vala is the *dolorosa* who, believing she loves him, always sacrifices him.

As all Blake readers know, Vala is one of Blake's most

complicated characters. Her name means "vale" as in "valley," and as Nature she is the valley of the shadow of death, the declivity of the female genitals, and the membranous "veil" which preserves virginity, as well as the "veil" covering the tabernacle of the Old Testament. Like the chapel in "The Garden of Love" and the "chapel all of gold," she stands at the intersection between corrupt sexuality and institutional religion; thus she is also the veil of the temple which was rent when Jesus died, for Vala is the Nature we worship when we should worship Christ, she is Fortuna, Babylon, the Great Whore, enemy of Jerusalem. Where Enitharmon is a tease and a betrayer, Vala is the "Female Will" incarnate as killer. She is the chaste mistress who witholds favors so that her lovers will become warriors, and she is the blood-spattered priestess who with a knife of flint cuts the hearts out of men—all the while protesting that she craves nothing but Love. So powerful a figure is she that I expect we see at least as much of her in popular culture—where she is the voluptuous pinup on barracks walls, and she is the lady in black leather who will punish you—as in conventional fiction and drama. Pornography magazines offer us endless reproductions of Vala-Babylon, and, in the most high-chic phases of fashion design, the ideal fashion model is "cruel" Vala.

If we judge by Mario Praz' exploration of the "tormented, contaminated beauty" and "femme fatale" in western literature, this type of female seems—at least prior to Swinburne—to have been more extensively treated by French than by English writers.[13] Ste.-Beuve, Gautier, Baudelaire adore her. For Swinburne, she becomes the Venus of "Laus Veneris," Faustine, and Mary Stuart. But if we look earlier, she certainly figures in Jacobean drama, and in at least one play of Shakespeare's.

Late in *Jerusalem,* one of Vala's avatars has a warrior-lover whom she craves to possess completely. "O that I could live in his sight," she says; "O that I could bind him to my arm" (*J* 82.44). Concealing him under her veil, she wishes him to become "an infant love" at her breast. When she opens the veil, revealing "her own perfect beauty," her lover has become "a winding worm." Blake hopes at this moment to show that Female Will is ultimately self-defeating. The winding worm is a further degeneration of helpless infancy, so that her wish has come true beyond her intention, as in folktales. The worm is also the phallic worm (cf. Yeats' "Chambermaid's Song," where "Pleasure has made him/ Weak as a worm") and the devouring worm of the grave. The parallel story is of course *Antony and Cleopatra.* There, too, Woman reduces Warrior to absurd infantile dependency, out of pure erotic possessiveness. She then dies by the instrument of a worm that she describes as an infant—"the baby at my breast/ That sucks the nurse asleep (V.ii.308–309) and that she croons to as lover. Without the aid of Blake, we might not think to identify the asp in *Antony and Cleopatra* as the last essence of Antony himself. With Blake, the identification seems compelling. At the same time, with the aid of Shakespeare, we may see Vala more clearly as the fallen form of female desire.

As the individual characters of Zoas and Emanations differ, so do the plots of their reconciliations. Los-Enitharmon's begins earliest in *The Four Zoas,* and involves a channeling of their arrogant energy through suffering. Following the binding of Urizen they have sunk, exhausted, to their nadir, "shrunk into fixed space . . . Their senses unexpansive" (V.57.12–18). Redemption starts with the painful birth of Orc, and the grief that follows the Los-Enitharmon-Orc Family Romance. Though repentance and sorrow over their mutual failure to free Orc are apparently useless, Enitharmon's heartbreak (V.63.10–14) triggers a process of imaginative re-expansion and re-unification that continues through the complex episodes of Spectre-Shadow and Spectre-Los reunions (VIIa.81.7–86.14) and the "six thousand years of self denial and of bitter contrition" during which Los builds Golgonooza and Los and Enitharmon finally labor together as partners in the Art which gives regenerate form to all of life (VIIa.90.2–57). At the opening of Night IX "Los and Enitharmon builded Jerusalem weeping" and at no point thereafter are separated. In the final two pages the regenerate "dark Urthona" has reclaimed them both.

Reunion of the other Zoas and Emanations completes the Eternal Man's awakening and resumption of control over his warring "members." Ahania revives at the moment of Urizen's rejuvenation. She bursts with excess of joy, sleeps a winter and returns in spring as Kore, and finally takes her seat "by Urizen" (i.e., not enshrined) "in songs & joy." Next, when Orc's passion burns itself out, Albion takes the somewhat-charred Luvah and Vala in hand and admonishes them: "Luvah & Vala henceforth you are Servants obey & live" (IX.126.6). They enact their obedience first in the ensuing pastoral episode, with its idyllic evocation of a new Golden Age, and then in the Last Vintage, where human grapes are orgiastically crushed in the winepresses of Luvah. The episode concludes with Luvah and Vala described as a couple linked to the seasons; together they sleep, wake, and are "cast . . . thro the air till winter is over & gone" while the "Human Wine" they have made "stood wondering in all their delightful expanses" (IX.137.30–32). Finally Tharmas and Enion, first pair to be seen in collapse and last to be seen regenerate, also undergo a double transformation. They are initially reborn into Vala's garden as naive and wayward children, as befits their innocent character. But a fully renewed and humanized Enion and Tharmas embrace and are welcomed by the Eternal Man (IX.132.10–133.1) to the final feast.

For the Blake who conceived of humanity as androgynous, the division of Zoas from Emanations signified human disorder and disaster. His poetry describing sexual division is some of the most anguished in the language. By the same token, re-couplings precipitate and are accompanied by all the images for joy and order Blake knew: a seasonal cycle culminating in harvest, vintage and communal feast; a painful bread-making and winemaking which issues in happiness; music and "vocal harmony" concluding in human "conversing"; and a beaming morning sun.

To trace the lineaments of Blake number three, we must return to the very outset of the poet's career, and the extraordinary lyric "How sweet I roamed from field to field," where an unidentified winged speaker is lured and trapped by "the prince of love." The poem is in a quasi-Elizabethan diction, but with the swoon of eroticism and ecstatic surrender we associate with Keats. Keatsian too are the lushness and fertility of the natural setting, and the painful close:

> With sweet May dews my wings were wet,
> And Phoebus fir'd my vocal rage;
> He caught me in his silken net,
> And shut me in his golden cage.

He loves to sit and hear me sing,
  Then laughing, sports and plays with me;
Then stretches out my golden wing,
  And mocks my loss of liberty.

Un-Keatsian is the ambivalent gender of the speaker and the personification power of love as male not female. Although the theme of romantic enthrallment of a woman by a man is relatively unusual in English poetry, Irene H. Chayes argues convincingly that the speaker is Psyche and the manipulator of "silken net" and "golden cage" is Eros.[14]

But in later versions of this scenario, the instruments of entrapment and enclosure—net, cage, locked box—will be the sexually symbolic props of females who imprison males. "The Crystal Cabinet," "The Golden Net" and "The Mental Traveller" are all versions of this theme, and the "Woman Old" of the last of these is a brillant portrayal of the *vagina dentata* in action, for she torments male vitality simultaneously by nailing and piercing, and by binding and catching. As if correcting his own earlier naiveté, one of Blake's *Notebook* poems asks rhetorically "Why was Cupid a Boy?" and answers that the illusion of a male Cupid who inflicts sexual suffering "was the Cupid Girls mocking plan," part of a scheme to keep real boys who "cant interpret the thing" unsuspecting while she shot them full of darts (E 470). Along similar lines, "My Spectre Around Me" envisages a war between the sexes dominated by female pride, scorn, jealousy and lust for "Victory" imaged as possession and enclosure: "Living thee alone Ill have/ And when dead Ill be thy Grave." The solution is a Spectral threat of rejection and retaliation:

Till I turn from Female Love
And root up the Infernal Grove
I shall never worthy be
To step into Eternity

And to end thy cruel mocks
Annihilate thee on the rocks
And another form create
To be subservient to my fate.

(E 468)

This brings the Emanation round, for it is either she, or Emanation and Spectre in duet, who "agree to give up Love" for "the world of happy Eternity."

Among the engraved poems, "To Tirzah" is a furious repudiation of female sexuality in its maternal aspect as that which encloses and divides man from Eternity. To appreciate the impact of "To Tirzah" in its original context we should probably see it as the contrary poem to "A Cradle Song" in *Innocence.* Where in *Innocence* a mother sings lullingly to a sleeping infant of the "sweet" smiles and tears that Jesus as "an infant small" sheds and shares with herself and the child, in *Experience* the child responds, ironically using Jesus' adolescent rejection of Mary (John 2.4) for his punch line:

> Thou Mother of my mortal part
> With cruelty didst mould my Heart,
> And with false self-decieving tears
> Didst bind my Nostrils Eyes & Ears.
>
> Didst close my Tongue in senseless clay
> And me to Mortal Life betray:
> The Death of Jesus set me free,
> Then what have I to do with thee?

A second strong repudiation is *Europe,* where erotic entrapment both maternal and sexual, the former expressing itself as possessive, the latter as seductive manipulation of male desire, takes place so that "Woman, lovely Woman! may have dominion" during the corrupt centuries of Enitharmon's reign. Here Enitharmon's "crystal house" is analogous to the crystal cabinet, and within it there is a constant claustrophobic movement of nocturnal binding, circling, cycling, broken only by the dawn of European revolution.

How well do these poems fit the Blake who praises "gratified Desire" and insists that "Energy is the only life and is from the body"? Rather poorly, I think. However allegorically we interpret the thing, sexual love in these poems is neither gratifying nor capable of gratification, and the poet consistently associates "sensual enjoyment" with cruelty, imprisonment, illusion and mortality instead of liberation, vision and immortality. Morton Paley has pointed out that Blake's Lambeth books involve "a sort of involuntary dualism, a myth with implications that in some ways conflicted with his own beliefs. Blake's intuition of the goodness of the body in general and of sexual love in particular had not weakened . . . but . . . the Lambeth myth seems to imply that physical life is inherently evil."[15] If, in other words, we have one Blake for whom physical life is type and symbol of spiritual life and fulfilled joy in one leads us to the other, there is also a Blake for whom body and spirit are as irreconcilably opposed as they are for any Church Father. But the contradiction is exacerbated rather than resolved in the later books, where the anatomical image of the enclosure vastly expands to become a whole world, the realm of Beulah, a dreamy moony place presided over by tender females, which is both comfort and trap.

To a fallen and depleted consciousness, Beulah is the source of poetry and our one hope of returning to Eden. The "Daughters of Beulah" are reliably compliant "Muses who inspire the Poets Song" or nurse-figures who comfort and protect the weary and distressed. That "Contrarieties are equally true" in Beulah makes it seem an obvious advance over single vision and Newton's sleep. Yet as another Crystal Cabinet writ large, Beulah inevitably means confinement, limitation, illusion. It can never mean Infinity. Where Eden is fourfold and human, Beulah is merely threefold and sexual, the vacation spot for beings who cannot sustain the strenuous mental excitement of Eden and need "repose":

> Into this pleasant shadow all the weak & weary
> Like Women & Children were taken away as on wings
> Of dovelike softness, & shadowy habitations prepared for them
> But every Man returnd & went still going forward thro'
> The Bosom of the Father in Eternity on Eternity.
>
> (*M* 31.1–5)

Of the double potentialities of Beulah, benign yields to malign in successive works. In *The Four Zoas,* Beulah is purely protective. *Milton* begins to emphasize not only its pleasantness but also its delusiveness. In *Jerusalem,* where the Daughters of Beulah have been replaced as muses by a single male muse and lover, "the Saviour . . . dictating the words of his mild song," Blake firmly identifies "the lovely delusions of Beulah" (*J* 17.27) with the terrors of sexuality. Thus Vala, claiming precedence over the Savior, hypnotizes Albion with her concave allure and her usurped phallic power:

> The Imaginative Human Form is but a breathing of Vala
> I breathe him forth into the Heaven from my secret Cave
> Born of the Woman to obey the Woman O Albion the mighty
> For the Divine appearance is Brotherhood, but I am Love
> Elevate into the Region of Brotherhood with my red fires
> (*J* 29.48–30.1)

Responding to Vala's triumph, Los laments:

> What may Man be? Who can tell! But what may Woman be?
> To have power over Man from Cradle to corruptible Grave.
> There is a Throne in every Man, it is the Throne of God
> This Woman has claim'd as her own & Man is no more! . . .
> O Albion why wilt thou Create a Female Will?
> To hide the most evident God in a hidden covert, even
> In the Shadows of a Woman & a secluded Holy Place
> (*J* 30.25–33)

Beulah itself seems at fault, in Los's agonized cry:

> Humanity knows not of Sex: wherefore are sexes in Beulah?
> (*J* 44.3)

And again, anticipating Keats's yearning description of a work of art "all breathing human passion far above," redeemed

> Humanity is far above
> Sexual organization; & the Visions of the Night of Beulah
> (*J* 79.73–4)

For, as Blake in his own persona tells us, however tender and pleasant and full of "ever varying delights" the "time of love" passed in Beulah may be, where "every Female delights to give her maiden to her husband" and

> The Female searches sea & land for gratification to the
> Male Genius: who in return clothes her in gems & gold
> And feeds her with the food of Eden, hence all her beauty
> beams
>
> (*J* 69.17–19)

Love in Beulah inevitably brings a depletion of energy and the advent of jealousies, murders, moral law, revenge, and the whole panoply of inhuman cruelties the poet has taught us to struggle against. In visionary contrast, Blake imagines a love that transcends sexuality because it is a mingling of male with male:

> I am in you & you in me, mutual in love divine:
> Fibres of love from man to man thro Albions pleasant land . . .
> I am not a God afar off, I am brother and friend;
> Within your bosoms I reside, and you reside in me.
>
> (*J* 4.7–19)

Such is the opening promise of the Saviour, and if in Eternity "Embraces are Cominglings from the Head even to the Feet" (*J* 69.43), we well may wonder whether such embraces can ever occur between male and female. For if the Blake who celebrates desire sees it as equally distributed between genders, the Blake who fears desire sees sexuality in general and sexual threat in particular as a female phenomenon. This third Blake gives us an array, culminating in *Jerusalem,* of passive males subject to females who seduce, reject, betray, bind, lacerate, mock and deceive them. After *Visions of the Daughters of Albion,* though Blake continues strenuously to oppose the idea that woman's love is *sin,* he increasingly describes it as *snare.* There is no comparable depiction of males seducing and betraying females.

This brings me to Blake number four, who is perhaps not quite a classic misogynist—though he sometimes sounds like one—but someone who believes that the proper study of woman is the happiness of her man, and who cannot conceive of a true woman in any but a supportive, subordinate role. In the margin of his 1789 edition of Lavater's *Aphorisms on Man,* Blake wrote, "Let the men do their duty & the women will be such wonders, the female life lives from the light of the male, see a mans female dependents, you know the man" (E 585). Females, in other words, may be wonders, but only if men are: and to be female is to be dependent.

Examining Blake from this point of view, and returning to *Visions,* we notice that Oothoon is good, and she is wise, but she is completely powerless. So long as her menfolk refuse enlightenment, she will be bound hand and foot, imprisoned in a passivity which she does not desire but to which she must submit. Looking at *The Four Zoas,* we see that Enion and Ahania are likewise good—indeed, they represent precisely the goodness of selfless love and compassion—but passive, while Enitharmon and Vala are active and evil. In *Milton* and *Jerusalem* the story is the same: female figures are either powerful or good; never both. The late prophecies may even constitute a retreat from the point Blake arrived at in *Visions,* for the better the late females are, the more passive, the more submissive and obedient they also are.[16] When Ololon finds Milton, she tearfully apologizes for being the cause of Natural Religion. And when Milton concludes his splendid final speech on "Self-annihilation and the grandeur of Inspiration" with a peroration against the "Sexual Garments, the Abomination of Desolation," Ololon responds by dividing into the sixfold Virgin who dives "into the depths/ Of Miltons Shadow as a Dove upon the stormy sea" and a "moony Ark" who enters into the fires of intellect

> Around the Starry Eight: with one accord the Starry Eight
> became
> One Man Jesus the Saviour. Wonderful! round his limbs
> The Clouds of Ololon folded as a Garment dipped in
> blood
>
> (*M* 42.9–11)

At the climax of *Jerusalem* there is a similar self-immolative plunge when "England" awakes on Albion's bosom. Having blamed herself for being "the Jealous Wife" who has caused all the troubles of the poem:

> England who is Brittania enterd Albions bosom rejoicing
> Rejoicing in his indignation! adoring his wrathful rebuke.
> She who adores not your frowns will only loathe your smiles
>
> (*J* 95.22–4)

But this somewhat gratuitous-seeming passage lacks—since we have not met "England" until now—the systematic quality of Blake's treatment of his chief heroine.

The poet's final and most fully-idealized heroine "is named Liberty among the sons of Albion" (*J* 26.3–4), yet we seriously mistake Blake's intention if we think Jerusalem is herself a free being, or even a being capable of volition. She is the City of God, bride of Christ, and man's Christian Liberty, to be sure, but that is only in Eden, and even there she does not act; she simply is. What happens to Jerusalem within the body of the poem at no point involves her in action or in protest. At its outset she is withheld by Albion from "the vision & fruition of the Holy-one" (*J* 4.17) and is accused of sin by Albion and Vala. Unlike Oothoon she does not deny the accusation, nor does she defend her own vision with anything like Oothoon's exuberance. Patiently, meekly, she explains and begs Love and Forgiveness from her enemies. That is her last initiative. Subsequently she is rejected as a whore, cast out, imprisoned, driven finally to insanity, and becomes wholly incapable even of remembering her original self without being reminded of her origins by the voice of her pitying and merciful God. Even this comfort does not help; for at the poem's darkest moment, just before the advent of the Covering Cherub, Jerusalem passively receives a cup of poison from the conquering Vala (*J* 88.56).

The final movement of *Jerusalem* evokes its heroine twice, when "the Universal Father" speaking through "the vision of Albion" echoes the Song of Solomen:

> Awake! Awake Jerusalem! O lovely Emanation of Albion
> Awake and overspread all Nations as in Ancient Time
> For lo! the Night of Death is past and the Eternal Day
> Appears upon our hills: Awake Jerusalem, and come away
> (*J* 97.1–4)

and when the poet's vision of "All Human Forms" is complete:

> And I heard the Name of their Emanations they are named
> Jerusalem
> (*J* 99.5)

Yet however amorous, however reverential our attitude toward this "persecuted maiden"[17] redeemed, we do not and cannot encounter the "awakened" Jerusalem directly. As *A Vision of the Last Judgment* explicitly tells us, and as the whole of *Jerusalem* implies, "In Eternity Woman is the Emanation of Man; she has no Will of her own. There is no such thing in Eternity as a Female Will" (E 552). If we wonder what the Emanative role in Eternity is, Blake has already told us:

> When in Eternity Man converses with Man, they enter
> Into each other's Bosom (which are universes of delight)
> In mutual interchange, and first their Emanations meet . . .
> For Man cannot unite with Man but by their Emanations . . .
> (*J* 88.3–9)

Is femaleness, then, ideally a kind of social glue? Susan Fox argues that although "in his prophetic poems Blake conceives of a perfection of humanity defined by the complete mutuality of its interdependent genders," he nevertheless in these same poems "represents one of these equal genders as inferior and dependent . . . or as unnaturally and disastrously dominant," so that females come to represent either "weakness" or "power-hunger."[18] Anne Mellor has observed that Blake's ideal males throughout the major prophecies are creative and independent while his ideal females "at their best are nurturing . . . generous . . . compassionate . . . all welcoming and never-critical emotional supporters," and that "in Blake's metaphoric system, the masculine is both logically and physically prior to the feminine."[19] But at its most extreme, Blake's vision goes beyond proposing an ideal of dominance-submission or priority-inferiority between the genders. As a counter-image to the intolerable idea of female power, female containment and "binding" of man to mortal life, Blake wishfully imagines that the female can be reabsorbed by the male, be contained within him, and exist Edenically not as a substantial being but as an attribute. Beyond the wildest dreams of Lévi-Strauss, the ideal female functions as a medium of interchange among real, that is to say male, beings.

And what are we as readers to make of Blake's contradictions?[20] Morris Dickstein, noting the shift from the "feminism" of *Visions* to his later stress on "female Will," calls it "a stunning change that seems rooted less in politics than in the nearly unknown terrain of Blake's personal life."[21] Diana George believes that Blake became entrapped in a culturally mandated sexual typology which he initially intended to "redeem."[22] Although all our anecdotal material about the Blakes indicates that Catherine adored her visionary husband even when he was not bringing home the bacon, much less adorning her in gems and gold, marital friction looks like a reasonable source for many *Notebook* and other poems. Perhaps, too, Blake had a model for Oothoon in Mary Wollstonecraft, whose vigorous equal may not have been encountered in his other female acquaintances after Wollstonecraft's death.[23] At the same time, we should recognize that the shift in Blake's sexual views coincides with other ideological and doctrinal transformations: from a faith in political revolution perhaps assisted or exemplified by Art to a faith in Imagination as that which alone could prepare humanity for its harvest and vintage; for what looks like a love of nature that makes him one of the great pastoral poets in the English language and extends as far as *Milton,* to a growing and finally absolute rejection of nature and all fleshly things; and from an immanent to a transcendent God.

Yet to say that Blake's views moved from X to Y would be an absurd oversimplification. It would be truer to say that X and Y were with him always—like his Saviour—in varying proportions, and that the antagonism between them is the life of his poetry. One of the idols of our tribe is System, a Blakean term signifying a set of ideas bounded by an adhesive inflexible consistency, cognate of the "bounded" which its possessor soon loathes, the "Circle" that any sensible God or Man should avoid, and the "mill with complicated wheels." If "Unity is the cloke of Folly" in a work of art, we might make it our business as critics not only to discover, but also to admire, a large poet's large inconsistencies—particularly in an area like the meaning of sex, where the entire culture, and probably each of us, in the shadows of our chambers, feel profound ambivalence.

If "without contraries is no progression," I think we should be neither surprised nor dismayed to find in Blake both a richly developed anti-patriarchal and proto-feminist sensibility, in which love between the sexes serves as a metaphor for psychic wholeness, integrity, and more abundant life, and its opposite, a homocentric gynophobia in which heterosexual love means human destruction.[24] "If the doors of perception were cleansed everything would appear to man as it is, infinite." What then if we concede that Blake's vision, at least part of the time, was fogged to the degree that he could perceive Man as infinite but could not perceive Woman as equally so? Blake understood that it is impossible for any prophet finally to transcend historical time. He understood so of Isaiah and Ezekiel, he understood the same of John Milton. "To give a Body to Error" was, he believed, an essential service performed by mighty intellects for posterity. We might, with gratitude for this way of comprehending great poetry, see him as he saw his precursors. To paraphrase Emerson and the *Gita,* when him we fly, he is our wings.

Notes

1. Northrop Frye, *Fearful Symmetry* (Princeton: Princeton Univ. Press, 1947), p. 14.

2. Quotations are from David V. Erdman, ed., *The Poetry and Prose of William Blake* (New York: Doubleday, 1970).

3. I am disagreeing at this point with Morris Dickstein's otherwise excellent essay, "The Price of Experience: Blake's Reading of Freud" in *The Literary Freud,* ed. Joseph Smith (New Haven: Yale Univ. Press, 1980), pp. 67–111. Dickstein (pp. 95–96) sees "The Garden of Love" as "angry polemical simplification," arguing that the speaker "thinks of repression in terms of a very simple etiology: *They* have done it to him," and that there is no question of "delusion or projection" here. A persuasive reading of the poem's Oedipal dimension is in Diana George, *Blake and Freud* (Ithaca: Cornell Univ. Press, 1980), pp. 104–106.

4. For a harrowing account of the phenomenon of the youthful harlot in nineteenth-century England, see Florence Rush, *The Best-Kept Secret: Sexual Abuse of Children* (Englewood Cliffs, N.J.: Prentice-Hall, 1980), ch. 5.

5. W. H. Auden, "Psychoanalysis and Art To-day" (1935), in *The English Auden,* ed. Edward Mendelson (New York: Random House, 1977), p. 339.

6. Analysis of Freud's rationalist and scientific pessimism, versus Blake's imaginative and artistic optimism, is a primary theme in *Blake and Freud,* which argues that in other respects the two men's diagnoses of western man's psychosexual ills were close to identical. Politically of course Freud remained conservative; the close parallels between Blake and Reich as radical psychopolitical thinkers are discussed in Eliot Katz, "Blake, Reich and *Visions of the Daughters of Albion,*" unpub.

7. *The Centenary Edition of the Works of Nathaniel Hawthorne,* vol. 1 (Ohio State Univ. Press, 1962), p. 263.

8. C. G. Jung, "Archetypes of the Collective Unconscious," *Collected Works,* ed. Herbert Read, Michael Fordham, Gerhard Adler and W. McGuire, trans. R. F. C. Hull, Bollingen Series (Princeton: Princeton Univ. Press, Bollingen Series

XX, 1967–78), vol. 9, part 1, p. 27. Jung also discusses the anima and the anima-animus "sacred marriage" in "Two Essays on Analytical Psychology" (vol. 7) and "Aion: Researches into the Phenomenology of the Self" (vol. 9, part 2). Among his less predictable parallels to Blake is Jung's idea that the anima-animus marriage is always accompanied and completed by the figure of a Wise Old Man—who I am ready to presume is "Old" in the same sense that Albion is an "Ancient" Man; i.e., he is Urmensch, not elderly. Among the critics who identify anima with emanation are June Singer, *The Unholy Bible: A Psychological Interpretation of William Blake* (New York: Putnam, 1970), p. 212, and W. P. Witcutt, *Blake: A Psychological Study* (Port Washington, N. Y.: Kennikat Press, 1946), pp. 43ff. Christine Gallant, in *Blake and the Assimilation of Chaos* (Princeton: Princeton Univ. Press, 1978) disagrees, arguing that although "the anima in Jungian psychology is a personification in a symbol, or in an actual human being, of those aspects of his unconscious of which a man is most ignorant, usually his emotional, irrational qualities," Blake's emanations are not animae because "if they were . . . they would have characteristics as differentiated as those of their Zoas" (pp. 53–54). It is my contention that they do. Although Jung in general diverges from both Freud and Blake in uncoupling psychological issues from socio-historic ones, he departs from Freud and coincides with Blake in at least three major respects: his insistence on the validity of spirituality in human life, his belief in a collective unconscious, and his relatively non-phallocentric exploration of female identity.

9. That Deucalion-Pyrrha and the Noahs are flood-survivors who renew the human race, and that the fallen Tharmas-Enion are identified with water and Tharmas in Night III struggles to take on Man's form, is a coincidence I do not pretend to understand but feel obliged to notice. My *primary* point here is that these couples are all parental, and all naive. The relation of Dickens' Gargeries to Tharmas and Enion seems to me particularly charming in that Joe Gargery is rather a perfect Tharmas throughout, but is given two wives by Dickens—as it were to parallel the quarrelsome and the redeemed Enion.

10. Gallant (p. 54) notes the Poseidon-Demeter/Tharmas-Enion parallel (another coincidence) and points out that the questing Demeter disguised herself as an old woman.

11. See, for example, Mary Daly, *Beyond God The Father* (Boston: Beacon Press, 1973), Marcia Landy, "The Silent Woman," in *The Authority of Experience,* ed. Arlyn Diamond and Lee Edwards (Amherst: Univ. of Massachusetts Press, 1977), Susan Griffin, *Woman and Nature: The Roaring Inside Her* (New York: Harper and Row, 1978), Sandra M. Gilbert and Susan Gubar, *The Madwoman in the Attic* (New Haven: Yale Univ. Press, 1980), chaps. 1 and 2. The contention of these and other feminist writers in America, England and France is that western religion and philosophy, by consistently associating power and authority with masculinity, have deprived women of access to authoritative speech and muted their ability to "voice" female experience authentically. The critique of rationalism in such works for the most part tallies very well with Blake's.

12. Ophelia's selfless "O what a noble mind is here o'erthrown" speech nicely resembles Ahania's memory of "those sweet fields of bliss/ Where liberty was justice & eternal science was mercy (*FZ* III.39.12–13). Later, when Hamlet has rejected her and slain her father (cf. Urizen's rejection of Ahania and his defiance of Albion), Ophelia's "speech is nothing." Both Ophelia and Gretchen, of course, express profound admiration for their lovers' intellects.

13. Mario Praz, *The Romantic Agony* (1933; rpt. Cleveland: World Publishing Co., 1956) pp. 28ff, 189ff. Among Praz' many valuable observations is a remark

on Ste.-Beuve which is particularly relevant to the Vala-Jerusalem relationship: "Whenever it happens that a writer feels admiration for [female] passionate energy—particularly if this energy have fatal results . . . it is always the diabolical . . . who ends by occupying the whole stage and causing her angelic rival . . . to appear a mere shadow" (p. 191).

14. Irene H. Chayes, "The Presence of Cupid and Psyche," in *Blake's Visionary Forms Dramatic,* ed. David V. Erdman and John E. Grant (Princeton: Princeton Univ. Press, 1970), pp. 214–43.

15. Morton D. Paley, *Energy and the Imagination: A Study of the Development of Blake's Thought* (Oxford: Clarendon Press, 1970), p. 90.

16. A partial exception is the prophetic figure of Erin in *Jerusalem,* yet in a sense Erin is an exception that proves the rule; for though her voice is inspirational without passivity or subordination, she remains undeveloped as a character, lacking the internal struggles and self-transformations of the other major figures in the poem.

17. The term is from Praz, who suggests Clarissa and Sade's Justine as two examples of the type.

18. Susan Fox, "The Female as Metaphor in William Blake's Poetry," *Critical Inquiry* 5 (Spring 1977), 507 [reprinted in the present collection].

19. Anne K. Mellor, "Blake's Portrayal of Women," in *Blake/An Illustrated Quarterly* 16.3 (Winter 1982–83), pp. 148–155.

20. For some readers, of course, no contradiction worth noticing exists. Consider, for example, the following: "Some modern women may have much to object to in Blake's latest thought about the relations between the sexes. But it is hard to believe that *l'homme moyen sensuel* would reject the hearty bread and fullbodied wine the late Blake is offering him. Or his wife either, for that matter: 'let men do their duty & the women will be such wonders.' " Such is Jean Hagstrum's pleasant conclusion in "Babylon Revisited, or the Story of Luvah and Vala," in *Blake's Sublime Allegory: Essays on The Four Zoas, Milton and Jerusalem,* ed. Stuart Curran and Joseph Anthony Wittreich, Jr. (Madison: Univ. of Wisconsin Press, 1973), p. 118. David Aers, in "William Blake and the Dialectic of Sex," *ELH* 44 (1977), 500–14, feels that in *Visions* Blake "may have slipped toward an optimistic, idealistic illusion in his handling of Oothoon's consciousness. The illusion lies in assuming that revolutionary consciousness can ever be as uncontaminated by dominant structures and ideologies as Oothoon's appears to be" (p. 505). By stressing female will in later poems, Blake "is casting out the vestiges of optimistic delusions," having discovered that "it is utopian and undialectical to imagine a female consciousness like Oothoon's" (p. 507). Since Aers does not seem to reflect that Oothoon's inventor himself must have been as "uncontaminated" as his invention, and that Los in *Jerusalem* seems likewise, I take Aers' position to be that we can believe in a male uncontaminated consciousness but that it is undialectical to believe in a female one.

21. Dickstein, pp. 77–78.

22. *Blake and Freud,* chap. 6, includes this argument in a larger discussion of Blake's treatment of "the feminine."

23. See Alicia Ostriker, "Todd, *Wollstonecraft Anthology,*" *Blake/An Illustrated Quarterly* 14 (1980–81), 129–31.

24. The mirror image of this view appears in a number of contemporary lesbian feminist works. See, for example, Griffin, pp. 207–27.

RONALD CLAYTON TAYLOR

Semantic Structures and the Temporal Modes of Blake's Prophetic Verse

"Aspect" is the traditional grammatical term for temporal "contours" or "schemata," as opposed to temporal "locations," for which the traditional term is "tense."[1] The semantics of aspect is thus particularly useful in stylistic analysis. An aspectual consideration of Blake's later prophecies reveals three basic modes, which vary the rate and kind of temporal "schemata" predicated line by line, thereby varying the rate and kind of the reading experience. Moreover, there is a significant correspondence between the underlying semantic features of aspect and certain important Blakean ideas.

A correspondence between semantic categories that figure importantly in a poet's style and the expressed categories of his thought need not have been a conscious construction on the part of the poet. Any connection of this kind is interesting, even if the results of stylistic analysis seem to differ surprisingly from what would have been projected from the poet's dicta on the subject. What Blake has to say about style, in pictorial and in verbal art, bears an oblique rather than a direct relation to his stylistic practice. Blake invariably contends for the definite and determinate in style, but there is in fact much that is "indefinite" in the

---

This essay first appeared in *Language and Style* 12 (1979): 26–49. Reprinted with permission.

temporal schemata of his verse. In the end, however, his own execution does follow his pronouncements for appropriateness, which insist that "Ideas cannot be Given but in their minutely Appropriate Words."[2] If considered in the light of his poetic purpose, Blake's aspectual indefinitudes do appear to have been definitely delineated.

Previous work on Blake's style has noted the importance of participles in the texture of his verse. As Josephine Miles has put it, "The participial sort of meaning is a major meaning for him, the motion observed in process and seen as qualitative rather than as active."[3] The participial forms, both progressive and perfective, function primarily to communicate aspectual meanings. But there is much more to aspect than participles. The semantic features of aspect may be seen to operate in verbs, in noun phrases, and in certain prepositions and adverbs. Indeed, the semantic layout of the entire sentence is often relevant to the determination of its aspectual import.

The internal semantic structures of individual verbs, for example, contain features that mark them as *state* verbs or verbs of *change:*

. . . the Mills were silent (M 8.23)
And all Eden descended into Palamabrons tent (M 9.1)

The first of these sentences predicates a state,[4] the second a change. It is the lexical structure of each verb that signals the difference in temporal "contours." Verbs of change are further differentiated into verbs of *definite change,* of *process,* and of *indefinite change:*

Satan fainted beneath the artillery (M 5.2)
Satan wept (M 7.33)
His tears fell incessant (J 62.36)

Verbs like *faint* are called verbs of *definite change* because in every case they predicate changes that are complete from beginning to end. Verbs like *weep* always predicate continuous process or activity; they are accordingly called verbs of *process.* Verbs like *fall* always predicate change, but the exact kind of change is determined by their semantic complements, so they are called verbs of *indefinite change.* With a singular subject, for example, *fall* predicates a *definite change,* a discrete event: *A tear fell.* Yet in the sentence above, with a plural subject and an adverb, it predicates an indefinitely ongoing process.

The semantic structures of noun phrases are also relevant in the predication of different temporal "contours." For example, if the semantic object of a change is indefinite in amount or extent, a reading of ongoing process will result:

> Thus the terrible race of Los & Enitharmon gave
> Laws & Religions to the sons of Har . . . (SL 4.13–14)

Laws & Religions, as an indefinite plural, is indefinite in extent, and inasmuch as it is the semantic object of the change predicated in this sentence, the change is felt to continue indefinitely or to have been repeated indefinitely in the past. It is important to note here that the "semantic object of the change" need not be identical with the syntactic object of the sentence. In the following two sentences, the semantic object of the change is represented by the syntactic subject:

> . . . tears/ Fell down as dews of night (M 9.36–37)
> Life in cataracts pourd down his cliffs (U 13.55)

In the first sentence, the object of the change is represented by an indefinite plural, and in the second by an indefinite mass noun. In both cases the indefinite extent of the object of the change renders the change incomplete and, thus, an "activity" or "process."

Prepositions and adverbs can also be criterial in determining the aspect of a sentence. Adverbial "particles" have long been known to operate "perfectively," that is, to modify a verb so as to effect a definite change:

> all sat attentive to the awful man. (M 2.24)
> Michael sat down in the furrow (M 8.37)

In the first of these sentences, *sat* predicates a state. In the second sentence, however, *down* forces *sat* to take a change interpretation, by specifying the point of completion for the change. Thus the combination *sat down* predicates a definite change.[5]

Prepositions work in a similar way. A single instance may be taken from the following comparison. Notice how the change of a preposition radically alters the nature of the temporal phenomenon predicated by the sentence as a whole:

> And as they went in folding fires & thunders of the deep
> Vala shrunk . . . (FZ 42.14)
> And as they went into folding fires & thunders of the deep
> Vala shrunk . . .

In the second sentence, *went* seems to represent a single discrete movement from one place to another, but in the first, it clearly represents a continuous motion. This is because of the aspectual difference between the prepositions *in* and *into:* the former is durative, the latter is perfective.[6] *Go,* as a verb of indefinite change, is compatible with either type of preposition, and the aspect of the predication as a whole differs accordingly. Thus the combination *go in X* constitutes a process predicate, and the combination *go into X* constitutes a predicate of definite change.

Aspectual semantics is based initially on a distinction between a pure notion of *state* and complementary notion of *change of state*, the one being of endless duration, the other being the durationless divider between states, the momentaneous shift into a new state. The combination of these two categories accounts for durative change, or *process*—an indefinite repetition of single changes, which "fills" the indefinite duration with activity. In addition to these three concepts, aspectual semantics utilizes several other well known language properties, among them definiteness, indefiniteness, and mass. I consider it significant, beyond the stylistics application itself, that some of these concepts figure prominently in Blake's prose writings.

Blake's idea of states, for example, is familiar to all Blakists. Blake metaphorically describes temporal experience as a journey through a succession of "Eternal States":

> These States Exist now Man Passes on but States remain for Ever he passes thro them like a traveller who may as well suppose that the places he has passed thro exist no more as a Man may suppose that the States he has passd thro Exist no more Every Thing is Eternal (546)

The states exist eternally, and the individual who passes through them exists eternally; time is the linear intersection of the two. The "events," or changes of state, of this scheme are, then, the enterings and leavings of the various states that one experiences.[7] Rather than a flow around and over one, time, according to Blake, is one's own journey through eternity. The striking thing about this conception is that Blake represents as a dynamic progress what we normally assume to be a passive acceptance of whatever states and events come our way.

More important than the state concept for the study of Blake's style is the way he uses the word *definite* and its synonyms. *Definition* is the term used among technicians of the visual media to describe the degree to which a certain area of the visual field is set off from the rest to form an *image.* Thus the *definition of the image* is the relative sharpness of its demarcation from the background. This is a relatively modern usage, but Blake was using the word *definite* in essentially the same sense in the late eighteenth century.[8] "Definite Outline" (628 et passim) was the essential quality of art for Blake, and we find references to it throughout his writings, using not only *definite* and *outline,* but such words as *determinate, discriminate, articulate, lineaments,* and so on.

Notice that Blake does not reserve this concept for the realm of pictorial aesthetics and technique. He extends its application to all life: "The great and golden rule of art, as well as of life, is this: That the more distinct, sharp, and wirey the bounding line, the more perfect the work of art" (540). He does not tell us how the rule is to be applied to life; but just after these words, he links it to the mental process of conception—"The want of this determinate and bounding form evidences the want of idea in the artist's mind"—and again to some rather mundane pursuits—"What is it that builds a house and plants a garden, but the definite and determinate?"

Blake also extends the sphere of definite outline to include the composition of verse. In many places he makes analogies between execution in poetry and execution in picture; in the following instance he applies the idea of the definite to verse:

> Nor can an Original Invention Exist without Execution Organized & minutely *delineated & Articulated* Either by God or Man. I do not mean . . . blurrd & blotted but Drawn with a

> *firm and decided* hand at once like Fuseli & Michael Angelo Shakespeare & Milton (565; italics mine)

Blake goes into much further depth about pictorial technique than he does about poetic technique. This is no doubt because he was trained in visual art and worked in it as a recognized professional. Had Blake (or anyone else at that time) been equipped with a semantics of aspect, he surely would have described the role of the definite and determinate in language just as minutely as he did for drawing. We know that he was able to *use* "The Words Mechanical Power" (641); but like many poets, he only intuited the theory behind his practice.

The indefinite also turns up in Blake's prose, usually mentioned in contrast to the definite and determinate. In one passage, the indefinite is collocated with *mass,* a word that, like *indefinite,* represents an important feature in aspectual semantics. The passage referred to is Blake's eulogistic commentary on the drawings of Thomas Heath Malkin:

> They are all firm, determinate outline, or identical form. Had the hand which executed these little ideas been that of a plagiary, who works only from the memory, we should have seen blots, called *masses;* blots *without form,* and therefore without meaning. These blots of light and dark, as being the result of labour, are always clumsy and *indefinite;* the effect of rubbing out and putting in, like the progress of a blind man, or of one in the dark, who feels his way, but does not see it. . . . All his efforts prove this little boy to have had that greatest of all blessings, a strong imagination, a clear idea, and a determinate vision of things in his own mind. (671; italics mine)

This passage is an amazing and most fortunate concentration of Blake's ideas on the strict correspondence between style and meaning. He frames the correspondence in terms of the definite versus the indefinite, of the determinate versus the indeterminate, of lines and boundaries versus masses, and finally of undecided wandering versus clear thought.

The identification of mass with the indefinite also enters into Blake's poetry, as when in *Milton* he speaks of "The rocky masses of The Mundane Shell" being "deform'd into indefinite space" (17.19–23). Blake means his words literally: the deforming of something is divesting it of clear purpose, of existence as an "Eternal Image & Individuality" (545). As he says elsewhere, "Both in Art & in Life General Masses are as Much Art as a Pasteboard Man is Human" (550). For Blake, there are forces in the universe that work to destroy the clear manifestation of thought, to obfuscate its purpose by scattering its "form" into vague masses:

> The stars of Urizen in Power rending the form of life
> Into a formless indefinite & strewing her on the Abyss
>
> (FZ 93.26–27)

But there are also forces that work to counteract the obfuscation; such are the Sons of Los:

> Delightful! with bounds to the Infinite putting off the
> Indefinite
> Into most holy forms of Thought: (such is the power of
> inspiration)
>
> (M 28.4–5)

Thus the definite and the indefinite are not only categories of the poet's thought, they also participate in the central dramas of his works.

In the semantic structure of language, as in the structure of Blake's cosmos, there are indefinite masses and definite forms. English nouns are marked as being either "mass" nouns or "count" nouns. Mass nouns are undifferentiated, uncountable: they have no inherent "unity," or natural divisions, as do count nouns. The difference can be quite important aspectually:

> he sang a song of death (464)
> He sang songs of death.
> He sang death music.

The first of these sentences contains a count noun as the syntactic object. This singular count noun represents a semantic object of change with definite bounds, so the change predicated is accordingly definite. The third sentence contains a mass-noun object, with no delimiting quantifier like *some.* Hence the change predicated is of indefinite duration—a process. *He sang a song of death* describes a single "act," while *He sang death music* describes an "activity." As the second sentence shows, it is possible to use count nouns in the predication of process. But the count noun must be indefinite and plural, thus generating an indefinite repetition of the "act" of singing a single song.

It may be argued that the difference between "act" and "activity" as shown above is a difference of meaning rather than style. I would contend, however, that it is the kind of meaning difference that distinguishes one "style" from another. It is in many cases a subtle poetic choice to represent a certain narrative arising as a definitely complete event rather than an ongoing process. Such it would be, for example, if a poet were to make his character *finish plastering* rather than *stop plastering.* Both *stop* and *finish* seem on the surface to predicate the simple end of the activity of plastering; at least, this is what would normally be considered "narratively important." But *finish* entails the understanding that the activity ended has had a predestined end, that it has been directed toward a goal, at which it has now arrived. *Stop* requires no such understanding; indeed, it implies that the activity has been "interrupted," and hence that it is likely to resume.[9] Such a choice is clearly a choice of one meaning over another, but the semantic difference is one that usually is not consciously noted by the reader and is therefore called "stylistic." As Blake puts it, "All but Names of Persons & Places is Invention both in Poetry & Painting" (639). I take it that this includes the semantic distinctions of aspect.

Moreover, if a poet should choose consistently one type of aspectual predicate over others, this fact would be reflected in our sense of his style, our sense of the temporal "texture" of his verse. So it is with Blake's verse. An initial foray may be made by way of the distinction between mass nouns and count nouns, which as we have noted helps to determine the aspect of predicates. In Blake's use of mass and count variants the stylistic relevance of aspect is especially clear.

There are some nouns in English that may be either mass or count, depending on their immediate context. *Time* is one such noun, and it ranks among Blake's favorite words: "With awful hands she took/ A Moment of Time, drawing it out with many tears & afflictions" (J 48.30–31). In this instance, *Time* is the "mass" of which the unit, *A Moment,* is composed. When Blake says, however, that "Every Time less than a pulsation of the artery/ Is equal in its period & value to Six Thousand Years" (M 28.62–63), *Time* is a discrete unit, a countable quantity with definite bounds.

It is interesting stylistically that Blake frequently insists on using the count version of *time* in the natural place of the mass version. Consider this line: "Times rolled on o'er all the sons of Har, time after time" (SL 3.20). The indefinite plural, *Times,* could just as well have been a mass noun—*Time rolled on o'er all the sons of Har:* the narrative import would have been the same. Indeed we expect a mass noun; the count version sounds odd. Blake must have had his reasons for "articulating" the "mass" of *time* into an indefinite plural, however, for he counts out the units one by one at the end of the line—"time after time." Such instances are not uncommon; the above line may be compared to one in *Jerusalem:* "Times Passed on" (61.48).

In such lines Blake is certainly playing with linguistic boundedness, suggesting that it belongs to time, the mortal realm of measurement, of beginnings and ends, of the demarcation of mass. His use of superfluous count nouns, as above, is a strong hint in this direction; yet the same poetic intent is unmistakably asserted in the phrasing of some passages:

> Falling, falling! Los fell & fell
> Sunk precipitant heavy down down
> Times on times, night on night, day on day
> Truth has bounds. Error none: falling, falling:
> Years on years, and ages on ages
> Still he fell thro' the void, still a void
> Found for falling day & night without end.
>
> (BL 4.27–33)

Not only is boundlessness overtly specified in these lines, it is overemphasized with indefinite plurals piled on indefinite plurals—*times, years, ages.* Though *end*less, these nouns are hyperarticulated, measured indefinitely. There is a commonality expressed in these lines between boundless, continuous process as represented by a verb form—*Falling, falling!*—and boundless though articulated plurals. Such passages convince me that Blake knew what he was doing in "the rough basement," that he understood something about "the stubborn structure of the Language" (J 36.58–59).

THREE MAJOR MODES

Blake's style is not a wholly consistent flow. It shifts gears every so often, from one mode into another, and the modes are strikingly different in their effects. These modes differ principally in their aspect, which is usually consistent throughout any one passage in a given mode. Therefore I have sorted the treatment of Blake's style into three basic aspectual modes, with variations to be discussed as they arise.[10]

The first of Blake's three modes is composed of universalizing states. It is essentially didactic in rhetorical function:

> In Eden Females sleep the winter in soft silken veils
> Woven by their own hands to hide them in the darksom grave
> But Males immortal live renewd by female deaths. . . .
>
> (FZ 5.1–3)

There are many such passages in the later poetry. They seem to report universal truth to the reader directly, as if, between one line and the next, Blake has turned aside from the narrative to tell us "how it is" in Eternity.

Another aspectual mode (the last to be discussed below) is the predication of definite and determinate acts:

> He took off the robe of the promise, & ungirded himself
> from the oath of God
> And Milton said, I go to Eternal Death!
>
> (M 14.13–14)

Acts like these are manifestations of the free will of the Divine Humanity, expressed in their most clear and foreshortened form.

Blake's most prominent aspectual mode, however, consists of unending process. An incredible quantity of goings-on is sometimes amassed in the verse, without any feeling of resolution:

He hovered over it trembling & weeping. suspended it shook
The nether Abyss in tremblings. he wept over it, he cherish'd it
In deadly sickening pain . . .

(M 3.31–33)

In the many passages composed exclusively of process predications, the reader is given neither rest nor satisfaction. Blake is always in the "going"; only rarely does he "get there." The immense mass of tremblings, quakings, and hoverings keeps the reader busy, but gives him neither a sense of achievement nor anything definite by which to order his experience. It is for this reason that we come so to value the moments of static calm on the one hand and the moments of decisive action on the other. The one is a "mild and pleasant Rest" (M 30.14), the other an inspiration, an awesome provocation to acts of our own.

UNIVERSALIZING STATES

Blake often breaks away from a narrative passage in the past tense, unexpectedly starting a stanza (a verse paragraph) with stative predications in the simple present tense, expounding the eternal nature of some part of the Blakean cosmos:

> In Eden Females sleep the winter in soft silken veils
> Woven by their own hands to hide them in the darksom grave
> But Males immortal live renewd by female deaths. in soft
> Delight they die & they revive in spring with music & songs
>
> (FZ 5.1–4)

These clauses form a description of conditions that are asserted to hold true universally within "Eden." When we read that "In Eden Females sleep the winter," we assume that any and every female in Eden sleeps for the winter—regularly, as a habitual practice. It is the combination of the simple present tense with certain kinds of complements that results in a predication of generic temporal scope.

The simple present has only three aspectual uses: with verbs of state to predicate present states, with verbs of change (whether definite, indefinite, or process) to predicate habits, and with verbs of change in performative utterances ("speech acts," to be discussed below). Of these three uses, only performative utterances predicate single, complete changes. "Habits" consist of the indefinite recurrence of some change, and thus are more "static" than "active" in effect. For instance: "Los reads the stars of Albion! the Spectre reads the Voids" (J 91.36). Though this sentence superficially predicates change, it establishes certain characteristics of Los and of the Spectre in the same way that "His horses are mad" (M 8.18) establishes a characteristic of "his horses," and the verb in the latter sentence is obviously stative. A habit is as it were a state that finds expression in an indefinite number of "occasions"; it is the surface predication of the event or act that constitutes relevant expression of the given state. Except for performative utterances, then, the simple present is used to predicate static characteristics; its temporal "scope" is generic.

The tensed verbs in the passage above are all in the simple present. They are also verbs of change: *sleep* and *live* are verbs of process,[11] and both *die* and *revive* are verbs of definite change. As these verbs are used in the lines above, the element of change inherent to each verb is taken to be indefinitely recurrent. Each of the clauses predicates a kind of eternal "habit." The females "die" and "revive" again and again indefinitely; it is their way, their lot in the universe.

It is the context and the complements to the verb that decide for us that a given instance of a verb of change in the simple present is to be interpreted as a habit predication (rather than a performative utterance). If the context contains any elements that allow for recurrence, then the habit interpretation is given to the sentence. There is no lack of semantic context for the habit interpretation in the above passage. The subjects of the tense verbs are indefinite plurals—*Females, Males*—and the adverbs suggest indefinite extension in time—*the winter, immortal, in spring.* Thus not only do the clauses predicate eternal habits, but in this passage Blake has heavily emphasized the infinite recurrence of the activities and events predicated. Even the auxiliary elements (instrumental and locative phrases) contain indefinite masses and plurals: *in soft silken veils, in soft Delight, by female deaths, with music & songs.*

The passage also contains a strong thematic appeal to indefinite recurrence. The second line, for instance—"Woven by their own hands to hide them in the darksom grave"—evokes universal feminine cyclicity. An organic cycle of growth has been set up: the females actively weave an external product, which then becomes a covering for their seasonal sleep, and then grows to them in death, a cocoon for the interval before the "after-life," when they "revive."

Not always is the thematic material of a passage in Blake's stative mode so very interwoven with its aspectual effect as it is in this one of Females and Males, of eternally recurrent life, death and weaving. Yet the effect of eternal recurrence is always present when verbs of change are used in the simple present in the company of state verbs or in a context that does not force a singular interpretation of the act or event predicated by the verb. Moreover, the stative predication of universal constants suits Blake's poetic purpose. So much of his verse is uneasily moving, violently pulsing, and full of unexpected arisings that the certainty found in passages composed of stative predications presents an enormous contrast. Blake's reader is both surprised and relieved by the security of the universalizing statives; he is very willing to rest quiet and be taught.

The most striking examples of Blake's universalizing asides are the most abruptly introduced. A good example occurs in *Milton,* where the past tense of the narrative is suddenly disregarded:

> Onwards his Shadow *kept* its course among the Spectres; call'd
> Satan, but swift as lightning passing them, startled the shades
> Of Hell *beheld* him in a trail of light as of a comet
> That travels into Chaos: so Milton *went* guarded within.
>
> The nature of infinity *is* this: That every thing *has* its
> Own Vortex; and when once a traveller thro' Eternity
> *Has* passd that Vortex, he *percieves* it roll backward behind
> (15.17–23; italics mine)

The strength of the shock is created both by the abruptness of the change of tense and aspect and by the lack of any readily apparent connection in the subject matter.[12] Such a lack is yet another mystery for an already insecure reader, causing him to cling hopefully to the universality of the ensuing stanza. "That every thing has its/ Own Vortex" sounds to him like a very welcome axiom—though he may, as we all know, become lost irretrievably in Blake's explanation of the Vortex.

There is never a warning to prepare the reader for such interruptions by the universalizing present tense, but sometimes there is a didactic introduction:

And this is the manner of the Daughters of Albion in their beauty
Every one is threefold in Head & Heart & Reins, & every one
Has three Gates into the Three Heavens of Beulah which shine
Translucent in their Foreheads & their Bosoms & their Loins
Surrounded with fires unapproachable: but whom they please
They take up into their Heavens in intoxicating delight
(M 5.5–10; italics mine)

This passage is from the Bard's Song of *Milton*. Again there is a complete break of tense and aspect and of subject matter. Everything about the passage gives an impression of universal permanence. Nothing is transient; the finite verbs are stative presents *(is, is, has)* or eternally continuing processes *(shine)* or acts *(take up),* and the nominal complements are representatives of generic classes (*every one, whom they please).*

The introductions to such passages can become even more openly didactic. In the first book of *Milton,* the didacticism mounts along with the frequency of stative asides, until in the final plates of Book the First Blake devotes himself entirely to instructing his reader. He goes so far as to assume that his reader is at his elbow with ready ear, and turns to him, addressing him directly:

Thou seest the Constellations in the deep & wondrous
Night
They rise in order and continue their immortal courses
Upon the mountains & in vales with harp & heavenly song
With flute & clarion; with cups & measures filld with
foaming wine.
And the calm Ocean joys beneath & smooths his awful
waves!
(25.66–71)

such passages are always a rest to the reader of Blake's prophecies, and on occasion they are extremely beautiful as well.

ENDLESS PROCESS

Blake's style of unending process is quantitatively the predominant mode, and its overall effect is to entrap its reader continually in the meanderings of Time. It is composed of process predications, formed both by process verbs with their complements and by the progressive construction. There is also an auxiliary function for this mode, which I shall call the semantic "frustration" of single definite events.

The progressive construction, and the progressive participle by itself, enjoy particular prominence in Blake's verse. As was remarked at the outset, others have brought attention to this fact—most notably, Josephine Miles and Roger Murray.[13] Both Miles and Murray focus on the "simultaneity" of the happenings and processes in Blake, attributing it in large part to the abundance of participles. It is clear that participles have something to do with the "speed" or with relative amount of "action" in the verse:

> The following instances . . . show how few and recessive the verbs are and how the gerunds and participles cluster to form contained "narrative" material. The actions are thus divided into greater and lesser. The epic action of the verbs is slow and cyclic; the verbals agitate the interstices between the verbs in an epicyclic motion. (Murray, 101)

Though Murray points to perfective as well as to progressive participles, it is the progressive participles that are responsible for the sense of "agitation."

The progressive participle has three essential semantic characteristics: its inherent process aspect, its temporal dependence on the tense of the clause to which it belongs, and its sense of transience.[14] The sense of transcience may be seen by contrasting the present progressive with the simple present. The simple present, used in all but special cases for the predication of habits and states, communicates permanence, the permanence of generic predications. Consider one of Blake's passages of universalizing:

Oshea and Caleb fight: they contend in the valleys of Peor
In the terrible Family Contentions of those who love each
    other:
The Armies of Balaam weep—no women come to the field
Dead corses lay before them, & not as in Wars of old.
For the Soldier who fights for Truth, calls his enemy his
    brother:
They fight & contend for life, & not for eternal death!
But here the Soldier strikes, & a dead corse falls at his feet
Nor Daughter nor Sister nor Mother come forth to
    embosom the Slain!
But Death! Eternal Death! remains in the Valleys of Peor.
(J 38.37–45)

If we now substitute the present progressive for the simple present of the original, the effect is obviously a change from eternal characterization to transitory activities:

Oshea and Caleb are fighting: they are contending in the
    valleys of Peor
In the terrible Family Contentions of those who are loving
    each other:
The Armies of Balaam are weeping—no women are
    coming to the field
Dead corses are lying before them, & not as in Wars of old.
For the Soldier who is fighting for Truth, is calling his
    enemy his brother:
They are fighting & contending for life, & not for eternal
    death!
But here the Soldier is striking, & a dead corse is falling at
    his feet
Nor Daughter nor Sister nor Mother are coming forth to
    embosom the Slain!
But Death! Eternal Death! is remaining in the Valleys of
    Peor.

I have chosen lines with verbs of change, where the present progressive can offer a meaningful alternative to the simple present: the state verbs of the surrounding context are ungrammatical in the progressive (e.g., line 22: *All broad & general principles are belonging to benevolence). Note however, in this regard, that *love* in "those who love each other" is stative, and that "those who . . ." is a generic reference, but the progressive forces the verb to signify activity ("those who are loving each other") and changes "those who . . ." into a specific group of individuals. The same shift from generic to specific occurs throughout the passage. The Soldier of "Truth" and the Soldier "here" both become specific individuals in the second version, and the fight of Oshea and Caleb as a whole becomes a scene happening now, not "always." Passages of stative predications do present visible scenes, of course, but they are not the transient scenes encountered in Blake's mode of process. The effect of the second version above is to create an immediate scene in a narrative, rather than a description of general conditions in Peor. The temporal frame is specific, not generic, not eternal.

The other semantic characteristics of the progressive may be exemplified by considering a passage cited by Murray. Murray says of such passages that "the epic action of the verbs is slow and cyclic," and that of the participles is "an epicyclic motion":

> . . . Albion rose
> In anger: the wrath of God *breaking* bright *flaming* on all sides around
> His awful limbs: into the Heavens he walked *clothed* in flames
> Loud *thundering* . . .
>
> (J 95.5–7; italics following Murray)

Murray's remarks about the different kinds of "action" follow from the semantic properties of the progressive participle. To be sure, the perfective participle *clothed* represents a change of becoming clothed, which occurred prior to the reference time indicated by the tense of *walked,* but its force at the reference time and therefore in the experience of the passage is static, as with all perfective participles.[15] The sense of motion in the phrase as a whole comes rather from the "flames/ Loud thundering" of which Albion's clothing consists.

As for the progressive participles of the passage, it is their process aspect that is responsible for the sense they have of "agitation" or continuous motion, of indistinctly blending in and out as the narrative moves on. For the construction obligatorily signifies process; even if the lexical root of the verb represents a definite change, an event, this event is necessarily understood to be incomplete and continuous. Thus, reading "the wrath of God breaking," we attempt to imagine a continuous motion of something splitting or shivering itself. Certainly it is difficult to form a clear mental picture of "wrath" breaking, but whether visualizable or not, this mass must "break" continuously, in innumerable streams of some sort. *Break* itself is a verb of definite change; inserted into the progressive participle with its continuity, the verb produces innumerable unitary "breaks." There is continuous motion, with no distinct end, instead of a single, discrete "break," as would be predicated by the simple-tense form *(it broke)*. The progressive, because it cannot predicate definite change, can never establish a definite sequence, which is the essence of narrative.[16]

Progressives take their temporal reference point from the finite verb on which they are syntactically dependent. Indeed, they do not really have a time reference of their own; they merely represent some process, and this temporal schema is in every case located in the temporal continuum by virtue of the time reference of some other sentence constituent, usually the tensed verb. In the progressive construction with *be,* the "auxiliary verb" is the tensed verb and anchors the process of the participle to a definite "temporal location" in the given context. Consider this version: "Albion rose; the wrath of God was breaking around his limbs." The past tense morpheme of *rose* establishes a definite (though unspecified) point in past time, and the time reference of *was* is assumed to be simultaneous with the time reference of *rose.* The process of *breaking,* being syntactically dependent on *was,* is simultaneous with the time reference of both *was* and *rose.* In the passage itself, no auxiliary verb is present, but the same relations hold.

The process or activity represented by the participle continues throughout the reference time, and is totally "contained within" it, but it does not have distinct boundaries, as a single, complete act like *Albion rose* does. Thus in the passage above "the wrath of God breaking bright flaming" necessarily "broke" and "flamed" all the while that "Albion rose." Furthermore, process consists, conceptually, of an indefinite repetition of infinitely divisible replicas of the definite change that a predicate like *break* would represent if it were "singular." Consequently, we are required by the verse to imagine an infinite number of "breaks" and an infinite number of "flames" realizing themselves during the time of the single act of Albion's rising.

This relation of time-reference dependence and of the co-happening of process and act can be represented in a diagram, interpreting S, the "point of speech," as the time of reading, and R as the "point of reference":[17]

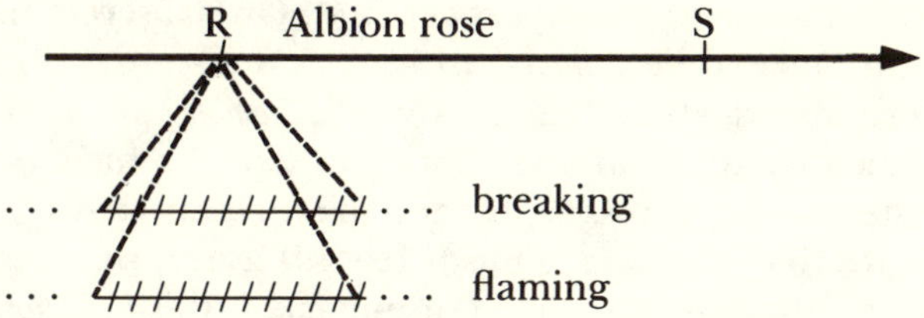

A single slash (/) represents a discrete change of state; a solid line with indefinite ends (. . . ——— . . .), for state, combined with innumerable slashes represents a process of indefinite duration (. . . /// . . .). This diagram thus shows a relation of many-to-one at a point of time (the many changes of process and the one of definite change), or, rather, a relation of the infinite telescoped into a singular finite unit. It is this kind of relation that creates the effect of packing the verse with "action."

Josephine Miles has established statistically the quantitative importance of participles in Blake's verse,[18] and, as I have indicated, the semantic qualities of progressive participles contribute to the line-by-line buildup of simultaneous processes. But process predication is a much broader category, and consideration of the prophecies in the light of it reveals the importance also of process verbs and of noun phrases. Indefinite repetition, in whatever form, is the semantic dynamo of Blake's uneasy motion. Consider these lines, which combine participles and process verbs:

> He hoverd over it trembling & weeping. suspended it
> shook

The nether Abyss in tremblings. he wept over it, he
cherish'd it
In deadly sickening pain . . .

(M 3.31–33)

Hover is a verb of process. It can never partake in a definite change, because it cannot take a direct object or a goal—it is always an indefinite motion of the subject alone, a vague, suspended vibration. *Tremble* and *weep* are the same kind of verb, as may be shown by a conventional test for complete changes: **It took him ten minutes to tremble; *It took him ten minutes to weep* (compare *It took him ten minutes to finish*). Only discrete temporal units can "take time"; *hover, tremble,* and *weep* are indefinite, undifferentiated—they "refuse form." *Tremble* and *weep* are in the participial form in the first line above, which especially emphasizes their process aspect and makes their activity simultaneous with that of *hoverd.* Thus three different processes are set in motion with only one finite tense-marker (the *d* on *hoverd*), all in less than a single line of verse. The buildup of process may be represented diagrammatically, using the same conventions as above:

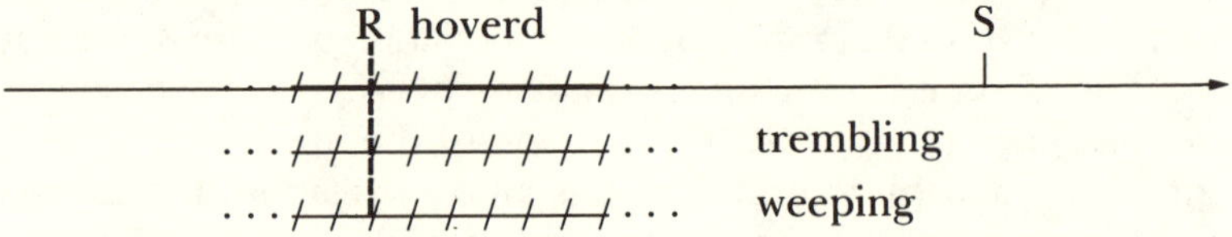

After *hover, tremble,* and *weep,* we encountered the words, "suspended it shook." *Suspend* is capable of predicating *definite change,* but here it is in the static form of a perfective participle. "It shook/ The nether Abyss" contains a deep intransitive of the same kind as *hover, weep,* and *tremble,* which is discoverable in the semanticist's paraphrase [It CAUSED (The nether Abyss shook)]. This embedded intransitive, moreover, is responsible for the shift in interpretation between the first and the second lines. First we read, "suspended it shook," thinking that "it" was shaking. On reading the next line we balk for a second, then revise the semantic interpretation to make "it" the instrument that effects shaking in "The nether Abyss." It is only after going through the whole of this process of reinterpretation that we begin to wonder just how it is that a "nether Abyss" can shake at all.

It is interesting also (and by no means uncommon in Blake) that Blake stretches out an already processive *shook* with *tremblings. Tremble,* on its own power, represents indefinite vibration, but Blake puts it into the progressive form, thus compounding the on-goingness, adding a process simultaneous to other processes in the context. Furthermore, Blake unitizes the participle as a noun ("gerund"), the object of a preposition, *in.* It is difficult to locate precisely in time even one "trembling," but Blake insists that the shaking happened "in" an indefinite number of "tremblings." Here we have yet another instance of Blake's penchant for articulating indefinitudes, noted earlier in a passage from *The Book of Los.* After the "tremblings," there come two finite verbs, "wept" and "cherish'd." They are process verbs, parallel to "hover'd" and "shook."[19] On the whole, the lines above contain so much process, so much indefinite motion, that we wonder, as we read, when there will occur a movement. We look for resolution of the vibrations, and find none.

Blake can keep up this kind of shaking for a long time. The passage above is rather short, though it is a good example of pure process aspect. Other passages sustain the effect and add a great variety of elements, giving the impression of the passage of time, though nothing "definite" happens. This is the effect of a stanza in the Bard's Song of *Milton,* where a feeling of the passage of time is needed to give duration to the "day of mourning":

> They *plow'd* in tears! incessant *pourd* Jehovahs rain, &
> Molechs
> Thick fires *contending* with the rain, *thunder'd* above *rolling*
> Terrible over their heads; Satan *wept* over Palamabron
> Theotormon & Bromion *contended* on the side of Satan
> *Pitying* his youth and beauty; *trembling* at eternal death;
> Michael *contended* against Satan in the *rolling* thunder
> Thulloh the friend of Satan also *reprovd* him; faint their
> reproof.
>
> (8.27–33; italics mine)

This passage describes how Los's train of mourners spent the time during "this mournful day" (line 24); it represents the temporal mass of mourning that "filled" that day, differentiated into the indefinitely many things that transpired from the time that Los said "follow with me" (line 21) to the time when "Michael sat down in the furrow" (line 37). As soon as the stanza ends, the "action" of the narrative starts up again. The effect of "many-things-going-on" results not only from the process predications (note the italicized words), but also from the indefinite numbers of things that extend the indefinitude of the predicates in a boundless multiplicity. Note for instance the "tears," and the "fires" that engage in pseudohuman activity with the mass of "rain." Notice, moreover, how the noun *thunder,* in the locative phrase "in the rolling thunder," becomes a meteorological process simultaneous with the activity of "contention." The reader feels that he too has "spent some time" when the stanza closes and the real "action" takes up again.

There is another side to Blake's process mode, involving the semantic "frustration" of single events (definite changes) rather than process predications or indefinite repetition. I class them together because they so often occur together and because the effect is in both cases the same: the arousal of the reader's spirit to action by continual prodding, but the putting off of any end or sense of fulfillment, even of any definite event on which a sequence might be based. The reader is often led to hope that the predication of a change will "perfect," or complete, itself, and thereby give him something definite with which to establish a narrative chain. Yet almost never does Blake present a complete and coherent sequence; usually the bottom falls out just as we approach completion.

The effect may best be seen in a brief example from the Bard's Song:

At last Enitharmon brought forth Satan Refusing Form, in vain
The Miller of Eternity made subservient to the Great Harvest
(M 3.41–42)

In most cases the defaulting of a complete event is through semantic anomaly. Only sometimes is there also ungrammaticality, as we have here in "Satan Refusing Form." *Brought forth* predicates a complete change, a movement from inside the womb to outside it. Moreover, it requires a direct object. The object of the change must be definitely quantified if the change is to be complete and single. The reader's narrative sense (as well as his grammatical instinct) looks for such an object for *brought forth,* so that he may rest secure in the knowledge that a birth has definitely occurred.

In the present case, the reader is given everything short of a complete act. The object of *brought forth* is not only singular and definite, it is human, and well known to the reader—the perfect completion to a history-making event. But the participial phrase, *Refusing Form,* spoils the completion of the act. Notice that even *Satan dancing* would be ungrammatical, unless *dancing* could be understood to modify *Enitharmon* instead of *Satan.*

Just which grammatical laws are being violated here is difficult to say. It is clear that *Refusing Form* modifies *Satan,* and not *Enitharmon,* for as a modification of *Enitharmon* it makes no topical sense (in addition to the fact that it is closer to *Satan*). As a modification of *Satan,* there may be multiple reasons for its unacceptability. On the one hand, *Satan* is the object of *brought forth* and cannot, with a clause conjunction, function as the agent of *Refusing Form.* On the other hand, and perhaps more cogently, the object of *brought forth* must be a grammatical unit and a concrete entity. *Satan Refusing Form,* as a grammatical unit, is an abstract entity, in effect an embedded sentence. If *Satan* alone is taken as the grammatically unitary object, then the participle must modify Enitharmon.

These being the semantic conditions, *Refusing Form* clearly frustrates any sense of a proper "birth." And in doing so, it constitutes a "token-reflexive" stylistic device. "Refusing Form" characterizes Satan as a master of deceit, of the Indefinite, and at the same time describes what is going on in the semantic structure of the sentence. By "Refusing Form," Satan refuses to perform his proper function as the object of *brought forth.* By its very nature, organic birth creates forms, and we require a "form," a definite quantity, in order to complete a narrative event. "In vain" is rather apt in this context, for no matter how much Satan refuses, the predication insists (if it is to make any sense at all) that he has been "brought forth."

Semantic oddities of this kind occur throughout Blake's later verse, but they vary in degree. They may simply consist of an expectation that is aroused, then ignored and left behind, without any ungrammaticalities. *Woo,* for example looks forward to a result—a winning, or a rejection:

> In Female beauty shining in the unformed void & Orc in
> vain
> Stretch'd out his hands of fire, & wooed: they triumph in
> his pain
>
> (M 18:44–45)

The abrupt shift to the simple present tense and its temporally generic frame of reference leaves Orc with his arms stretched out, empty-handed, and "habitualizes" the interaction (him wooing, the Females ignoring his pleas and delighting in his suffering). The shift is unexpected and stylistically shocking, in spite of the cues, "unformed" and "in vain."

The verb *build* sometimes participates in the semantic frustrations of Blake's prophecies; his buildings are rarely stable. Consider, for example, the use of the passive in the following lines:

> Unfathomable! without end. But in the midst of these,
> Is built eternally the Universe of Los and Enitharmon:
>
> (M 19.24–25)

Is built eternally can be read either as "is being built eternally" or as "has been built, for the duration of eternity." Jespersen observed that *be* plus the perfective participle is ambiguous between the passive and the perfect (*His bills are paid* is either a habitual occurrence—the present passive—or a state resulting from a single past event—the perfect with *be*).[20] In the line above, *Is built* can represent either a present state resulting from a single past event or an ongoing process. Inasmuch as the context is composed of stative predications in a didactic aside (explaining the geography of the fallen Zoas), the stative reading is favored. But stative predicates cannot be modified by *-ly* adverbs of time or manner. In order to keep the stative reading, *eternally* must be given a special interpretation—it must be taken as a "Miltonism," meaning, in effect, "for eternity." The surface syntax, with *-ly,* therefore favors the process reading ("is being built eternally"), but this reading has its problems, too. *Build* is a verb of definite change, so that if a single, definite object (*the Universe of Los and Enitharmon*) is built indefinitely, as necessitated by the adverb, the *whole* of the object must be built over and over again. To *build* a thing is to bring it into existence. The reader is thus required to conceive of the Universe of Los and Enitharmon as a "building" which comes into existence continually—apparently without ever going out of it. The conception is an impossibility, and the reader returns to wondering if Blake rather intended the stative reading. Blake seems to have intended us to conceive of a thing solidly located in "the midst" of the Zoas, which nonetheless comes into existence continually; such a strange, existentially pulsing entity is ideal for Blake's idea of the "Universe of Los and Enitharmon," the world of Generation.

Another instance of semantic frustration is found in the Jacob-style wrestling match between Milton and Urizen, the scene of struggle that appears intermittently in the middle plate of *Milton.* We find many times in Blake what seems to be an anomalous application of the spatial and aspectual schema of MOTION + GOAL = DEFINITE CHANGE. Consider the following two lines:

Silent they met, and silent strove among the streams, of Arnon
Even to Mahanaim, when with cold hand Urizen stoop'd down
(19.6–7)

There are two kinds of striving. One can *strive with (against)* someone else, in a fight, or one can *strive at* or *toward* something, and this something can be journey or a goal, so that one can *strive to* somewhere. "Even to Mahanaim" is compatible with the latter kind of striving, for it could be thought that Milton and Urizen "strive" side by side and arrive together at Mahanaim. But every reader is confused by this phrase, for he supposes that Urizen and Milton strive *with each other,* in one place (the indefinite place which "among the streams" denotes). He is led to this by the context and also by the alliteration, which associates their striving with their meeting.

Moreover, *among* normally serves to obviate any idea of a definite destination or end point (it marks the location rather than the goal of a movement),[21] thereby forcing the predication of an activity. *Even to Mahanaim* thus clashes semantically with *among the streams.* One could, of course, assume that in their striving *with* each other the two inadvertently moved *to* Mahanaim, but this requires the mental substitution of another predication of *they strove* for the second line, precisely because the two prepositions, *among* and *to,* force different aspects for the whole clause. Nor can the reader interpret "of Arnon/ Even to Mahanaim" as meaning (archaically) "*from* Arnon to Mahanaim," modifying the "streams," for the following *when* clause with its definite event requires a single *point* of temporal reference, which is supplied by *to Mahanaim* (the point of completion for the putative movement by striving). In short, the anomaly created by the juxtaposition of the process aspect in the first line and the syntactically dependent eventive aspect in the second line is irresolvable, and the reader suffers. Blake's reader must go on, though never sure exactly what happened at Mahanaim. Like Milton, he moves on, though "his feet bleed sore" and though he leaves thoughts "infixed" in his path.

THE DEFINITE AND DETERMINATE

The overall picture of Blake's style that results from a consideration of two important modes is that of a great mass, characterized generally by "endless" strings of process predications mixed with semantically "frustrated" events. The whole is uneasily pulsing with activity; the reader is exposed to process after simultaneous process, each of which starts to vibrate as he cognizes it, but few of which are resolved, and even fewer of which result in something temporally solid. Amidst this mass of conceptual motion, there are isolated moments of static calm, varying in frequency depending on the poem and the section of the poem. These moments are very welcome to the reader, whose time-sense is buzzing with process-lag or still perturbed by unresolved events. He finds relative clarity in the moments of calm, and consequently he listens closely to the universal assertions that come direct from the author.

Yet to call Blake a "poet of process" because the majority of his predicates are imperfective would be unfair, and, I believe, quite incorrect. Blake was the one poet in his century who especially championed action—action stylistic and narrative as well as political and "mental." Blake's veneration for "mental acts" is well known; he also extends this attitude to the evaluation of historical narrative: "All that is not action is not worth reading" (534). It is significant for the analysis of his style, however, that in discussing history, narrative, and art, Blake customarily uses the discretely bounded, countable version of "action": "*Acts* themselves alone are history" (534 italics mine). That Blake intended to follow this direction in his own writing is evident, first, from the fact that in *Jerusalem* he asserts that Eternal art consists of unitary acts: "All *things acted* on Earth are seen in the bright Sculptures of/ Los's Halls" (16.61–62; italics mine). Second, his own "visions of Eternity" consisted largely of "acts": "the Eternal Form/ Of that mild Vision; wondrous were their acts by me unknown/ Except remotely" (M 40.1–3). Third, the Bard's Song, a poem within a poem, is thought to consist of "acts" subject to verification: "Others said. If it is true! if the acts have been perform'd/ Let the Bard himself witness" (M 13.49–50). There is no doubt, then, that acts have a place in Blakean poetics. It remains to be seen that they have a place in Blake's style.

In the midst of the incessant howling, thundering, and trembling of the great mass of Blake's prophetic verse, there are a few predications of single, definite acts. "Events," which are nonagentive, are usually "frustrated," aspectually or otherwise; those definite changes that fulfill themselves are acts—they result from human agency. The acts in Blake's verse are remarkable for their grand simplicity, which exists only in relief, foregrounded from the indefinite mass. They strike like cool, single bolts of lightning out of the storm. Such is Blake's own act, in response to the "appearance" of the "Vegetable World" on his foot:

> I stooped down & bound it on to walk forward thro' Eternity
> (M 21.14)

The predication of definite action is not hampered by any participial accoutrements or qualifying adjectives; unlike the semantic frustrations and endless meandering discussed above, it is simple and direct. The clauses are short, concise, and the motion is outward, as opposed, for example, to the recessive activity of the Females who eternally weave cocoons around themselves. Note moreover that the activity *walk* is not predicated in the above line, it is merely referred to. The finite predications, *stooped down & bound it on,* are single and complete acts. *Down* and *on* are perfective particles that ensure that the stooping and the binding are "fulfilled" as distinct changes from up to "down" and from off to "on." The aspect of the acts may be tested by adding a *for* phrase for duration: *I stooped down for hours* and **I bound it on for hours.* The one is no longer single, but is repeated indefinitely, and the other, because it cannot be repeated, is ungrammatical. It is the definiteness of these two acts that gives one the impression that the activity of "walking" that is to follow is not going to be the aimless motion characteristic of so much activity in Blake's prophecies. The effect may be paraphrased thus: "I did this and I did that. I do not act randomly; as I walk forward through Eternity, I walk as a man, I have direction."

Also grand and also foregrounded is the Bard's act at the end of the Bard's Song in *Milton.* Indeed, the very end, the exact instant, is what I refer to. For the Song closes like an iron door, in three single-syllabled words: "The Bard ceas'd." The lines immediately previous to these words had woven us into "Intricate labyrinths of Times and Spaces unknown," and before we know it, the Song is all over:

> . . . Times and Spaces unknown, that Leutha lived
> In Palamabrons Tent, and Oothoon was her charming guard.
> The Bard ceas'd.
>
> (M 13.43–45)

Cease is a verb of definite change, and in the context there is a singular definite activity which may be ceased—the singing of the Song. Hence the sentence predicates a definite change. Note, also, that it is part of the shock of these words to realize that the activity which is summarily "ceas'd" has constituted our experience as readers for thirteen plates. The past tense of *Leutha lived* and *Oothoon was her charming guard* has a reference point different from that of *ceas'd.* The former are the words of the Bard; his song is a direct quotation. Without quotation marks, the only signal we have for the change of time reference is the definite reference to a Bard of whom we have previous knowledge. The change awakens us; we have become absorbed in the story of the Song, which stands temporally in a relation of prehistory to the narrative of the poem as a whole. The abrupt shift of time reference makes us palpably aware of this relation, but, more important, of the fact that we have forgotten it.

Inspired by the Bard's Song, a few lines after its "cessation" Milton performs a series of definite acts:

> Then Milton rose up from the heavens of Albion
> ardorous!
> The whole Assembly wept prophetic, seeing in Miltons
> face
> And in his lineaments divine the shades of Death & Ulro
> He took off the robe of the promise, & ungirded himself
> from the oath of God
>
> (14.10–13)

Rise up predicates a complete change, consisting of moving in an upward direction to a static position, which is signalled by *up* and understood in context to be the upright, standing posture of the human body. The subject of the verb (in this case the semantic object of the change) is obviously definite and singular—*Milton.* Consequently the sentence predicates a single, definite act. The same is true of "He took off the robe" and "He ungirded himself." *Take* is a verb of definite change, and in this case it has a definite, unitary object, *the robe. Off* is a perfective particle signifying complete removal of one unit from another unit. *Ungird* implies a "girdle," and *un-* signifies removal. *From,* which requires the presupposition of two separate units, functions perfectively like *off,* stressing the completeness of the removal. Thus Blake does not merely predicate singular acts, when he wishes to foreground some "act of Eternity." He over-predicates them; but the semantic redundancy is not tedious: it fills the peaks and troughs of the rhythm; the *offs* and *ups* and *froms* punctuate the acts, both semantically and aurally.

In the reading experience of *Milton,* the above series of acts, however emphatic the acts may be in themselves, is only a drum roll for Milton's vocal act: "I go to Eternal Death!" (line 14). Each of his three foregoing acts is a definite movement predicated by a verb of motion plus a definite object of motion and some kind of marker to indicate a complete change of location. The same would be true of *I go to Eternal Death* (object of change + motion + goal), were it not also in the simple present, with a first-person subject. Given these factors, though the predication in its surface form is only a definite change of location, the utterance of it in this context is "performative."

A performative utterance is an utterance that enacts in the saying of the words themselves the act that the utterance describes. *I pronounce you man and wife* is a good example. The minister, in the act of saying the words, does indeed marry the couple. A number of semantic factors are required to make such a "speech act" valid—proper authority in the speaker, and so on.[22] The simple present tense is one of the formal features that can signal a performative utterance, and the simple present happens to be especially important in poetry. As George Wright has noted, the simple present is much more frequent in poetry than in speech or in prose, and it is "significantly expressive"—we feel in it "a portentousness, a freedom from singleness. . . . The actions described seem suspended, removed from the successiveness of our ordinary time levels, neither single nor repeated but of a different dimension entirely."[23] Wright neglects the aspectual evidence, however, and aspect reveals the performative force of many poetic uses of the simple present. The simple present has a significant aspectual distribution: state verbs normally occur in the simple present, but when verbs of change occur in it, they must predicate either habits or single, definite *speech acts.* Milton's utterance is of the latter type.

In choosing not to use a "performative verb" (like *pronounce*), but rather to force a mere verb of motion into performative use, Blake increases the forcefulness, the daring of the act. Normally, when a non-performative verb is used in this way, a future time adverbial is added, as in *We go tomorrow,* and the implication is that although the "going" is to happen "tomorrow," the act is already decided, and is a fact. It thus constitutes a speech act of "announcing." In Milton's announcement, the absence of a future time adverbial leaves us only the deictic tense-marker, and we suppose that he means to "go" immediately. We already see him starting to move, though he has not finished his speech. (Significantly, he utters the same words again when he *does* leave, at the very end of his speech.) Thus it is that the verbal enactment, "I go to Eternal Death," is commonly identified with the posture of the frontispiece, which shows Milton stepping with raised arm into the dark, reddening clouds.

It is acts such as these that make it difficult to call Blake either a "poet of process" or a "poet of stativity," although both of the latter modes are extremely important and quantitatively predominant in the prophetic verse. Rather, it seems that these modes promote in Blake's reader a value for durationless action, for single acts which manifest in their durationless spark the power of Humanity in Eternity. Such acts cannot quite be sensibly called a "mode" in themselves, for they each stand alone, and do not mix with their surroundings to form a composite stream of words. But they are definitely Blakean, and the majority are unforgettable, with their own kind of beauty.

Hence it is difficult, using the parameters of aspectual semantics, to find a handy catch-phrase by which to typify Blake's style. He used a combination of distinct modes to a decided effect. Yet his cannot be called a "composite" style, either. Blake said, in response to Joshua Reynolds, "There is No Such a Thing as A Composite Style" (641), and that is certainly true for his own style. His is rather a studied alternation of keys or modes than a "composition" of continuous texture. The closest he comes to a continuous texture is in what I have called his "style of process," the mode of unending activity, feverish and rolling.

It is a curious thing that there should be so much indefinite activity in a poet who so venerated the definite and determinate line of change, of time, of action. Again and again he maligns the indefinite, but there is an abundance of it in his verse. I am convinced, however, that this was part of Blake's design. He says that "Ideas cannot be Given but in their minutely Appropriate Words nor Can a Design be made without its minutely Appropriate Execution. The unorganized Blots & Blurs of Rubens & Titian are not Art" (565). The indefinitudes of Blake's style are *organized* blots and blurs, organized to lead the reader on, to excite him, confuse him, even tire him. All of the process makes the reader only too aware of the temporal nature of his experience and very grateful for the quietude of the static asides. Within this background, the singular acts are the fulfillment of the definite, which is always spoken of, but rarely seen. Blake did not say that he did *not* use rough edges and dark shadings. He said, regarding his verse, "Every word and every letter is studied and put into its fit place: the terrific numbers are reserved for the terrific parts—the mild & gentle, for the mild & gentle parts, and the prosaic, for inferior parts; all are necessary to each other" (J 3). Clearly this dictum applies to the aspectual semantics of the style also. For if Blake had made his verse replete with definite acts, they would be nothing to us. Nor could there be that marvelous simultaneity of which Miles, Murray, and others have spoken: definite acts form definite sequence, as in any pure narrative of events, while processes and states pile up in one reference-time.[24] Blake said, "I defy any Man to Cut Cleaner Strokes than I do or rougher when I please" (571). It is one of the findings of an aspectual analysis of Blake's prophecies that he cut very clean and very rough strokes indeed.

Notes

1. I am indebted to Donald Freeman for helpful comments on an earlier version, and to Julian Boyd, Charles Fillmore, Donald Ault, Morton Paley, and others for criticism of the preparatory work.

2. *The Poetry and Prose of William Blake,* ed. David V. Erdman (Garden City, N. Y.: Doubleday, 1970), p. 565. All citations of Blake will be from this edition, with page numbers for prose and plate (or MS page) and line numbers for poetry. Blake's poems are indicated by the following abbreviations: BL, *The Book of Los;* FZ, *The Four Zoas;* J, *Jerusalem;* M, Milton; SL, *The Song of Los;* U, *The Book of Urizen.*

3. *Eras and Modes in English Poetry* (Berkeley: Univ. of California Press, 1964), p. 85.

4. The reader should not think that adjectives are always stative. According to tests proposed by George Lakoff, some adjectives are non-stative: *Don't be noisy* (imperative); *What I'm doing is being noisy* (do-something); *I'm being noisy* (progressive)—*Irregularity in Syntax* (New York: Holt, Rinehart and Winston, 1970), p. 121. Note, however, that we must be careful in applying such tests: the context itself can force a normally very static adjective into active service, as in *Be silent!* or in *They were being silent.* In the Blake line, the inanimacy of "Mills" and the absence of the progressive leave us with a stative interpretation.

5. Thus there are some verbs, like *sit,* that are indeterminate for aspect, or that perhaps have aspectual variants, depending on the context. For further discussion, see Ronald C. Taylor, "The Semantics of Time in the Later Poetry of William Blake: A Stylistic Study" (Berkeley: Univ. of California Ph.D. diss., 1976), p. 44 and p. 63 n. 13; see also Ronald C. Taylor, "The Aspectual Structure of the English Sentence," *Doshisha Studies in English,* 15 (Dec. 1976), 164–98.

6. This characterization of *in* applies only to its use with spatial nouns. With nouns representing temporal extents, the situation is quite the reverse, as in *He finished in ten minutes,* where *in* requires that the predicate be perfective.

7. Regarding Blake's ideas on "events," see Taylor, diss., pp. 8–10.

8. To be sure, there were early uses of *define* (and its cognate forms) that associated it with spatial and visual outline—most notably by Newton in 1727 and by Wordsworth in 1815. But its use in a technical sense in the visual media stemmed from its use in the science of optics, for which it became common only after 1859, the only earlier instance being that of *Difinitor* for "a kind of surveying instrument" in 1664 (OED).

9. Domenico Parisi and Francesco Antinucci, "Lexical Competence," in *Advances in Psycholinguistics,* ed. G. B. D'Arcais and W. J. Levelt (Amsterdam: North-Holland, 1971), pp. 197–210.

10. There is a fourth mode, not treated here for lack of space and because it is relatively minor. It consists of "stacking" discrete events one "on top of" the other in a dense series, and it gives an impression of incredible speed and abruptness. This "rush of events" is somewhat more important in the style of the earlier, short-line prophecies; the handiest example, however, is from *The Four Zoas:* "down rushd the Sun with noise/ Of war. The Mountains fled away" (15. 14–15). Taylor, diss., pp. 47–55.

11. *Live* seems to be one of those verbs that depend on their complements for their aspectual denotations (cf. n. 5). I have called it a verb of process here because the modifier *renewd by female deaths* entails a sense of active duration. Cf. *He lived at Felpham,* which predicates a state, and "he Lived on Bread & Apples" (626), which indicates what "he" *did* during the time he was alive, so that it necessarily implies activity.

12. For a discussion of the underlying subject-matter connections between these asides and their contexts, particularly in *Milton,* see Taylor, diss., Chap. V.

13. Miles, op. cit.; Roger Murray, "Blake and the Ideal of Simplicity," *Studies in Romanticism,* 13 (1974), 89–104.

14. Taylor, diss., pp. 31–34. Cf. John Anderson, *An Essay Concerning Aspect . . .* (The Hague: Mouton, 1973); Dwight Bolinger, "The Nominal in the Progressive," *Linguistic Inquiry,* 2 (1971), 246–50; Wallace Chafe, *Meaning and the Structure of Language* (Chicago: Univ. of Chicago Press, 1970), pp. 168–77; John Lyons, *Introduction to Theoretical Linguistics* (Cambridge: Cambridge Univ. Press, 1969), pp. 315–17, and references therein.

15. Taylor, diss., pp. 34–35.

16. Ibid., pp. 47–55. Cf. E. L. Epstein, "Blake's 'Infant Sorrow'—An Essay

in Discourse Analysis," in *Current Trends in Stylistics,* ed. Braj B. Kachru and Herbert F. W. Stahlke (Edmonton: Linguistic Research, 1972), pp. 231–41.

17. This symbolism is a modification of Hans Reichenbach, *Elements of Symbolic Logic* (New York: Free Press, 1966), pp. 287–98.

18. *Eras and Modes,* pp. 86–87, and *Renaissance, Eighteenth-Century, and Modern Language in English Poetry—A Tabular View* (Berkeley: Univ. of California Press, 1960).

19. The situation with *cherish* is similar to that with *live,* as described in n. 11.

20. *The Philosophy of Grammar* (London: Allen & Unwin, 1924), pp. 273–74; *A Modern English Grammar on Historical Principles* (London: Allen & Unwin, 1949), IV, 100–03.

21. But compare *He ran among the trees,* which is ambiguous between "He ran into and among" and "He ran around in." Perhaps this ambiguity is partially responsible for the semantic dilemma described below.

22. John Searle, *Speech Acts: An Essay in the Philosophy of Language* (Cambridge: Cambridge Univ. Press, 1970).

23. "The Lyric Present: Simple Present Verbs in English Poems," *PMLA,* 89 (1974), 564, 565.

24. Taylor, diss., pp. 47–48, 52–54.

STEVEN SHAVIRO

"Striving with Systems": Blake and the Politics of Difference

"I must Create a System, or be enslav'd by another Mans," cries Los at a crucial moment early in *Jerusalem*, "I will not Reason & Compare; my business is to Create" (10:20–21, E151).[1] The emphasis in these lines is upon "Create" rather than upon "System," but it is in the conjunction of the two terms that the problematic of Blake's text may best be situated. On the one hand, what might be called Blake's systematizing mania is a major stumbling block for any reader of the longer poems; *Jerusalem*, with its bewildering cast of metamorphosing characters and its discontinuities of place and action, can scarcely be read apart from the commentary which it has generated, that of the elaborate mapping so painstakingly worked out by S. Foster Damon, Northrop Frye, and their successors.[2] Yet on the other hand, as such systematizing critics themselves never tire of pointing out, Blake's elaborate constructions are themselves only means toward the end of liberating the poet and his readers from any such limitations of system or of perspective. Systematization must remain subordinated to the process of creation of which it is nevertheless the result and the symptom. In the long run, any completed system, including even Blake's own, must be destroyed in order to be freshly recreated.

This problematic may be stated in another and starker way

This essay first appeared in *boundry 2* 10 (1982): 229–250. Reprinted with permission.

by noting the contradiction between the two most commonly received images of the poet: that of Blake as systematizer, as sage and teacher, as essentially doctrinal poet, and that of Blake as dramatic poet and master of irony who rarely or never speaks *in propria persona.* These opposed conceptions intersect or interfere at the moments (such as Los's resolution to "Create") in which the systematizing compulsion is dramatized as such within Blake's text. At such moments, a prior knowledge of Blake's system in its totality is needed in order to approach a point prior to that system and from which the system as such is generated. The poem itself dramatizes, and thereby reflects back upon and limits, the process of its own systematization. The poem suggests that any System is an object of desire, and needs to be constructed; but such an insight is available to us only if we ignore its applicability to the overarching Blakean System in which, e.g., the function of Los as figure of Imagination is first defined. Any such identification of the role of Los depends upon a previous conception of Blake's myth or System as a coherent and organized totality. This means that Blake criticism, like the systematizing movement within the poetry itself, is able to validate itself only to the extent that it already assumes what it then sets out to prove.

In consequence, there seem to be two alternatives for any reading of Blake. On the one hand, we may move within the familiar paradox of pre-knowledge and the hermeneutic circle. Blake is interpreted systematically because it has been assumed not only that Blake's works do in fact constitute a System, but even that the contents or broad outlines of the System (such as the identities and functions of the characters) are already known prior to the act of reading. This accounts for what Thomas Weiskel has called "the charmed circularity of Blakean hermeneutics,"[3] the maddeningly cultish, self-referential and self-congratulatory tone of all too much Blake criticism. Or else, if the *a priori* postulate of totalization and systematic coherence is abandoned, then the contradictory perspectives and ironic reversals of Blake's text are resolved into some form of infinite regress, in which any System refers back, in its contingency, to the act by which it was created, while creators and acts of creation are themselves determined and made possible only within the context of previously existing Systems. Blake's dramatic ironies are regulated and distributed by his overarching System; but that System is itself only produced as an effect in the course of an essentially ironic dramatic interplay.

These alternatives exist for every critic of Blake because they are already contradictory features of Blake's text itself. In exploring this problematic, my own commentary will therefore not resist the temptation to function, at the same time, as an allegory of the critical process itself. In Blake's poetic discourse as in the discourse of criticism and of critical theory, an infinitely ironizing movement disqualifies and subverts, while at the same time establishing the possibility and preconditions of, any systematization or totalization. It would be misguided and premature, however, merely to invert traditional criticism by postulating a reversed hierarchy, in which irony occupies the place of mastery. In Blake's poetry, it is not subversion by means of irony, but rather precisely the contradiction between an ironic and self-limiting rhetorical and dramatic stance, on the one hand, and the conceptual, totalizing thrust of a mythopoeic system, on the other, which most needs to be explored. I will argue that it is this gap between irony and representation, between production and conceptualization, between desire and mastery, which constitutes Blake's discourse; and I will suggest the consequences which such a view of the interplay of irony and totality in difference has for current critical debates.

At one point in *Jerusalem,* Los is described as "Striving with Systems to deliver individuals from those Systems" (11:5, E153). Let this phrase stand as an emblem for the contradictory determinations of Blake's poetry. For "with" must be read as meaning both 'against' and 'by means of,' while "deliver" must be read as meaning both 'rescue' and 'aid in the birth of'. Thus creating a System is conjoined with attacking, destroying, or evading a System; and an Individual is constituted both as one whose individuality is realized only in the process of being freed from the constrictions of a System, and as one who is only produced or defined as individual within and by virtue of such a System. Blake is deliberately not a systematic writer, in that he characteristically and repeatedly overloads the same words, overdetermines the same symbols, with both positive and negative connotations. The declaration of desire: "I must Create a System" must be grasped in its immediate dramatic context (Los's struggle with the Spectre), which is rendered ambiguous by the possible multivalency of the "I" as much as by that of "Create" and of "System." The question is to what extent the dramatic and contextualizing principle which differentially distributes such valorizations is itself subject to the interplay of contraries.

Insofar as Blake's mode of presentation is dramatic and differential, it is always suggesting opposing perspectives, "Contrary States of the Human Soul" (E7), Innocence and Experience, Heaven and Hell, Beulah and Generation. The problem of systematization in Blake's text is thus one regarding the logic of binary oppositions. How is it possible to move from the radical perspectivism of the contrary states of the soul to the total System in which each of these states has its proper place? For Blake's Contraries are not dialectical. "Without Contraries is no progression" (MHH, E34), but also "Negations are not Contraries" (J17:33, E160). Dialectical progression always implies the "Abstract objecting power" (J10:14, E151) of negation and comprehension, whereas Blake insists upon the positivity of both contraries, their active and continuing opposition. "Progression" thus has a very special meaning for Blake, implying the continuation of a lived tension of opposites, rather than any sublation or furthering resolution.

Such a refusal of dialectics marks Blake's rejection of the intellectualizing and conceptualizing procedures of rationalistic philosophy. Yet such a rejection paradoxically presents itself in the form of a conceptual or cognitive moment within Blake's own text. The doctrine of Contraries, as put forth in *The Marriage of Heaven and Hell,* is differential and anti-discursive in terms of its polemical content, but universalizing, conceptual, and systematic in terms of its form. It becomes necessary simultaneously to read Blake's text both in terms of its System, or conceptual unity, *and* in terms of its anti-conceptual differentiality, or ironic perspectivism and dramatic contextualizations. But such a double reading reveals a fundamental *dissymmetry* which precedes and organizes the strife of Contraries as equal and binary opposites. This dissymmetry arises from the fact that the alternate readings are not of equal status, but may instead be hierarchically articulated. The systematic approach, as a claim to totality and to truth, transcendentally compares and organizes the disparate perspectives. The differential approach is founded upon the insistence of minute particulars which resist such a sublimation. A tension is maintained because Blake prohibits any dialectical movement from one level to the other.

The strife of Contraries is thus necessarily articulated in language which is itself contradictory; but in this latter case the contradiction is not one of binary opposition between equals, but rather a sort of Russell's paradox, a conflict between two different levels of discourse, between content and form or between statement and meta-statement. Gregory Bateson has claimed that the double bind resulting from such a conflict is constitutive of schizophrenia,[4] and we shall see that the principle of authority in Blake's poetry, the Urizen figure on one hand and the creative and System-building figure on the other, is always schizophrenic in precisely this sense. But at the same time, it is this dissymmetrical contradiction which generates the active tension of equal and opposed Contraries. The "marriage" of Heaven and Hell indicates at once the equalizing reconciliation and the differential irreconcilablity of the opposed states.

We are told, in a passage which cannot be attributed to any particular voice, that the Contraries "are always upon earth, & they should be enemies; whoever tries to reconcile them seeks to destroy existence" (E39). The rhetoric of this statement is quite interesting. First, the eternal existence of the Contraries is presented as a given fact (they "are always upon earth"). But second, the enmity of the Contraries is presented not as a fact, but as an imperative ("they should be enemies"). What is in question is not their existence, or the existence of the world, but the mode of their relationships. Then third, the reconciliation of the contraries is presented as an empty and illusory desire, a project as impossible as it is pernicious: "Religion is an endeavour to reconcile the two," but the words "endeavor," "tries," and "seeks" imply an exertion which goes contrary to fact (since the Contraries "are always upon earth," the world continues to exist, existence is not destroyed). The paradox of a conflict between incommensurable levels of discourse is here reproduced more concretely in the contrast between the imperative "should" and the less forceful wording of "tries" and "seeks." "Should" at once invokes a necessity and confesses (since it is conditional rather than indicative) that that necessity may not in fact be the case. The statement "they should be enemies" is at once the expression of a particular perspective (one of the Contraries) and a meta-statement which thereby surpasses that, or any other particular, perspective. But its hypothetical contrary ("they should be reconciled") is presented only in much weaker terms, which disqualify it from attaining legitimacy as a meta-statement.

Blake's text thus establishes a hierarchy of authority at the same time that it overtly denies the possibility of such a hierarchy. This is possible because of the circularity whereby the content of each Contrary reflects back upon the mode of being of the system of Contraries as such. "Attraction and Repulsion, Reason and Energy, Love and Hate, are necessary to Human existence" (E34), but it is always also a question of whether Attraction and Repulsion are attracted to or repulsed from one another, of whether "the passive that obeys Reason" and "the active springing from Energy" are actively or passively opposed to one another, of whether the relationship between the class of men who love and the class of men who hate is one of love or of hatred. The discourse of *The Marriage* is consistently dramatic and ironic, limited to the perspectives of specific speakers (so that it is inaccurate simply to identify Blake's own voice with that of Hell and the Devil); but to the extent that that discourse refers back to and founds the very perspectivism or doctrine of Contraries, within which and by means of which it is itself situated, it validates itself as a transcendent principle of authority. Blake's logic thus at once remains within the ironic limits of perspective and context, and yet escapes beyond them. No dialectical reconciliation of the Contraries is permitted, and yet it is in an authoritative statement, one which would have to transcend the contradiction, that the Contraries are maintained *as* Contraries, as states defined in opposition to and by means of struggle with one another. The rhetorical strategy of exalting one Contrary over the other, insofar as it is that which founds both, while at the same time maintaining the Contraries in the strict equality of binary opposition, permits Blake to have things both ways, to establish a position of transcendence, free from the limitations of any given perspective, and yet to maintain opposed perspectives in their minute particularity, free of any dialectical subsumption or sublation. It is an authoritative voice which warns the reader that no voice is authoritative, that every statement has a context and a perspective and must be actively and positively opposed by another statement made in another context and from another perspective. The principle which grounds and articulates the system of contradictory perspectives is itself located within that system as one of its contradictory terms, and it is precisely this infinite regress of the principle of authority which founds the self-validating circularity of the system as a whole.

A similar hermeneutical problematic is at work in the Preface to *Milton* (E94). Once again, the structure of Blake's argument is that of a dissymmetrical binary opposition. The Bible is opposed to the classics, Inspiration to Memory, "Painters! . . . Sculptors! Architects!," the "Young Men of the New Age," to the "Ignorant Hirelings." The latter class of men is defined, in contrast to the former, as containing those "who would if they could, for ever depress Mental & prolong Corporeal War." The opposition between the inspired and the hirelings is thus an opposition between mental warfare and corporeal warfare, a strife between a non-dialectical strife in which the tension between Contraries is maintained, and a finite or concludable strife culminating in a violent suppression, in which one Contrary is destroyed or swallowed up in the victory of the other. Once again, the leap to meta-statements implies a dissymmetry in the relationship of Contraries, a dissymmetry which in turn produces the equality of opposing Contraries. The hirelings "would if they could" defeat the ideal of the inspired (mental warfare), and replace it exclusively with their own ideal (corporeal warfare). Yet their own ideal is itself only this formal condition, its own proper triumph over its adversary. The grammar of the phrase "would if they could" implies a condition not only contrary to fact but logically impossible; the hirelings do not depress and destroy mental warfare because they cannot, because the strife of Contraries always subsists. Mental warfare and corporeal warfare both continue to exist. This state of co-existence is precisely the principle of mental warfare, and in contradiction with that of corporeal warfare. Hence the co-existence of mental and corporeal warfare is in fact the triumph of the former over the latter, even though it is only the principle of the latter which would authorize such a one-sided resolution. It is this reversal which generates Blake's aggressively polemical stance, his speaking from the side of one of the Contraries, and his implication that that side of the opposition is original (artists working by inspiration) whereas the other side is derivative ("hirelings" act only for money, not out of inspiration or conviction), at the same time that he proclaims the mutual and eternal necessity, the strict equality, of those Contraries.

Thus Blake's system of Contraries is generated by a movement which is endlessly contradictory, inadmissible by the standards not only of formal logic but also of Hegelian dialectical logic. In Hegelian terms, both the overt doctrine of Contraries which are never reconciled or sublated, and its underlying and determining double bind structure, are instances of what Hegel calls "the wrong or negative infinity," an undialectical fluctuation between the finite (Blake's corporeal war) and the merely quantitative infinite (Blake's endless mental war), an opposition which "sets up with endless iteration the alternation between these two terms, each of which calls up the other."[5] Put more positively, the structure of Blake's argument reveals a differential and rhetorical movement which necessarily precedes and determines *any* argument based upon a logic of opposition (whether the argument be Blake's own, or—by anticipation—Hegel's). This unresolvable differential movement thereby also accounts for the polemic against Reason or philosophical logic which is so prominent a feature of Blake's text. Within the system of Contraries, Reason has precisely the same status as does corporeal war in the Preface to *Milton* or religion as an effort to reconcile the Contraries in *The Marriage:* it is the term which, as a meta-statement, would seek to put an end to the eternal strife of Contraries, and which is therefore itself suppressed in that proclamation, by the other Contrary, that neither Contrary may ever be subsumed or suppressed.

This generative differential movement exhibits in the first instance the rhetorical form of the chiasmus, since by virtue precisely of their dissymmetry the Contraries incessantly refer back to one another, taking one another's place without ever achieving any reconciliation or teleological subsumption, in that movement of endless circularity which founds even as it exceeds the possibility of the hermeneutic circle. But in the second instance, insofar as this movement is one of the infinite regress from statement to meta-statement, the closure presupposed in any systematization (whether it be that of Blake's own System, or that of the classificatory system of classical rhetoric), and implicit in the very notion of the hermeneutic circle, is itself disqualified and breached. The Contraries can be neither exhaustive nor mutually exclusive. The regress from statement to meta-statement continues; the differential movement which generates the doctrine of equal Contraries also goes beyond it, denying it the stability of a fixed law or final regulating term.

Blake's System, as the systematization of this untotalizable differential movement, is thus intrinsically incomplete. It is the positivity of this perpetual lack of closure which Blake privileges as Creation or as Imagination, the transcendent term nonetheless at the same time immanent to the System it founds and surpasses. If it is the Imagination which founds any systematization, it is also the Imagination which then goes beyond it, in the positive movement of the "wrong infinity" of the chiasmic-regressive figuration. Such a figuration, operating in accordance with the schizophrenic double bind structure of the meta-statement, at once enforces the closure of Blake's discourse, producing its systematic and conceptual coherence and its polemical force, and yet leaves it perpetually incomplete and open. Such a structure or movement has more than merely formalistic consequences, as I shall proceed to demonstrate by means of a detailed close reading of one brief poem, "The Tyger." But first, in order further to clarify the points which have been raised so far, I will hazard a brief comparison between the differential functioning of Blake's text and that of the (non-)concept of *differance* expounded by Jacques Derrida and his followers, in terms of their respective relations to the movement of dialectical logic.

Derrida remarks that "if there were a definition of differance, it would be precisely the limit, the interruption, the destruction of the Hegelian *relève [Aufhebung] wherever* it operates."[6] On one hand, the *Aufhebung* "is *the* concept of history and of teleology."[7] On the other hand, "except [for his] eschatology,. . . Hegel is *also* the thinker of irreducible difference."[8] Differance could be determined, therefore, as the inversion of the *Aufhebung* into mise en abîme, the movement of negativity always already suspended or interrupted, so that the totalizing and teleological negation of the negation is never realized. It is in terms of this suspension that Derrida neither accedes to nor simply steps beyond the logocentric enclosure. Yet it is because of this ambiguous positioning that Derrida's writing takes the form of a critique of philosophy, so that it necessarily becomes at times critical and polemical, that is to say, itself negative, itself carrying out the negative movement which it declares to have been suspended in the text to which it refers. Whenever deconstruction operates as ideology-critique, whenever the deconstructive reader critically isolates and denounces a logocentric moment in a given text, he or she thereby performs a movement of pure negation, simply surpassing the logocentric enclosure and for that very reason remaining trapped within it. In Derrida's own terms, *any* critical or polemical gesture (including especially that of the limitation/suspension/destruction of the *Aufhebung*), however inevitable, is itself nonetheless a totalizing and sublating movement, itself as much a part of the movement of the *Aufhebung* as that which it attacks and of which it is the negation. Hence the privileging of irony in Derrida and in other deconstructive critics, most notably Paul de Man. But conversely, insofar as differance 'precedes' any origin or any metaphysical determination of Being, it is already operative in any given context, so that it should become impermissible to make the privileging and hierarchizing distinction, as Derrida does, between what a text "declares" and what it "describes,"[9] or to establish, as de Man does, a dialectic of "blindness and insight."[10]

While Derrida, in disqualifying all polemic, reintroduces the necessity of polemical error, Blake is freely polemical in such a way as to render the very issue of polemic and necessary error entirely irrelevant. Blake makes no attempt to suspend or limit the *Aufhebung,* but overtly performs the totalizing sublation in the very act of polemicizing against it. The *aporia* or ultimate undecidability of the text is not, in Blake, that which qualifies, limits, and 'decontructs' a teleological and totalizing movement. Rather, *aporia* and *Aufhebung* are dissymmetrically opposed and intricated meta-statements, simultaneous effects of pure difference, of the non-cause which is the chiasmic-regressive figuration. Although there is an affirmative side to deconstruction, the deconstructive operation tends ultimately to express difference only negatively and critically, as the limitation or unmasterable contradiction subsisting within any teleological and totalizing project. Blake's text, however, expresses difference positively and affirmatively: not as that which compromises the totalizing project from within, but as that which, after the totalization has in fact been accomplished, still remains irreducibly exterior and prior to it. Deconstruction in effect grants priority to that which it at once opposes and declares to be inevitable and insurpassable, the ever-unsuccessful project of hermeneutical and cognitive mastery. But Blake's text can afford to be overtly polemical and overtly systematizing because it is ultimately not cognitive or hermeneutical at all, not even negatively. The Urizenic project of interpretative mastery and its failure, are indeed inevitable consequences of the chiasmic-regressive figuration: this is the schizophrenia constituted by the double bind situation. But the figuration, as structure of pure difference, cannot be reduced merely to this cognitive aspect. Imagination is *not* ultimately undecidable: not because anything can be determined or decided, but precisely because there is finally nothing to decide. Imagination is fundamentally irreducible, in that it is not to be determined as any essence but also not to be negatively determined as the undeterminable or undecidable.

While deconstruction ironically privileges interpretation as infinite regress, for Blake the infinite regress is an affirmative movement of difference, that which is always other than (rather than merely that which contradicts or undoes) the will to closure and the will to interpretation. Deconstruction finally remains (despite its disqualification of such terminology) a thought of interiority and of internalization, of the ever-increasing internality of contradiction, which it represents as the contradiction of internality. Blake's discourse, on the other hand, remains open to exteriority: it can afford to be unashamedly polemical because, in its differential play, its constant movement between incompatible levels of affirmation, another perspective always arises elsewhere. The governing metaphor of deconstruction is always the negative one of repression; the distinction between intent and content, or between a given text's self-representation and that which it in fact represents or reveals, is the one metaphysical binary opposition which never gets 'deconstructed.' In Blake's discourse, however, the play of different perspectives is open and affirmative: they are juxtaposed so as to disrupt any project of stable hierarchization, and the movement between them is not one of repression and its undoing, of a psychoanalytic symptomatology, but one of accumulation, of positive expansion, of the reproduction of the same differential nexus on a larger scale.

It is in the light of these distinctions that I would like, finally, to turn to a reading of "The Tyger" (E24–25). This poem moves toward a moment of hermeneutical indecidability, even as it lends itself to a certain psychoanalytic vocabulary. But at the same time it delineates the limits both of the hermeneutic impasse and of the psychoanalytic metaphor. Totality is put into question in the poem not insofar as it is internally contradictory, or insofar as it symptomatically bears the traces of the exclusions which it has operated (although both of these situations are also the case), but finally insofar as its claim to the power of determination is itself assigned only a determined and determinate context. Indeed, such a problematic is explicitly articulated by the speaker of the poem, who frames his own discourse with a repeated question about the significance of an originating and contextualizing framing: "What immortal hand or eye/ Could [or, Dare] frame thy fearful symmetry?" The word "frame" has at least two major senses in the poem. Most obviously, it means to construct or build, to design or fabricate, to create. The poem is concerned above all with the tyger's creator, and with the process of the tyger's creation or framing. But at the same time, to frame means to contextualize or delimit, as a picture frame sets off and defines the space of a painting. In this sense, the frame is what establishes a particular perspective. We can only interpret the linguistic signs which make up the poem, confront the tyger as a "thou" or treat it as a signifier or metaphor, by virtue of the context within which, or the background against which, the tyger is placed.

The interplay between the two senses of "frame" reproduces the differential structuration with which we are already familiar. In a first, overly naive but unavoidable reading, framing/delimiting, as confining the object within specified limits, seems to be only one phase of the greater task of framing/making. The poem narrates a series of creative acts: seizing the fire, twisting the sinews, beating with the hammer, and so on. The completed tyger is only then placed within the "forests of the night," against whose background it is seen "burning bright." Similarly, the poem "The Tyger" had first to be hammered out by Blake in his Notebook, before being framed physically by the picture which surrounds and supposedly illustrates it, and conceptually by the entire series of "Songs of Innocence and of Experience."

But in a less naive and equally inevitable reading, these priorities are reversed. Metaphorically, at least, all the creator's (and the poet's) acts of framing/making are aspects of a more fundamental process of framing/delimiting. Blake insists throughout his writings that in art "all depends on Form or Outline" (E520). To form/frame the tyger means to abstract the flame from the "distant deeps or skies" and to confine it within a frame or determinate outline. The rhyme words "grasp" and "clasp" suggest that the "deadly terrors" have been seized and trapped. The brain, during its creation, is sealed in the furnace, even as the created tyger is set down to shine "in the forests of the night." Similarly, the poem "The Tyger" must be read in terms of its context as a song "of Experience" and as a dramatic utterance reflecting, even as it creates, the surrounding character and circumstances of its presumed speaker.

To frame/create, then, always means first of all to frame/delimit. Unbound energy (distant fires) is mastered and spatially confined by the creator. The tyger's energy exists only within and by virtue of the determinate outline which defines and frames the tyger. The tyger itself burns bright only against the background of the "forests of the night" (it is notorious that in Blake's illustration, framed this time by the pink of the dawn and only by a single leafless tree, the tyger has entirely lost its nighttime fierceness).

The double meaning of "frame" thus frames (delimits) the creative act which is the subject of the poem. To frame/make usually refers to the process of bringing something into being; whereas to frame/delimit is to define, confine, or appropriate that which already exists. In "The Tyger," the act of the creator is deeply equivocal, since creation is associated not with the primary energy of the fires but with the secondary repression or binding of that energy. Blake's longer and more systematic poems portray the Creation and the Fall as virtually the same event, and the phrase "the stars threw down their spears" recurs specifically in the context of Urizen's fall.[11]

Yet the differential interplay of the two senses of "frame" also undermines, even as it suggests, the hierarchal labels of 'primary' and 'secondary' which I have just employed. The oxymoron "fearful symmetry" implies an intrication within which priority cannot be determined or assigned. The distant, uncontained fires are "fearful," and the "symmetry" is that imposed by the container or frame. A symmetry which is itself fearful is then a container composed only of the uncontainable and unconfineable which it nonetheless confines and contains. The speaker at once admires the uncontrolled energy of the distant fires—"portions of eternity too great for the eye of man" (E36)—and the creator's framing energy, which masters, confines, represses, and gives definite outline to those frames. The power of an impersonal or pre-personal field of energy is both confused with and separated from power personified in the figure of the creator. Each logically precedes and determines the other.

On one hand, the tyger is nothing apart from its frame. It becomes possible to speak of an object, or to speak to it, to locate it as a "thou," as the object of the speaker's discourse, only because an undefinable and undecidable something (which I have been calling energy, but which strictly speaking cannot be named, but only referred to indirectly through the metonymy of "fire" in "distant deeps or skies") has been objectified, contextualized, framed. This frame is at once spatial (the forests), temporal (the process of creation), and conceptual (the speaker's moral and intellectual categories). Yet on the other hand, the frame itself (meaning both the already existing frame, and the process of framing or of bringing the frame into existence) is not the object, is not a definable object at all, but rather that which the object is not, the contrast of its surroundings, its outline. An outline cannot exist as such apart from the thing outlined, while the thing 'in itself,' apart from the outline, is formless and ungraspable. The creator has to first "seize the fire" and "grasp" the "deadly terrors" in order to create the tyger; yet the fire and the terrors can be apprehended only as attributes of the already-created tyger.

The argument of "The Tyger" is thus founded, like the doctrine of Contraries, upon a movement at once circular and regressive. The circularity is aptly figured by the near-repetition of the opening stanza at the close; while the nuance of change from "could" to "dare" indicates the regressively spiralling nature of the speaker's reasoning. Attention is diverted from the object to the frame and the process of framing; yet framing and frame can only be discussed in terms derived, in turn, from the object which they create and define. It thus becomes impossible to assign priority precisely because the poem is so explicitly concerned with questions of origin. Insofar as each of the inseparably intricated terms is posited as the origin of the other, the circle becomes an infinite regression.

This combined movement could perhaps best be defined as one of displacement or evasion. The figure of the tyger itself is strangely absent from the poem, despite its being repeatedly addressed and invoked by the speaker. It is never directly described; its physical characteristics, and the affects which it evokes, are assigned elsewhere by means of rhetorical dislocation. The "deadly terrors," for instance, logically should be those of the tyger's brain, but syntactically seem rather to be those of the anvil upon which the brain was beaten into shape. The bizarre discontinuity of "What dread hand? & what dread feet?" may similarly be read as a not entirely successful attempt at displacement on the part of the speaker.[12] The poem regresses from foreground to background both in space (from the tyger itself, to the forests which frame it, to the "distant deeps or skies") and in time (from the actual night to the night of creation). By evoking ever more distant contexts, the speaker escapes, or diverts attention away from, his immediate situation.

Kenneth Burke notes that it was typical of nineteenth-century thought to use "origin" as a trope for "essence"[13]; the poem parodies this intellectual trend in advance with its systematic transfer of terms and attributes from essence to origin. In the eighteenth century, such reasoning was the basis for the argument from design of natural theology. In the argument of "The Tyger," characteristics of the tyger as existent being are ascribed to the supposed process of its creation. A further inference leads from creation (process) to creator (substance). Finally, or to put a halt to the regression, the creator is endowed with being independent of his creation, so that he may observe it from the outside after having completed it: "Did he smile his work to see?" Causal connections have been entirely reversed. The hypostasis of the creator is founded exclusively upon, and yet exceeds and denies, the actual presence of the tyger. Tyger and creator are mutually dependent, since each is conceived through the other; yet since the two are disproportionate, each is also conceived independently of, and prior to, the other. The creator is the origin of the tyger; but the tyger is no less necessarily the origin of the creator. The assumptions about the creator which underlie the speaker's questions exceed anything which can be rightfully inferred from the mere appearance of the tyger. But these questions are themselves unanswerable because they demand, in turn, an insight into the nature and purpose of the tyger which exceeds anything that can be inferred from what we know or believe about the creator. Thus creator and creation exchange places in the fallaciously circular logic of the chiasmus.

The static circularity of the poem's logic is supplemented on what might be called the psychological level by a one-way movement of regression. On the level of argument, the essentialistic discourse of natural theology is disrupted insofar as the origin which is supposed to ground and validate the claim for essence is instead itself implicated within the problematic of essence, and thereby lost in an infinite regress. But the movement of difference which disqualifies any simple assertion of presence, including the speaker's own implicit assertion of self-presence, is nonetheless also psychologized, as the speaker's (unconscious) intentional strategy for evading or eliding what is for him the tyger's overwhelming presence. "The Tyger" thus offers itself to a reading in psychoanalytic terms; although at the same time, and for the same reason, the chiasmic-regressive figuration posits the limit of any reading which is subject-centered or psychological.

The circularity and mutual reference of the dissymmetrical relationship between creator and creation is transformed into a linear regression from the point of view of the presumed intentionality of the speaker, who moves the argument in one direction only: always away from the tyger, away from the dramatic present. This ambiguity is precisely that of the Freudian mechanism of dream-formation. According to Freud, displacement and condensation are at the same time basic features of primary process thought and devices whereby the contents of such thought are censored and repressed. The id is characterized by the endless circularity of substitution along the signifying chain, without goal or direction; but the pressures of repression are selective, and thus impose the semblance of teleology and order. The selectivity of censorship isolates those substitutions which move in directions acceptable for conscious representation; or, it may be that a governing teleology is itself the condition which makes a given series of substitutions acceptable to consciousness. In "The Tyger," similarly, an underlying circularity becomes the basis for a teleological argument, and an endless series of displacements is selectively transformed into a linear movement of evasion.

In psychic terms, the tyger is a primary object of anxiety, or, better still, the object of what Freud calls primal repression:

> a first phase of repression, which consists in the psychical (ideational) representative of the instinct being denied entrance into the conscious. With this a fixation is established; the representative in question persists unaltered from then onwards and the instinct remains attached to it.[14]

The primal repression is thus an originary act for any given psyche, since all subsequent movements of instinct and of defense may be referred back to it. It posits and defines the hidden centrality, the simultaneous presence and absence, of the supposed lost object, the ideational presentation which, having become bound to the instinct, is the repression's object. When the circle of substitutions is frozen at a specific point, the image thus chosen "persists unaltered" as a terminus for all subsequent series of substitutions, precisely because it cannot itself be displaced along any such series. The tyger is the one object which cannot be described or directly presented by the speaker of "The Tyger," but only addressed by him, and for this very reason it governs the entire movement of the poem.

The explicit teleology of the speaker is thus the correlate of a repressed teleology or intentionality moving in the opposite direction. The process of repression encompasses these two movements linked by a chiasmic inversion. On one hand, the speaker transforms the tyger from ultimate and psychic origin to contingent and external effect. The unknowability of the supposed creator is merely a reflection of the unspeakability of the repressed tyger. Each framing or recontextualization of the object serves only to hide it yet more fully. On the other hand, it is only by virtue of these evasive framings that the tyger is defined as such as an object, and that it is furthermore granted its central or primordial status. It is precisely this repulsion of the tyger, the impossibility of its appearance, which reinstates it as the primal lost object, the "thou" to whom (rather than to the creator himself) the poem is addressed.

The famous questions raised by the speaker can thus be situated as rhetorical effects of the double and chiasmic structure of repression. Questions about the creator of the tyger lead inevitably back to the tyger itself, which is in turn only constituted as such insofar as those questions evade it. The fixation which isolates and designates the tyger is also the repression which renders it inaccessible. It is abstracted from the circle of endless substitutions only to be reinstated as the unreachable terminus of a supposedly teleological chain of displacements which is in fact an infinite regress. The object of primary anxiety and primal repression is itself not primary and not an object. Ever absent although constantly addressed and referred to, the tyger signifies not any particular contents which have undergone repression, but rather the process of repression itself. A reading of the poem, therefore, must be founded not upon an uncovering of what has been repressed, but upon a theory of repression.

Freud's final theory of repression and anxiety was based upon the recognition that "it was anxiety which produced repression and not, as I formerly believed, repression which produced anxiety."[15] Terror and awe, both transforms of anxiety, are the dominant affects in "The Tyger," and the change in Freud's theory parallels a necessary movement in any reading of the poem, from a hermeneutical approach which ironically contextualizes the speaker's questions to a positively differential one which places and displaces them.

If repression precedes and produces anxiety, then the speaker's anxiety may be traced back to the primal repression which founds his psychic identity; and the aim of critical analysis, following Blake's own implicit polemic, is to overcome the speaker's repression and self-alienation and recover the truth of his perspective. Such an enlargement or framing recontextualization may be exemplified by returning to the interpretative history surrounding the most famous couplet in the poem, the questions of lines 19–20: "Did he smile his work to see?/ Did he who made the Lamb make thee?" Northrop Frye has summarized the traditional critical alternatives:

> Scholars will assert that the question . . . is to be answered with a confident yes or no: yes if Blake is believed to be a pantheist, no if he is believed to be a Gnostic. Most of those who love the poem are content to leave it a question, and they are right.[16]

In a way, of course, pantheists and Gnostics are also both right: as a figure of repression, the tyger ambivalently partakes of both repressing and repressed forces, and its history is necessarily one which "has been adopted by both parties" (E34). That the terrors of repression and the fires of organic revolt are not all that far apart in the psychic economy is a point made explicitly by Blake in his poems of the so-called "Orc cycle."[17] The speaker is able to pose his questions only by means of a violent and arbitrary stoppage of the circular-regressive movement which determines his discourse; the tyger is a fixed object only insofar as it is repressed and inaccessible. To lift the repression, to identify the tyger, is also to destroy its status as identity, to return to the interminable and undeterminable movement of primary process, ambiguously both repressing and repressed. The interpreter can either reproduce the undecidability of the tyger in the very act of determining it one way or the other; or else, as Frye recommends, the question can be left in its original indeterminacy.

The poem thus functions as a kind of trap for the reader, since any hermeneutical manoeuver is drawn, by a process of identification, into the chiasmic-regressive figuration of the schizophrenic double bind. The tyger as such is inaccessible; even the contextualizing postulation of an absolute origin is open, inconsistent, and incomplete. To attempt to answer the speaker's questions, or even to leave the questions open and undecidable, is to identify one's own position as reader of the poem with the limited position of the speaker as reader of nature (the delusion of 'natural theology'). The tyger then functions as an empty signifier, a screen or mirror which reveals only the desires and fears of its interpreter. Gnostics and pantheists alike impose their own visions and obsessions upon the poem, just as the speaker can himself be defined in terms of a hidden obsessional structure projected first upon the tyger and then upon the entire cosmos. Similarly, even Frye's more modest suspension of the question evidences an astonishment and awe, baffling interpretation, before "The Tyger" and its creator which exactly reproduces that of the speaker before the tyger and its creator. As a figure of primal repression, the tyger cannot be tied down to any given and specified content, but rather draws to itself whatever secondary repressions, or repressed contents, the reader is able to supply.

Thus any reading of the poem, whether it asserts or eschews hermeneutical mastery, falls into the double bind paradox: because it represents an attempt, on the one hand, to free the poem from perspectivist limitations, while remaining bound, on the other hand, to a specific perspective. Since it is precisely such a double bind which similarly determines the position of the speaker of the poem, the interpretative movement takes the form of an identification as well. Indeed, the structure of psychic identification, in which the subject posits itself as an ego only by virtue of a schizophrenic alienation, is unresolvably contradictory in precisely the same way as the logical double bind.[18] And this identification is strongest, the alienation most complete, in that reading which attempts to transcend its own perspective the most, to be the most universal. The most sophisticated reading of the speaker's questions, and of the poem, is the ironic and dialectical one, which puts those questions themselves into question, and thereby explicitly criticises the speaker's own perspective. The speaker, in this reading, attempts to invent or discover a context which will confine and delimit the tyger, and in so doing defines the tyger and its presumed creator in a context which confines and encompasses himself. The speaker is at once both repressor and repressed; it is the alienating act of repression which splits his being into contradictory segments, and transforms him from "the Universal Man" (E297) absolutely present to himself into a specific character in a particular dramatic context. The speaker's error is his self-alienation, his apprehension of his own power as something frightfully separate from, and either indifferent or actively malignant with regard to, himself. The speaker's anxiety is thus only a consequence of his prior repression or fall. What the reader recognizes, precisely because the speaker fails to, is that (in Harold Bloom's words) "all deities, for [Blake], resided within the human breast, and so, necessarily, did all Lambs and Tygers."[19]

In such a humanistic and dialectically totalizing reading, the reader no longer identifies with the actual speaker, but thereby identifies all the more strongly with the speaker's unfallen potentiality, or with what might be termed both the speaker's and the reader's ideal ego. To the extent that the poem disengages itself from, reflects back upon, and ironically undermines, from a distance, the delusions of the speaker, it is also this very act of critical disengagement which itself generates these delusions. The speaker can only be criticized, and his perspective transcended or sublated, insofar as the doctrinal principle of authority is not itself inscribed within, but rather transcends, the speaker's own systems of repression and defense. But this transcendence, this separation of authority from immediate dramatic context, is precisely the speaker's complaint. It is the reader's (and allegedly the poet's) external judgement, from the point of view of Eternity and of the Blakean System, which, in comprehending the speaker, condemns him to the delusive limits of his terror and alienation. The ironic and dialectical reading of the poem, by exposing the falsity and limitations of the speaker's conceptions, renders those conceptions true. Such a humanistic and totalizing reading of "The Tyger," precisely because it is the reading truest to Blake's overall System, objectifies and distances, rather than working through, the poem's own system of repressing and repressed forces, thereby enforcing its own claims for human universality only by excluding the speaker from its project of recuperation.

The largest implication of this reading, and of the inevitability of such a reading, as a necessary lure of the project of hermeneutical mastery, is that it is impossible to escape the logic of mastery, repression, and domination by a greater counter-act of mastery and domination, impossible to locate the spot at which factional and repressive mastery ceases and human self-mastery begins. The project of hermeneutical recovery, linked ideologically to the humanistic exaltation of a transcendent but reified Imagination, remains in complicity with that against which it is a reaction and from which it strives to escape, since it shares with its opponent a common logic of representation. "The Tyger" overtly implicates its audience in the differential movement which generates but is then suppressed by its own discourse. The reader, no less than the speaker, and even (or especially) when critical of the speaker, is drawn, by the desire of mastery or comprehension, into the schizophrenic logic of the meta-statement, the identification of one's own particular perspective with the position from which both that very perspective and those which contradict it may be judged and distributed. The schizophrenic act of interpretation takes the psychological form of an identification of oneself and one's own position with that which can only be conceptualized, nevertheless, as something external and superior to oneself. A structure of alienation can only be overcome insofar as it is simultaneously objectified, eternally fixated as a structure, as an alienation. The speaker's 'error' lies in his hypostatization, as an eternal structure, of the difference which separates the power he apprehends from himself. The naive reader identifies with the speaker and thus enters into and replicates his delusion. The advanced reader, in pointing to the speaker's error, repeats that error in inverted form, identifying with the power at the speaker's expense.

In the differential movement of the circular-regressive figuration, there can be no self-identity, but for the same reason no permanent or fixated structure of alienation, and no reification. Yet this differential movement both generates and is in turn repressed by a series of fixating identifications from which the speaker, the readers, and even the poet himself (insofar as he is projected as the guarantor of the text and of the System in which it is an expression, and as the master of its ironies) may not be excluded: identifications in an ascending series with the tyger, with the tyger's creator, with the speaker, with the poet, finally with the function of the Imagination, the truly human, itself. This latter function is conventionally associated with Blake's visionary program of political, aesthetic, and sexual liberation. But the series of alienating identifications which characterize the process of reading "The Tyger" seems rather to confirm William Hazlitt's far gloomier political assessment of the imaginative function: "the language of poetry naturally falls in with the language of power. . . . [The imagination] is a monopolizing faculty, which seeks the greatest quantity of present excitement by inequality and disproportion."[20] For the ironizing, dialectical and humanistic reading of "The Tyger" functions in precisely this way: it is a sublimation, which does not disperse the repressive concentration of power, but only—insidiously—shifts the locus of power. The rhetorical and conceptual sublimity of the poem may not be ascribed to unknown gods or "distant deeps or skies," but instead, in the ascending series of identifications, is appropriated to the poem's authorial and systematizing functions. The speaker is oppressed by the alienation, via repression, of his creative powers from himself; but the poem, and the poet, figure the overcoming of such alienation only to the extent that they establish art, and the processes of its creation, as a new totalitarian myth. The making of the tyger is no less awful and awe-ful for being a self-referential metaphor. The differential structure of the poetry is transformed, in the humanistic myth, into a duplicity in which the overcoming of man's self-alienation authorizes the aware readers to claim for art, or for the artist and his initiates, the very fulfillment (of the phantasy of an alien and fearful creative power) which has been denied to the speaker in the name of the same humanism and overcoming. The functioning of Imagination is here entirely negative and destructive, since its fulfillment is at the same time its self-contradiction, the hermeneutical triumph an *aporia*.

A hermeneutical approach to "The Tyger," since it attempts to locate the point of repression in the poem and to recover that which has been repressed, is necessarily in solidarity with the earlier Freudian theory in which repression precedes and causes anxiety. But such a reading culminates in the deconstructive impasse in which no lifting of repression, no comprehending sublimation, is sufficient to dispel anxiety. Rather, repression is the repetition of the differentiality which it represses; and the reversal of repression is yet again its repetition on a larger scale. Deconstructive criticism points to and privileges this negative moment, the infinitude of the task of comprehension, the irreducibility of a paradoxical anxiety of pure difference. Irony at first implies a privileged perspective, a superior mastery; yet this mastery is itself subject to the subversive action of irony.

But alongside of this irony, and not exhausted by it, there subsists what might called, following Gilles Deleuze, the *humor* of "The Tyger": the positivity of imaginative differentiality in an interplay of sense and nonsense from which fixity of signification and the hermeneutical project which attends and presupposes it, together with the correlate unities of subject and object, had been abolished.[21] If the hermeneutical understanding proceeds by a series of fixating identifications, leading to a neurotic rigidity doubled in the schizophrenic delusions of mastery which are unmasked by deconstruction, then the positivity, the affirmation, of Imagination consists in its active perversity, its dispersion and setting askew of its own presumably totalizing claims by means of the renewed insistence of the circular-regressive differential structure on every level and within every context. The humanistic reading claims to undo repression; the deconstructive reading, as its limit, reveals the continuation of repression as precisely that which is still repressed. The humorous, affirmative reading, in assigning priority to a non-localizable, differential anxiety rather than to any constituting movement of repression, carries the notion of repression itself to its limit, and puts it into question. The distinction between manifest and latent, or between what Blake declares and what he describes, or between the totalizing humanistic project which he supposedly means to put forward and the impossibility of such a project which his text actually does illustrate—all these oppositions are themselves merely instances of the differential movement which precedes and exceeds them. The positive differentiality of Blake's poetry is not that of one of these levels (the deep or repressed structure) as opposed to the other, but precisely the movement from one to the other, the interaction between them and their irreducible heterogeneity. Thus the question of Blake's own intentionality and will to presence, and concommitantly of his repressions and evasions, cannot be regarded as ultimately determining or constitutive. For the entire psychic structuration designated as "Blake"—his guiding presence as author, together with the divisions, repressions, and unconscious insistences which traverse, divide, and 'deconstruct' that presence—is itself the real and positive, but secondary, ontological effect of an impersonal differential movement.

"Man must & will have Some Religion" (J52, E198): and if Imagination, in its systematic functioning in Blake's work, seems to provide such a religion, then in the humor of its minute particulars it ridicules any such ambition, putting into question the subject "Man" no less than the predicate "Religion." This fundamental ambiguity yet again instances the irreducible movement of dissymmetrical difference. And again, to distribute these differences so that either aspect of Imagination is privileged as the unconscious determinant or hidden truth of the other is merely to deny the positivity of difference in the very act of repeating it. The liberatory effect of Blake's discourse cannot be reduced merely to its negative or critical aspect, its 'deconstruction' of ideologies and of the totalizing drive which calls forth such ideologies. For it is by its positive, affirmative force that Blake's discourse not only demolishes ideologies but also moves apart from the entire horizon of ideology and of meaning. Similarly, Blake's political and cultural radicalism cannot be reduced to his "apocalyptic humanism,"[22] to his active imaginative synthesis and creation of a unique System. For the humanistic ideology which accompanies his myth of Imagination is coordinated with a continuing project of hierarchization and mastery. In part this is a consequence of Blake's historical position after the triumph of the bourgeois ideals of the Enlightenment, but before industrial capitalism had completed the proletarianization of the lower classes. On the broadest historical level, Blake's discourse may be lodged in the contradiction between what the Enlightenment promised in the way of liberation and what the capitalism of which it was the harbinger actually produced. The contradictions of Blake's System are those of all modern humanism. The speaker of "The Tyger" imagines terrifying powers and ascribes them to God conceived as absolute Other; but the poet or reader, in reclaiming those powers for the human, necessarily arrogates to an idealized image of humanity the unapproachable prestige of that Otherness as well. That mastery which is the triumph of the Imagination is utterly dependent upon the very model and authority of religious totalitarianism which, in order to validate itself, it first has to destroy. The triumph of the Imagination in Blake's poetry is thus as sterile as it is magnificent. In thus circumscribing the ideological operation performed by the Age of Reason, Blake on the one hand foregrounds the unacknowledged limitations and exceptions to liberal humanism's claims of universality, while on the other hand suggesting that such limitations and exceptions are inevitable consequences of the very claim of universality itself.

Finally, the extravagance of humanistic claims for the Imagination is a symptom of an overwhelming despair and anxiety: a despair and anxiety born in the realization that the humanistic shifting of values from God to Man is on the one hand not enough of a change, since the same or equivalent structures of oppression persist, and too much of a change, since the attempt to ground within Man those hoped-for certainties whose religious sanction had been undermined by the Age of Reason is doomed to failure. "He who replies to words of Doubt/ Doth put the Light of Knowledge out" ("Auguries of Innocence," 95–96, E483): what could be more desperate, or more despairing, than this dread of even the merest suggestion of scepticism? In its nostalgia for certainty and its disingenuous transformation of the textual, social, and political movement of difference into an intellectualized crisis of belief, the Blakean imaginative faith is as modernistic, that is to say as regressive and as much of a dead end, as is, for instance, T. S. Eliot's retreat into a more orthodox form of religious consolation.

But in its affirmation of difference, Blake's text does more than merely expose and delimit the contradictions experienced by later writers such as Eliot as crippling external constraints. "The Tyger" enacts a violent scene which conditions all interpretation and representation but cannot itself be interpreted or represented. This scene is not a scene and not an origin, and can only be constituted as such, or apprehended at all, by recourse to an act of interpretation or representation which it in advance disqualifies. Imagination as the movement of differentiality does not simply disqualify these acts of interpretation or representation, but also situates them in their difference from themselves and thus liberates the violent (im)possibility of the non-scene of non-origination as that which, in the positivity of its affirmation, is other than all interpretation and all representation. "The Tyger" is the production or reproduction—even as it is at the same time, to the contrary, the repression, representation, and interpretation—of that pre-originary anxiety which precedes repression. An anxiety which precedes repression is that movement which is not open to mastery or even to the failed attempt at mastery, even though it is that which calls forth repression or the (failed) project of mastery. To liberate that anxiety (despite the literal impossibility of such a liberation) is a political, no less than a literary, act, albeit one which lacks an author. Blake's discourse does not merely challenge liberal humanism, but also challenges, in reproducing it, the very fatality to which humanism is always subject, the inevitable process of identification whereby a challenge finds itself in solidarity with the totalization or indeed totalitarianism which it challenges. Blake's discourse affirms the positivity of alterity and of alteration within the problematic which Western civilization is still in the process of confronting, and which in our own time has been formulated most succinctly, perhaps, in the texts of Michel Foucault: "you may have killed God beneath the weight of all that you have said; but don't imagine that, with all that you are saying, you will make a man that will live longer than he."[23]

Notes

1. All quotations from William Blake are taken from *The Poetry and Prose of William Blake,* ed. David V. Erdman (Garden City, 1965), and identified by 'E' and page number. For certain works I have also listed plate and line number, using the abbreviations M *(Milton)* and J *(Jerusalem).*

2. See especially S. Foster Damon, *William Blake: His Philosophy and Symbols* (New York, 1924, rpt. Gloucester, 1958); S. Foster Damon, *A Blake Dictionary* (Providence, 1965); Northrop Frye, *Fearful Symmetry: A Study of William Blake* (Princeton, 1947, 1969); Harold Bloom, *Blake's Apocalypse: A Study in Poetic Argument* (Garden City, 1963, rpt. Ithaca, 1970).

3. Thomas Weiskel, *The Romantic Sublime: Studies in the Structure and Psychology of Transcendence* (Baltimore, 1976), p. 65.

4. Gregory Bateson, "Toward a Theory of Schizophrenia," in *Steps to an Ecology of Mind* (New York, 1972), pp. 201–227.

5. *Hegel's Logic* (Encyclopedia Logic), trans. William Wallace (Oxford, 1975), p. 137. Maurice Blanchot suggests the importance for literature of this "wrong infinity" in "L'infini littéraire: l'Aleph," in *Le livre à venir* (Paris, 1959, 1971), pp. 139–44.

6. Jacques Derrida, *Positions,* trans. Alan Bass (Chicago, 1981), pp. 40–41.

7. Jacques Derrida, *Of Grammatology,* trans. Gayatri Chakravorty Spivak (Baltimore, 1976), p. 25.

8. Derrida, *Of Grammatology,* p. 26.

9. Cf. Derrida, *Of Grammatology, passim.,* e.g., p. 313.

10. Paul de Man, *Blindness and Insight: Essays in the Rhetoric of Contemporary Criticism* (New York, 1971), and especially "The Rhetoric of Blindness," pp. 102–41.

11. *The Four Zoas,* Night the Fifth, 64:27, E337; and see Harold Bloom's commentary, E874.

12. Blake experimented with alternate readings of this line (textual note, E717); but the speaker's bizarre strategy of displacement is still evident in the illogical associations of the alternate version: "And when thy heart began to beat,/ What dread hand formd thy dread feet?"

13. Kenneth Burke, quoted in Stanley Edgar Hyman, *The Tangled Bank* (New York, 1962), p. 366.

14. Sigmund Freud, "Repression," in *The Standard Edition of the Complete Psychological Works of Sigmund Freud,* trans. and ed. James Strachey (London), Volume XIV (1957), p. 148.

15. Sigmund Freud, *Inhibitions, Symptoms, and Anxiety,* in *Standard Edition,* Volume XX (1959), pp. 108–09.

16. Northrop Frye, "Blake After Two Centuries," in M.H. Abrams, ed., *English Romantic Poets: Modern Essays in Criticism* (Oxford, 1960), p. 57.

17. The "Orc cycle" is Frye's term for the myth of death and rebirth, organic revolt and its unending interaction with repression, figured in the history of Orc, especially in *The Book of Urizen* and in *The Four Zoas.* See *Fearful Symmetry,* pp. 207–35.

18. I am thinking particularly here of Jacques Lacan's description of the ego as a schizophrenic construct, formed precisely by alienating identifications with an idealized mirror image. See his "The mirror stage as formative of the function of the I as revealed in psychoanalytic experience," in *Ecrits: A Selection,* trans. Alan Sheridan (New York, 1977), pp. 1–7.

19. Bloom, *Blake's Apocalypse,* p. 139.

20. William Hazlitt, "Coriolanus," in *Characters of Shakespeare's Plays,* in *The Complete Works of William Hazlitt,* Centenary Edition (London, 1930), Volume 4, p. 214.

21. Gilles Deleuze distinguishes between the ascending movement of irony, which subverts meaning and law by recourse to a higher principle, and the descending or horizontal movement of humor, which perverts law and meaning by tracking them into their furthest and minutest consequences and effects. See *Présentation de Sacher-Masoch* (Paris, 1967), pp. 81–91, and *Logique du sens* (Paris, 1969), pp. 159–67 and *passim.*

22. "Apocalyptic humanism" is Harold Bloom's phrase: see *Blake's Apocalypse, passim.*

23. Michel Foucault, *The Archeology of Knowledge,* trans. A. M. Sheridan Smith (New York, 1976), p. 211.

SANTA CRUZ BLAKE STUDY GROUP

What Type of Blake?

Blake is no longer the prophet of *écriture.* Perhaps the single statement that some young critics of the new age found most compelling in Blake, his remark in the Preface to *Jerusalem* that "the Ancients entrusted their love to their Writing," has literally been obliterated in David V. Erdman's "Newly Revised Edition," *The Complete Poetry and Prose of William Blake* (Berkeley: University of California Press, 1982; cited hereafter as E). Or, leaving open a recuperative strategy, could these young critics say that *Jerusalem*'s traces have achieved a new dissemination? The line now reads: "the Ancients acknowledge their love to their Deities." The alteration may serve as a lesson for all of us who were—or become—wholly one with the Editor's text: CAVEAT LECTOR, even when that text—as is this most recent edition—is sanctioned and approved by the Modern Language Association Committee on Scholarly Editions (MLACSE).

Comparing Erdman's "text" with examples of the productions by Blake that it re-presents, we realize again with added force the absolute justice of the Editor's admission that "In print it is impossible to copy Blake exactly: his colons and shriekmarks [!] grade into each other; he compounds a comma with a question mark; his commas with unmistakable tails thin down to unmistakable periods." We realize as well the profound contradiction in the subsequent disclaimer that "In Blake the practical

---

This essay has been extracted from a review which first appeared in *Blake/An Illustrated Quarterly* 18 (Summer 1984): 4–31. Edited, titled, and reprinted with permission.

difference between comma and period, however, is almost unappreciable" (E 787). Contradictory, because the reader of the "complete" Blake is never "in" Blake, but is rather in the editing and altering "I" that has "been inclined . . . to read commas or periods according to the contextual expectations." The Editor does offer the reader without access to originals or facsimiles one check on his calibration, for one of the book's illustrations (following p. 272) reproduces plate 10 of *America* (copy not specified) which has twelve lines of text. Lines 7–9 of the printed version (E 55) offer the following:

> Because from their bright summits you may pass to the
> Golden world
> An Ancient palace, archetype of mighty Emperies,
> Rears its immortal pinnacles, built in the forest of God

But the reader of even the reproduction included in *The Complete Poetry and Prose of William Blake* will probably perceive:

> An ancient palace. archetype of mighty Emperies.
> Rears its immortal pinnacles, built in the forest of God

We cannot do too much with this one instance, however, because as Erdman notes, he has prepared a "collected" edition "as against transcripts of individual copies." The study of an individual copy of an illuminated work cannot call into question a collected transcript that has been produced as the fruit of the Editor's compositing art. But for those several works that exist in only one copy, the individual transcript *is* the basis of the collected edition. One such, *The Book of Ahania,* offers a kind of introductory exemplar, and has the further virtue of having been printed in intaglio, which gives to its text more clearly defined lines than the usual relief etching. "Editing the works that Blake etched and printed himself," writes the Editor, requires first of all "precise transcription." The MLACSE has stated that it "signifies" by its emblem (which appears on the dust jacket) that this volume "records all emendations to the copy-text introduced by the editors," according to "explicit editorial principles." In Erdman's printed text Ahania remembers, towards the conclusion of the book:

Chap: II:

1: But the forehead of Urizen gathering
And his eyes pale with anguish, his lips
Blue & changing; in tears and bitter
Contrition he prepard his Bow.

2: Formd of Ribs: that in his dark solitude
When obscurd in his forests fell monsters,
Arose. For his dire Contemplations
Rushd down like floods from his mountains
In torrents of mud settling thick
With Eggs of unnatural production
Forthwith hatching; some howld on his hills
Some in vales; some aloft flew in air

3: Of these: an enormous dread Serpent
Scaled and poisonous horned
Approachd Urizen even to his knees
As he sat on his dark rooted Oak.

4: With his horns he pushd furious.
Great the conflict & great the jealousy
In cold poisons: but Urizen smote him

5: First he poisond the rocks with his blood
* Then polishd his ribs, and his sinews
Dried; laid them apart till winter;
Then a Bow black prepard; on this Bow.
A poisoned rock placd in silence:
He utterd these words to the Bow.

6: O Bow of the clouds of secresy:
* O nerve of that lust formd monster!
Send this rock swift, invisible thro'
The black clouds, on the bosom of Fuzon

7: So saying, In torment of his wounds.
He bent the enormous ribs slowly;
A circle of darkness! then fixed
* The sinew in its rest: then the Rock
Poisonous source! placd with art, lifting dif-
-ficult
Its weighty bulk; silent the rock lay.

8: While Fuzon his tygers unloosing
Thought Urizen slain by his wrath.
I am God. said he. eldest of things!

9: Sudden sings the rock, swift & invisible
On Fuzon flew, enterd his bosom;
His beautiful visage, his tresses.
That gave light to the mornings of heaven
Were smitten with darkness, deformd
And outstretchd on the edge of the fo-
-rest

10: But the rock fell upon the Earth,
Mount Sinai. in Arabia.

Chap: III:

1: The Globe shook; and Urizen seated
On black clouds his sore wound anointed
The ointment flow'd down on the void
Mixd with blood; here the snake gets
her poison

2: With difficulty & great pain; Urizen
Lifted on high the dead corse:
On his shoulders he bore it to where
A Tree hung over the Immensity

3: For when Urizen shrunk away
From Eternals, he sat on a rock
Barren; a rock which himself
From redounding fancies had petrified
Many tears fell on the rock,
Many sparks of vegetation;
Soon shot the pained root
Of Mystery, under his heel:
It grew a thick tree; he wrote
In silence his book of iron:
Till the horrid plant bending its boughs
Grew to roots when it felt the earth
And again sprung to many a tree.

4: Amazd started Urizen! when
He beheld himself compassed round
And high roofed over with trees
He arose but the stems stood so thick
He with difficulty and great pain
Brought his Books, all but the Book
Of

The Book of Ahania, pl. 3. Rosenwald Collection, Library of Congress.

> My ripe figs and rich pomegranates
> In infant joy at thy feet
> O Urizen, sported and sang
>
> (5.26–28, E 89)

Erdman's version leads us to think that Ahania reports to Urizen how her fruits acted, because of the comma which makes "O Urizen" into an apostrophe. But no such punctuation is visible in Blake's plate. As with her exclamation six lines before ("O! eternal births sung round Ahania") so here, in less exclamatory fashion, Ahania jumps to the catching memory that "Urizen sported and sang." Further: evidently Ahania suggests a strange time when her fruits were the feet of Urizen. The syntax then, the mere absence of the comma, complicates considerably our image of Urizen. Such proliferating complication, struggling against "contextual expectations," is at the core of our vision of Blake's work. To appeal to "contextual expectations" as a neutral and universal given is to avoid the possibility that the difference between a period and a comma, or between a comma and nothing at all, is "the difference we see—and, by seeing, make."[1]

The possible complications suggested by letter configurations can be equally prolific. Consider the lines that Erdman transcribes to report that Urizen "fixed/ The sinew in its rest" (*BA* 3.32–33). This "sinew" was addressed six lines earlier in the poem: "O nerve of that lust form'd monster!" A comparison of " 'sinew' " with the "sinews" of 3.21 (in Blake's text) suggests that the second instance may be trying *graphically* to become—as it is conceptually—both "nerve" and "sinew" at once, a "sinerv" [see illus.]. Certainly the eighteenth-century semantics of "nerve" allows us to think of a "nerve of sin," a new sin constituted with the advent of the Rock:

> So saying, In torment of his wounds.
> He bent the enormous ribs slowly;
> A circle of darkness! then fixed
> The sinerv in its rest: then the Rock
> Poisonous source!

The Rock is, of course, "Mount Sinai. in Arabia." (Erdman reads "Mount Sinai," *BA* 3.46). The (material, graphic) nature of "Sin" is itself problematic. According to Erdman, in *BA* 2.34 Urizen names Ahania: "He groand anguishd & called her Sin,".

Those who delight in dread terrors may see additional complexities in the text Blake printed. The first chapter of *Ahania* is much involved with "astronomical" cosmology—that is, with the "Globe of Wrath." The first stanza ends with a description of Fuzon and/or his wrath as "Son of Urizens silent burnings" (2.9), and the last stanza concludes with the picture of the fiery beam of Fuzon seized by Los and "beat in a mass/ With the body of the sun." (2.47–48). The reader's "contextual expectations" must point to the multiple possibilities in calling anything, especially "his parted soul" (sol—"*so n*ame his parted soul"),[2] "S_n." The graphics of 2.34, through the novel "n" shape and the absent dot for the "i" bear out the possibilities. Perhaps what we see happening to Urizen, his so[u]lar failing is, indeed, *identified* in almost all its forms as sui-sun-sin, seen one on top of the other rather than linearly. The reader's probable query here is our answer: you reason it out.

Lest this seem too much quibbling over trifles, we should reemphasize one of the basic rules of the typographic game: that to change anything that physically appears in Blake's work to an editorial alternative is to "emend" the text in favor of an editorial line of interpretation. It is for this reason that the terms of the MLACSE approval state "explicit editorial principles" which include the recording of "all emendations to the copy-text introduced by the editors" (E VI). In his longest comment on any word or line in *Jerusalem* (*J* 21.44, E 809–10), Erdman explains why he did not emend his reading of "warshipped" to "worshipped" which would follow the common assumption that the "a" is a simple spelling mistake on Blake's part (this reading is discussed in greater detail below). G. E. Bentley, Jr., on the other hand, prints "worshipped" in his edition without comment, leaving open the question of whether he *saw* an "a" and silently changed it or instead simply saw and recorded an "o." For Urizen 19.46 Bentley notes that " 'Enitharmon' is spelt 'Enitharman'" (*William Blake's Writings*, 2 vols. [Oxford: Clarendon, 1978] I, 266) and presents what he assumes to be the correct spelling in his printed text. In his text Erdman prints "Enitharmon" at this point without comment. Did he *see* the "a" and silently correct it?

If so, was it truly a "correction" or was it an unrecorded emendation to the copy text in violation of the MLACSE code? In his note to *Milton* 10.1, Erdman, having printed "Enitharmon" in his text, announces explicit disagreement with those who see an "a" at this point instead of an "o." ("Not misspelled 'Enitharman' despite Bentley, following Keynes" E 807.)

There are two levels of interpretation intertwined in these examples. One is the graphic at the level of physical perception ("Of course an 'a' can look something like an 'o,' " Erdman observes). The other level is the still more difficult one of authorial intention, which raises the issue of whether or not the letter in question may be a "mistake." These problems are compounded by the issue of editorial policy or principle with respect to the category of "mistakes," and the editorial prerogative—or presumption—to make a better "text" than the author/printer William Blake. We believe that the reader has the right to know that Blake made "mistakes," and the even more important right to weigh the possibility that what looks like a mistake may not be one—that "Enitharman" and "warshipped" and "sinerv" might be meaningful or provide clues to meaning. But first one must *see* the "a" in the place of the "o" and the "rv" in the place of the "w." Erdman does not give us the option of seeing the "a" in "Enitharman," and Bentley does not give us the option of seeing the "a" in "warshipped." Neither Editor gives us the synergetic possibilities of seeing "sinerv."

Another curiosity in the "precise transcription" of Blake's printing is the practice Erdman shares with other Blake Editors of disregarding Blake's original line shape. Presumably to suit the exigencies of typographic economics, Editors often permit short, hyphenated lines to be printed straight through, while they gratuitously double Blake's "long resounding" line to suit the dictates of their formats. This is inconsequential if the letters and lines are merely abstract linear vehicles of sense; but if this is not the case then the practice does violence to the visual semiotics of Blake's printed text. In Blake, perhaps more than most poets, the arrangement of words on the printed page has a graphic potential that should not be ignored. Words (and subunits of words) can be meaningfully associated by a vertical contiguity and patterning as well as by the more obvious syntagmatic syntactic order exhibited by the text. Consider this minor instance from *Urizen* as printed in Erdman's text:

> 5. But no light from the fires. all was darkness
> In the flames of Eternal fury
> 6. In fierce anguish & quenchless flames (5.17–19, E 73)

In Blake's text—disregarding the diacritical figures and connection-lines which we grant to be outside the typographical concern—the reader will find a different experience:

> 5. But no light from the fires. all was
> darkness
> In the flames of Eternal fury
> 6. In fierce anguish & quenchless
> flames

The text reads up and down as well as across; vertical relationships imply a connection between "no light / darkness," "darkness / flames" and "fierce / flames" which is repeated five lines later:

> In howlings & pangs & fierce madness
> Long periods in burning fires labouring

The cumulative effect of such encoding asserts the existence of the "fires" as another presence, so that when "Los shrunk from his task":

> His great hammer fell from his hand:
> His fires beheld, and sickening,
> Hid their strong limbs in smoke.
> (13.21–23)

Such connections lead to the core-text of 5.32–24:

> . . . eternal fires . . .
> . . . Eternity . . .
> . . . sons . . .

So too the first appearance of that son of Eternity, Los, is more problematic if, rather than reading the line straight across, we encounter Blake's arrangement:

8. And Los round the dark globe of
    Urizen

(5.38)

(round Los = the dark globe of Urizen? = like a black globe . . . like a human heart?) The differences seem even more telling when we compare the Editorial version of *Urizen* 4.24 with a version that follows what Blake printed:

6. Here alone I in books formd of metals
6. Here alone I in books formd of me-
    -tals

It is appropriate enough, in this book so polysemously predicated *of* Urizen, for the protagonist, speaking of his books, to describe them and himself as "I in books formd of me-." This mind forgery is one alloyed me-tell.

The transition to type also alters Blake's spacing, and so obliterates many significant effects. In Blake's *Urizen* 20.1–2 the exact correlation (and thus contrast) of:

. . . eternity:
. . . Eternity.

becomes in Erdman's text:

Stretch'd for a work of eternity;
No more Los beheld Eternity.

For another example in this vein, we note that Blake's "Ah !SUN-FLOWER" (not Erdman's "Ah! SUN-FLOWER") begins "Ah Sun-flower ! weary of time." rather than "Ah Sun-flower! weary of time," as in Erdman (and Bentley and Keynes).

. . . .

i.

Format: general plan of physical organization or arrangement.

No matter how unconscious we are of the effects on our mode and mood of perception, we are constantly influenced in our reading by how a poem looks on the page. Our first glance at a new poem can reveal a traditional form printed in metrically-regulated neat stanzas, suggesting among other things how the poem will sound or feel to our ears. A glance at a poem in free verse with a wide variety of line lengths will create quite different expectations of the nature of what we will be experiencing as we read the words. As John Hollander remarks in *Vision and Resonance:* "The very look of the received poem on the page jingles and tinkles today the way neat, accentual-syllabic rhyming once did" (New York: Oxford University Press, 1975, p. 240). Part of the formal content and context of any poem, then, will be perceived in our encounter with the image made by the words as they are printed on the page which represents our field of vision. For the most part the effects these visual arrangements stimulate do not receive our direct attention. We only notice them in a printed book when they obtrude themselves upon our consciousness, disturbing the generally bland and neutral matrix of subordination that is supportive of the often desired effect of reading the poem through a transparent medium.

The normative tendency in letterpress or offset printing seems to be the disposition of words on the page in a way that is essentially arbitrary and meaningless in itself, with page breaks simply coming when the available space has run out. With printed prose, only paragraph indentations break the monotonous scanning motion of the eyes; with poetry a few more flexible and varied options are accommodated by the format, but financial expediency and typographical proprieties tend to keep these at a minimum. The form of the book is extensively and efficiently coded by the nature of the processes involved in its production, and the finished result operates to structure the reading process in ways that are compatible with that code. Since reading involves the ability to distinguish functional units through visual identification, anything we perceive as surrounded by white space will be a semiologically significant unit. In conventional typography the units are almost exclusively semantic ones: words, lines, paragraphs or stanzas.

A growing body of research suggests that much of perception, even up to fairly high interpretive levels, is automatic and independent of conscious awareness. The effects of peripheral vision are especially powerful in this regard, and it has now often been shown that what we are unaware of seeing is nonetheless influencing what we see and how we feel about the content of our consciously focused vision.[3]

Further understanding and appreciation of Blake's poetry calls for more attention to conceptual structures in his visual semiotic and to what might be called the visual syntax of his written work. "Vision" is a key term for Blake, and the visual form of his poetry, especially as it violates traditional linear forms, is an important functional element of his work—though even W. J. T. Mitchell, who has advanced our understanding of Blake's "composite art" more than anyone else, still accepts a primary distinction between the (non-visual) poetry and the illustrations.[4] To explore the visual syntax of Blake's poetry and to grasp the visual statements he creates requires paying attention to a variety of features that are unavailable in the conventionally presented editions of his work.

Among these, perhaps the most fundamental to the emergence of visual form are figure-field relationships. Every semantic unit is seen with respect to its background, and it establishes its own particular visual presence in terms of its magnitude (both size and shape), position, and orientation perceived against this background. Some of the main factors which influence our reading of figure-field relationships, as pointed out by Arnheim, include texture, spatial proximity, the qualities of enclosed forms, vertical distinctions between bottom and top, horizontal vs. oblique positioning, convexity of forms, suggestions of overlap, and consistency or simplicity (or their opposites) in shape.[5] Even if the visual stimulus is physically two-dimensional, it contains clues that influence the viewer's perception and evoke a reading of implied depth, making the figure-field relationship a distinctive aspect of the syntactic meaning.

Reading Blake's work in the original or in facsimile takes time, which leads most of us to try to "get" the poetry from a printed edition while studying the plates for purely visual information. Our ability to read has been conditioned by our familiarity with traditional linear text forms and the consistent and powerful appearance they present, which stimulates and rewards certain conventions of reading, while affecting the dynamics of the reading experience. In this experience the poem presents itself to the reader as centered within or on a single abstract plane. We engage the visual composition at the upper left and scan line after line horizontally while picking up information and rhythmic impact visually from variations in line length and from variations in typographic forms (e.g., capital letters) and punctuation. The margins framing our encounter with the text are typically large, neutral, and relatively consistent. The figure-field relationship of the poem is one of neutrality, and the interior visual syntax of the poem is empty of significance, with maximum consistency in spacing between letters, words, and lines. Where variations in spacing are required to justify line-endings they are often made as subtle as possible in the attempt to keep them below our threshold of perception. Blake's poetry, in contrast, persistently violates and challenges our assumptions about the proper orientation of visual symbols in a field, as well as about their shape, size, orientation, color, physical material and texture. There is crucial information of a visual-semiotic nature in Blake's disposition of individual letters, words, sentences and other semantic units on his printed page, and in the visual boundaries that make such disposition possible. At least some of these effects can be hinted at even within the physical and economic constraints of the typographic medium, and Editors of Blake should be much more imaginative and insistent in their attempts to do so.

The format of individual pages in a book is of course only part of the impact made by the material form of the text on the reader. There are numerous intrinsic properties attendant upon the design and order of books and their component parts. The effects generated by the emblematic characteristics of the book will constitute a significant part of the terms on which the contents of the book are offered and received. In the conventional printed book the assignment of text to a given page is arbitrary or even accidental; yet the turning of a page is a vital act performed by the reader, one which is structured in relation to the poem's form and meaning by where and how the text has been separated by the printer. To quibble over commas and periods, while randomly introducing "punctuation" on the magnitude of page division, is a bit like swallowing the camel and choking on a gnat, in terms of the impact on the visual and semantic structure of the work. Divisions that Blake made are not functionally present, while divisions he did not make are operative—and juxtapositions can be as significant as divisions. How are we to measure the impact of Erdman's page 144, where the "Finis" of *Milton* is separated from the title *Jerusalem* by only 3/4 of an inch and the intervening two-leafed tendril that he used at tops of pages in *The Illuminated Blake?*

Blake's constant attention to the overall form of his "books" and to minute formal nuance within them should pose a challenge to the Editor to try to achieve as many of Blake's effects as the typographic medium will allow (as David Erdman does, for example, in his remarkable edition of *The Notebook of William Blake*), rather than disguising those effects and lulling the reader into believing that she is getting the "book" as well as the poetry in the book. This might lead to expensive decisions about blank space in some cases and non-blank space (e.g., narrow or minimal margins) in others. It might not be considered worth it to print *Urizen* on only one side as Blake did, but the possibility should be considered before going to press, along with the possibility of presenting the text in the original bicolumnar form which constitutes one of its most conspicuous and meaningful features. *The Book of Urizen* is an especially important case in point, because in it Blake was concerned not only with "writing" but also with the "bookishness" of the book, with the problem of the book as an object, a volume which offers its contents *in terms of its physical and formal properties as an object.* Blake's *Urizen* is designed within a specific historical and contextual field of purposes, conventions and assumptions; yet while designed within them, it is also engaged with them in intellectual warfare. Blake's books are addressed to the "Reader!   of books!"[6] Blake did not "write texts"—he made books which posed a critique of the book-making practices of his own era, and which challenge all future readers and editors to confront the nature of books as material embodiments of texts.

. . . .

ii.

Let us return to the problem of Blake's punctuation, with the honest and grateful acknowledgement that David Erdman has done more than any previous editor to free us from our programmed desire for conventional syntax. Erdman is, in places, not at all uncomfortable with Blake's short periods:

> 2. That Energy. calld Evil. is alone from the Body.
> & that Reason. calld Good. is alone from the Soul.
>
> (*MHH* 4, E 34)

Such periods break up completion. logical syntax, and invite the reader. to a more active, participation in the production of text. Blake could use commas elegantly when he chose, as in the following quotation (where our reading of *MHH* copy D tallies exactly with that offered on E 39):

> But first the notion that man has a body distinct from his soul, is to be expunged; this I shall do, by printing in the infernal method, by corrosives, which in Hell are salutary and medicinal, melting apparent surfaces away, and displaying the infinite which was hid.

But still, there are more periods in Blake than in Erdman, and we need to accept them as such if we are truly to grapple with the at times discontinuous folds of Blake's syntax. "Truth can never be told so as to be understood. and not be believ'd." (E reads "understood,"). "I must Create a System. or be enslav'd by another Mans" (E reads "System,"). Periods can be banished completely, rather than be demoted to commas, if Erdman finds them "intrusive" (E 808), as he does the one after "dance" in *Milton* 26.3:

> Thou seest the gorgeous clothed Flies that dance & sport in summer
> Upon the sunny brooks & meadows: every one the dance[.]
> Knows in its intricate mazes of delight artful to weave:
>
> (E 123)

With the removal of this "intrusive" period vanishes the mazing possibility of weaving not only a dance of Flies, but also a dance of sunny brooks and meadows. So vanishes, perhaps, another

"Period" in which "the Poets Work is Done", that startling stop in which, by which, "Events of Time start forth & are concievd in such a Period" (29.1–2). In Blake's "London" (E 27), we can instructively compare lines 5–8 as transcribed by Erdman with what appears in copy C:

In every cry of every Man,
In every Infants cry of fear,
In every voice: in every ban,
The mind-forg'd manacles I hear

In every cry of every Man.
In every Infants cry of fear.
In every voice: in every ban.
The mind-forg'd manacles I hear

The next stanza of the poem, amplifying the unending line of the preceding one and the first line of the last, gives us an example of Blake's vertical ordering that does not elude the typographic medium:

The mind-forg'd manacles *I hear*

*H*ow the Chimney-sweepers cry
*E*very blackning Church appalls,
*A*nd the hapless Soldiers sigh
*R*uns in blood down Palace walls

But most thro' midnight streets I *hear*
(E 27, emphasis added[7])

Another minute particular involves what Erdman calls "one kind of *silent* insertion"—the occasional addition of an apostrophe to the possessive of Los. Without the apostrophe, Erdman notes, we are "otherwise subject to confusion with 'Loss'" (E 787). So, for example, we have this Editor's Spectre "driven to desperation by Los's terrors & threatning fears" (*J* 10.28, E 153) rather than by "Loss terrors & threatning fears". Yet the Spectre speaks precisely out of an intense sense of loss ("Where is my lovely Enitharmon," "Life lives on my/ Consuming"). Blake knows as well as Milton or Lacan that our feeling of "loss" feeds ("unwearied labouring & weeping") our emotional and imaginative life. Los's possession is loss (to our profit);[8] and these references can be connected to the solar aspect of Los's name as well, for when we can go inside out and see even our sun as a loss, then we have solace.

iii.

I have a disease: I see language (Barthes)

For the weak, merely to begin to think about the first letter of the alphabet might make them run mad forthwith. (Rimbaud)

For A is the beginning of learning and the door of heaven. (Smart)

For that (the rapt one warns) is what papyr is meed of, made of, hides and hints and misses in prints. Till ye finally (though not yet endlike) meet with the acquaintance of Mister Typus, Mistress Tope and all the little typtopies. Fillstup. (Joyce)

One would not presume to speak of—or practice—*editing* a painting or a sculpture, no matter how valuable and useful the attempt to represent such objects in photographic and book form may be, because of the essential materiality of their mode of existence. Nor, we would assume, would anyone try to correct Joyce's spelling in *Finnegans Wake* in order to make it easier for the reader to get at the "text" of Joyce's work. The problems with the Erdman edition and related matters we have been discussing so far have all been within the context of exploring and recommending what is *possible* in attempting to achieve a typographic representation of Blake's work. In this disgression we will emphasize even more the negative (the Loss) in any edition of Blake that uses typography. We do so not in the spirit of fetishizing the unique original as a sacred relic, or of endowing it with some magical authority because it was physically assembled by Blake, but rather from the conviction that a significant part of the *complete* poetry of the illuminated books is a visual-verbal semiotic in which form and meaning cannot be separated from material substance, or the adequate representation of the materiality of substance.

We wish to call attention to the visual aspects of linguistic communication in writing in general, but more particularly in Blake, as our concern moves from an awareness of graphic space as a structural agent on a large scale (page format and "book") to the minutiae; from an emphasis on the spatial-structural relationships of the linguistic materials to the actual materiality of the signifiers: their "concreteness" in a perhaps metaphorical sense, their "visibility" in a literal sense.

There seems to be a pervasive cultural and intellectual tendency to suppress the graphic element of writing, its graphology. For the general linguistic approach to the study of language, the primary function of writing systems (with the occasional exception of ideographic or hieroglyphic forms) is to give phonological information. But *ink*—like air disturbed into sound and patterned into words—can also be a linguistically patterned substance, a different medium, and one which by its very nature is not invisible or transparent. Yet the typographic production of books in the usual manner strives for invisibility or transparency of its signifiers in the service of the idealized "text." If we print or write the word "red" in red ink, there may be a non-arbitrary relationship between the *graphic* signifier and its signified; and this is only a simple and obvious instance. As soon as we come down with the Barthesian dis-ease of "seeing language" we enter a combined semantic and visual semiotic field in which an enormous range of meaningful effects becomes possible. For Blake this was not a neutral possibility, but a poetic necessity: "Writing/ Is the Divine Revelation in the Litteral expression" (*M* 42.13–14, E 143), and the *literal letter* (Lat. *littera*) is the medium of the revelation, as doubly indicated by Blake's spelling. Earlier we mentioned that Mitchell, in his valuable book, has separated the poetic text from the visual text in his dialectical approach to Blake's composite art. We want to suggest that something like Mitchell's "dialectic" is going on within the poetry itself, and that more attention to and respect for that visual form is long overdue, to appreciate a different form of "composite" art which combines a heightened visual and acoustic attention to Blake's signifiers (i.e., *not* to his "text").

To "see" words can be considered a disease because it is non-normative. It may be typical, as Freud said, of the state of consciousness present in dreams, but it is a deviational mode of attention verging on epistemological error in our ordinary state, much as attention to particulars was aesthetic error for Reynold's aesthetic of the grand style. Linguistics tends to share this attitude through its definition of the mode of existence of language, with graphological forms as purely arbitrary indicators of phonological acts. The historical theory and practice of typography are complicitous with the same set of assumptions and values. The fundamental aim of typography as a practical discipline is to achieve a state of invisibility, a type so "legible" that the reader looks *through* it not *at* it. How are we to understand this self-effacement? The goal in this practice is to make print a perfectly functional *language medium,* which is to ignore the difference between spoken and written utterance—to ignore the fact that the necessity of vision is built into the production of writing, the reproduction of writing, and the reception of writing in the literate mind.

It is one of the strongest conventions within the dominant mode of book production that the materiality of the printed sign-vehicle be ignored as non-iconic. It is not printing per se that is at issue, for Blake printed his own work from what he called "stereotypes," adopting the word from conventional printers' usage. It is rather the desire to make the medium transparent in the service of a disembodied "text" which negates Blake's persistent efforts to exploit the materiality of his mode of production as a significant part of the potential meaning of his work. The form of Blake's work signals a change of sign-function, with its marked departure from linear printing, and challenges the reader to a different mode of reading. We are arguing that it is neither a "service" to Blake nor to the reader of Blake to make the experience of reading him easy or convenient. It may at first seem fanciful to suggest that to "buy" meaning from Blake requires—in the sense of classical economics—an exchange of labor of comparable value. But Blake could easily have "written" his works for the typesetter and saved himself and us enormous labors—especially us, since his writings would very likely not have been published at all. How much of what he put into his "works" can we get out if we continue to make things as easy as possible?[9]

What we mean by the "iconic" dimension of Blake's writing is not a naive privileging of the authority of the author's own handwriting as authenticating "signature" of presence. It is more like the definition that Peirce gave of a motivated relationship between the iconic sign and its object, where the iconic sign is "like [some]thing and used as a sign of it."[10] We would not limit our use of "iconic" as Peirce does, to cases where the qualities of the iconic sign must "resemble" those of its denotatum and "excite analogous sensations in the mind for which it is a likeness" (p. 168), because resemblance is too narrow a limit to assign to the iconic-function potential. Resemblance is only the most obvious of the motivating connections that can exist between the shape of individual letters, their combination into words and larger units, their color, material substance and form, and what those letters mean, or stand for, or represent, or signify.

To maintain that Blake's writing is visible or iconic means that a signifying process is functioning which cuts through, disrupts, and challenges the ordinary reading process without necessarily destroying it or superseding it. Blake's signifying practice must be sensed through both auditory and visual means, and there is no reason why the same writing cannot give evidence of both operations simultaneously at work—or play. In this context we want to return to the instance of "warshipped" mentioned above, and the difficuty in determining whether it is, in Erdman's words, "*an error for* worshipped" or "*possibly a punning coinage.*" What we have here is not simply a physical question of seeing, but a complex perceptual field which includes the possibility that a problem of seeing ("o" or "a") may relate to a mode of hearing. Tony Tanner has argued for a conceptual relationship between puns and adultery in the novel, suggesting that two meanings that don't belong together in the same word are like two people who don't belong together in the same bed.[11] Tanner's is an important comparison, because there is in each case a "law" of propriety that is being broken. The overdetermination of a lexeme by multiple meanings that it does not carry in ordinary usage violates a cultural sense of textual and linguistic propriety. When this happens in Blake, the visual lexeme can be an important functional component of the auditory experience, and provide a simultaneous violation of the linearity and univocity of discourse.

We want to emphasize that we are not dealing here with a trivial textual crux, which may or may not be resolved definitively by improved photographic techniques. We are dealing with an editorial practice (relaxed in this case by Erdman), with ontological notions of the "text" that call for a typographical transparency in the material manifestation of that text. When Byron yearned for words that are things, he was using a metaphor implying a non-human language, the unmediated generative speech of God, or at least a long-lost referentiality of language. But the Blake text insists on the materiality of its words as things in a *literally literal* sense, the sense in which Freud could say that "Words are a plastic material with which one can do all kinds of things," and the sense in which W. H. Stevenson is ironically *not* being literal when he changes Blake's "Litteral."[12] Freud frequently uses metaphors of writing in his representation of the unconscious. In *The Interpretation of Dreams* he speaks of the symbolism of dreams in general as a cryptography or rebus, a hieroglyphic or pictographic script, but notes more specifically that "It is true . . . that words are treated in dreams as though they were concrete things, and for that reason they are apt to be combined in just the same way as presentations of concrete things. Dreams of this sort offer the most amusing and curious neologisms."[13] For Freud words are presented in the unconscious in ways that must be distinguished from the perceptual mode of consciousness, which looks through the word only for its lexically coded signification. Something that is ordinarily invisible to consciousness is ordinarily visible in the unconscious, and the interpreter must see language differently, must stop short before the accepted or expected meaning of a word in order to perceive language in its material density. A certain amount of regression may help the interpreter in this enterprise, since "the habit of still treating words as things" is most common in children, and is "rejected and studiously avoided by serious thought."[14]

When Freud moves on in Chapter V of *Jokes and their Relation to the Unconscious* to consider the general question of the subjective determinants of jokes, he makes some interesting speculations on the relationship between joke-work and the infantile as the source of the unconscious, suggesting that "the thought which, with the intention of constructing a joke, plunges into the unconscious is merely seeking there for the ancient dwelling place of its former play with words. Thought is put back for a moment to the stage of childhood so as once more to gain possession of the childish source of pleasure" (p. 170). But playing with words, like playing with feces, is not countenanced by authoritative parents (or editors). Thus, "it is not very easy for us to catch a glimpse in children of this infantile way of thinking, with its peculiarities that are retained in the unconscious of adults, because it is for the most part corrected, as it were, *in statu nascendi*" (p. 170). It may well be that a large part of the editor-work is operating over against something like Freud's joke-work in the production of the idealized Blake "text." Freud emphasizes that the "laugh" can function as a confirmation of the possibility that *Witz* has a profound relationship to instinctual drives already at work in infancy. Laughter can dismiss as "children's 'silliness' " that which the adult must reject and studiously avoid when he makes "serious use of words." In this context the laughter advocated by a serious arbiter of the arts takes on a certain nervous resonancy: "One would laugh at a writer who would wish his text to be printed now in small unspaced type fonts, now in large spaced ones, or in ascending and descending lines, in inks of different colors, and other such things."[15]

What we can see and hear in Blake is influenced by what we expect to see and want to see; our desires for a purely phonological information and a "pure" lexical codification of that information make it difficult both to see and to accept the unexpected. To put a letter different from the expected one is a disruptive act, one which has the effect of engaging with other signifiers in the near vicinity. This engagement can be visual (we can see "ear" in "hear" or "orc" in "force" or "los" in "close") and phonetic. The surrounding visual and phonemic area becomes charged and structured (or unstructured and skewed) in ways not immediately or ordinarily available to consciousness in conventional reading. Such disruptions hint at the force of a desire which is ordinarily censored, a desire for play, for unconfinedness, for regression, perhaps even for subversion. But to speculate on the identity of the force of desire requires a recognition of the effects of that desire, and an unconscious mode of censorship that screens out "what ought not to be" in the text, in language, in the psyche—with hints of an uncanny gap between the subject and his discourse in which "language" seems to be acting on its own, or where the unconscious usurps language as the servant of a subversive desire rather than the servant of well-mannered thought and the communication of sharable meaning. As Wordsworth observed, in commenting on how words can be "things": ". . . they are *powers* either to kill or animate . . . a counter-spirit, unremittingly and noiselessly at work to derange, to subvert, to lay waste, to vitiate, and to dissolve."[16] At times editing can seem to a kind of toilet training of the text, or the work of a normalizing or idealizing airbrush removing all blemishes on its pure surface. Too often with the "blemishes" go a whole range of potential semiotic effects produced at the level of the letter, rather than the word or the sentence.[17]

If we are right in our emphasis on the integral semiotic significance of the visible signifier in Blake, a number of consequences follow. For example, the question of "format" raised above becomes even more complex. If we load the individual letters with significant visibility, then the contextual field in which they appear will be changed also, with an even greater emphasis on the complete two-dimensional page over against the more limited linear path traced through the page by the normal itinerary of the printed text. Printing itself is not the problem, as we have said before. The main criterion for print is simply the existence of an "image carrier" that allows large numbers of nearly identical images to be produced from it. The image carrier can be anything from an engraved plate to a letterpress form to a photographic film or magnetic tape. The unique feature of Blake's printing in the illuminated books is that he was printing traces or representations of marks he himself had made ("Grave the sentence deep"—and print it).

Thus although he produced printed works, they retained—even before he did additional work on the prints—evidence of what Arnheim has called "writing behavior," pointing out that "to the extent to which a reader perceives written material as the product of writing behavior, kinesthetic overtones will resonate in the visual experience of reading," producing kinesthetic connotations that tend to transform our perception of the field from a vertical to a horizontal field of action. The implied *motor behavior* of writing thus emphasizes the surface of the page "as a microcosm of human activity, dominated by the symbolism of relations to the self: close and distant, far and near, outgoing and withholding, active and passive."[18] Blake's writing behavior when he was engraving words on a plate was different from his manuscript activity when working on *The Four Zoas,* which poses additional considerations of its own—some of which will be taken up in the next section. But his mode of production insisted on making that writing behavior visible, with the consequences that we have been trying to emphasize. It is unusual, more difficult to read, calls for a different mode of attention, and reminds us that the body was involved in the process of production. When Blake invokes his muses, he asks them to descend "down the Nerves of my right arm" (*M* 2.6, E 96).

iv.

The complexities of the ms, in short, continue to defy analysis and all assertions about meaningful physical groupings or chronologically definable layers of composition or inscription must be understood to rest on partial and ambiguous evidence. (Erdman on *The Four Zoas*)

What if we then accept Erdman's new revision as the major edition, accept its inevitable errors or questionable readings, accept its concessions to print technology—is that all one need say? One's belief in the necessity of such concessions is dependent on a sense of the necessity of print editions themselves; and if we read Erdman's *as if* it were Blake's own text, even knowing that it is not, it will be in order to avoid a constant consideration of the concessions, or in order to induce one's students into a more immediate, unmediated confrontation with the text. But this review continues to exercise lingering doubts about editing and typography themselves, about their very necessity.

A Shakespeare editor must be concerned that variations between the Folio and Quarto editions of *King Lear* represent different and perhaps irreconcilable notions of how the play was written or performed at different times. With differences in performances, print is resubmerged in subsequent productions; these productions tend not only to reinterpret but to re-edit the play as well. The problem is not simply one of editorial methodology but of fundamental differences between performance and print situations, differences obscured or obliterated by the phenomenology of print itself. In the case of Blake the problem is just as striking, for here we are obviously faced with different forms of print, materially different values of production. Blake's production is itself a performance situation, a "scene of writing" which continually draws attention to itself as graphological production. The possible "sinerv" of *Ahania* or *Urizen*'s "books formd of me-/ -tals" are not only polysemous, they also rouse the reader to such a graphological awareness. Someone is/was actually writing. If print is so fixed and final and regular as to be virtually self-effacing, Blake's writing is self-reflective or reflexive as material production and multifold in both meaning and form. It is now commonly believed that Blake's methods of engraving and copperplate printing purposefully set themselves apart from industrially-determined print technologies; his practice may even have constituted an active critique or subversion of what Walter Benjamin has called the age of mechanical reproduction, anticipating Brecht's combined aesthetic and ideological insistence on exhibiting—rather than hiding—the means of producing the artistic effect.[19] The variety in the existing copies of the *Songs* may lead us to constitute, in part, a sense of a kind of metamorphic variance under a general controlling aegis or governing form which we call "the" *Songs*. But in another sense, those varieties undermine and contradict the very notion of such a generality. It is difficult to speak of the *Songs* entirely as if "it" were a single text, and such a difficulty can be very useful for Blake's readers. The printed hybrid editions, however, rob the reader of that difficulty by presenting an editorial fiction based on the implicit assumption of the existence of an "ideal text" which they are representing in the most adequate fashion. If this is the case, then *any* print edition, no matter how "accurate" to the letter of the text, will necessarily represent a counter subversion, a recuperation of Blake's text by the very forces it sought to oppose.

One of Erdman's many virtues as an editor is that he has always tended to be hospitable to minute graphological particulars. If print forces the necessity of compromise, he makes fewer than most editors. Earlier editors were so accommodating to the standards of print and public taste that they often seemed like schoolteachers correcting a messy or overly-inventive child. Where Keynes, for instance, regularly normalized spelling and punctuation, one always feels a greater confidence in Erdman because he tends *not* to normalize, because his editions look more like the original texts, even though not as much like them as print technology might allow if fully exploited. If we have taken occasion in this review to indicate passages where Erdman is not fully consistent with this practice, where he does normalize, it should not be taken as a sign that we fail to appreciate his work as the considerable advance over previous editions which it often is. Indeed, if anything, we might express the fear that these virtues constitute a danger if they lull the reader into a false confidence that he now has the Blake "text" in his hands, lacking only the illustrations for a full encounter with the author.

Editorial sensibility and technological strictures weigh heavily on this new edition, and are perhaps nowhere so evident as in Erdman's treatment of *The Four Zoas*—especially Night VII, which provides also the single most radical editorial change for the old E. The problems here are exceedingly complex, and in some ways might be considered exemplary: a history of editorial approaches to Night VII alone could provide a useful study of the ways in which Blake's text has been processed and disseminated. There are too many approaches to describe them all in the space of this review, but readers who need a fuller sense of the issues involved should consult *Blake/An Illustrated Quarterly*

46 (Summer 1978), which contains studies of the Night VII problem by John Kilgore, Andrew Lincoln, Mark Lefebvre and Erdman, and which provides indispensable aid for a full understanding of what Erdman calls his "drastic rearrangement" of Night VII.

The problem, of course, is that Blake left two Nights titled "Night the Seventh," and no fully reliable clues to their probable order or priority; the editor's task is to find ways to present them in print. Erdman's earlier solution had what was called VIIa (ms pp. 77–90) written "later than and presumably to replace" VIIb (ms pp. 91–98); VIIa was printed between VI and VIII, and VIIb left as a kind of appendix after IX. Erdman's decision reflected a wide tendency in the past generation of Blake scholarship to treat VIIa and VIIb as *units,* a practice which made it impossible to fit either or both into the text in a narratively coherent way. Of course narrative coherence in *The Four Zoas* is generally problematic and, insofar as one understands coherence in anything like the terms of linear logic or "realist" novels, a false issue.

The textual studies of Kilgore, Lincoln and Lefebvre made it possible to redefine the problem: VIIa and VIIb were no longer described as units but as sets of two which could be reshuffled in at least three ways.[20] Erdman's textual note is a handy summary of the choices:

> Andrew Lincoln, arguing from an impressive hypothetical reconstruction of the evolution of the ms, would insert VIIa between the two portions of VIIb (as Blake rearranged them). Mark Lefebvre and John Kilgore, arguing mainly from fit, propose inserting all of VIIb between the two portions of VIIa (taking the first portion of VIIa as concluding with 85:22, originally followed by "End of the Seventh Night"). Kilgore would return the transposed parts of VIIb to their original order; Lefebvre would keep them in the order of Blake's transposing. In the present edition I have decided to follow the latter course. (E 836)

Erdman does not fully explain here why he prefers Lefebvre's theory, but from his article in *Blake* 46, with its fascinating system of notation, it would seem that he does so on the basis of best possible fit. But the concern with fit is itself problematic. As Erdman himself reminds us, when Ellis and Yeats first "discovered" the manuscript it was unbound, entirely a pile of loose leaves. In other words, to conceive VIIa and VIIb as either single *or* bipartite units is highly speculative. In *The Four Zoas* in general, unity is not *a priori* but the result of interpretive and/or editorial theory.

To call unity theoretical is not to say that it is wrong, but that it does require us to examine the theory more closely—a difficult task, since many decisions are not based on strict textual evidence but on inadequately articulated assumptions of, or *desires for,* a unity beyond the manuscript's actual state. These assumptions and desires are frustrated by what appear to be conflicting notions of poetic unity in the poem itself. It is likely, and often suggested, that Blake's difficulties in completing the *Zoas* arose from changes during its composition in his own sense of appropriate unity, that the poem represents a series of transformations leading from the never-ordinary narratives of the Lambeth books to the even more radical procedures of *Jerusalem.* The manuscript evidence of such transformations has led many readers to consign *The Four Zoas* to the category of brilliant failures.

The point is crucial, for what the manuscript exhibits in the most graphologically explicit fashion is an ongoing, unfinished process of self-editing, a process which print ordinarily shuts down. The process would be even more evident in the manuscript had not its keepers in London deemed it necessary to bind the leaves. This should be restated: the manuscript's editor must be responsible to the phenomenological closures of print, but this is not to say that Blake's editors always seek unity like that of the most ideally ordered classical epic. Rather, the editor seeks unity by attempting to extend the interrupted trajectory of Blake's compositional process in such a way as to create a "Blakean" unity, in this case in order to salvage both Nights VII and approach a hypothetically Blakean conclusion of this infamously unfinished poem. One could describe this procedure as an editorial version of the intentional fallacy: a compositional fallacy, perhaps, or at least a compositional fiction. Passages like the following one from John Kilgore—who, as Erdman says, is concerned mostly with "fit"—are virtually standard in editorial commentaries:

> It is as if Blake could not content himself with completing *The Four* Zoas as such, but had to go on to attempt a wholesale demonstration of the poem's consistency with its offspring; as if, after a certain point, everything had to be said over again from the standpoint of *Jerusalem.* Nights I and II contain certain late additions which suggest that Blake may have decided to work through his six Nights yet again, installing passages which would anticipate the new vision, before tackling the problem of VIIb. Yet at the same time, judging by the virtually atemporal structures of *Milton* and *Jerusalem,* Blake was undergoing a crisis of disenchantment with narrative itself. . . .

We have selected this passage from Kilgore (p. 112) not because he is the worst offender, merely the handiest practitioner of the compositional fiction. In fact, with his rhetoric of "as if" and "may have decided," Kilgore's speculations are a great deal more modest and palatable than the assertive certainties of several other commentators.

Would it be such apostasy to say that *none of this matters,* or that it matters only because unities we more or less subliminally associate with printed editions, with print itself, demand that it matters? The plain fact is that this Night VII is not Blake but Erdman "on" Blake; but however obvious this fact is, Erdman on Blake will tend to be read and taught *as* Blake. If Night VII reads more easily as narrative in new E than it did in old E; if the reshuffling of the two Nights VII better accommodates certain links between VI and VIIa[a] and VIIa[b] and VIII by inserting a transposed VIIb between them; if this "drastic rearrangement" more closely approximates a coherent theory of Blake's intention or at least one probable arc of that intention, in another sense the gains of new E are also a loss, for it even more effectively obscures the nature of the text as manuscript, its writing of *still-latent* choices, its graphological, poetic uncertainties. If Erdman has produced a more accessible version—accessible in the double and related senses of wide availability and surface coherence—we must also ask what has been lost.[21] Consider, for a minute particular, the following passage from Night the Seventh:

the howling Melancholy
For far & wide she stretchd thro all the worlds of Urizens journey
And was Ajoind to Beulah as the Polypus to the Rock
Mo[u]rning the daughters of Beulah saw nor could they have sustained
The horrid sight of death & torment But the Eternal Promise
They wrote an all their tombs & pillars
(94.55–95.5, E 367)

Like other editors, Erdman emends 95.3, but a consideration of what sense that alteration is designed to save offers tangible evidence of Blake's manner of expanding a line's reference. Do the daughters see "Mourning" rather than a more violent "howling Melancholy"? or "Mourning" rather than "death & torment"? If the daughters themselves, through inverted predication, are "Mourning," what did they see, and how are they able, a few lines later, to wait "with patience" and to sing "comfortable notes"? Perhaps the daughters see a morning that lightens the horrid sight of "black melancholy." If critics are correct in feeling that the passage calls for emendation, it seems more likely—since the text offers a situation "when Morn shall blood renew" (93.19)—that "Morning the daughters of Beulah saw [*not*?] nor could they have sustaind/The horrid sight of death & torment."

Surely Blake must have wished to "finish" *The Four Zoas,* whatever that finishing might have turned out to mean, but at the same time the very strangeness of the manuscript fascinates us: its surface chaos, its false starts, its palimpsestuous revisions and deletions are invitations to a kind of labor which is itself deleted from the print edition. Erdman prevents his reader from enjoying the difficult pleasures he himself experienced; the reader's participation at certain graphological levels is itself edited out because the editor assumes, and must assume, that such participation is inessential to reading. To correct the graphic traces of a struggle for resurrection to unity is to assume that they are irrelevant to the reader's experience of the text as a struggle *in writing,* an energetic exertion of talent including a potential grammar of mistakes which might advance reading.[22]

And what if the manuscript's unfinished form is somehow appropriate to the unfinished world it explores? By resurrecting the manuscript to an editorial unity, the editor interferes with the reader's capacity for taking the manuscript as a call for and challenge to unity on other levels. Of course this disruption cannot be total, since most of the text's disruptions remain, so to speak, intact. If *The Four Zoas* as manuscript is not yet resurrected to unity, neither are the Zoas themselves; and it is perhaps a probing recognition of the strangely discordant harmony of graphological form and spiritual content which will produce the richest readings. Perhaps our best hope as readers of *The Four Zoas* is still to find a copy of the Bentley facsimile and apply a razor to its binding, or to wait for the promised edition ("made from infra-red photographs") being prepared by Erdman and Cettina Magno.

We wish again to emphasize that we fully appreciate E as the best available printed edition, an accomplishment so remarkable that to object to it at all seems ungrateful. But we remain troubled by the hidden power to distort in the editorial praxis and the typographic medium; if print editions are necessary to accommodate a reading public, we must nonetheless question their efficacy, and point out that "reading" Blake in this edition is as far from *experiencing* "the Divine Revelation in the Litteral expression" as the "performance" on a synthesizer would be from a choral and symphonic rendition of Beethoven's Ninth Symphony. And if E is the best available edition, we wish to question the notion of best edition. If E becomes, as it is likely to do, the major if not universally accepted edition, problems such as that of the two Nights VII will continue to demonstrate that for the serious reader the matter of editing must remain a conscious issue, that this is *not* Blake's text, that at the very least one must always attempt to triangulate, so to speak, Blake's text through as many editions and editorial theories as one can lay hands on. This edition is one more possible text, one more hypothetical unity to be placed in the field of all other possible unities in order to prevent oneself from ever assuming a single and final unity. The reader must never accept the authority of print at typeface value, never allow the editor and his medium to become invisible, but always raise the question of mediation, of how Blake's works are processed and disseminated, under what aegis, according to what ideologies and economic imperatives, what assumptions of unity, what interpretation, what Zoic impulse.

It may well be, as Randall McLeod has suggested, that traditions of editing are maintained by pedagogy "in which the teacher's role mediates the students' confrontation with art, and shapes it according to various intellectual and social paradigms, which impose ideal order on recalcitrant facts."[23] There are of course even more profound philosophical and ideological factors at work, but for the moment, we wish rather to emphasize that—whatever the reasons—there has been too little concerted effort to exploit the syntax of concrete ideas offered by photography in bringing the work of Blake to the audience Blake deserves in a form closer to what the audience deserves. *The Four Zoas* is perhaps the least available of all Blake's major works and yet, except for size, it poses fewer problems of photographic reproduction than the engraved works. In an age of photographic transmission almost every reader of *The Four Zoas* must still seek an encounter with Blake's writing through the elaborate and expensive mediation of editorial and compositorial middlemen.

Reproduction by print, even of a photographic image, may not be the best answer technology has for the multitude of problems posed by Blake's work. Even the best photographic facsimile of the ms of *The Four Zoas* would not bring out the details and editorial clues that X-ray photography and related technologies may help uncover—but the unaided eye with the original ms would be almost as much at a loss for these traces as with a photograph of it. In addition to the possible solutions to textual problems offered by new technologies, there are also vistas of promise for the goal of providing "eye" access to Blake. We imagine future Blake students examining the illuminated books and the ms materials from video discs and high-resolution screens, comparing variants in split-screen images, isolating and magnifying cruces and details, jumping instantly from plate to plate and copy to copy, having access to images of all the works without having to travel to the various collections. Once the images were actually encoded on disc, the cost of reproducing multiple copies would be minimal. This is not a utopian proposal: if print editions necessarily involve formal compromises and the interference of a technology Blake's project was designed to circumvent, then with such video reproductions we will no doubt be trading one set of compromises for another. But we could also provide ourselves with a much richer range of readings unmediated by editorial assumptions of unity, and untransformed by print.

. . . .

Notes

1. Stanley Fish, *Is There A Text In This Class?* (Cambridge: Harvard University Press, 1980), p. 148. Two chapters in Fish's book are especially pertinent to our discussion here: "Interpreting the Variorum," where what Erdman calls "contextual expectations" are discussed by Fish as the "hazarding" of what he calls "interpretive closure"; and "Structuralist Homiletics," where an extended analysis of a passage from Lancelot Andrewes gives more detailed examples of how an unfolding verbal and semantic structure is answerable to and shaped by our expectations for its form and meaning.

2. Or, to invoke the French Blake might have known: "so name": *son âme*: "his parted soul."

3. Cf. Tony Marcel, "Unconscious Reading: Experiments on People Who Do Not Know That They Are Reading," in *Visible Language*, 12.4 (Autumn 1978). Julia Kristeva, among others, has emphasized the importance of visibility as a component in establishing the semiotic modality and meaning of a work: "The lines of a grapheme, disposition on the page, length of the lines, blank spaces, etc. . . . contribute to the building of a semiotic totality that can be interpreted along multiple paths, a substitute for thetic unity." *La Révolution du langage poétique* (Paris: Seuil, 1974), p. 219.

4. See *Blake's Composite Art* (Princeton: Princeton University Press, 1978). At the "Blake and Criticism" Conference held at Santa Cruz in May 1982, Mitchell remarked that while working on Blake's illuminated poetry he "had to have a printed version of the poetry in order to read it."

5. Rudolf Arnheim, *Art and Visual Perception* (Berkeley: University of California Press, 1954), pp. 32–81.

6. Or to the "Reader! [*lover*] of books!" or to the "Reader! *lover* of books!" (the first from E 145; the second from the Trianon Press typographical reprint included with its facsimile [1952]).

7. For further discussion, see Nelson Hilton, *Literal Imagination: Blake's Vision of Words* (Berkeley: University of California Press, 1983), pp. 63–66.

8. On this still much neglected pun, see also Aaron Fogel, "Pictures of Speech: On Blake's Poetic," *Studies in Romanticism*, 21 (Summer 1982), 224.

9. Cf. the policy of the Longman Annotated English Poets Series, as written by F. W. Bateson: "the series concerns itself primarily with the meaning. . . . whatever impedes the reader's sympathetic identification with the poet . . . whether of spelling, punctuation or the use of initial capitals—must be regarded as undesirable" (*The Poems of William Blake,* ed. W. H. Stevenson [London: Longman, 1971], p. ix). Although this edition is described on the title page as having "text by David V. Erdman" (i.e. poems *of* Blake, text *by* Erdman), the policy of the series produces (and, of course, copyrights) a "text" *out of* the "text"—a "text" which asks us to identify sympathetically with its text-destroying pretense that "writing/ Is the divine relation in the literal expression—."

10. Charles Sanders Peirce, *Elements of Logic, Collected Works,* vol. 2, ed. Hartshorne and Weiss (Cambridge, Mass.: Harvard University Press, 1932), p. 143.

11. ". . . we may say that puns and ambiguities are to common language what adultery and perversion are to 'chaste' (i.e., socially orthodox) sexual relations. They both bring together entities (meanings/people) that have 'conventionally' been differentiated and kept apart; and they bring them together in deviant ways, bypassing the orthodox rules governing communications and relationships. (A pun is like an adulterous bed in which two meanings that should be separated are coupled together). It is hardly an accident that *Finnegans Wake,* which arguably demonstrates the dissolution of bourgeois society, is almost one continuous pun (the connection with sexual perversion being quite clear to Joyce)." *Adultery in the Novel* (Baltimore: Johns Hopkins University Press, 1979), p. 53.

12. Sigmund Freud, *Jokes and their Relation to the Unconscious* (New York: W. W. Norton, 1960), p. 34; on Stevenson, see note 9, above.

13. Sigmund Freud, *The Interpretation of Dreams,* tr. James Strachey (New York: Basic Books, n.d.), pp. 295–96.

14. Freud, *Jokes and their Relation to the Unconscious,* p. 120. Freud's formulation here suggests that the "habit" is not automatically outgrown. It must be rejected and studiously avoided, and "when we make serious use of words we are obliged to hold ourselves back with a certain effort from this comfortable procedure" (p. 119).

15. Alain, *Systeme des Beaux-Arts,* in *Les Artes et les dieux* (Paris: Gallimard, 1958), p. 439, quoted in Leon S. Roudiez, "Readable/ Writable/ Visible," *Visible Language,* 12.3 (Summer 1978), 240.

16. "Essay on Epitaphs II," in *The Prose Works of William Wordsworth,* ed. W. J. B. Owen and Jane W. Smyser (Oxford: Clarendon Press, 1974), pp. 84–85.

17. When such effects can't be censored *in statu nascendi* as Freud suggests, they can be laughed at as childish. If they can't be laughed at, the metaphors that become available for describing them are revealing. Susanne Langer has argued against the possibility of a "marriage" between the visual and the verbal in art, asserting that there are "no happy marriages . . . only successful rape" (*Problems of Art: Ten Philosophical Lectures* [New York, 1957], p. 86, quoted in Mitchell, *Blake's Composite Art,* p. 3). The metaphor of rape is even stronger than Tanner's analogy between puns and adultery. Under the rubric of the "concealed offense," Kenneth Burke discusses various puns and sound effects among "the many modes of criminality hidden beneath the surface of art" (see *The Philosophy of Literary Form* [Berkeley: University of California Press, 1973], pp. 51–66).

18. "Spatial Aspects of Graphological Expression," *Visible Language,* 12.2 (Spring 1978), 167.

19. For an excellent discussion of Blake's practice in the context of the

commercial norms of the time, see Morris Eaves, "Blake and the Artistic Machine: An Essay in Decorum and Technology," *PMLA* 92.5 (October 1977), 903–927 [included in the present volume].

20. Kilgore, however, believes that previous editions were "undoubtedly correct in presenting each Night as a unit, rather than attempting to reintegrate VIIb into VIIa or VII or both, for such an attempt would be highly presumptuous, and would *obscure a problem it could not solve*" (p. 112, emphasis added). Our own argument, it will be seen, moves along somewhat similar lines.

21. In a similar light, the practical value of Erdman's "Editorial Rearrangement" of "Auguries of Innocence," retained in this edition, might be less in its treatment of the poem than as a vivid synecdochic reminder of a more general editorial presence.

22. The phrase, "grammar of mistakes," is from Henri Frei, cited by Roland Barthes in his essay on "Flaubert and the Sentence," in *New Critical Essays,* tr. Richard Howard (New York: Hill and Wang, 1980), p. 71.

23. "UN Editing Shak-speare," *Sub-stance* 33/34, 12.1 (1982), p. 38.